# LEGISLATURES IN DEVELOPMENT

# PUBLICATIONS OF THE CONSORTIUM
# FOR COMPARATIVE LEGISLATIVE STUDIES

**Malcolm E. Jewell**
*General Editor*

G. R. Boynton and Chong Lim Kim, Editors, *Legislative Systems in Developing Countries*

Abdo I. Baaklini, *Legislative and Political Development: Lebanon, 1842–1972*

Allan Kornberg and William Mishler, *Influence in Parliament: Canada*

Peter Vanneman, *The Supreme Soviet: Politics and the Legislative Process in the Soviet Political System*

Albert F. Eldridge, Editor, *Legislatures in Plural Societies: The Search for Cohesion in National Development*

Michael L. Mezey, *Comparative Legislatures*

John D. Lees and Malcolm Shaw, Editors, *Committees in Legislatures: A Comparative Analysis*

Joel Smith and Lloyd D. Musolf, Editors, *Legislatures in Development: Dynamics of Change in New and Old States*

# LEGISLATURES IN DEVELOPMENT: DYNAMICS OF CHANGE IN NEW AND OLD STATES

Edited by

**JOEL SMITH and LLOYD D. MUSOLF**

**Duke University Press,   Durham, North Carolina   1979**

*For Barbara and Berdyne*
*Two very patient and tolerant people*

# CONTENTS

## PART III. LEGISLATORS AND DEVELOPMENT

# FOREWORD

Perhaps the fundamental question faced by legislative scholars is simply: What difference does the legislature make? The question can be expanded: How does the legislature affect the decisions made by government and the impact of government on the lives of citizens? Do the activities of the legislature promote or obstruct the economic, social, and political development of a country, and do they improve the welfare of the ordinary citizen? Because the effects of legislative activity differ from country to country, we want to know: What factors cause these differences and determine what kinds of impact the legislature will have on development?

Too often in the past the limited number of legislative studies that have been undertaken have focused on the internal operation of the legislature and have ignored the consequences of its actions as well as its interaction with other components of the political and economic system. Students engaged in comparative legislative analysis have, however, become increasingly interested in these issues, and public officials, including those who have sponsored comparative legislative research, have persistently raised questions such as these. The sponsors of the Carmel Conference set out deliberately to encourage legislative students to confront these questions. This book, based on the revised papers presented at that conference, is the result.

The reader will quickly discover that it is easier to raise these questions than it is to answer them. It is also easier to compare legislative institutions or procedures or the characteristics of legislators than it is to compare legislative impacts on policy and on development. The most thorough method of analysis would be to examine, in a single legislative body, one policy area, perhaps even one bill at a time—a case study approach. But the task of constructing theories of legislatures and development from the cumulation of such case studies is prohibitively slow and difficult. Obviously one must engage in comparative analysis and risk losing the descriptive and analytical detail that is possible in case studies. Even if a legislature handles different policies in different ways, one must look for the commonalities that will make possible some generalizations. Some of the studies in this volume examine one legislature's impact on several aspects of development. One deals with a single policy area (population control) in a number of legislatures. Others seek to explain the factors affecting the viability of legislatures; in some cases the conclusion is that a legislature seeking to expand the scope of its influence on development becomes more vulnerable to suspension or abolition.

Perhaps the greatest value of a volume such as this is that it illustrates a variety of approaches to the study of legislatures and development. It is reasonable to expect that other scholars will find some of these approaches useful to their work. It also illustrates the variety of factors that affect how the legislature copes with developmental issues, and it proves that the questions we have asked will have no easy or uniform answers. This volume illustrates the vulnerability of legislative institutions, for example in Thailand, Chile, and several African nations; but it also shows the resilience of the legislature in countries as diverse as Malaysia, Kenya, India, and Spain.

*Malcolm E. Jewell*, General Editor
Comparative Legislative Studies Series

# PREFACE

This book is about legislatures in developing countries throughout the world. It is concerned with the efforts of these legislatures to achieve changes that will help provide their constituents with a better life. It has been common practice to call most such efforts development, but not as common to raise questions about the existence of legislatures or about the roles they might play in the developmental process. Why is it that there are such governmental institutions as legislatures? Why do they exist only in some countries? Why do they often cease to function in many of those developing countries that have them? Why, after they are discontinued, are they often reconstituted? Moreover, since they obviously are not like the U.S. Congress or the British Parliament, what are they like? And, finally, what is it in their actions, inaction, and very being that relates to or interacts with development? To begin to answer these questions our contributors have taken a variety of approaches to an array of specific issues. Some survey the world, others survey regions, and still others report on single nations. They draw upon materials and experiences from first-hand research and from familiarity with a broad spectrum of literature. Many of them, perhaps the majority, work with developing countries that are new nations, and the special character of such situations is a theme of the volume.

The chapters are grouped in three sections after an introductory essay by the editors, and they may be divided between two types. There are those that are concerned primarily with features of larger systems that influence whether legislatures exist, and, if they exist, constrain or promote participation in developmental activities. The first section of this volume contains five chapters that fall primarily into this category. In contrast the remaining seven chapters emphasize the consequences of legislative action and inaction. While they all deal with this second issue, these seven can be divided between those that primarily emphasize the consequences of action by legislatures as a whole and those that focus on consequences of the activities of individual members. Hence the second section deals with the roles of legislatures as institutions and collective bodies, and the third with their members' roles. Since no thorough analysis can avoid calling upon a range of data, however, the assignment of chapters to the different sections reflects our judgment as to the arrangement that heightens the primary value of each chapter.

A word is in order concerning the introductory essay. From the beginning of this enterprise we were concerned with avoiding the lack of focus that besets so many ventures in collective scholarship. Moreover, because of the nascent state of inquiry on this topic, we found it difficult to communicate with potential contributors to get them to bring their experience and data to bear on an unfamiliar issue not in the forefront of their attention. To counteract this communication difficulty and to coordinate individual efforts, we drafted a review essay almost twice the length of the version now included as the Introduction. We felt it would be helpful to the reader to see at least a version of the statement that provided the first stimulus to the contributors' efforts. Since it preceded their preparation, it contains no specific references to the essays, but when the reader finishes the volume, the connections among the chapters should be obvious.

We believe this to be the first work to relate legislatures to efforts for change in developing nations. We trust that the reader also will find it refreshing to see in a new light an old familiar institution that usually is perceived from the perspective of our own. Indeed, the novelty of this perspective extends to what our contributors find these legislative members to have done in their national offices. The nature and meaning of the activities stray far from Western experience and convention. We hope that we have succeeded in conveying our enhanced awareness, derived from this research, of how important are value judgments in any assertions about the centrality, importance, and direction of legislative actions in developmental efforts.

Most of the papers that make up the chapters of this book were prepared for and presented at a Conference on Legislatures and Development held from August 11 to 15th, 1975, at the Highlands Inn at Carmel, California. They subsequently were revised and then edited extensively on the basis of the discussions at the conference. Two other papers eventually were invited to fill certain gaps. For all these efforts we want to express our deepest gratitude to our contributors as well as to other colleagues too numerous to mention who either attended the conference or subsequently rendered service. They will know who they are and the full extent of our debt to them.

Our sincere thanks also go to Meri Gibb, Valerie Hawkins, David Jackson, Alfreda Kaplan, Andrea L. Kawai, and Joel King, without whose help this volume would still be a dusty pile of undecipherable, half-referenced, and half-indexed manuscripts. Reynolds Smith of the Duke University Press eased the last pains of creating a book with a most efficient and professional editorial assist. Finally, we must pay special note to the contribution of Allan Kornberg, a founding father of the field of comparative legislative studies and a primary force in the creation of the Inter-University Consortium for Comparative Legislative Studies, as well as a valued friend and colleague. In addition to encouraging us to organize the Carmel conference and, subsequently, to prepare these materials for publication, he willingly offered invaluable aid as an editor of our own work when we were no longer sure we would be able to face our own manuscripts again. Support for our work has been provided by both the Duke University Program in Comparative Legislative Studies and the Inter-University Consortium for Comparative Legislative Studies with funds provided by a grant from the Agency for International Development. While the choices for contributions to the conference and the editorial decisions for this volume were ours, we do wish to express our deep appreciation for this encouragement and support.

*Joel Smith*
*Lloyd D. Musolf*

# CONTRIBUTORS

*Alia Abdul-Wahab*
Department of Political Science
State University of New York at Albany

*Abdo I. Baaklini*
Associate Professor of Political Science
State University of New York at Albany

*Joel D. Barkan*
Associate Professor of Political Science
University of Iowa

*Raymond F. Hopkins*
Professor of Political Science
Swarthmore College

*R. B. Jain*
Associate Professor of Political Science
University of Delhi

*Allan Kornberg*
Professor of Political Science
Duke University

*Victor T. Le Vine*
Professor of Political Science
Washington University

*Juan J. Linz*
Professor of Sociology
Yale University

*Terry L. McCoy*
Associate Professor of Political Science
University of Florida

*David Morell*
Research Political Scientist and Lecturer
Department of Politics
Princeton University

*Lloyd D. Musolf*
Professor of Political Science and
Director, Institute of Governmental Affairs
University of California, Davis

*Kennieth Pittman*
Department of Political Science
Yale University

*Richard Sisson*
Professor of Political Science
University of California, Los Angeles

*Joel Smith*
Professor of Sociology
Duke University

*Leo Snowiss*
Professor of Political Science
University of California, Los Angeles

*J. Fred Springer*
Lecturer in Political Science
University of California, Davis

*Arturo Valenzuela*
Associate Professor of Political Science
Duke University

*Alexander Wilde*
Research Associate, Latin American Program
Woodrow Wilson International Center for Scholars

# INTRODUCTION

*Chapter 1*

# INTRODUCTION: SOME OBSERVATIONS
# ON LEGISLATURES AND DEVELOPMENT

JOEL SMITH
LLOYD D. MUSOLF

The effort to learn how legislatures relate to development is an ambitious undertaking. The extensive literature on both topics rarely places them in juxtaposition. Specialization is the style, but it is often bought at the price of a broad understanding of complex interrelationships. In these introductory remarks, we hope to avoid this failing by treating both legislatures and development as flexibly as possible, there being an enormous diversity in what goes under the name of each and the relationship between them inevitably being an integral part of an intricate process of survival and change. Accordingly it will be necessary to be somewhat more encyclopedic than may seem essential, but we have deemed this approach more appropriate than setting forth typologies or hypotheses, not only for reasons of flexibility but also because of the more specialized character of the chapters that follow.

## LEGISLATURES AS INSTITUTIONS IN NEW STATES

Phrased most broadly, the relationship between legislatures and development might be stated as follows: "Under what conditions will there be legislatures? When they exist, what roles will they play in: (a) recognizing the need to change, (b) anticipating problems in and opportunities for change, and (c) managing change?" So phrased, the topic may avoid distortions engendered by Western ethnocentrism. Living in countries with relatively mature institutions and a measure of political stability, Westerners incline toward overrefined conceptions of legislatures' relation to development. There may be a tendency to treat legislatures as given and countries as in a state of flux. In consequence, investigations may center on the roles of legislatures in such efforts as opening an interior to settlement, creating new industry, or achieving agrarian reform. Though these are legitimate and pressing concerns, they often overlook the larger context. In states that have achieved a degree of growth or stability, perhaps it is realistic to concentrate narrowly on the capabilities of designated institutions for carrying out specific development programs. As emerging institutions in developing countries, however, legislatures have an existence at least as precarious as other institutions. They may, in fact, be more vulnerable because often their lineage can be traced more easily to former "colonial" powers than can that of other institutions. In any event, to facilitate an approach to the relationship between legislatures and development in the broadest possible terms,[1] we shall attempt to sketch some background aspects of both phenomena and their possible interaction. The discussion is organized under four headings: legislative origins and history, articulation of the legislature with other salient national structures and processes, the political system and process, and the internal systems of legislatures. These are large topics, and we make no pretense at comprehensive coverage; we strive simply to highlight some aspects of their relevance to understanding legislative roles in developing countries.

## LEGISLATIVE ORIGINS AND HISTORY

Both Max Weber's (1967) and Sir Henry Sumner Maine's (1931) writings on the origin of formal law surmise that, in their first appearance, laws were canons to deal with problems involving personal rights, property ownership claims and rights, personal conduct and behavior that violated established group norms or inconvenienced others, and the management of intergroup conflict (Maine, 1931:22–23; Weber, 1967:11–40). Thus, law-giving was a central group function to supplement or replace increasingly ineffective traditional customs, and the process had to be rooted in power if it was to be accepted. Agreements arising from consultation among group (e.g., families, tribes, villages) leaders or their representatives were central to the process by which legal canons could be established (Maine, 1931:24; Weber, 1967:83–86; also cf. Kendall, 1960:317–345).

This hypothetical generalized account of the origins of legal canons is not, of course, a reliable historical guide to the establishment of national legislatures. We know, for example, that the British Parliament evolved over centuries after the Norman Conquest and that it often dealt with matters other than law-giving. The type of analysis advanced by Maine and by Weber is relevant principally because it may help account for the prestige and sense of importance of law-making assemblies down through the centuries. That is, legislative-like rule-making may well have provided an effective alternative for resolving problems in circumstances where social order was threatened with disruption and custom and tradition were proving inadequate.

Undoubtedly, the roles of legislatures can be influenced by the circumstances of their origin and their age. Since so many countries are new states, the birth pangs accompanying the establishment of their legislatures are reflected directly in their performance and roles. Older legislatures, in contrast, have rich traditions on which to draw in justifying both their present activities and their legitimacy. They profit from the inattention of being taken for granted and derive the benefit of having been part of the governmental way of life for so long that they escape the sort of serious and extreme criticism that might lead to their dissolution. But legislatures in new countries are not taken for granted and accorded acceptance, almost solely through inertia. Their sins of omission and commission are not only obvious to other power centers in new states, but also weigh in the balance in decisions about institutional efficacy and necessity, decisions that usually never arise and rarely are rendered for more established bodies. Moreover, they have not yet been able to acquire the institutional charisma of a British Parliament or a United States Congress by having become associated in popular belief with heroic roles in the state's transformation or formation. A legislature's age also modifies the importance of other circumstances concerning its origin that may have had overriding significance for its workings and fate in its infancy.[2]

One of the most important of these circumstances is whether the legislative form continues or extends indigenous institutions or is borrowed or imported from the former metropolitan colonial power or from some dominant friend or ally in the struggle for national freedom. Such beginnings influence a legislature's initial legitimacy in the public eye and its compatibility with established beliefs, values, and customary ways of doing things.[3] Legislative bodies whose rules and functions continue those that have been operating traditionally and effectively prior to statehood—often at provincial, tribal, or local levels—have greater chances to be effective and successful because their members will understand better how to behave in such systems and citizens will be more familiar with what to expect.[4] The probabilities of overt conflicts or serious discontinuities in government functions are somewhat lessened.[5] Where, for example, the military has been accustomed to set policy and perform executive functions, or the executive customarily has served legislative functions, a new legislature entrusted with either or both these tasks is not likely to survive long without having considerable independent power or accommodating its organization and activities to these others (see Nordlinger, 1970:1131–1148; Tachau and Good, 1973:551–573; Steiner and Trubeck, 1971:464–479; Shils, 1962:7–67). However, since new legislatures are not firmly established and have little that is sacrosanct about them, they are vulnerable to being swept aside as "foreign" in waves of xenophobic nationalism.[6]

A second (and related) condition of legislative origins is the character and level of national development at the time. Particularly important is the extent of overlap between the dominant society and the boundaries of the country. This sets the extent to which cultural pluralism is a major national concern, and, accordingly, the extent to which the representation and participation of various groups is a problem to be dealt with in the organization of governmental institutions. How this problem is handled—that is, whether by representation of all groups on a fair or unfair basis or by the exclusion of some or all subordinate groups—will influence in obvious ways the extent of support for a new legislature and whether it becomes an embattled institution.

The nature of the economic base and the level of economic development at the time of a legislature's origin are also important to its subsequent fate. Economic base and level of development can threaten internal stability seriously by limiting goals and by fostering the sort of pervasive sense of relative deprivation that spawns revolutionary discontent. They limit a political system's ability to provide services and the ability of any legislature that is a part of that system to satisfy the needs and demands of constituents. If the country is poor, legislatures that appear to do little of importance can be judged superfluous, and disbanded. But even if poor economies do not lead directly to the demise of legislatures, they probably help keep the legislature an "underdeveloped" institution. Bankrupt countries can pay legislators only very little, and poverty also limits the extent and type of legislative infrastructure, and limitations on these facilities, in turn, influence legislative effectiveness.

Since developing countries so often are new states (with many obvious exceptions in the Middle East and Latin America), two qualities of new states that strongly impinge on the roles and fates of their new legislatures deserve special mention. One is the extent of national social and cultural homogeneity and the other is prenational political status. With respect to the former, stress-inducing threats to national integration can arise from conflicts among various groups that coexist within national boundaries. Even when such differences do not produce continuous overt conflict—and the experiences of Canada, Switzerland, Belgium, Spain, France, and the Netherlands all attest to the possible latent survival of these conflicts despite appearances of accommodation if not actual assimilation—they set needs and problems with which new legislatures must cope both nationally and within their own walls.[7] Problems can arise from differences in language, religion, and custom that interfere with the conduct of even the most mundane and routine legislative business.

At least as important as the connection of a legislature and its origins to the events and processes of state making is the preindependence status of a new country. Whereas in the past new states tended to emerge through agglomerative processes—the expansion of a dominant group's hegemony by dynastic intermarriage, warfare, colonizing settlement, political bargaining, conversion, and similar techniques that tended to create regimes exercising dominion over large areas and in turn afforded economies of organizational scale—the new states of the twentieth century tend to have been born through dismemberment—the dismemberment of empires or the disintegration of countries (Black, 1966:90–94, 95ff.). In most cases, the birth of the new state is not so much the culmination of cultural and organizational development following a long period of uninterrupted identity and growth. It is rather a traumatic lurch into self-reliance and self-responsibility by a psychologically ready but otherwise ill-prepared people (though the degree of unreadiness varies with the sort of domination to which the new state was subject, i.e., according to, the extent of control by functionaries from the mother country, or, contrastingly, the extent of training of indigenous colonials for positions of high responsibility). Also important to legislative stability is whether the colony previously was a historical society and/or national entity, or was a contrived administrative unit of convenience to the needs of the colonial power. Similarly, conceptions of the relation of a colony to the colonial power have varied drastically. Such aspects of the preindependence experience obviously affect preparedness for statehood, the organizational and integration problems of the new state, and the ease and peacefulness of the transition to independence. They have obvious pertinence to whether legislatures are likely to be established, their organization, their prescribed functions and personnel, and the basic set of issues to which they must attend as vital parts of a government.[8]

### ARTICULATION WITH OTHER SALIENT INSTITUTIONS AND PROCESSES

The development, functions, and fates of legislatures are often seriously affected by their interrelations with the military, bureaucracy, and executive groups. If efforts to exercise certain prescribed or asserted rights become sources of conflict, they can lead to the demise of institutions as fragile as are the new legislatures of new states. Leaders have popularity, bureaucracies have expertise, and the military have weapons. All are fairly effective means for backing up claims in any contest over roles. Legislatures have only constitutional legitimacy and/or popular support, and both are entirely too new and unreliable to provide much strength for waging such conflicts. For example, when the Thai legislature in 1971 sought to cut the military budget, annoyed military leaders abolished the legislature. For their own survival, then, legislatures in developing countries may find it necessary to build networks of formal and informal relationships with authoritative elements in the society.

In addition to the need to relate to such powerful well-established entities, new legislatures must articulate with the various salient groups within the society. In a traditional society these may be castes. Certainly they will be interest groups—collectivities that share one or more attributes like religion, tribal affiliation, and language that define common concerns. Equally important may be corporate groups that share less persistent but more immediately salient attributes like occupation, land-holder status, or employer status. More generally, interest groups emphasize sectoral rather than total national needs.[9] The satisfaction of such disparate groups requires bargaining and the allocation of scarce resources, and potentially troublesome inequities may well result. It is not clear how divisive interest groups may be for new national units, but the question certainly needs to be addressed, as does the question of the potential role of legislatures in ameliorating such potential sources of internal stress by their involvement in the distribution process.[10] An important corollary question is whether representation on some equitable proportional basis averts strife among interest groups.[11] Clearly, if these answers can be positive and if the principles employed in the organization of legislatures enhance such roles, the chances for the survival and effectiveness of legislatures in new states may be improved. And whether the legislature, as a colloquy of representatives of conflicting interest groups, serves as an arena for conducting the conflict or, instead, as a place for bargaining and accommodating it, has much to do with the basis and proportionality of representation, the roles allotted to the institution and its members, and their emphasis on and interpretation of these roles.

Legislatures' fates also may reflect their nations' positions in international affairs. To varying degrees that depend on the exigencies of the times, the existence of legislatures reflects prevailing international expectations. The decision of President Thieu to hold senatorial elections in the former Republic of South Vietnam at the height of hostilities may have been a classic instance of responding to such outside expectations. When outright pressure is not being exercised, mimicry of admired ideals or models may have similar effects. As in all human life, even at the national level, there is much reference group behavior and it pertains to the existence of institutions and their organization and functioning. Indeed, it may not be too much to claim that organizations like the Inter-Parliamentary Union and international development banks and assistance agencies generate pressure to have legislatures and provide models as to how they should be organized or what they should do. Directly and indirectly, the legislature's existence in a world of legislatures and the country's existence in a world of countries both offer a variety of models and a complex of pressures, some supporting, some threatening, and some molding legislatures.

## THE POLITICAL SYSTEM AND PROCESS

We have selected for discussion three aspects of the political system that have import for legislatures—political parties, legislative representation, and selection for legislative seats. Party systems vary in many ways—the number permitted, the degree to which membership is formal, their ideological basis, the degree of personal autonomy allowed or conformity expected of members, the selective basis of membership, and the like. Perhaps the most important of these for the legislatures of developing countries is the number of parties. In all countries, the more parties the greater the difficulty in establishing a government or reaching majority positions on issues. New states with multiparty systems have special difficulties because they have little experience in accommodating legislative stalemates and must cope with them while national existence hangs precariously in the balance. (Thailand affords a good example of a country that has been faced with this kind of predicament.[12] ) Legislatures in states with multiparty systems also can become weak and ineffective if partisan conflict impedes or guts legislative activity. The legislature may acquire and perpetuate a reputation for irresponsibility, destructiveness, and ineptitude if it produces a string of stalemates.

A polar alternative to multiparty fractionation is the one-party system. Single-party states suffer from a lack of alternatives if the party fails. Surveillance and criticism of the government, and the provision of reasonable alternatives to it, tend to be hampered in most one-party situations.[13] The extent to which party discipline is expected or required of its elected representatives also has salience for legislatures. In parliamentary systems, an erosion in disciplined party loyalty will generally foreshadow the fall of a government. If legislative performance offends public expectations because parties cannot keep their members in line, public unhappiness may be directed to legislative rather than party inadequacy and unreliability.

Parties obviously differ in the extent to which they are ideological or pragmatic. As collectivities, ideological parties may be less likely than others to negotiate and bargain freely, and more likely to hamper legislative effectiveness by submerging national (and) legislative goals to partisan goals. With less party discipline, however, representatives from nonideological parties may be freer to subvert national interests and serve their own self-interests. Either situation hampers legislative effectiveness and can expose the institution to public disrespect, disdain, and ridicule.

Finally, membership selectivity of parties can be a considerable factor in their legislative performance. Some parties are "mass" parties in the sense that they generate support and membership widely, even if unequally, from all strata of the population.[14] Others, in contrast, largely attract support, recruit membership, and even may be named on the basis of a distinctive characteristic of a sector of the population such as occupation, landowning status, or religion. The legislative activities of the latter may easily be considered segmental and in the interests of special groups rather than the country as a whole regardless of whether the charge is deserved.

The basis of legislative representation is equally germane to legislative performance. Basically, seats are assigned to either territorial areas (i.e., districts) or groups (i.e., parties or corporate entities in the state). Territorial seating may be particularly germane to the regional approach to development. If, as is often the case, holistic national development is impeded by a scarcity of resources, prior regional development of the best-endowed area seems to offer an advantage by generating new capital for developing less fortunately endowed and situated areas later without having to borrow externally. Territorial representation, however, may lessen legislative support of such regional development tactics because, if the representatives of less endowed areas are under pressure from "the folks back home," they will feel their incumbencies threatened if they vote to promote another part of the country while getting little or nothing for their own.[15]

A major problem that is particularly important to developing countries is that territorial representation tends to perpetuate schisms such as those among regions, rural-urban divisions, or tribes and ethnic groups if they have not dispersed through the national territory. Such divisions are basic threats to national integration, and national legislatures, as representational bodies, provide settings in which these tensions may be exacerbated or ameliorated (Lipset and Rokkan, 1967:12–13). Representation on the basis of functional groups like caste, religion, occupation, ethnicity, tribe, or social stratum can create the same potentially divisive problems for developing countries as can territorial representation, though group representation may be both a more lasting and less fluid cause of problems. While migration can dilute or alter the character of the population homogeneity of districts and, thereby, rob them of particular selfish and divisive local interests, social categories are, by definition, homogeneous, and the mere fact that they are recognized tends both to maintain them and to reinforce their significance and power. In contrast to territorial divisions, which are usually exhaustive and provide at least some minimal representation for all locations in the national territory, functional groupings need not be and can omit important sectors of the population.[16] The consequences for the quality of legislation may be severe.

Though election is the usual method for choosing legislators, selection by appointment and/or qualification by some personal attribute is still employed. Such systems are based on some variant of the philosophy that there is a small group of people who are more deserving than others or will make better members of the assembly. In a social system where trained ability is concentrated and it is known who would be a good office holder, such a selection process may be appropriate. Legislative membership by appointment may even be desirable in developing new states where few qualify on the basis of literacy, the electorate is illiterate, unschooled, and inexperienced in the electoral process, and, rightly or not, there is felt to be very little margin for error in governmental processes if the country is to survive. Indeed, the lack of confidence of those in power that election outcomes will support what seems obvious and necessary to them, even when the franchise is exercised only by a highly literate and politically experienced electorate, may account for the relatively frequent practice of suspending or postponing elections during wars and other national crises.

A problem faced by nonelective legislatures is that their actions may lack the legitimacy that derives from public support. In circumstances where popular participation in elections is the norm, it is understandable that appointed bodies have little power, for their members cannot claim that they have the confidence of the voters and are vulnerable to charges of a lack of public concern. In developing countries the problem is not merely that of a legislator's election or survival in office, but also that of the basic survival of the legislature as an institution and its contribution to the survival of the country. Thus, the alternatives of legislator appointment and election may be viewed as equally attractive and dangerous alternatives that pose a most difficult choice. Such reasoning may help account for the practice of mixing selection systems in some countries, such as Tanzania and Malaysia.[17]

To the extent that restricted membership in legislatures is desired, but the appointment of elites would offend populist sentiments, the same goals may be achieved approximately by restricting the electorate explicitly or through practice. For example, in Dahl's classification of polyarchies, the United States and Switzerland qualify only marginally because of the informal constraints placed on voting by blacks in the former and the legal exclusion of voting by women in a number of cantons of the latter (Dahl, 1971:28–29). Even if the rationale for restricting the electorate is genuinely to obtain well-qualified voters, selecting the criteria to index expertise can be a most difficult task. If, instead, voter exclusiveness really is meant to serve vested interests, any such qualification will remain useful to the nation only so long as the group defined maintains its homogeneity and shares as its common quality an attribute that somehow leads to goals whose achievement contributes positively to national concerns.

Voter eligibility, then, has a crucial impact on the legitimacy of legislatures. Just as nonelected legislative bodies may have extreme legitimacy problems, those selected by relatively small eligible electorates from exclusive sectors of the population may have similar problems in securing wide public support for their activities. In the short run, the absence of public support can be compensated for by the use of raw force, but that is an unreliable and expensive way to produce public compliance. In the long run, the actions of governing institutions need to be accepted and complied with voluntarily.

The composition and, hence, both the performance of legislatures and the acceptability of their actions (within the limits of prescribed and traditional roles and prerogatives) are also affected by the voting system employed. For example, various systems of proportional representation encourage the inclusion of most social sectors among the elected representatives. Proportional representation can create problems if, as is sometimes the case, its complexity makes it incomprehensible to most of the electorate (Rae, 1967:114–125). In essence, while voting and counting systems can be constructed so as to maximize the chance of representation of all people's choices at the time of election, in countries in which the institutions involved are novel and lack traditional and strong support, such gains may be won at the potential expense of popular acceptance of outcomes.

## INTERNAL SYSTEMS OF LEGISLATURES

All legislatures are constituted by and operate under systems of rules that govern everything from who and how many may serve for what length terms to how they will organize themselves and proceed with their work and what resources will be available to them. The basic prerogatives of legislatures are usually prescribed by a national constitution or charter, or through long-established tradition. The constraints on the actions of members go to the heart of such fundamental matters as whether a legislature can be an institution for creating policy directly or whether it can function in this sense only indirectly through activities like questioning, consulting, amending, and appropriating. Likewise, many major functions of legislatures are constrained by the system under which the legislature operates. In the parliamentary system the legislature and the executive are two arms of a winning party or coalition of parties and, accordingly, legislative functions like government surveillance and accountability are more easily exercised because cabinet ministers also sit as legislative members. In a congressional-presidential system of the American model, separate membership is the rule, and where there is also a real or understood norm of separate *and* equal branches of government,[18] surveillance of the higher levels of the executive and administrative branches can be difficult. In the national assemblies of one-party states, the rights of individual assembly members are likely to be quite severely constrained as far as innovation is concerned, but the legislature may be the regime's most important mirror of public opinion even if its members do not speak in public session (Stultz, 1970:303–333; Hakes and Helgerson, 1973:335–362).

Almost as important as the explicit, though sometimes ambiguous and changeable (Macridis and Brown, 1960:276–279; deGrazia, 1962), prescriptions and proscriptions of legislatures' prerogatives (Herman and Mendel, 1976) are the rules that order their proceedings. These rules help determine legislative decorum. They may affect the quality of the legislation produced or otherwise dispensed with. They also may affect the public respect accorded that legislation and the institution generally. Rules that specify the number of times bills must be read publicly and the length of time between readings are particularly important in impeding the passage of irresponsible legislation or blocking strongly supported legislation. In the new legislatures of developing countries, the rules can assume even greater importance because they are neither well established and, hence, accepted as custom, nor are they widely well known or understood. The effect may be to increase any appearance of disorganization, chaos, and irresponsibility in legislative proceedings.

Every aspect of legislative scheduling has obvious import. Whether sittings are continous, annual, biennial, or simply at the call of the executive is important to both the nature and quality of work legislatures can do. Session scheduling also can impede or facilitate participation by members from different locations or social strata. In Cyprus, for example, the small size of the island and the ability to restrict meetings to two days a week made it possible for any elected representative who could get to Nicosia to serve and return home each day. By contrast, while sitting, Malaysian MPs from Sabah and Sarawak are separated by hundreds of miles of water from their districts and usually do not get home during the short parliamentary meetings. Wherever they occur, short sittings require that basic investigatory spade work be done either prior to a session, poorly, or not at all. Moreover, but less obviously, the shorter a sitting, the less time there will be for members to get to know each other and members of the government and to begin to exercise effectively their various ancillary informal service and influence functions with the bureaucrats in the central executive. This circumstance will tend to give political advantages to representatives close to the capital area because they will be around the central government regardless of whether the legislature is in session. Because new developing countries tend to be poor, they can ill afford long and/or frequent sessions and, thereby, may adopt schedules that help ensure the ineffectiveness of the institution. Moreover, if a schedule tends to magnify the opportunities of the capital area, as it so often does, it is likely to result increasingly in the sort of unbalanced regional development that never is fed back sufficiently into national development.[19]

Another aspect of legislative organization that is a major influence on what and how well a legislature does is its committee system (Herman and Mendel, 1976:468–527). Committees may be standing, or ad hoc with broad or narrow mandates, or they may not exist at all. In different governmental systems, committees vary in their powers to gather evidence, interrogate witnesses, draft legislation, amend legislation, and recommend or quash legislative proposals. An obvious advantage of a highly developed committee system is that it may facilitate the focusing of interest and serve to develop legislator expertise. An effective committee system also may permit the average member to rely on recommendations that capitalize on the skills and expertise of his colleagues. A problem with the system is that committees and, even more, their chairmen, can amass tremendous power and squelch minority expression. The possibilities of secrecy and exclusion from participation are always present in committee systems, but they are heightened in the underfunded legislatures of developing countries where the resources for notification and recording of proceedings are minimal.

Committees are not the only route to enhanced personal influence for members, but regardless of how a virtuoso legislator operates, the skills and power that can come only with seniority are a necessity. Accordingly, every factor that enables individual legislators to build tenure in office has an important bearing on the operation of legislatures and their output. Some of the most important forces that contribute to tenure are beyond a legislature's direct influence. The longer terms are and the less frequently an incumbent is "at risk," the greater the chances of continuing in office and the likelihood that members will see legislative service as a career rather than a passing interlude. However, "careerism" may change the character of legislative behavior for, while it builds members' skills and expertise, it also reduces their contact with and sense of closeness to constituents.

Committee systems and the presence of experienced careerists are primarily relevant to the drafting and passage of bills that set important national policies and major programs. Such activities also require established and well-developed infrastructures that may include such features as staffs for each member, legislative libraries, bill-drafting facilities, and debate and vote recording systems (Robinson, 1970: 366–390). If legislation is to have the opportunity to succeed and not be invalidated for conflicting with constitutional or other standards, legislators need help in understanding, drafting, and checking proposed bills. Most of the developing legislatures of new countries cannot afford or have not evolved such infrastructures. This may place them in the position of having to borrow the experience of others.[20] While such services can expedite a legislature's abilities to act on a wide variety of national problems, the members are more or less at the mercy of their own weaknesses in adapting to local circumstances whatever is provided in good faith but with little sensitivity to the local situation.[21] Nonetheless, legislators in developing countries do express the need for assistance in doing their work. For example, the Agency for International Development and the Inter-Parliamentary Union receive requests from legislatures in developing countries (and not necessarily new bodies) to provide help in tracking bills or in checking whether proposed legislation duplicates or contradicts existing statutes.

This brief consideration of various constraints on legislatures' activities and products indicates that there is always some difference between a legislature's manifest roles in its own political system and the functions it actually serves. Accordingly, since legislatures' activities reflect their members' activities, it can be expected that there will also be considerable variation in what individual members actually do. Recognition of this fact has led to widespread investigation of legislative roles (i.e., the interaction among prescriptions for activities and functions, members' values and interests, their conceptions of their role, and the meaning for others of these various activities), the distribution of these various roles, and how all this relates both to the legislature's institutional structure and the larger political system and national system. LaPalombara (1974:177–185) suggests that this has led legislative scholars to divide between those who emphasize the behavior of members in role activities on the one hand, and those who emphasize a systems approach to organizational behavior, on the other. Actually, an overemphasized role approach would seem to run the risk of violating the sociological truism that organizations exist and continue independently of their personnel, and that systems have some impact on their personnel.[22] Although an approach to the study of legislatures that emphasizes legislators' role behavior may not be the single most generally useful approach to the study of legislatures (Packenham, 1970:521–582), it may be particularly important in understanding the roles of the developing legislatures of the states we are considering, since they operate in questionably effective and largely nonindigenous frameworks, and depend on frequent change, evasion, and manipulation for effectiveness and survival. Consequently, we should expect that they would have to include significant non-law-making activities that serve to link citizens to their new and unfamiliar governments and to meld various antagonistic interest and ethnic groups into a fragile national entity.

## LEGISLATURES AND THE DEVELOPMENT PROCESS

There has been considerable terminological confusion in discussing the process by which nations struggle to improve the conditions under which their people live. Though the term "development" is used in this paper for the sake of convenience, it has been criticized frequently as too value-laden to be useful.[23] Some have preferred to employ "modernization," but this raises questions as well. Whether there is any necessary relationship between modernization and development and, if so, whether either is necessary but not sufficient for the other has not been resolved. Efforts at resolution have called into question some of the presumed basic components of modernization (e.g., empathy, future orientation, adaptability) as well.

However, "change" is a more generic term that subsumes both of these terms. Despite the notion that some societies are static, change is a normal feature of all social life. If social forms are the arrangements by which groups solve the problems spawned by the environmental settings (in the most general sense of the concept) in which they exist, then group survival in changing environmental circumstances necessitates at least some minimum flexibility and change in these arrangements, be they political or economic or social in the narrower sense of each term.[24] Even a concerted effort to maintain the social environment in a static state (e.g., cutting contact with the rest of the world, as Japan did for over two centuries) could not prevent change in a viable social group because the physical environment and demographic structure can change independently, and they are important aspects of the environmental problem to which social arrangements are a dynamic response and solution. It goes without saying that such other factors as growth in knowledge through induction from accumulating experience, spatial mobility, and similar alterations in social reality also stimulate social change.

If change is omnipresent and universal, we must isolate some of its variable features in order to begin to understand it. One such aspect whose variability seems obvious is the rate at which it occurs. A related but different aspect is how cataclysmic it seems to those upon whom it bears. That is to say, the time span of changes and the perceived magnitude of their consequences are analytically separable even if they are empirically intertwined.

What are developing countries from this perspective? They seem to be the loci of all the forces and pressures for change, writ large and exaggerated. As new states, their formal systems are relatively makeshift and ramshackle Rube Goldberg-like inventions, doomed to rapid obsolescence and failure. Accordingly, they exist in seemingly constant states of crisis. Simultaneously, however, most of them still possess the resources whose value in the past disproportionately failed to reach the populace, either because colonial exploitation removed the wealth to the metropolitan power or because closed stratification hierarchies channeled wealth to a small and exclusive ruling elite. Their present statehood is promising insofar as these resources can be harnessed, their value redistributed, and the country survive while this is happening. For these countries, then, there normally is a felt need to articulate new goals with respect to the level of national product, the distribution of the value of that product, the rules that govern individual rights and expectations of achievement and access to the appropriate channels for exercising them, and the extent of participation in the political life of the state. Normally, they also sense both the opportunity and need to manage and control that change; that is what development is all about. Until such ideals can be achieved, there is the spectre of the problems of survival—of protecting the social fabric from tensions within and threats from outside.

Experience since World War II shows a depressing lack of progress toward development, particularly if it is conceived as the promotion of human welfare. Recently the progressive disillusionment of students of development with its ease of attainment has been documented carefully by Irma Adelman and Cynthia Taft Morris (1973). On the basis of a careful analysis of economic and political data from seventy-four developing countries for the years from 1957 to 1968, Adelman and Morris found that "development is accompanied by an absolute as well as a relative decline in the average income of the very poor" (1973:189). Greater income equality is associated with those countries, such as Dahomey, Chad, and Niger, that have undergone virtually no development or, at the opposite extreme, those like Argentina, Chile, Taiwan, and Israel that have achieved a high level of economic development. They also note that another easy assumption of development specialists in the immediate postwar era—that there is a historical association between successful economic growth and the spread of parliamentary democracy—has been refuted by experience. Their study revealed no significant association between short-term growth rates of per capita gross national product and political participation, though it did identify some indirect connections. That is to say, "countries that have introduced changes in social structure conducive to greater individual upward mobility are also likely to have generated some channels for expanded individual participation in political associations and institutions" (Adelman and Morris, 1973:192). There is a price to be paid for this kind of development, however. The price is that "increases in social mobility unfortunately occur at the expense of higher rates of growth of per capita GNP" (Adelman and Morris, 1973:192).

If the governments of developing countries are to be effective in articulating and establishing national goals, they themselves have to be well established and responsible in their own right. However, research suggests that the very problems with which developing countries must deal also affect the stability and effectiveness of their governments (Cutright, 1963:253–264; Lipset, 1960; Haug, 1967:294–304). We shall review briefly these aspects of society in developing countries and suggest their relationship to the development and maturation of effective political institutions. In particular, this review could also serve as an agenda for the policy and program foci of these legislative institutions, and incidentally as an introduction for the chapters on this topic that follow.

By definition, all independent states have a territory and a population. The relationship of the two is density, and density is a central component of any ecological theory of social organization because it establishes both the needs of and the limits to effective social organization.[25] From this perspective, failure to maintain a balance between the two in terms of gross overall density ratio and actual distribution of the population over areas of differing carrying capacity is a constant problem for new states. Depending on which is easier to change, the problem may be put: either the population is too large or small or maldistributed for the area, or the area is too large or small or insufficiently endowed with resources for the population. Inadequate or insufficient territory can be expanded by colonization or warfare, but since virtually all of the land area of the world is now national territory, warfare (or some covert, similarly aggressive tactic) is the major means of expansion available. A large apparently sufficient land area inadequately endowed with natural resources (e.g., arable land, ports, fuel, mineral resources) poses the same dilemma. Since new states are latecomers and basically weaker than most established powers, they are particularly susceptible to the problem of territorial need and the lack of power to do much about it. These circumstances go far in accounting for the frequency with which developing countries have become pawns in the power politics of the major powers. The national territory is also a problem in the sense that it has to be physically linked.[26] Many new states have large relatively uninhabited areas and habitable sections largely unconnected with each other. (In the case of prepartition Pakistan, two major noncontiguous areas were separated by a hostile country.)

In view of the relative intractability of the geographic problem, population has more often than not been the focus of national attention. In this regard national actions reveal great ambivalence. On the one hand, manpower is often the greatest national resource; on the other hand, inability to support the population and dissatisfaction with a mean way of life create an interest in population limitation. The developed world stands close to the sidelines as an interested observer, muddying the waters by imposing preferences that exacerbate the problem. The modern West, for example, abhors traditional population control practices such as infanticide and abandonment of the aged and infirm that once served as population checks. On the other hand, by improving diets the nations of the West may have increased fecundity.[27] In a variety of ways (e.g., improvement of public sanitation, malaria eradication), then, length of life and, consequently, population size have grown in countries unable to sustain increases. With mounting concern that the world is approaching its capacity to sustain large populations, Western countries have become more than interested bystanders and have participated energetically in developing techniques and disseminating programs for family planning and birth control (Meadows, Meadows, Randers, and Behrens, 1972). However, as demographers have long known, in situations governed by natural population growth checks and high infant mortality, cultural values usually support high fertility behavior and resist any innovations that seem to impose unnatural checks on conception and delivery.[28] The resistance of developing countries to population controls is also deepened by a suspicion that the West is being unfair in criticizing them, and resentment is sometimes expressed passionately as a charge that fertility control is a form of genocide practiced by whites on people of color. A feeling sometimes articulated is that Western countries emphasize the relation between overpopulation and scarce resources but underemphasize the contribution that their own high living standards make to the depletion of the world's natural resources. There is certainly merit in this view. Developing countries, nevertheless, may have no alternative to coming to terms with their own problem of limited natural resources and swiftly increasing population growth.

Health care and public health practices are a closely related concern in developing countries. Dating from colonial days when public health and health care were promoted by ruling powers in the interests of the survival of colonists, troops, missionaries, and administrators, concerted efforts have been directed to disease control. Their impact on increasing length of life and population size has already been indicated. Moreover, improved public health has also decreased the incidence of debilitating but nonfatal diseases. Therefore, curtailing modern health practices to reestablish old ecological balances would cause the loss of some tangible economic benefits to improved health. In any case, choice of the most appropriate public health strategies is a considerable and chronic problem in these countries and appears in various forms—whether to train domestically, who should receive care, whether to implement public health programs or to treat individual illness, and the like. But the basic issue is that health programs largely determine the make-up of the population and its levels of energy.

   The initial concern of most development specialists after World War II was economic development, with a heavy emphasis on the creation of Western style industry (Bendix, 1969:5–12). Regardless of the possible naiveté of many of the schemes that were tried and of their underlying analogical reasoning (i.e., Western countries with high standards of living had highly developed modern industry, so what they needed was the same), in reality many countries lack sufficient natural resources to acquire much foreign exchange by the export of raw materials, and, nevertheless, at least some manufactured goods must be obtained. Developing countries are also acutely aware of the wide fluctuations in the world prices of the raw materials they produce. These circumstances create real but varying needs for some industrial development in new and developing states. The motivation no longer need be emulation. It is more likely to be to achieve a higher level of living without being forced into the camp of a major world power. If any surplus manpower can be absorbed in other ways, then industry can be more efficient than agriculture for converting manpower into wealth.

   The pressures on developing countries to decide upon and implement policies of territorial organization and integration, demographic processes, and health care and public health practices can be described as rationalistic in the sense that they call for identification of needs and goals and assessment of the efficacy of various means to reach these goals. The actions selected involve innovation and openness to new ideas, and if there is to be change there also must be opportunities for individuals whose minds are not already settled in traditional ideals and modes of thinking to assume positions of importance and even leadership.[29] Moreover, if, as is sometimes claimed, mastery of modern Western modes of thought and knowledge requires intelligence (see, e.g., Cropsey, 1963:109–130), there have to be opportunities for social mobility. In many new and developing countries, however, the systems of stratification are quite rigid and traditional. They award prestige and social position on ascriptive bases, and do not easily afford opportunities for individual free mobility. Relatively closed stratification systems can be particularly dysfunctional for new and developing countries, for they tend to assign large sectors of the population to fixed social positions and interpersonal relationships on ascriptive bases rather than on personal qualifications (Singhví, 1970:179–227).

   Traditional stratification systems not only tend to impede necessary social mobility but also may exacerbate citizen dissatisfaction with their general lot in life. In a great many new and developing countries, the large bulk of the population still lives at an almost Malthusian margin of existence. There is much poverty and deprivation, a low level of security, and few saved resources to fall back on in hard times.[30] Life at its best is often marked by deprivation, denial, and insecurity. Regardless of whether the promises of developmental change are realized, the idea of change and improvement has been introduced and the masses look forward to sharing in its benefits. If these expectations are not satisfied, and particularly if extreme discrepancies in wealth, life style, and power remain visible, considerable social and political unrest tends to develop. In order to avoid the detrimental effects of both debilitating civil unrest and the inability to reward talent or to use it where and how it is needed, systems of stratification must be altered to facilitate relatively open social mobility and the realization of the ideal of comparable rewards for like achievement.

But traditional stratification systems are not so easily changed. They rest on tradition and, hence, have the advantage of familiarity, and they tend to be considered sacred, thus having neither to be explained nor justified. Moreover, through generations of existence they have created extreme inequalities in power and wealth resources that can be used to block changes in the system (Davis, 1949:495–498). This is one reason for stiff opposition to programs for land reform, tax reform, and the like, and why it is that much change in developing countries, when it does occur, can be described better as revolutionary than evolutionary (Huntington, 1969:388–396). The rigidification of an established stratification system is particularly hard to deal with, not only because members of the upper strata acquire a monopoly over wealth and knowledge, but also because members of the elite usually control the mechanisms of government and know how to use them to reinforce their positions even when subjecting the system to apparent change. Legislatures are particularly susceptible to control by advantaged classes because their memberships can be influenced through voting eligibility rules (in those cases where appointment is not employed as an even more effective tactic), candidate eligibility requirements, membership resource requisites, and constituency definition. Indeed, this may be why it has been suggested that legislatures become the entrenched bastions of the conservative power groups of developing societies and exercise their powers to inhibit and impede innovative social change. Whatever is really the case, articulation with and opening of established systems of social stratification are major challenges to the legislatures of new and developing countries.

Regardless of the rigidity of established systems of stratification and power, once there is any real effort to change toward modernity educated citizens are needed. For a while professionals and skilled technicians can be imported, but they are expensive and there is always the feeling that they represent an inadequate temporary arrangement. Eventually local systems of education at all levels must be provided to sustain any innovations that involve abstract technical principles. By promoting literacy, education facilitates extralocal non-face-to-face communication, and thereby may stimulate more general participation in national politics and social affairs and, ultimately, generate pressure for governmental forms that promise and actually achieve social equity and social justice. While the development of educational systems raises the national literacy level, and, thereby, stimulates pressure for social change, popular involvement, and, perhaps, national unrest, specific aspects of that educational system have very different but equally important consequences. Schools may have vocational or general education emphases, or they may be employed purposefully to disseminate a consciousness of the state as an entity and its traditions and goals; these are two examples of specific alternatives for enhanced public educational systems that have obviously important different consequences. At the university level decisions are of comparable magnitude.

If legislators participate in such decisions, they do so from the perspective of prejudices rooted in their own educational experiences. If they themselves lack much formal education, they may be either handicapped in doing their own legislative work or prejudiced against instituting opportunities for others that they themselves never had a chance to enjoy or both. Particularly in view of the visible radical activism of student groups in various nations, it is understandable that governments in general and legislatures in particular cannot always be counted upon to deal with a developing country's higher educational needs in the maximum national interest.[31]

A final aspect of social organization in new and developing countries, one that bears directly on their survival and simultaneously affects their capacity for self-government, is pluralism—the existence of diverse linguistic, racial, ethnic, and religious groups in the same nation. Politics may be organized along lines that reflect these latent schisms (e.g., religion as a basis for parties in the Netherlands) (Lijphart, 1968) or the schisms may break out in conflict without apparent reason (e.g., French separatism in Berne canton; Flemish and Walloon conflict in Belgium) even where pluralism has been managed by providing equity and opportunities for participation to all groups, and the possible effectiveness of coalition governments has been enhanced (by such factors as a commitment to the principles of coalition governments and system maintenance, a belief in the possibility of external threats, and a maintenance of government effectiveness in doing its work [Dahl, 1971:112–121; Daalder, 1974:604–621]). The importance of pluralism is clarified both by Dahl's interpretation of Haug's analysis and by Cutright's research on relationships between pluralism, socioeconomic level, and effective governmental development (Haug, 1967; Cutright, 1963). They show that low socioeconomic development and pluralism are positively associated, and that pluralism is negatively associated with legislative independence and positively associated with governmental ineffectiveness. These relationships suggest that governments are not likely to be able to reduce pluralistic strife without institutions for accommodating the interests in conflict and that perhaps legislatures, being representational, can become such institutions (Dahl, 1971:121–123). For legislatures to be effective in this fashion and develop public legitimacy and autonomy, however, they will have to protect the integrity of the groups involved and legislate to guarantee equitable participation in both the benefits and the costs of their actions.[32]

In order to achieve these goals it may be necessary to reserve seats for the various ethnic, linguistic, and religious groups, as is done in Yugoslavia (Dahl, 1971:12), or to district to achieve a very high correlation between the boundaries of legislative districts and the distributions of these groups. For the provision of safe seats to the disparate groups of a plural society to be meaningful, there also may have to be some equity in numerical representation and some accommodation to the desires of small groups to secure representation for which they might not be eligible on a strictly numerical basis. Some gerrymandering (i.e., setting of boundaries on an obviously contrived basis so as to favor some groups and disadvantage others) is probably unavoidable, and this will inevitably bring a legislative body under fire from some group in a pluralistic situation. Moreover, representation problems can reappear at any time in district systems if there is free migration, for boundaries that formerly assured group representation can easily become barriers to it. Indeed, when spatial mobility is not only free but people can move anywhere as individuals rather than in groups, if the resulting residential desegregation is not accompanied by assimilation and social acceptance, pressures for group representation will remain. In sum, social pluralism is both a condition that must be accommodated in developing and new states and a parameter that impinges directly on the organization and likely legitimacy and effectiveness of a legislature.

## WHAT MAY BE THE ROLES OF LEGISLATURES IN NEW AND DEVELOPING COUNTRIES?

These comments may suggest that there is more of an established literature relating legislatures to development than is the case. Actually, as we noted, very little has been written. Furthermore, existing materials tend to be skeptical that any connection between the two is constructive in nature. There seem to be two rather contradictory views of legislatures and development, the first that legislatures are weak and ineffective, and the second that legislatures impede development. Though each will be considered in turn, it will help to review how some of the roles suggested for them relate to some of their most pertinent features.

Three organizational qualities of legislatures that impinge on both their law-making and other roles will be singled out for comment. (a) They are councils (de Grazia, 1962:63). Thus they provide opportunities for consultation, discussion, and advice among delegates who are representatives with delegated authority to act on behalf of constituents, and between them and their clients and counterparts. (b) Since they often are the sole political institution in a country compelled by its own rationale to admit and accept opposing forces (de Grazia, 1962:71), every legislature is somewhat geared to accommodate conflict. (c) Because they have been established either on constitutional grounds, by charter, or by long-standing tradition, and assuming their members have been selected legitimately, the institution and its acts potentially begin with legitimacy and moral force behind them.

In addition to taking account of structure, identifying the roles of any institution makes it necessary to recognize that not everything that happens within the legislative system is prescribed. Often important unintended consequences do follow from prescribed actions. This distinction between formally recognized and legitimated activities and their consequences and other undesignated or unintended positive or negative consequences of the activities of a unit is the essence of the conceptual distinction between manifest and latent functions (Merton, 1957:19–85). While the former are usually designated explicitly, in the process of legislating they may easily become confused lost, or ambiguous since the language of public debate (which usually makes at least socially acceptable intentions explicit) often is not the same as that of formal legal specifications. Indeed, much of the business of courts is to clarify the legality of marginal activities by interpreting ambiguous or inadequate legislative wording by referring to the contemporaneous language of expressed intentions.

One further difficulty in identifying the roles of legislatures arises from national differences in specifying their necessary and possible activities. The Inter-Parliamentary Union's compendium on legislatures identifies no legislative roles shared by all, a few served by a large number of them, and many roles served by only a few (Ameller, 1966:263–315; see also Herman and Mendel, 1976:571–958). Aside from functions being present or absent, the manifest functions of some legislatures may prove to be latent functions of others. In view of both international and temporal variation, and in order to avoid making lists of the latent and manifest functions of each national legislature, we shall consider as manifest in our judgment only those functions that occur frequently in a variety of legislatures. The criterion is general recognition that these functions can be served by a legislature regardless of whether they actually are served. The identification of latent functions also must be limited arbitrarily since, being unintended, they are indefinite in number and their importance varies with time, place, and circumstance. Therefore, we shall focus mainly on those that relate to the distinctive qualities of legislatures in new and developing countries and are pertinent to efforts at managing change.

Scholars of political institutions are well aware of the nuances and variety in legislative activities.[33] However, lists of legislative functions can be misleading, for there is a tendency to mix statements about activities (e.g., pass laws, hold debates, provide speeches, appropriate, ratify, and the like) with statements about their meaning (e.g., require executive accountability, formulate policies, create programs). In studying legislative systems, this real but fine distinction is difficult to sustain. For example, in parliamentary systems, when failure to support the government on a particular issue involves a vote of no confidence, the particular issue is usually secondary and the decision not to enact proposed legislation is simultaneous with and inseparable from the act of bringing down the incumbent government. In all systems, specific legislative acts potentially may have such confusing multiple meanings. Despite such difficulties we shall risk some suggestions of each sort of function.

Since, whatever else, a right and obligation of all legislatures is to legislate on the matters they are privileged to or must act on, no action on these matters has legitimacy without their concurrence. In this sense legislating also constitutes the legitimation of the actions called for in bills enacted. Regardless of how bills are introduced, and taking cognizance of constraints on the right to amend, legislatures can abort, redirect, delay, or accept executive proposals. In political systems whose governments would fall if their legislatures failed to support legislation basically as proposed, the mutual dependency between legislators and executives works to give the former leverage in securing favors and services for their constituents and the latter a sense of reliable support. The legislative process itself functions as much to inform the government of public opinion through debates and questioning as to legitimate by approving. In "people's democracies," legislative bodies have less autonomy, but apparently they still serve as channels of information about the citizenry for the leadership (Dix, 1973:261–303; Foltz, 1973:143–170). In these countries the leadership finds it increasingly difficult to prepare adequate domestic legislation without input from legislators, and, in these areas, at least, legislative bodies seem to be making more inputs.

The private members' bills permitted in most systems typically pertain to relatively minor matters involving only a few constituents (Herman and Mendel, 1976:595–601). With the exception of the United States Congress and a few well-endowed counterparts, private members can do little more on their own even if they have the right to introduce any sort of bill, because they rarely have the help, facilities, or time to prepare adequate legislation. In congressional systems with well-endowed facilities, legislators who exercise these powers can compete for power with members of the executive even if in theory the legislature was to have been less powerful. Since such assemblies usually appropriate their own funds, they can also provide the support facilities that permit serious involvement in drafting and introducing major legislation. For various reasons, however, including both the fact that the head of state usually has been given a more massive show of popular electoral support than any legislator and the fact that the legislature includes the opposition, legislators tend to let attributed powers slip away to other branches of government.

Because so many systems prohibit legislative members from introducing much legislation and force their support for executive-sponsored bills, and because legislators in congressional systems often relinquish prerogatives, it is widely held that much legislative activity deals with relatively trivial matters and usually has no significant role in either general policy making or major program delineation (Blondel, 1973:137–138). It is claimed that members lack the experience, expertise, and consensus to formulate appropriate national policies, and the technical knowledge to formulate programs to implement these policies successfully. United States experience clearly suggests that this need not always be the case, and that, even if legislatures do not create policy and enact programs on their own (a doubtful assertion at best), they can make important original inputs. Indeed, Blondel (1973:119–131) has asserted that legislatures clearly have a role in policy making, and Bendix (1969:196–197) interprets Weber as having suggested that historically legislatures were established expressly to break the monopoly of bureaucracies in setting policies.

In many countries legislatures help keep the activities of the executive in the public view. In the parliamentary system it is common to schedule regular questioning periods which public officials must attend to answer legislators' questions, and in congressional systems departmental executives or their aides usually can be requested to appear before committees (Herman and Mendel, 1976:661–674, 854–877). While there is considerable variation among all such systems in the mechanics and mandatory character of the process, at least some executive activities can be exposed to public scrutiny in these ways. Moreover, this exposure gives legislators both public and private means of confronting executives with their own and their constituents' concerns.[34]

Almost all legislatures appropriate funds (Herman and Mendel, 1976:731–800). If, in the process of appropriating, legislators can change government budget requests, legislatures ultimately can determine the fates of proposed organizations and activities. Depending upon the appropriations process, a legislature may even be able to share credit for innovations by passing enabling legislation or assure failure by making insufficient appropriations. The appropriation function not only can give legislatures a major role in policy formation, program creation, and foreign affairs by determining how much money is appropriated for activities, but it also can enhance the political careers of members who may help friends by judiciously allocating government funds to them and providing them with relief from taxes and other levies. Although the magnitude of such selfish activities may seem minor and the consequences relevant only to the careers of legislators and the pockets of their friends, if they become common practice the cumulative diversion of funds and conflicting exceptions provided by special privilege legislation can inadvertently undermine general policies and programs which the legislators may support. The dangerous consequences for new and poor states are obvious.

This sketch of legislative structural qualities and manifest functions also suggests some of their major latent functions for developing countries. Admittedly some pertain to national survival rather than to development, but the difference is a fine point, for in a new state with a crushingly poor economy and low standard of living, mere survival may be construed as development. Certainly, any organization and reorganization that introduces efficiency and decreases waste would be so construed. The first latent function, symbolization (cf. Edelman, 1964:95–113), is most encompassing of all sectors of the country given that representative legislatures may symbolize the participation of all members of national society in rule-making processes. Relatedly, if there is some public awareness that established countries have legislatures, they may also symbolize some of the prestige of statehood. Bendix suggests that modern legislatures based on citizen suffrage also serve to break down divisive local communal orientations and instill broad extralocal orientations (Bendix, 1969:112–114). Heads of state, the military, bureaucrats, and other executives may not be elected directly, but legislators usually are. Bendix argues that prior to modern states social groupings found their expressions in estates with ascriptive membership. If people participated, it was within the estate and not nationally. Voting for legislatures, he suggests, can extend and focus such participation to the country as an entity. Hence, legislative elections can further the sense of nationhood and, thereby, decrease national fragmentation and insecurity.

Most of the specific latent functions of legislatures that are germane to development relate to how their members play their roles in dealing with the country's need to resolve discordant pluralism—to develop both a sense of nationhood and physical and psychological national integration out of chaotic conditions, a weak or nonexistent national identity, and a fragile unity. The most important of these functions, then, is probably conflict resolution—the satisfaction and accommodation of differences between opposing social groups and strata—through brokerage or bargaining activities. Although every bill acted on could be interpreted as a resolution of differences, we have in mind here conflicts not on the legislative agenda. In this process legislators trade the rights or resources of their groups to achieve a maximum of satisfaction. Regardless of each legislator's motives, in new states the truces and mutual dependencies such deals produce buy badly needed time and relative tranquility which may give the national system a chance to provide more satisfactory services and promote greater citizen allegiance.

Two derivative aspects of these activities important for national development are interest articulation and need perception. In the former, the publicizing of constituents' interests by their representatives promotes the realization of common and complementary interests while working out coalitions and mergers among uncoordinated groups. Realization of complementary interests can also facilitate development of cooperative mutual support through the provision of specialized services. Thus, if legislatures can be public forums for legislators to present the problems and interests of their groups as needs which the state must satisfy, then they can also become market places in which discordant groups discover common interests or complementary advantages while advancing initially private and selfish claims (see, e.g., Coleman, 1970:1074–1087).

Where designated legislative activities are minimal, or their prerogatives considerably greater than their ability to act, clever legislators come to understand that their own tenure in office depends on what they deliver to their constituents. Particularly where citizens lack access to government because they do not understand how the new state is organized or how it operates, and/or because they are too distant from governmental officials to represent their own needs, legislators also often can help them obtain special legislation, permits, licenses, tax relief, waiver of military service, and the like. Such functions provide legislators with frequent opportunities for demonstrating to high government executives and bureaucrats their close and congenial contacts with the populace. This can help build their potential personal power and influence. The satisfaction of personal need can be most important for development, if, as has been suggested, it requires a future orientation and deferment of immediate gratification (see, among others, Lerner, 1958; Banfield, 1958). If most citizens of developing countries cannot await indefinitely the realization of the rewards of newly won statehood without spasmodic relief from their privations, legislators' abilities to provide small services that relieve constituents' privations and pressing personal problems, unwittingly or not, defuse potentially volatile unstable situations and buy the time needed for national organizations and planning to become effective.

Finally, countries exist in an environment of countries, the more established of which have legislatures. These countries are both the evaluators and reference groups of new states, and, as such, are likely to be emulated.[35] They are also involved in the new state's future. One factor in their decisions to support a new weak state is the likelihood that the client will survive in relative stability. The presence of a legislature in a new state may suggest regime legitimacy and national stability by implying citizen participation in government and the likelihood of voluntary rather than coerced public order. Even though there is the risk that the legislatures of a new or developing country can be chronically irresponsible, frequently impede action, and promote harebrained schemes, thereby creating a bad reputation that spreads quickly and widely, the ability of a government to hold legislative elections, seat the winners, and permit that body to conduct its business in a relatively unpressured and orderly fashion can serve the rest of the world as a symbol of a country's maturity, dependability, and stability.

These considerations may provide a useful context for assessing the conflicting claims concerning the roles of legislatures in development policy. These roles, while potentially important, are not exclusive. What, then, is the basis of the criticism that legislatures are weak and ineffective in development policy because they probably are not crucial in the making of policy or program decisions? It is pointed out that legislatures lead a chancy life at best, that they are sometimes prorogued, and that even when they succeed in staying on the scene it makes little difference to policy making. There is much truth in the view that legislatures, particularly in developing countries, have little real power over decision making. It is also true, however, that judgments about the potency of legislatures tend to center on their decision-making function at the expense of the many others they might have. This way of looking at legislatures undoubtedly originates in the West where problems are different. In the United States, it is strengthened by the enshrinement of the separation of powers in the national constitution and the constitutions of the various states. Even though parliamentary democracy fuses the legislative and executive powers, the venerable British system, attenuated though it may be in practice, rests upon the supremacy of Parliament in decision making.

The practice of judging legislatures in terms of their decision-making potency has affected even scholars who employ a functional approach. Finding that in developing countries other political instruments were usually more crucial than legislatures in "the authoritative allocation of values," they tend to dismiss legislatures as a focus of study. Holding to this point of view has led one student of legislatures to assert that "the institutional analysis of elected assemblies outside the Western world often becomes an exercise in triviality" (Grumm, 1973:12). Nevertheless, others assert that a proper functional approach "assumes that sociological phenomena (e.g., structures, roles institutional patterns, norms) may be explained by the part they play in meeting the demands of the social system in which they exist" (Mezey, 1972:687). In an effort to reorient the predominant identification of legislatures with decision-making activities, Riggs has urged that the term legislatures be dropped in favor of territorial, mainly elected representative assemblies (Riggs, 1974).

All this having been said, the fact remains that legislatures usually are not at the heart of decision making. The swift-moving twentieth century has been hard on the concept of legislative decision making. If representative assemblies are a compromise between autocratic rule and direct democracy, then the diminishing vitality of the concept poses enormous problems. As Blondel has pointed out, "governments which want to bypass or curb the legislature may justify doing so by claiming that such action *increases* democracy" (Blondel, 1973:4). In addition, the difficulty of drawing a firm boundary between legislative and executive matters permits aggrandizement by the latter. The "decline" of legislatures is thus noted whenever these ambiguities come to the fore.

The infrequency of decisive actions hides a role of legislatures for decision making that may be overlooked. They may dither and dawdle, they may seem outmoded, but they do at least have a potential for representing sentiments that governments, no matter how powerful, can afford to overlook only at their peril. The impatience that the presence of a legislature can evoke in the minds of a modernizing elite is understandable. In the interest of persistent accomplishment, however, national planning in all areas may benefit from further scrutiny; the disappointments that have plagued the planning process should give pause to planners and their bosses (see, e.g., Faber and Seers, 1972). It is conceivable that added inputs from legislators whose roots extend back into the remote areas of a developing country is a needed antidote if planning has been based largely on capital city thinking and received economic theories.

When not being criticized for being ineffectual in development, legislatures often draw fire for the opposite reason—their effectiveness in blocking development. Samuel P. Huntington has summarized a number of cases in which land reform was slowed or halted by landlord-dominated legislatures (Huntington, 1969:388–396). Robert Packenham has offered evidence to support the proposition that "legislatures tend to represent, all over the world, more conservative and parochial interests than executives, even in democratic polities" (Packenham, 1970:578).

On this question of legislative obstructionism, there is an obvious need for more research. Where the landed elite is overrepresented in the legislature, it is scarcely surprising to find agrarian reform treated badly. One of Professor Packenham's students has put the matter well: "There is a need for a study of the consequences of legislative activity by a fairly apportioned, strong, independently elected legislative body in the context of strong political parties and interest groups providing representation of the masses. Such analysis would help determine whether legislatures are by their nature status-quo oriented or rather is it primarily the social structure and the electoral system that give legislatures this characteristic." [36]

## SOME FURTHER REFLECTIONS ON KNOWING ABOUT LEGISLATURES AND DEVELOPMENT

The innumerable uncertainties just reviewed would dissipate if we had valid and reliable answers to the question, "Under what condition will there be legislatures and what roles will they play in efforts to manage change?" It is hard to anticipate the content of such research because there cannot be controlled experiments in which legislatures are created or terminated as experimental stimuli in controlled national and international contexts. Even before substitutes can be devised for experiments that address incisive and specific hypotheses, many detailed case studies will be needed to specify the variables being considered. Our preliminary efforts to do such case studies indicate a variety of general and specific problems that will arise. Some of these bear mention.

First, sampling is necessary. In sampling certain relevant variables must either be controlled or allowed to vary under controlled conditions by either stratifying or some other analogous process. Largely, these other control variables can be grouped under the term "context." The problem, as our colleagues contributing case materials well know, is that the list of possible contextual variables is almost endless and there is no compelling theoretical perspective for uniformly selecting among them. Without uniform selection, comparative analysis is difficult, if not impossible.

A second consideration is that studies to identify the actual roles of legislatures in development cannot be restricted only to countries where legislatures are permitted to play a wide variety of roles. The possibility of bending rules and of latent functions makes the discovery of unexpected roles plausible. Moreover, when we know what legislatures do, it may turn out that essentially the same sorts of policy decisions are made and implemented in much the same fashion with about the same results in countries lacking legislatures. If so, these are not necessary roles of legislatures. To establish necessary roles, cases of countries without legislatures will have to be examined to see whether or how outcomes differ. Eventually it would be desirable to separate those roles of legislatures in development that have been real but not necessary from those that, for whatever reason, only legislatures can serve. Are there roles that only legislatures can play because of their unique qualities? If so, what are they? For what aspects of development are they pertinent?

Furthermore, there are problems in relating concepts to reality. By way of example, perhaps the general view that legislatures have lesser roles in government—particularly in new and developing countries—reflects the belief that policy decisions are made largely by heads of states and executives with inputs from technocrats. Even if legislators do influence implementation, given the priority of policy over program, that activity is relatively minor. The name of the game and the location of the playing field have already been decided. Our concern as scholars is that even if this view of things is correct, it needs to be established on a systematic empirical basis, not by argument with anecdotal information. Consultation with experts in development programs and discussions with sample informants affirm that the distinction between policy and program lacks clarity in real life. Certainly few people argue that development efforts might not be more orderly if policies and programs could be separated and the relationship between them evaluated directly. However, even if such separation could be achieved, the hiding or innocent unawareness of purposes will obfuscate investigators' ability to maintain the distinction in research. Indeed, even though the effective management of change could be enhanced by adhering to such a distinction, it is difficult to make because the practice of inferring policy from program is flawed, employing as it does the assumption that there must be a consistent logic. Such an approach always must lead to the conclusion that programs are appropriate implementations of the policies to which they relate, and further that there are no programs without policy. Since one basic question posed by legislative scholars is whether legislatures ought more appropriately to be involved in policy or in program formation, the implications of applying the distinction in research are obvious.

Another problem in relating concepts to reality may involve the notion that legislatures are bounded, impermeable entities. In practice, not only is institutionalization of developing countries' legislatures often woefully weak but there is frequently a limited cast of characters in the government drama and these individuals appear in a variety of roles. If the boundaries of these assemblies are as permeable as their existence is vulnerable, we should be studying, on the one hand, institutions incorporating features that make legislatures distinctive and, on the other hand, actions of those whose authoritative legitimacy includes legislative membership at some time.

Such phenomena complicate the concept of legislative roles and the evaluation of their relative importance. Roles are judgments about the functional meaning of actions and, as such, must be highly subjective (by contrast, responsible research on what legislatures do is somewhat less debatable). In practice, then, assessing the importance of specific legislative roles requires that subjective judgments be made about data that may become accessible only when the institution has ceased to exist and sufficient time has elapsed for the consequences to be apparent. A tendency to reestablish legislatures often prevents these consequences from emerging clearly.

Whatever the obstacles, the question of assessing legislative roles must ultimately be faced. A number of other difficulties inevitably will arise in specifying and weighing the extent of these roles accurately. There is not likely to be official, verbatim record keeping or voting records, for this requires a technology that many developing and new nations lack. Moreover, since political processes often are resolved outside in the halls or elsewhere, the investigator's net has to be cast widely.

In collecting and interpreting information, investigators must be able to separate respondents' recounting of events from interpretations of them. In one country the head of the national planning agency never wavered in his verdict that the legislature's role in establishing legal town planning requisites and standards was trivial, but his judgment contradicted information he and others provided that, before passage, the legislature sat on the bill for four years before finally adopting it with a series of amendments that completely altered its intent and applicability. In such circumstances the protective coloration of informed expertise well-laced with ingenuousness and naiveté may be the only effective guise for investigators who must rely on willing but opinionated informants to report fully the information needed.

## CONCLUSION

It is clear that individual legislatures vary within the wide power range from "rubber stamps" to major power blocs. All uniformly share the legitimating function. That range also suggests a continuum from a small number of functions of little tangible importance, on one extreme, to a large number of significant roles, on the other.

The possibility that legislatures in new states can contribute to their survival and development is a central theme or hypothesis of this volume. It is certainly not original with us. For example, the idea was suggested to one of the authors in two entirely separate conversations. In one, an American executive of an international development bank expressed the conviction that development programs tended to fail in Latin America because legislatures were not involved in their preparation and adoption. In his opinion, no such programs could succeed there without the legitimation provided by legislative involvement. In addition to mentioning the symbolic value of legislative approval, he also stressed that the legislative process increased the possibilities that programs related to real needs. Almost a year later an eminent African geographer opined that since so many of the problems of developing countries are distributional, national legislatures must be involved in them because, for better or worse, they are the only institutions in these countries that cover and represent the entire national space. While both the logic and facts in these two expressions may be unclear and even wrong, both are responses to the representational and inclusiveness problems that beset new and developing countries, and reveal an acute, if emotional, sensitivity to the general absence of other institutions that are as inclusive and representative.

Legislatures in developing countries are probably here to stay. However, the path down which legislatures are likely to evolve will entail only limited traces of decision-making power; simultaneously their bureaucratization will be encouraged. Although in some regimes the legislature will serve simply as a political symbol, both domestic and international, other regimes, more adventurous and flexible in their development aims, may begin to realize that the legislature has the potential to be a resource well beyond symbolization. Based throughout a country, legislators can provide feedback on how development programs are working. Their ability to do this can be greatly enhanced if they also sit on committees that help implement programs in their constituencies. So situated, they can provide questions that will keep administrators alert, private suggestions to ministries in the shaping of legislation, or (more riskily from the government's viewpoint) amendments in legislative debate. Needless to say, the involvement of legislators in this manner also enhances their possibility for mischief. Yet, despite this very real possibility, such involvement may hold the key to the future of legislatures in developing countries.

## NOTES

*This chapter was prepared for the Conference on Legislatures and Development at Carmel, California, August 11–16, 1965. Support for this work was provided by A.I.D. Grant #csd–3295 to the Comparative Legislative Studies Program of Duke University and to the Consortium for Comparative Legislative Studies. We wish to thank Allan Kornberg in particular for his wise and discerning assistance in bringing this chapter to its present form. The authors alone, of course, are responsible for its content.*

1. Because development is a nationwide concern (albeit there is a propensity for differential growth captured in such phrases as "dual society" and internal colonialism) there is reason to focus attention on the role of national legislatures in developmental processes. We would be wrong if we implied that provincial assemblies or tribal or village councils are not also legislative bodies with important roles to play in the development of these countries. Indeed, there is considerable evidence to suggest that they may play some particularly important roles (Micks, 1961; Whitaker, 1970; Miller, 1969; Kilson, 1966; Ashford, 1967).

2. Problems faced by the U.S. Congress and British Parliament during their formative stages are discussed by Young, 1966; Mansfield 1965; and Polsby, 1968:144–168.

3. Malcolm Jewell, for example, has related the fate of new national African legislatures modeled after the Westminister system to their initial fit with the national circumstances at the time of independence and with their ability to make subsequent rapid adjustments to bring their structure and workings more in line with the national system (Jewell, 1973:208–210).

4. India is probably an outstanding example in this regard. See the discussion of Nehru in Geertz, 1963:105–106.

5. Where, for example, the military has been accustomed to set policy and perform executive functions, or the executive customarily has served legislative functions, a new legislature entrusted with either or both these functions is not likely to survive long without either having considerable independent power or accommodating its own organization and activities to these others (see Nordlinger, 1970:1131–1148; Tachau and Good, 1973:551–573; Steiner and Trubeck, 1971:464–479; Shils, 1962:7–67).

6. While omitting phrases like "xenophobic nationalism," the transitory nature of such institutions is discussed by Almond and Coleman, 1960:362.

7. For a review of literature discussing countries practicing this "politics of accommodation," see Daalder, 1974:604–621.

8. Many of these problems regarding the founding of modern regimes in former colonies are discussed by Rustow, 1970:337–363.

9. Not even membership on the basis of nation-wide criteria has been able to purge members of their sectoral interests (Proctor, 1973:3ff.).

10. *The Federalist* was frequently concerned with this problem in defending the set of institutions proposed for moderating such groups in the design of the American system (Rossiter, 1961: Papers 10, 51). On their anticipations regarding proportional representation see Paper 35.

11. It has been shown that electoral arrangements such as PR do have consequences for the mediation of conflict in the polities which adopt them (Rae, 1967; Rae and Taylor, 1970).

12. The impact of extreme party fractionization on legislative paralysis and consequent instability is reviewed in Rae and Taylor, 1970: chapter 2.

13. Indeed, it may be that the types of guarantees which would protect these activities in a single party state are exactly the kinds of conditions which would permit the rise of additional parties (Dahl, 1956:15).

14. Lipset and Rokkan, 1967:26–29. Some observers feel that the differential strength of "mass" parties among various sectors of the populace approximates a cleavage structure in society. Cf. Oakeshott, 1961:151–170.

15. That they sometimes may not experience such pressure is suggested by Stauffer, 1970:354; Kochanek, 1968a:272; Payne, 1968:219.

16. And such omissions are not always accidental. See the discussion of Kenya and Tanzania elections in Bretton, 1973:198.

17. See Cliffe's discussion of the 1965 Tanzanian elections for one account of the workings of such an elective/appointive system in Cliffe, 1967.

18. It is interesting that even in the United States this has come to be understood as the norm even though Rossiter (1961:Paper 51:322) notes clearly that "in republican government, the legislative authority necessarily predominates." Indeed, the primary fear of *The Federalist* was legislative tyranny.

19. Weinbaum, 1972:72. Lloyd Rodwin's (1970:70–106) discussion of the Turkish experience in urban growth policy makes it clear that only Ankara could develop relatively successfully in the effort to find an antidote to Istanbul's dominance as a "primate city," and that this was because it had the advantage of attention and personnel that comes with being a capital.

20. For example, the World Health Organization will provide model public health codes for interested countries not in a position to draft their own statutes.

21. The naiveté that may characterize such proffered services was exemplified in the remark to one of us by an officer of an international agency that it had never occurred to him that enacted laws were the product of the interaction between technocrats' general knowledge and intentions, and ongoing political processes.

22. Reissman (1949:305–310) demonstrates the impact of structure on role and person. Weber (1967:82–86; 1947:363–386) discusses an analogous phenomenon in his remarks on the routinization of charisma. Weber (1947:329–341) discusses the rationality norms under which bureaucracies operate. More contemporary sociological studies, of course, have questioned the extent of the success of bureaucrats in developing such characteristics. See Bonjean and Grimes, 1970:365–373; Kohn, 1971:461–474.

23. For a review of the critical literature, see Kornberg, Hines, and Smith, 1973:471–491.

24. The change from wet to dry rice culture among the Tanala and its implications for change is a classic case. Linton, 1947:45–51.

25. Hawley presents a classic statement of the need of social units to adapt to their environment. See Hawley, 1950:3–11.

26. This problem of territorial integration has been discussed often in developmental literature since Coleman and Rosberg, 1964.

27. A case analysis of the relation of improved diet to fecundity is provided by analyses of the case of !Kung. Cf. Lee, 1973:329–342; Kolata, 1974:932–934.

28. Parsons, 1971:23–35. The extent to which such values are implicated in developing countries has led Kingsley Davis (1967:158) to state that their "social structure and economy must be changed before deliberate reduction in the birth rate can be achieved."

29. National manifestations, of course, vary. Contrast the evolutionary change in Turkey described by Lerner (1958) in *The Passing of Traditional Society* with the hostility to external influences expressed by the Burmese in Pye, 1962: chapter 8.

30. Even modern technology encounters difficulty fighting the Malthusian problems. See Wade, 1974:1093–1096.

31. Most of these questions, and some of the problems involved in any answer to them, are addressed by the various authors in Piper and Cole, 1964.

32. Nonetheless, coincident with the social scientific analysis of "consociational" politics, the consensus underlying such polities may be breaking down. Daalder, 1974.

33. From his comparative study of political systems, LaPalombara suggests five main latent and manifest functions in the activity sense (1974:chapter 5). Blondel devotes four chapters to their functions, in the sense of consequences. LaPalombara, 1974:134–166; Blondel, 1973: Chapters 2, 8–10.

34. LaPalombara, 1974:161–166, discusses the supervisory function.

35. Cropsey, 1963, defines "backward" countries as those which are receivers of both material aid and ideas.

36. Robert Widell, quoted in an unpublished paper by Robert A. Packenham presented at a seminar on legislative development in Rio de Janeiro, August 12–14, 1974.

# PART I
# POWER, LEGITIMACY, AND LEGISLATURES

*Chapter 2*

# LEGISLATIVE VIABILITY AND POLITICAL DEVELOPMENT

## RICHARD SISSON
## LEO M. SNOWISS

Governments based upon strong legislative institutions are rapidly becoming a rarity among the former colonial or "new" nations of Asia and Africa and in the Third World generally (cf. in this volume the chapters by Kornberg and Pittman, McCoy, and Le Vine). Perhaps the decline of these parliamentary regimes should not have been unanticipated. There is, after all, an extensive literature which suggests that stable democratic institutions cannot be sustained in the absence of an elaborate configuration of cultural and socioeconomic conditions.[1] It is well known, moreover, that modern parliamentary regimes were nurtured under largely specifiable historical circumstances in a number of Western societies (Huntington, 1969; Rokkan, 1968; Sisson, 1973), and that successful institutionalization seems to have coincided with particular stages or thresholds of national integration, industrialization, urbanization, and mass political participation (Pye, 1966; Deutsch, 1953; Black, 1966; Binder, 1971; Bracher, 1964).

But the persistence of parliamentary forms in Anglo-American countries and in Western Europe has never been a simple artifact of socioeconomic development. The survival of these institutions has always depended upon their adaptability to changing political and socioeconomic circumstances. The great variety of legislative structures and their concomitant party and electoral systems testify to the plasticity of the institution in Western societies. Similarly, the decay, decline, and reassertion of legislative authority and influence in various of these "modern" or "advanced" societies would seem to imply that "stages" or "prerequisites" of socioeconomic and political development, while suggestive, do not determine the vitality of representative legislatures.

Thus, although legislatures in most non-Western nations have not succeeded in maintaining themselves, it is not at all clear that their decline has been foreordained by "societal conditions." Indeed, the "failure" of representative legislatures in these nations was at least partly precipitated by the widely shared view that such institutions were simply invalid and ineffective. If this is true, arguments which question the desirability and viability of legislative institutions are mutually dependent and ought to be reexamined.

In this chapter we shall argue that most analyses of the decline of legislatures have been misleading and that assertions of what legislatures can do and are intended to do have been inadequately assessed, especially in the context of the new and emergent nations. The problem as we see it is twofold. In the first place it must be understood that the functions performed by legislative bodies entail—indeed require—power. The more powerful the legislature, the more comprehensive its functions will be and the more extensive will be its societal impact, granted that the abuse of such power ultimately can lead to its loss of function, as in Chile (Valenzuela and Wilde, in this volume), or its fall, as in Thailand (Morell, in this volume). Obvious though the point may be, contemporary social science seems to have neglected it. The larger point is that institutions may organize power in very different ways. To talk about the organization of *legislative* power we must discuss its distinctive impact on the character and quality of the functions performed. Thus the first task of this paper is to explore the distinctive character of the legislative institution and to analyze the consequences which this distinctiveness entails for the character of political life and the distribution of public benefits. Indeed, that is precisely what a *viable* institution must have the capacity to do.

Secondly, the characteristic organization of power in particular institutions naturally affects the relationship between those institutions and the larger society. In so far as legislatures organize power in distinct ways, we shall suggest that there are specifiable conditions which facilitate their rise and persistence even under trying circumstances. But we shall also propose that legislatures may promote the conditions of their own persistence—again, in characteristic ways that reflect the organization of their institutional power. Thus an explanation of the viability of legislative institutions requires an analysis of the interaction between organized political power, social structure, and the goals and functions performed by particular institutions.

## THE ANALYSIS OF LEGISLATIVE FUNCTIONS

It has been suggested that legislative institutions are not "necessary" in "modern" (presumably industrial or postindustrial) societies (Huntington, 1966; Crick, 1970). Those who make this argument commonly assume that the days of individualism have been replaced by an era of collectivist or corporatist social organization in which the fundamental questions concerning the direction of society are no longer a matter of political dispute. In this view, public problems have become essentially technical or managerial. It is therefore the executive bureaucracy—the authority of which has always been justified in terms of technical and managerial expertise—which is said to be the most appropriate political institution for responding to the needs and demands of modern society wisely and efficiently. Legislatures somehow might be useful for "mobilizing consent" (in Beer's felicitous phrase) or serve as forums for public commentary, but they are not deemed essential to the formulation and review of law—since, it is argued, elected representative institutions cannot deal effectively with the complicated and intricate interdependencies which characterize modern social order.

Applied to the developing nations, these observations would lead one to assert that the role of legislative institutions is and ought to be marginal at best. We would have to conclude that the attainment of those conditions which are "required" for the establishment of viable democratic orders also renders legislatures, presumably the institutional heart of democratic regimes, obsolete. Indeed, if it is true that in most advanced or "modern" societies such institutions cannot govern effectively and, therefore, should be displaced by executive institutions, our attention and concern should be restricted to institutions other than legislatures.

But legislative bodies are complex institutions which mold as well as respond to socioeconomic conditions, and which have historically exhibited great adaptability in both functional and structural terms. Allegations concerning the "decline" of legislatures in contemporary regimes are based less upon an analysis of the functions which such institutions can or do perform than upon misinformed judgments about what they should be doing or what they are alleged to have done during heady moments in the past (Loewenberg, 1971b; Crick, 1968; Bracher, 1964). Even in a single polity, the structures as well as the functions performed by a legislative system will vary a great deal— not only historically or developmentally, but during any given period of time as the system responds to the demands put upon it in a variety of issue areas.

Nevertheless, legislative institutions are particularly vulnerable in the new and "modernizing" states[2] which are attempting to meet the problems of national integration and economic development. If legislatures are to endure and have meaningful roles in such inherently unstable contexts, they must acquire some capacity to influence the direction of these momentous processes. Without that capacity they would be reduced to serving secondary (or "minimal") functions—at best legitimizing decisions made elsewhere in the political system.[3] Indeed that is precisely what has happened in the great majority of the new and modernizing states which have created representative assemblies. With few exceptions, legislatures that have not been displaced by military governments have been turned into adjuncts of executive-centered single-party states.

Such legislatures, however, may perform functions of significance in a political system. Even at the height of the avowedly authoritarian Nkrumah regime in Ghana, for example, the National Assembly retained some independence as a forum for expressing grievances and dissent within the ruling Convention People's party. A number of irregularities in the operation of state corporations were investigated and exposed, and a few government bills were withdrawn because of backbench opposition (Apter, 1972; Kraus, 1971; Lee, 1963). Moreover, even in "minimal legislatures" seats may serve as prestigious rewards for the party faithful and as avenues of social mobility and political recruitment (Packenham, 1970; Payne, 1968)—functions which may have profound effects upon even the most rigid systems of social stratification.[4] Of course, one might wish to speculate on the long-term unintended consequences of such practices. But in all such cases the effect on *policy making* has been "minimal" indeed (Packenham, 1970). In point of fact, it frequently has been observed that, even in the older European and Anglo-American democracies, the policy-making capacities of legislatures have declined precipitously (Huntington, 1966; Crick, 1970; Loewenberg, 1971b; Beer, 1966).

Does it follow that we ought to discount the significance of policy making as a primary focus for analyzing legislatures?[5] One need not dispute the validity of these empirical observations to disagree with such a conclusion. The central question is whether it is sound to analyze the functions of legislative institutions by using their more diffuse and remote consequences as a primary point of departure. That would be a circuitous way of studying political power. Whatever its secondary effects, a *viable* legislature must have the institutional power to affect governmental decision making and the course of public policy.

## THE ORGANIZATION OF POWER
## THROUGH LEGISLATIVE INSTITUTIONS

Legislatures have demonstrated a remarkable resilience and capacity to persist. Once abolished, they almost invariably reappear, although often in altered form and frequently under the suzerainty of those who served as executioners.[6] The central reason for such persistence and recurrence is to be found in the nature of power itself, which, although it can be centralized, is first and inherently a plural phenomenon.[7] Indeed, conciliar institutions are characteristic of all regimes, both historical and contemporary. This is as true of bureaucratic and autocratic forms as of those that are more plural and libertarian. In fact, it is entirely proper to regard conciliar institutions as a universal and necessary means of organizing power for governmental purposes.

Given this understanding of political power, it is useful to envisage the development of distinctly "legislative" institutions as a transformation from "councils of convenience" to "councils of consent." The decision to "create" legislative institutions in the formal sense may therefore be regarded as a decision to acknowledge, enhance, and value the pluralistic side of power. Moreover, with the transformation from councils of convenience to councils of consent, a major qualitative distinction between the character of bureaucratic or executive-centered institutions and conciliar or legislative institutions is illuminated. The former, though plural, emphasize the legitimacy of centralized power and decision making, while the latter, although often displaying hierarchic features, engender and legitimize decentralization and the pluralization of power and interests.

It is necessary to emphasize that differences between legislative and executive-oriented institutions are not merely matters of degree. We must isolate as carefully as possible, therefore, the fundamental characteristics that distinguish legislatures from other forms of political association. This is a difficult task, if only because all institutions organize power and, therefore, are not generically distinguishable in purely structural terms. Both legislatures and executives, for example, are *multimember bodies* which may recruit members who are representative of and responsive to a wide range of popular and group demands. As a consequence, composition itself is insufficient for our purposes. It is also obvious that all institutions require and are characterized by some measure of *autonomy*. But upon reflection, differences in this regard are less matters of degree than of the ways particular institutions define the terms or conditions which distinguish them from other institutions and mediate relations among them. Finally, both legislative and executive institutions may be characterized by a great variety of *internal authority patterns*—legislatures are not uncommonly hierarchic and bureaucracies are often dispersed and decentralized. It is the qualitative distinctions inherent in each of these categories and not their structural or quantitative dimensions which are crucial.

1. *Multimembership and Representation.* Although legislative assemblies are plural bodies, it is neither their size nor their representativeness but the character of their relationship to their constituencies which is decisive and which distinguishes them from the much larger administrative apparatus of the state. Legislatures are intended to encourage the formation and articulation of social interests and to be responsive to them as a matter of right, and not merely of convenience. Hence the most important and perennial practical questions associated with representation include the type and size of constituency, the length of tenure, the extent of the franchise, and the mode of election—all important devices affecting the closeness and character of the relationship both within the legislature and between it and the larger society.

It is obvious, however, that legislatures have no monopoly on representation. Indeed, there are those who suggest that executives and their attendant administrative organizations can be more representative of important social needs and interests (Huntington, 1966; Shils, 1960; Friedrich, 1940). But there is an important difference between legislative assemblies and administrative agencies in this regard. Legislatures are intended to be collegial institutions whose members are selected by election so that they may be held accountable by their constituents. Administrative bureaucracies, on the other hand, typically are appointed without direct collective public participation. Because there is no means of institutionalized public choice, administrative appointments are a matter of personal and a priori judgments which are likely to be made in the interests of the appointing agencies. Even in regimes with elected presidencies, the definition of "representative" appointments is ultimately an assertion of personal fiat and not necessarily one of electoral choice or political necessity. This distinction is fundamental because without electoral accountability the ultimate responsibility will tend toward those who make the appointments rather than to the public which they are appointed to serve.

2. *Autonomy and Responsible Leadership.* Institutional autonomy is a sine qua non of all social organization or differentiation. But whatever one might say of societal institutions in this regard, it is tempting to associate the extent of autonomous decision making with the extent to which political institutions are autocratic. Autonomy alone, therefore, does not help us much. Although a central variable in most conceptions of institutionalization, an autonomous institution, taken to its logical extreme, would have no relationships with its environment or, at least, its relationships would be void of dependencies. Autonomous and therefore relatively impermeable legislative assemblies would most certainly lose their capacity for responsive, representative governance and acquire the endowments of a guardian class of rulers. In turn, the isolation of legislative assemblies from executive bureaucracies would make effective, workable governance impossible. This is not to argue against the necessity of some autonomy, the discretionary foundations of which are necessary for the independent decision making which any stable government requires. But it is less the extent of the autonomy than the conditions of institutional reciprocity and the character of "boundary exchanges" which are decisive. The terms on which legislatures claim autonomy are in fact claims upon essential areas of policy making. Such con-

siderations form the basis of any constitutional order which seeks to specify and limit the power and functions of particular governing institutions.

3. *Authority and Consent.* Legislatures would not be distinguishable in principle from other governing institutions if they were defined solely in terms of the formal structures of internal authority and organization that they exhibit. Whether they are governed through cabinets or committees, or make decisions through disciplined parties or shifting coalitions of individual members or blocs, the mode of decision making is decisively affected by the requirement that important decisions be ratified by majority assent. Thus, parliamentary or legislative governments somehow utilize roll call voting as a matter of right. In this minimal sense legislative assemblies are essentially collegial bodies designed to incorporate a wide range of societal interests into their deliberations. The necessity of majority rule, in turn, compels legislative assemblies to reconcile democratic consent with structures of internal authority that facilitate governance. Even in systems of cabinet government based upon disciplined parties, the right and necessity of obtaining consent among the elected members of parliament set limits upon the autonomy and authority of the parliamentary party leadership.

## THE VIABILITY OF LEGISLATIVE INSTITUTIONS

There is no reason to assume that the ultimate justification for the existence of legislative institutions must depend upon the discovery of "inherently" "legislative" functions—i.e., functions which are performed exclusively or primarily by legislative bodies. It is obvious that the most general societal functions, such as "conflict reduction," can be performed by innumerable institutions or social structures. Nor are the more distinctly political functions which legislatures may perform their exclusive domain even under ideal circumstances. We know, for example, that the role of the American executive and judicial branches in creating law is continuous and often more important than the contribution made by Congress. The same can be said for the mass media (and especially the press) with respect to the function of "legislative" oversight of administration. The question is not whether legislatures perform these and other functions exclusively but whether they do so differently, and, in so doing, contribute something distinctive and desirable to the regimes which encourage and utilize them.

In general terms, the most distinct functions that viable legislatures perform are a consequence of their peculiar capacity to centralize decision making while preserving pluralistic and often decentralized power. Legislative bodies more than executives tend to value localism and regionalism, and are more receptive to geographically based interests.[8] They are also more inclined than executives to use log-rolling and compromise as instrumental techniques (Davidson, 1969; Frey, 1965; Leites, 1959; Hopkins, 1970; Stultz, 1970; Hakes and Helgerson, 1973; Apter, 1972), and, therefore, tend to stress the value of popular consent and to perceive themselves as institutional bulwarks for the security of individual liberty.[9] Finally, because they are more dependent than executives upon societal pluralism, they are more likely to value interest heterogeneity and to seek to enhance the private sector and private interests.[10] Indeed, it is precisely these attributes or propensities that have led some students of political sociology to conclude that legislatures inherently resist change and, therefore, are impediments to socioeconomic development (Packenham, 1970; Huntington, 1969). Nor is it a coincidence that the political leaders who advocate single mass parties in the modernizing, developing nations almost invariably deprecate the value of independent legislatures and laissez faire approaches to economic development. The two are viewed as mutually reinforcing means of dispersing power and, therefore, as threats to the organic unit of society.[11] Thus, although executives certainly do legislate, the important point is that legislatures tend to do so differently—i.e., with different values and interests in mind and at stake.

Legislatures legislate differently because they organize power differently. But their distinctive organizational qualities would mean little if they were not also endowed with effective authority of a fundamental kind. Viable legislatures must have the capacity to influence significant dimensions of public policy in a competitive context. There are three dimensions to the problem as we see it.

1. *Legislatures as Law-Affecting Bodies.* The involvement of legislatures in the creation of law must be considered their central and most fundamental function, though certainly the initiation of law is not their abstract right or prerogative.[12] It is the overall *effect* on the making of law which is crucial, and in that regard the *power* which

legislative assemblies have to influence the direction and contours of public policy making is decisive. So fundamental is this process that it is difficult to imagine legislatures performing any other functions effectively without somehow participating in the formulation of law.

   2. *Legislatures and the Control of Executive Power.* The capacity to control the potential excesses of executive initiative and power has been considered a basic task of legislatures in modern theories of representative government (*The Federalist*, Rossiter; Mill, 1958; Pitkin, 1969; Mansfield, 1968a, 1968b). It is intrinsic to the idea of both cabinet responsibility in parliamentary systems and congressional oversight in presidential systems. In fact, contemporary theorists are prone to stress this function while deprecating the presumed obsolescence of legislatures as law-making institutions in modern "technocratic" or "managerial" society.[13] Yet these critics often are concerned that legislatures seem ill-equipped to exercise effective control over the activities of executive departments. The problem as we see it is that the control of the executive will be ineffective if it is no more than the assertion of a right, however sound the principle behind that right may be. In the long run, exhortation is no substitute for the power which legislatures must have to compel executives to supply them with the information they need to establish control. Executives, after all, readily can claim prerogatives to withhold essential information, even in polities with well-established constitutional traditions which seek to make them amenable to legislative control (Berger, 1974). Nor can we expect legislatures to establish effective staffs and committees without the certain knowledge that the information generated can be put to effective use in formulating policy alternatives to executive actions (Robinson, 1970; Patterson, 1970; Agor, 1971b, 1970; Stultz, 1970, 1969; Payne, 1968; Mezey, 1972). And those essential and inveterate sources of influence and information—interest groups and lobbies—hardly can be expected to associate themselves with assemblies whose oversight functions are fundamentally hortatory (Beer, 1966, 1965; Stewart, 1958). Only when popular assemblies participate in the molding of law can the necessary power for controlling the bureaucracy be built and expanded.

   3. *Legislatures and the Mobilization of Consent.* The advocates of strong executive-centered government for modern or modernizing societies assume that legislative institutions ought to serve as aux-

iliaries in mobilizing public support for policies advocated by executives (Beer, 1966). As Crick (1970:40) observes, England has "never had government *by* Parliament, . . . but always government *through* Parliament." The lesson, of course, is that contemporary legislatures can serve as organs of popular consent without participating in the creation of law—a lesson readily perceived by the leaders of numerous modernizing states.[14]

It may well be true that the origins of legislative assemblies in Europe are traceable to conciliar bodies created to foster consensus in the consolidation of monarchical power. But we must distinguish between those origins in absolute monarchies based upon principles of divine right and the fundamental change that occurs with the advent of secular parliamentary supremacy based upon popular sovereignty. To conceive of elective cabinet or presidential governments as functional substitutes for absolute monarchies is to misconstrue the locus of sovereignty grossly. In the modern democratic state, legislatures can perform effectively only if they have the power to compel executives to govern "through" them by governing with them. There is every reason to doubt that an essentially impotent institution would have the resources or the popular esteem needed to mobilize effective support for governmental programs. It is not, after all, simply a matter of generating propaganda—influential executives surely have more effective means of accomplishing that through access to the mass media.

The effective mobilization of consent through *legislative* institutions must be accomplished through a complex infrastructure of political support which ultimately is grounded in the capacity of the legislature to affect law making. It is the ultimate effect of legislatures upon public policy that transforms elections into vigorous systems which mobilize consent by encouraging the articulation of interests and the organization of groups to pursue those interests in the larger political system (Stauffer, 1970.)

### THE IRONIES OF LEGISLATIVE VIABILITY IN NEW NATIONS

It is apparent from these remarks that viable legislative regimes are compelled to resolve certain inherent tensions in the principles and structures of organization upon which they are founded. Put simply legislatures must maintain sufficient autonomy to be able to influence the course of national policy making without stifling or undermining their representative capacities. The contours of the problem are especially manifest in the circumstances of the new and developing nations. There the most institutionalized structures of governance tend to be relatively centralized, bureaucratic and authoritarian—the mass party of solidarity, the army, and the civil service or bureaucracy—all adjuncts of executive authority (Riggs, 1969; LaPalombara, 1965). The frequency of personalistic leadership in these states adds another centralizing force—one which cannot admit easily of vital institutions that intervene between the leader and the people. Legislatures, on the other hand, seem to become institutionalized less rapidly than the more centralized authority structures because they must obtain support through elaborate electoral systems and extensive infrastructures of independently organized societal interests (Sisson, 1973; Mezey, 1972). Although it has been argued that many developing nations do not possess "adequate" infrastructures of support in the "modern sector," it is nevertheless true that such regimes encourage legislative dependence upon powerful individuals and societal groups. In so doing they are likely to engender intense conflicts over the allocation of values affected by governmental decision making.

Even political elites presumably committed to parliamentary institutions have resorted to repressive measures to control the conflicts of interest that representative regimes naturally generate (Ghana, Apter, 1972; Ivory Coast, Zolberg, 1971, 1969; Kenya, Stultz, 1970; Nigeria, O'Connell, 1971; Pakistan, Jahan, 1973). We may well ask whether the political elites in parliamentary regimes are driven inexorably to transform their polities into variants of executive-centered one-party states. It is obvious that the problem of legislative viability is complex and does not turn simply upon the good intentions of political leaders—however important that factor may be. Nor is it enough to assert that legislative institutions are inherently incapable of coping with the problems of economic development and national integration. Rather, the difficulty is traceable to the tension which is generic to the structure of all viable legislatures—tension which precipitates the fundamental conflict between autonomous decision-making authority and dependence upon the consent or acquiescence of influential societal groups.

The resolution of this contradiction is manifest in three basic problems that legislative regimes must resolve. *First* and most fundamentally, as institutions that have the power to influence the course of public policy making, legislatures are at once *arenas* which affect the distribution of political power and *agents* of powerful clientele interests whose support necessarily limits their decision-making autonomy. Recently established legislatures are likely to be weakly institutionalized and, therefore, especially sensitive to the character of this supportive abridgement of their autonomy. If they are supported by narrowly based socioeconomic, ethnic, or regional groups, their agential function may jeopardize their capacity to maintain an open, pluralistic arena of power and their long-run institutionalization will be impaired.[15]

*Second*, although viable legislatures must be able to control executive power, they serve also as avenues of political recruitment and social advancement. But insofar as the advancement of major social classes is tied to such political recruitment, control over the agencies of governance may create new ruling classes based upon the holding of elective and appointive political offices and the control of political preferments. Under such circumstances the stakes are so high that governing elites cannot afford to retain open electoral and parliamentary processes. Thus, the conditions are established for the creation of single-party, executive-centered regimes, whatever the original intentions of the political elites. The problem is particularly acute in new and developing nations where the state is the single largest source of investment capital and public employment seemingly is an inexhaustible resource for partisan advantage.[16]

*Third*, democratic legislatures ultimately must be justified as organs of popular consent. The long run legitimacy of legislative regimes (or the "diffuse support" which they obtain) will depend on it. Yet a preoccupation with popular consent can be inimical to the survival of viable, policy-affecting legislatures, for where national integration is most problematic, incessant recourse to popular consent may be most pernicious, and institutions that encourage the expression of diverse and conflicting interests and sentiments may court disaster (Jewell, 1977). In such situations the viability of legislative governments may well hinge upon the capacity of political systems to provide legislative elites with sufficient autonomy to reach acceptable accommodations—a problem hardly unique to the new nations.[17] Ironically, the organizational device most commonly utilized to secure elite autonomy, the mass party, has always been regarded with suspicion by the advocates of legislative autonomy.[18] Indeed, extra-parliamentary party organizations in the European democracies generally have considerable influence over the internal decision-making structures of the legislatures they serve (Duverger, 1961; Jewell, 1973). The problem is especially acute in the new nations, where attempts to use the legislature may be inherently divisive and the resources for creating single-party regimes are readily available.

## THE CONDITIONS OF VIABILITY

How do legislatures acquire law-affecting capabilities? Two fundamental and closely related conditions appear to be necessary. In the first place, a polity must generate ideologies or conceptions of legitimacy that support an influential role for legislative institutions in the making of public policy. Second, important social groups or classes must develop clientele or utilitarian stakes in preserving parliamentary institutions to satisfy their own interests. Only when these conditions are met will legislators have access to the political resources needed to secure a policy-making role for the legislature against the appeals for mass support made by the administrative bureaucracies and party organizations.

### LEGISLATURES AS LEGITIMATE ARENAS
### FOR RESOLVING CONFLICT

It is eminently arguable that viable parliamentary institutions ultimately must rest upon the development of doctrines of constitutionalism and individual right (Rokkan, 1968). Such ideals, rooted in ancient European feudal practices, took centuries to germinate and grow into cogent theories of limited government and of the rights of citizens which could be afforded in courts of law administered by a legal profession. But, however significant these doctrines and institutions may be, viable legislatures require a separate and distinct notion of authority—viz., that some measure of law-making power should reside in the legislature as a matter of right. Parliamentary authority in this narrower sense was relatively late in emerging. Parliaments seem to have originated more as adjuncts of monarchy than as checks upon it (de Jouvenal, 1957; Beer, 1966, 1965; Crick, 1970, 1968; Loewenberg, 1973, 1971a, 1971b, 1971c, 1967; Packenham, 1970). Indeed parliamentary "legislative" functions did not emerge clearly in England until late in the sixteenth century, and the idea that Parliament might create law rightfully was not institutionalized fully until the great religious and dynastic questions were settled a century later (Hockin, 1972; Beer, 1966, 1965). The assertion of parliamentary authority over all aspects of law making, including foreign affairs, was not established doctrine until the eighteenth century.[19]

Such a lengthy development of constitutional and legislative authority is not commonly open to the new and developing nations. Where parliamentary institutions are either borrowed or inherited from colonial regimes, supportive ideologies are not likely to be well-developed. The question is whether an independently powerful legislature is accorded intrinsic value (or "diffuse" support)[20] by an influential stratum of the population.[21] Three models of legitimacy seem to have been especially influential in this regard.[22] Legislatures have been most influential where governing elites have embraced some variant of liberal democratic theory. In such regimes the attainment of independence and the pursuit of national integration and economic development have been predicated upon the establishment of representative legislatures. Limited constitutional government and a significant role for private enterprise have been stressed, at least initially, as in the Philippines, Kenya, the Ivory Coast, Nigeria, India, and (the classic and most durable case) the United States. On the other hand, advocates of corporatist models invariably deplore the conflicts of interest which are encouraged and enhanced by such regimes, and seek to effect social mobilization and economic change through the agency of a single mass party or the interlocking bureaus of the state. Perhaps the clearest examples of regimes instituted on these principles have been initiated in Ghana (under Nkrumah and the CPP), and Tanzania (under Nyerere and TANU) (Apter, 1972; Kjekshus, 1974). Finally, in countries with established traditions of administrative rule, legislatures have not always found ready reserves of support for law-making prerogatives. Legislative institutions have been especially unpopular in countries with entrenched bureaucracies (as in Thailand and Germany) or modernizing autocracies (as in Iran) (Mezey, 1972; Loewenberg, 1973, 1971a, 1967; Bill, 1971).

To the extent that viable legislatures have been instituted, one must look to particular elites and organizations as carriers and propagators of the more supportive ideals. There are two basic patterns of institutional transfer which are relevant in this regard. A number of countries obtained independence through relatively well-established legislatures and without the assistance of a well-organized and powerful independence movement or party. Sri Lanka and the Philippines are the most obvious recent examples of this process. In both cases the legislature seems to have been endowed with considerable prestige and legitimacy (Wriggins, 1960; Stauffer, 1970; Styskal, 1969; Grossholtz, 1970). The same can also be said for the significance of colonial legislatures and congresses prior to the American revolution.[23] Legislatures which are instrumental in securing independence from foreign domination seem to enjoy a special sense of popular legitimacy. Secondly, there are those instances where well-organized mass party movements have led the struggle for independence but have chosen to do so in cooperation with parliamentary institutions. In the process, such parties have had to adopt democratic practices of internal organization based upon pluralistic centers of power. The Congress party of India and (to a lesser extent) the Kenya African National Union are good examples of movements which endowed postindependence legislatures with considerable authority and vitality (Stultz, 1970; Kochanek, 1968a).

More frequently, however, legislative institutions were accepted by revolutionary leaders and mass parties simply as the price of obtaining independence from a colonial power. Such independence movements were organized as weapons of mass mobilization and their leaders rarely expressed much interest in the intrinsic value of parliamentary forms—"lawyer's regimes," as Nkrumah contemptuously called them. The Convention People's party was one of the best examples of this type of movement. The National Assembly in the Gold Coast was accepted by the CPP as the price of obtaining independence. It ceased to play a significant law-affecting role immediately thereafter and for as long as the CPP remained in power (Apter, 1972, 1965). But whatever the specific agencies of institutional transfer, ideological support alone is not an adequate or reliable means of preserving the authority of legislative institutions in new nations.[24] Indeed, it is often argued that new or emergent nations are lacerated by socioeconomic and cultural cleavages so deep that legislative institutions are rendered impracticable. More centralized and hierarchic structures of authority and less permissive norms of legitimacy seem to be necessary.

It is true, of course, that theories of liberal democracy tend to legitimize and encourage social and political conflict. But it is also true that regimes which subscribe to various versions of that theory tend to spawn norms and practices which can mitigate even severe cleavages. In other words, there is no reason to assume that social and political cleavage will be coterminous.[25]

Historically, two types of norms seem to be especially important in mitigating the effects of societal cleavage upon the capacity of elective parliamentary elites to govern. First, and most important, are those norms or attitudes that accord elected leaders the flexibility and autonomy which they may need to defuse (rather than to exploit) potentially divisive issues. In the Anglo-American democracies, a widely diffused sense of political "trust" appears to serve that function (Putnam, 1973; Christoph, 1965). But there are numerous examples of deeply divided societies which have maintained parliamentary institutions because political elites have been able to work out compromises without electoral retaliation. Since Malaysia obtained independence in 1957, Malay and Chinese political leaders have used a bipartisan consultative organization to effectuate agreements on economic, religious, and particularly vexing linguistic differences between their rival communities (Grossholtz, 1970; Esman, 1972). Similarly, "cartels of elites" have been successful in mitigating communal conflicts and stabilizing democratic regimes in Switzerland, Belgium, the Netherlands, and (until recently) Lebanon.[26]

Second, there are those more generalized norms which screen or depoliticize problems before they are translated into political issues and demands. The diffusion of Western secular values has, for instance, played a significant role in mitigating the political impact of religious communalism in India and ethnic communalism in Sri Lanka (Smith, 1963; Kearney, 1967; Nordlinger, 1972). Furthermore, a commitment to a free enterprise economy in some cases has deflected demands for governmental intervention and has encouraged groups to compose their differences in order to stabilize their own economic interests.[27]

### LEGISLATURES AS UTILITARIAN AGENCIES.

Whatever the ideological commitment of postindependence elites, legislatures will have to be nurtured by other means if they are to survive as viable law-affecting institutions. They must secure a social base of support to resist the inevitable incursions of executive-centered power (Von Vorys, 1959). In fact, it is tempting to argue that their fate may well hinge upon the extent to which they are supported by social groups and classes which perceive in parliamentary institutions a direct means of consolidating and furthering their own interests. Thus the law-affecting power of emergent legislatures may depend on the extent to which they are the captive agents of powerful and prestigious classes.

There is ample historical evidence for such a conclusion. Where viable legislatures have developed, the dominant impetus for their creation and enhancement has come from new social groups or classes which have seen the legislature as a useful agency for constraining or circumventing executive-centered authority. Where this process has resulted in limitations upon executive power and the enhancement of parliamentary authority, we refer to supportive societal abridgement of other political power centers for the enhancement of the legislature. A significant measure of autonomy from executive domination is gained, although the enhanced influence of clientele groups in the legislative process is a necessary consequence. This shift in the locus of power sets one stage for the development of a powerful, viable legislature.

The outcome of efforts at supportive abridgement is dependent upon several structural conditions in addition to the ideological dimensions discussed above. Supportive abridgement is most likely to occur where the organization of the executive rests upon a decentralized system of authority and where centralized bureaucratic institutions have not been able to establish a permanent and effective presence at the local level. Supportive abridgement is also enhanced where there is a tradition of local political autonomy and representation in public bodies. Such relatively autonomous and localized structures of authority constitute an institutional shield protecting social interests, a shield not to be dislodged by executive-centered authority. In such situations even the demands of the narrowest class and interest group for expanded legislative power can be expressed in terms of traditional principles of legitimation. This process of abridgement is a protracted one and occurs where the executive-centered elite does not or cannot respond positively to the demands of an emergent counter-elite—whether these demands are relatively narrow (such as for expanded employment in the government bureaucracy) or for broader and more effective influence in making policy.

The effectiveness of supportive societal abridgement, however, is also a function of class power and elite cohesion. The process occurred in particularly striking form during the seventeenth and eighteenth centuries in England. It was during the latter century that the convention of collective ministerial responsibility to Parliament finally developed—thereby emphasizing the primacy of the parliamentary arena in policy making. During this period the landed aristocracy and emergent commercial, industrial, and financial interests used Parliament as an indispensable means of extending their propertied interests at home and abroad, a propensity traceable on a much smaller scale to the latter sixteenth century (Guttsman, 1963; Bennington, 1968; Neale, 1963; Plumb, 1967; Judd, 1955; Namier, 1957; Laski, 1928a, 1928b; Thomas, 1939).

The process of supportive societal abridgement is also evident in certain Asian and African states. The Indian case is instructive. There, demands for the creation and subsequent expansion of legislatures into law-affecting bodies commenced in the latter part of the nineteenth century and derived from two new coalitions—new professional classes allied to indigenous commercial groups and upwardly mobile peasant and lower caste movements. The professional classes included for the most part lawyers, a number of educators, and journalists (Majumdar, 1965; Seal, 1968; Martin, 1961; Crane, 1964; McCully, 1940; Misra, 1961).[28] Commercial groups included families of substantial wealth who had business interests in the larger metropolitan areas, as well as smaller entrepreneurial groups in rural towns of the British Provinces. During the second and third decades of the twentieth century, lower status groups also became politicized and sought to breach the executive bureaucracies and political centers of state and local power controlled by traditional elites. Thus, the widespread anti-Brahman movement in Madras found political expression in the Justice party and controlled the legislative councils until 1935 and after. The anti-Brahman movement in Bombay Province was based in a large peasant caste, the Marathas, who eventually captured control of the Congress party and used it first as a means of access to the legislature, and ultimately to the cabinet. In Bengal, the rural Muslim peasantry found in the legislature a vehicle to circumvent the power that traditionally had been wielded by Hindu-dominated Calcutta, and by Hindu as well as Muslim landlords in the rural areas of eastern Bengal—classes which also enjoyed substantial representation in the administrative services. In the Punjab, a strong and hardy peasant caste, the Jats, found in the legislature a means of circumventing the conventional instruments of upper caste and class control (Irschick, 1969; Broomfield, 1968; Patterson, 1954; Washbrook, 1973; Gould, 1973; Bayly, 1971; Robinson, 1973).

Of course the support which legislatures receive as utilitarian agencies is not necessarily conducive to their long-run viability. Whether they survive this initial agency function as law-affecting bodies depends on the character of social stratification and its relationship to legislative politics at the founding of the regime. This point requires elaboration.

If the initial utilitarian support is confined to a narrow, distinct social base, those groups which control the legislature may be prepared to abandon the institution when it no longer serves their purpose, i.e. when their interests are threatened by newly mobilized groups. Thus, the 1970 military coup in Turkey was precipitated by a shift in legislative representation and power from a coalition of military and bureaucratic elites clustered in the Republican party to a new coalition of lawyers and merchant classes with locally based power organized through the Democratic party (Frey, 1965). In Pakistan, the national legislature was dissolved and military rule declared in 1958 with the support of the aristocrats and landlords of the western province who had long dominated the legislature in the face of an increasingly vociferous coalition of rural peasants and urban middle class elements centered in East Pakistan and rising refugee and peasant discontent in the west (Callard, 1957). In other cases, when legislatures were not abandoned outright, presidencies were instituted and used to repress opposition movements among disaffected classes or regions—as occurred in Ghana under Busia as well as Nkrumah, and in Uganda under Obote (Apter, 1972; Lofchie, 1967).

The extent of social differentiation or pluralism at the founding sets limits upon the stability which any political system can anticipate. Where there are deep and abiding primordial or class divisions, competition for political power is likely to become especially ferocious because class or communal interests appear to be affected by a wide range of political issues. Politics then resembles defensive warfare. In the absence of mitigating ideologies, legislative regimes tend to exacerbate such cleavages because they naturally encourage competition and the expression of group interests. In fact, liberal democratic theory assumes that social conflict can be converted into peaceful political competition which can be resolved in the legislative forum.[29] But during the initial agential stage of legislative development this is not a valid assumption. Control of the legislature is still viewed as a means of class or group survival (Nigeria, Vickers, 1970; Pakistan, Jahan, 1973, Chaudhury, 1975).

On the other hand, where social divisions are pluralized more extensively, as in postindependence India, coalition possibilities increase, the capacity of any single group or party to crush its rivals is thereby constrained, and individual groups need not fear that the loss of legislative power will be fatal—after all, they might be needed in the next coalition. Such conditions long typified the internal politics of the loosely organized, pluralistic Congress party of India (Kochanek, 1968a; Nicholson, 1972). There are, of course, limits to the benign effects of pluralized power, for in the extreme it can fragment governmental decision making and undermine the effectiveness of the regime—a recurrent problem in the Congress party (Sisson, 1972). In the long run, however, pluralistic power can be self-perpetuating and thereby supportive of legislative institutionalization. As Madison observed of the American founding, legislatures based on pluralized socioeconomic interests will tend to use political power to discourage the formation of deeply divided social classes (Rossiter, 1961; Papers 10 and 51). Under agential pluralism the regime might well be afforded time for ideologies that support legislative rule to develop (Patterson and Boynton, 1965; Putnam, 1973).

The new nations are also developing nations, a fact especially obvious with respect to their economies and in the context of rapid economic development, the political dynamics of societal pluralism do not necessarily guarantee an open legislative forum receptive to new and emergent interests. Rapid socioeconomic change can outrun even a relatively pluralistic regime if the interests of the dominant coalition appear to be threatened by new events. Thus, what appears to be a relatively broad coalition of agential support for a legislature may be truncated by the rapidity of social change. As we have seen, the Busia coalition in Ghana, fearful of urban working class discontent, resorted to repressive measures against organized labor. A similar problem confronts the Congress party of India. With its rural organizational support rooted in prosperous agricultural classes, and its urban base tied to entrenched commercial interests, Congress has been unable to be responsive to the increasing demands of landless peasants and a rapidly expanding urban proletariat (Kochanek, 1968b). As a consequence, strident peasant movements have arisen in Bihar and Eastern India, and urban unrest has been expressed in national strikes. In England, on the other hand, the transfer of power from a landed aristocracy to emergent middle classes with industrial and commercial interests was facilitated by kinship ties and a ruling class which was relatively open during the crucial period of economic development and social change in the late eighteenth and early nineteenth centuries.[30] In the process, parliamentary authority was preserved and enhanced and an ethic of open receptivity to political opposition became a fixed feature of British political culture. By the mid-nineteenth century the idea of a "loyal" opposition was accepted as an integral part of a belief that Parliament should be "the agreed arena" for the resolution of conflict (Hockin, 1971–72; Beer, 1966, 1965)—an idea that surely facilitated the electoral reforms which eventually brought the working classes into parliamentary politics.

## CONCLUSIONS

Ultimately a viable legislature is one that contributes to the maintenance of the fundamental values upon which liberal democratic regimes are founded. The power of the legislature must function in a way consistent with the protection of individual and minority rights and the maintenance of a sizeable, energetic sphere of private interests. Legislatures are crucial to liberal regimes not only because they can restrain the more authoritarian propensities of executive-centered power, but because they have a natural tendency to decentralize and disperse power. In other words, they can nationalize authority while enhancing the pluralistic side of power.

Such regimes have always been considered difficult to establish and perpetuate. In the context of the new and developing nations, they suffer two particularly grievous defects; their association with a colonial past, and their tendency to value and stimulate conflict. The first seems to undermine their legitimacy and the second their utility.

Thus, although legislatures are often (and rightly) considered static institutions which preserve the power and interests of dominant groups or classes, it is in fact their more destabilizing and dynamic propensities which render them suspect to leaders in the new states. Indeed, they do act as agencies of social mobilization which have propelled new groups into the political process; this is true not only at the national level, but also at the local level where the structure of power has often undergone profound change. With the reordering of power through the institution of the legislature, executive authorities have had to take the demands of the new groups into account. As a consequence, legislatures have served as effective instruments for the redistribution of the benefits of society.

Such tendencies need not be pernicious to national integration or to political stability. But in the context of the new states the dynamics of legislative politics can undermine both, and in so doing, contribute to the erosion of political authority. Indeed, it is the historically crucial utilitarian stage of development which is the source of the problem. Without a cushion of diffuse support, reliance upon essentially self-interested groups can turn the legislature into a fearsome instrument which exploits (rather than resolves) social cleavage. Under these circumstances, status, ethnic, and communal differences may be exacerbated as a general consequence of the increased demands that are placed upon government.

Thus, the most critical juncture in the development of representative regimes involves the transformation of legislatures from utilitarian agencies into constitutional forums. At least initially, legislatures may well have to be defended against powerful executives through the medium of supportive societal abridgement. But if a representative regime is to survive, the legislature must at some juncture cease to be the agent of restrictive classes and become the defined arena within which the competing forces of society seek to resolve their differences and participate in defining their common objectives. In short, it must derive an increasing measure of its support from a belief in its inherent rightness as part of the system of public authority.

## NOTES

1. The literature is very extensive; major contributions include Lipset, 1959, 1960; Almond and Coleman, 1960; Deutsch, 1961; Lerner, 1958; Cutright, 1965, 1963; Smith, 1969; Haug, 1967; and Thomas, 1974.

2. We are aware of the ambiguity of the term. See Kornberg, Hines, and Smith, 1973.

3. Mezey (1972) cites a number of examples. Packenham (1970) observes that after the military coup of 1964, the continued meetings of the Brazilian Congress served only to enhance the power of the president by supplying him an arena of legitimacy.

4. The effect was especially pronounced at the state level in India, although the state legislatures there are not "minimal" in our sense (Rudolph and Rudolph, 1967; Sisson, 1969).

5. A number of the most knowledgeable students of the legislative process have suggested that it does—and should (Huntington, 1966; Crick, 1970, 1968; Loewenberg, 1971b; Beer, 1966).

6. In 137 sovereign polities surveyed by Jean Blondel (1973) in 1970–71, all but 25 had legislative institutions or were in the process of creating them. Of those 25, at least two have since resurrected legislative institutions—the most notable case being Greece. In those regimes without legislative bodies, conciliar institutions within the framework of a military or single party regime generally exist, although with no claim to autonomous power or function.

7. For an elaboration of this conception of power see Lasswell and Kaplan, 1950; de Jouvenal, 1949; Dahl, 1962; Fleron, 1969.

8. For a general assessment in the developing countries see Packenham (1970). Perhaps the most obvious example is to be found in the "Old Tory" conception of the power of Parliament, which obtained throughout the sixteenth and seventeenth centuries in England. An explicit distinction was drawn between local and private legislation, which was the business of individual MPs, and "Great Matters of State" (succession, the church, and foreign policy)—the exclusive concerns of the crown (Hockin, 1971–72; Beer, 1965).

9. The theory that the security of liberty resides in representative assemblies is traceable to the ideal of a "balanced constitution" which emerged in the late seventeenth- and early

eighteenth-century English parliamentary practices. (Hockin, 1971–72; Mansfield, 1965). The argument is simply a structural version of that theory in terms of contemporary pluralist theory (Dahl, 1971; Rossiter, 1961:Papers 51–66 and 70–73).

10. Hence the Marxist observation that parliamentary government is inherently the weapon of the bourgeoisie.

11. For a general discussion of mass mobilization parties see Apter (1972:xv–xviii, 372–86). The Ivory Coast is the only prominent example of a single-party regime which explicitly rejects socialism and the organic view of a society mobilized by the party (PDIC) (Zolberg, 1969). An informative assessment of the two approaches to economic development is found in Elliot Berg (1971).

12. It is not easy to determine who actually initiates legislation even in American national politics. Policies advocated by the executive may in fact have emerged from the advocacy and lobbying of organized interests, or may have been incubated (to use Polsby's term) for many years in various congressional committees (Polsby, 1971; Moe and Teel, 1971).

13. The argument is made by Beer (1966) and Crick (1970), both of whom use the latter term. Also see Huntington, 1966; Loewenberg, 1971c; Goguel, 1971.

14. Nehru and Kenyatta espoused "mobilizing" conceptions of parliament remarkably similar to those found in Beer and Crick. Also see Hart (1971) and Stultz (1970).

15. This is precisely Huntington's (1966) assertion about the contemporary U.S. Congress For an insightful commentary on this and attendant issues, see Polsby (1975).

16. For general analyses of the problem of capital formation under state control in the new nation see Berg (1971) and Green (1971). The political consequences are analyzed in numerous studies of new nations (Vickers, 1970; Austin, 1967; Jahan, 1973).

17. It is often claimed that the survival of representative government in the "smaller" European democracies ultimately depends on such arrangements. For a review of the literature on such "consociational" democracies see Daalder (1974).

18. The works of Bryce and Ostrogorski have been most influential in this regard.

19. Even Locke, it will be recalled, reserved authority over foreign affairs to the monarch exclusively.

20. The distinction is usually made between "specific" (or utilitarian)) and "diffuse" (or legitimacy) support—terms derived from the works of David Easton. The mass/elite dichotomy may cut through both types of support. The most pertinent studies of legislatures include those of Patterson (1973) Loewenberg (1973, 1971a) Boynton and Loewenberg (1973), Wahlke (1971), and Patterson and Boynton (1969).

21. Mass support for crucial democratic and libertarian values seems to be relatively limited and unstable even in the United States and Britain. Hence the tendency among empirical democratic theorists to look to political elites as carriers of constitutional ideologies. The most pertinent studies include those of Prothro and Grigg (1960); Dahl (1961); Key (1964); Budge (1971); and Christoph (1965). For a general discussion of the problem and an analysis of the supportive ideologies of parliamentarians in two Western democracies, see Putnam (1973).

22. The analysis which follows is based upon the generally acknowledged division between two conflicting philosophic traditions. The first, founded upon the works of Locke, Bentham, the two Mills, and Madison, stresses individual rights, limited government, and the private sphere. The second, based upon the works of Rousseau and Marx, stresses social and economic equality and the use of the state to realize those goals. For especially good analyses see Sabine (1952), Sartori (1965:228–246) and Putnam (1973:159–236;). Apter (1972:xv–xvii, 330) points out that the Marxian tradition is especially appealing in the new nations because colonialism is associated with capitalism.

23. Madison hoped to rely on the popularity of the colonial legislatures to obtain loyalty for the new national Congress established under the constitution. See Eidelberg (1968) and de Grazia (1951).

24. For perceptive comments on the fleeting character of elite as well as mass ideological

support, see the comments by Austin (1967) and Goody (1968) on popular reactions to the fall of Nkrumah in Ghana. Also see Loewenberg (1973) and Feith (1962).

25. Even elites from similar social backgrounds have differed profoundly over the legitimacy of a particular regime. Perhaps the most striking example is to be found among the gentry in Parliament prior to the English civil war (Brunton and Pennington, 1954).

26. The term is Arend Lijphart's (1967). We rely upon the literature on "consociational democracy" here. For general reviews see also Daalder (1974) and Nordlinger (1972).

27. Belgium, Switzerland, Malaysia, and Lebanon (until recently) are examples of societies with politically influential commercial classes which successfully sought to overcome communal conflicts in order to preserve economic stability and growth (Nordlinger, 1972:46–48.)

28. Under the 1892 reforms 67 percent of those elected to provincial councils by district boards and 93 percent of those elected by municipal boards were lawyers. Under the reforms of 1909, lawyers constituted from 45–50 percent of those elected from "open" constituencies. Under the reforms of 1919, the proportion of lawyers in the legislatures varied from province to province but ranged from 30–45 percent. This was due in large part to the entry of landlord candidates who commanded considerable power in rural areas (Great Britain, 1930, 1918).

29. See Lijphart (1969) for a review of the literature on cross-cutting cleavages. For additional consideration of this problem, see Smith and Musolf, and Kornberg and Pittman, this volume. Also see Jewell (1977).

30. During this period the ruling class was in reality a close association between landed and commercial interests. Capital passed back and forth, as did persons (Judd, 1955:54–70). After 1832, as the industrial revolution began to take political effect, the number and influence of commercial MPs rose sharply (Thomas, 1939). For a general analysis see Guttsman (1963).

*Chapter 3*

# REPRESENTATIVE AND MILITARY BODIES: THEIR ROLES IN THE SURVIVAL OF POLITICAL SYSTEMS OF NEW STATES

ALLAN KORNBERG
KENNIETH PITTMAN

Military intervention in the internal affairs of government is a pervasive contemporary pattern. Of the more than 140 independent states currently in existence, more than half (75) experienced actual or attempted military interventions during the period 1946–75.[1] The causes, forms, and lengths of these interventions varied considerably. In Uruguay in 1973, military intervention was expressed as threatened withdrawal of support for civilian government, and in Turkey in 1961, as mediation of disputes between civilian government leaders. In Argentina in 1962 and in Kenya and Uganda in 1964, it took the form of mutiny to protest socioeconomic or political conditions. It has dissolved traditional bonds of authority (Egypt, 1952; Libya, 1969), substituted one elected leader for another (Brazil, 1964), and dispensed with popularly elected government altogether (Chile, 1973). The military can intervene swiftly and visibly as in Greece in 1967 and in Portugal in 1974, or its intervention can be protracted as in Ethiopia since 1974.

Between 1946 and 1975 there were 218 reported attempts by members of the armed forces of African, Asian, Latin American, and Southern European countries to change an existing political order. (There may well have been considerably more. For a variety of reasons, political leaders in power often are loathe to report aborted coups.) Of the successful attempts, only 5 percent were followed by an election which brought to power a new ruling group. In another 11 percent, a plebiscite or some other expression of public opinion was used to ratify (and presumably legitimate) the intervention. However, fully 84 percent of the successful interventions brought to power civilian, or most often, military rulers who subsequently governed without any indication that they were supported by the citizens in whose name intervention almost invariably is justified.

As Table 3.1 indicates, interventions have occurred most frequently in Sub-Saharan Africa and Latin America, and least often in the older states of Southern Europe. In only 8 percent of the successful interventions did the military limit itself to applying pressure on existing civilian authorities. In 17 percent the military replaced a current civilian government with a new cohort of civilian officials. In all other instances, members of the armed forces supplanted existing civilian or—in counter-coups—military leaders. At times the military rulers of a country exchanged their khaki for mufti. Frequently, however, they did not bother with even this kind of cosmetic action.

**TABLE 3.1**

**REPORTED MILITARY INTERVENTIONS AND THEIR CONSEQUENCES (IN PERCENT)**

|  | Southern Europe | North Africa | Sub-Saharan Africa | Asia | Latin America | Total |
|---|---|---|---|---|---|---|
| Unsuccessful interventions | 28.5 | 35.0 | 57.5 | 20.8 | 28.3 | 39.4 |
| Successful interventions | 71.5 | 65.0 | 42.5 | 79.2 | 71.7 | 60.6 |
| N = | (7) | (40) | (80) | (24) | (67) | (218) |
| Proportion of successful interventions that resulted in: |  |  |  |  |  |  |
| Pressure and influence on civilian authorities | – | – | 5.9 | – | 8.3 | 4.5 |
| Displacement of civilian authorities by other civilians | 40.0 | 26.9 | 14.7 | 31.6 | 16.7 | 21.2 |
| Replacement of current authorities by military and/or by military-civilian authorities | 60.0 | 65.4 | 79.4 | 68.4 | 75.0 | 72.7 |
| Revolutionary new regime | – | 7.7 | – | – | – | 1.5 |
| N = | (5) | (26) | (34) | (19) | (48) | (132) |

If the incidence of military intervention seems dramatic, it is noteworthy that governments incorporating legislatures or similar representative institutions are nearly as numerous (Lowenberg, 1971b; Kornberg and Musolf, 1970). Indeed, of the above-mentioned 140 independent states, only five have never included a representative body in their political structures.[2]

Unlike a junta's, a legislature's ubiquity cannot be ascribed to response capacity. As Blondel observes, "legislatures are rarely strong. Even in liberal democracies many complain about their impotence, their decline, their ineffectiveness; and if they are strong they are often blamed for their inconsistency, their squabbles, and thus the same ineffectiveness. On the other hand they rarely are abolished for very long: one prefers a subservient legislature to no legislature" (1973:3). These seemingly miraculous powers of regeneration have intrigued and occupied other students of legislatures (Sisson, 1973; Riggs, 1973).

In this chapter we will explore the bases of legislative resilience, the prevalence and variety of military intervention, as well as our belief that the two are closely related. Stated somewhat more heroically, our purpose is to provide a framework in which both the occurrence of military interventions and the establishment and reestablishment of representative bodies can be understood as integral parts of political development in new states.

## THEORETICAL ASSUMPTIONS

We begin by assuming that the rulers of new states seek above all else to avoid repudiation of the political systems they lead. To succeed they must be able to maintain political and public order, and if existing structures and processes prove inadequate for the task, we assume that leaders will attempt to change them. Public order includes protection of the lives and property of individuals and groups from others in and outside the country, and its maintenance requires at least a minimum of political order—the machinery of government must effectively mediate and regulate interpersonal and group conflict, marshal the state's human and environmental resources, and enforce decisions (Bienen, 1968:35). If a political system cannot perform these functions, its repudiation will be imminent.

Although political and social theorists have little difficulty identifying the raison d'etre of states, the leaders of new states experience great difficulty in maintaining the political order necessary for public order because the task invariably requires reconciling conflicting system-general and system-specific demands. The former, often external in origin, require "whole system" responses, regardless of potential costs to component subsystems, while the latter generally originate internally and require responses that may harm the political system as a whole. The two sets of demands are interrelated when resources are limited (a condition in almost every new state) for the political system's ability to respond to one type necessarily constrains its ability to respond to the other. (Morell's analysis of Thailand in this volume is an excellent case in point.)

Our second assumption is that compliance with the authoritative decisions of political leaders of a new state is fundamental to the maintenance of public order. Broad support engenders patterns of *voluntary* compliance. When support is initially absent, however, *forced* compliance to measures that produce popular outcomes also can lead to general support for the political system, and, ultimately, to voluntary compliance.

The loci of control distinguish the notions of support and coercion. The coercive mechanisms normally are under the immediate control of political leaders, unlike support, which is rooted in symbolic attachment and generally beyond their power to affect.[3] Support is time- and performance-dependent. It increases as leaders demonstrate they can maintain public order and meet the needs of a "critical mass" of the population.[4] It also is value-dependent, for it reflects the level of agreement on both the definition and goals of the community and the instruments and procedures that may be legitimately employed to realize those goals.

Third, we assume that the need for compliance encourages leaders to make the range of their authority congruent with the geographic boundaries of the state. In particular, the need to maintain the territorial integrity of a state motivates them to extend their authority to the periphery. In the relationship between the extension of authority and the maintenance of state boundaries, each depends on the other and both are crucial in maintaining the political system; the failure of one jeopardizes the effectiveness of the other. Even though new states at times have inherited colonial boundaries that disregard ethnic, cultural, and linguistic criteria,[5] national self-preservation requires the political center to draw into the state all groups within the national boundaries; to make from a de jure state a de facto nation.[6]

Where a new state is largely an aggregate of traditionally separate groups, each with a preexisting identity (e.g., traditional tribal groups), the nation is little more than an aggregate of conflicting groups bound in an involuntary union (Furnivall, 1948; Kuper and Smith, 1971). Although old symbols and loyalties need not be destroyed, new structures and processes almost invariably arise. Concerted efforts are then made by political leaders to develop public attachment to the new arrangements[7] —usually resulting in a crisis of integration.[8]

Three types of conflict—value, norm, and organization—have been identified (Parsons and Shils, 1962; Smelser, 1962; Kahane, 1973), and can be arrayed along a continuum of decreasing intensity. Value conflict reflects a lack of consensus, not only on the forms of political structures and the symbols of the state and its goals, but, over whether the state should even exist. Value conflict sharply reduces the possibility that disparate groups within a state can be integrated successfully. In situations where the trappings of nationhood have been forged from the values of one or more groups at the expense of others, the potential for disintegration is exceedingly high.[9] Norm-oriented conflict reflects disagreement over principles for organizing the nation and rules by which it is to be maintained. Norm-oriented conflicts, (e.g., federal versus unitary, unilingual, bi- or multilingual, secular or clericalist, socialist or free enterprise) can make the problem of integration severe and protracted. Finally, organizational conflict reflects clashes over who will control political institutions (e.g., disagreement among elites on representation, hierarchical ordering of institutions, allocation of resources to institutions).

Starting with value conflict, each level defines the parameters of those next in line. Where integration is not accomplished at the level of basic values, primordial differences persist and sustain almost total conflict. The political system is torn by increasing demands and reduced ability to fulfill them. With diminished political order the problem of maintaining public order becomes immense. Conversely, as more levels are integrated, the number of demands made on the political system decreases. Moreover, the number and intensity of *conflicting* demands are reduced.[10] Such conditions help political leaders maintain public order as major social groups are likely to comply voluntarily with their public decisions. There is less need for coercion, and force, if used, is more likely to be regarded as legitimate.

Legitimacy refers to the belief that a political system has the *right* to the obedience of its members, even if its specific decisions do not coincide with their perceived personal interests (Linz, 1975a; Apter, 1971:chaps. 2, 5; Eisenstadt, 1966:chaps. 1–3). Effectiveness refers to the capacity of the leaders to formulate goals and to develop means adequate for their achievement (Linz, 1975a). The relationship between the two is reciprocal (Lipset, 1963:chap. 3; Rose, 1969).

Even though a political system may be regarded as only marginally legitimate, the pressures to be effective remain. Therefore, its leaders may have to secure compliance from some of the groups that deny the system's legitimacy. To become both effective and legitimate (the former may possibly be at cross-purposes with the latter), political leaders must establish an effective balance between mechanisms of support and coercion. Two political structures which are used for this end are representative bodies and armed forces.

## REPRESENTATIVE BODIES AND THEIR ROLES IN THE SURVIVAL OF NEW STATES

In our view, the most important contribution a representative body can make to the political system of a new state is the generation of voluntary public support and, thereby, the bestowing of legitimacy on its central institutions and processes. This goal is furthered if the members adopt and follow appropriate procedural rules. Regularizing and systematizing procedures and adhering to them while transforming prospective policies into actual legislation helps instill a feeling—among elites and eventually among nonelites—that the political system is a "government of laws and not of men."

A second way in which a representative body can generate support for and legitimize a political system is by including in its membership adequate representation of the socioeconomic and cultural groups included in the state. A third way is to create transcultural symbols and mechanisms (e.g., flag, coat of arms, national anthem, new athletic stadium, new capital city, new place names, national airline, road system, radio network, national university, armed forces). Historically, these have generated increased citizen attachment and loyalty toward a political system, and facilitated the integration process (Kornberg and Hines, 1977).

New states typically have "low information" political systems. The political center generally lacks reliable information on "grass roots" attitudes and opinions whereas the outlying regions have even less knowledge about what a government does or is currently doing. The members of a representative body can provide valuable links between a political center and its outlying regions (see the chapters by Barkan, Hopkins, and Morell, for example). Individual members can perform service and ombudsmen functions for constituents; they can monitor and apprise the political center of local values and attitudes; they can ascertain local development needs and urge officials at the center to meet these needs; they can help "sell" the new system, its leaders, their ideologies, their policies and programs (current and prospective) to their constituents and, thereby, help create a feeling that the new system deserves support.

Representative bodies can contribute to public order if they are involved in the appropriations process (the Inter-Parliamentary Union suggests that most parliaments are). They can appropriate or approve funds for the armed forces to maintain security. They can generate or ratify laws that define personal and property rights and contractual responsibilities. Such laws regulate, stabilize, and make predictable the relationship of individuals and social groups to one another. If enforced adequately, passage of these laws contributes to a public feeling that the new political system is performing effectively.

A representative body's members may initiate or otherwise be involved in development programs and policies. Equitable development can contribute to the integration of the numerous social sectors into a nation, thereby encouraging the belief that the new system is legitimate and effective.

We have suggested measures that representative bodies are able to take under "optimum" conditions when they are already somewhat established. However, all political institutions and processes in new states—legislatures included—generally are in a state of flux. Frequent changes in their structures and functions and the selective application of their procedures generate confusion, frustration, and cynicism. Moreover, even when all socioeconomic and cultural groups are represented in a legislative body, if some are constantly ignored, they are likely to feel anger rather than obligation toward the political system. In addition, when there is little agreement over the values pursued, the norms established, and the organizations created (as often is the case in new states), the legislature can become a highly visible battleground. Constant bickering among spokesmen for competing interests is more likely to polarize a public than generate an impression that the system is effective and deserves support.

Similarly, although representative bodies can create transcultural integrating symbols and mechanisms, some may become white elephants. The four-lane highway with sporadic cart traffic dramatizes the fact that limited resources have been drained from local areas without any prospect of tangible returns. Representative bodies involved with white elephants may easily be associated with what seems to be unnecessary deprivation. Further, if the security forces for which they have appropriated funds act arbitrarily, or if they are used repressively, representative bodies will probably be viewed as agents of tyranny.

Representative bodies associated with failed development programs are as likely to be blamed as are other political institutions, regardless of the extent of their control over implementation. In fact, they may be regarded as more culpable because of the very qualities for which they are valued in Western societies—representativeness, fixed rules of formal procedure, and collective decision making based upon extended deliberation. The environment of crisis surrounding most representative bodies in new states may give them the image of standing by helplessly while the country burns, or of being willing to sacrifice national interests for the sake of the parochial interests they represent or their own self-interests (see Morell's analysis of the Thai legislature and its overthrow by the military).

## MILITARY BODIES AND THEIR ROLE IN THE SURVIVAL OF NEW STATES

Like representative bodies, the armed forces of a new state are political institutions.[11] Their function is to maintain public order and secure compliance with the leaders' authoritative decisions. In all societies, new or old, military and police forces have de jure monopolies over the use of instruments of physical coercion. However, in new states which lack substantial value and norm consensus, it is likely that other groups also will be armed. If they are large and have forcibly resisted integration, generally only the military has the numbers, armaments, and technical skills to maintain the public order necessary for political order.

Only the military is able to protect the territorial integrity of new states against external force. If effective, they contribute to the ascription of public support and legitimacy to the political system, as witness Israel. Israel also exemplifies how a new state's armed forces can mold social groups with widely different values and life styles into a nation. Particularly notable was the success of the Israeli military during the 1950s. The Israeli government utilized universal military training for both men and women to socialize and acculturate large groups of immigrants reared in traditional societies with authoritarian and nonparticipatory political systems into a society whose values, political institutions, and practices are predominantly Western, democratic, and participatory. Given the population transfers that have occurred since World War II, militaries have also been employed in other new states as instruments of social and political integration.

As the most visible emblem of the collective power of a state, the armed forces provide a symbol around which new attachments can be fostered and to which old loyalties can be transferred.[12] The hierarchical organization of the military is appropriate for the initiation and implementation of many developmental policies and programs (Janowitz, 1964; Lerner and Robinson, 1960:19–44). Moreover, the armed forces of new states (together with the civilian bureaucracy) frequently contain most of the educational and technical skills in the population.[13] If public compliance must be secured by force or its threat, the armed forces are equipped to do this. It should come as no surprise, therefore, that among most new states suffering shortages of resources, the military segment of society enjoys a preferred position—augmented by a disproportionate share of foreign assistance.

However, despite their potential for contributing to the survival of a new state, the creation of a de facto nation, and the support of a political system, it is the armed forces that have often precipitated the collapse of existing political structures. One reason is that some military forces are incapable of carrying out their basic functions of maintaining the state's order and territorial integrity as recent events in South Vietnam amply testify. Numerous successful military coups, counter-coups, and threatened coups in various Middle Eastern and Sub-Saharan states also can be attributed, at least in part, to conspicuous failures of military institutions either in containing serious internal dissident movements or in combatting external enemies.[14] An inept military can come to symbolize all that is wrong, inefficient, and ineffective in a state and foster feelings of individual and collective inferiority rather than pride and patriotism. Repeated military defeat also can generate anger toward and frustration with the political system. The performance of the armed forces of the several Arab states in conflicts with Israel in 1948, 1956, and 1967 is frequently cited to explain both the self-conscious inferiority expressed by individual Arabs and their collective hostility toward the West and their own governments.[15]

Second, militaries, like other political institutions, are subject to the conflict and consensus—value, normative, and organizational—that can beset a society (Mazrui, 1976:258–264). If important national subgroups are underrepresented in the officer corps, and if coercion is often necessary to enforce compliance with political decisions, the armed forces can be identified with the values and interests of dominant social groups. Even if representation is equitable, value and normative conflicts can reduce the military to a battleground for contending officer cliques (e.g., Nigeria, Uganda). The military is capable of intervening when other political structures falter because its disciplined hierarchical organization makes it particularly able to act decisively. That it does intervene, however, places it in danger of becoming enmeshed in the divisive issues that rend a society and necessitated the intervention initially (Rapoport, 1968:551). The conflicts that originally set military against civilian leaders can reappear as conflicts between the military *as an institution* and the military *as a government* (Stepan, 1971:chap. 12, pt. 4).

Third, despite foreign assistance military forces still place an enormous financial drain on a state's resources. Sophisticated weapons are extremely expensive and once military personnel have been trained to use them, demands for procurement almost invariably follow. Since 1945 more than one new state has been brought to the brink of financial ruin by the appetite of its armed services for ever greater numbers of bigger and better armaments. This perspective heightens the irony of military coups resulting from political leaders bankrupting their states.

Finally, although the military is geared to expeditious implementation of developmental policies, it cannot protect a new state against mistaken decisions (Nordlinger, 1970).[16] When the armed forces do participate in development efforts and disaster follows, however, it is the political leaders who are likely to be blamed for any ensuing crisis.

Since representative and military bodies are political institutions whose actions can be helpful to the continued life of a political system, it is safe to assume that political leaders of new states try to maximize positive contributions and eliminate negative effects. Why have events over the last thirty years demonstrated failure in this area? To answer we must look again at the assumptions with which we began. More specifically, we must examine some of the factors that affect the ability of leaders of political systems to avoid overthrow and secure support for their decisions.

## CHANGE AND THE RELATIONSHIP OF REPRESENTATIVE BODIES TO MILITARIES IN NEW STATES

Although armed forces and representative bodies are but two of the institutions available to political leaders to maintain order and garner support, their presence (and, in the case of representative bodies, their frequent reappearance) in most states regardless of political arrangements suggests they are institutional manifestations of a more fundamental social reality. Stated baldly, military interventions generally occur where coercion is necessary for stability, whereas representative bodies flourish where there is widespread voluntary support for the system. In a society of the first kind, both the scope and importance of military activity tend to expand and those of the representative body to contract. The opposite process characterizes a society of the second type. The explanatory value of the coercion-support ratio and of the military-representative body relationship is enhanced if we consider how they affect and are affected by the formulation of demands and the political system's response.

We noted previously that demands can be separated into system-general and system-specific types. Should these two conflict, our view is that the success of the political center (other than in the case of a state forcefully occupied by a foreign power) will be determined by its capacity to respond to system-specific demands. Excessive rigidity (i.e., favoring system-general solutions) can produce strains that destroy the structures of the new state, but a more common danger is excessive malleability (i.e., favoring system-specific solutions) which weakens the political center and leads to an implosion as the system collapses upon itself.[17]

The most powerful demand confronting a political system is the pressure toward a special combination of changes that binds system-general and system-specific demands in a complex series. These changes have been labeled "modernization."[18] Gabriel Almond suggests that modernization and its inherent movement toward mass integration is actively pursued " . . . because nations perceived or perceive in science, in technology, in education and communication, in bureaucracy and political association, a set of ways of realizing human potentiality and capacity more effectively than their own traditional ways" (1969:459). Almond's speculation may be valid, but a more obvious characteristic of modernization appears to be its inescapability rather than its desirability. Economic survival alone is a powerful inducement to modernize.[19] Modernization processes seem to be facilitated by societal integration, but integration is a system-general priority, and system-specific demands frequently militate against it.[20] This conflict can lead to political disorganization as well as to massive social and economic dislocation. Such problems have been encountered by all political systems but are notably intense in new states where value and norm conflicts are common.

Both representative bodies and militaries, but especially the former, are integration-dependent; the more consensus they enjoy with respect to existing values, norms, and organizations, the more both institutions are able to contribute to the performance of a political system's principal functions. When value consensus is great enough, the norms encompass the organizational dimension, and a representative body, in accordance with a constitutional prescription, may remove a chief executive without a breakdown of political and public order that would threaten the system.[21] In other societies (e.g., Egypt or Turkey), lower value and norm consensus may restrict representative bodies to informal mediating roles under similar conditions, whereas in still others (e.g., Dahomey, Mali) the existing consensus may be so low that only the *idea* of a representative body as a source of legitimate authority exists. The presence and reappearance of representative bodies in states with a variety of political arrangements does suggest that in nearly all new states value and norm integration have coalesced sufficiently to generate at least a symbolic attachment to the notion that a representative body is an integral part of a legitimate political system.[22] Problems arise, however, when the symbolic attachment to the idea of a representative body exists without a developed consensus regarding its actual role. There may be general acceptance of a representative body as a legitimate instrument of political action but little or no agreement on how the members are to be chosen, what powers they are to exercise, and how they are to exercise them. The less consensus there is on such essentially organizational matters, the less effective a representative body is likely to be.

All political systems obviously need institutions to channel demands and direct energies toward the achievement of societal goals. In new states the need is especially great because of scarce resources and the heavy demands from largely inescapable pressures to modernize. Hence, their political leaders frequently turn to the military for assistance because, given its hierarchical organization, discipline, and skills and resources, the military is likely to be the most efficacious organization available. Once involved, however, it is difficult to restrain.[23] Even if it does not become an overt participant in governmental affairs, it still can exercise substantial influence over the content and direction of public policy. As indicated in Table 3.1, military establishments of Africa, Asia, Latin America, and Southern Europe at various times have: (1) pressured civilian political leaders by threatening direct and forceful action if their wishes were not considered; (2) displaced one set of civilian political leaders with another that promised to realign system goals and adopt policies and programs more congruent with military preferences; (3) replaced civilians, in part or in whole, with their own officers; and (4) carried out a revolution. Here the emphasis was on fundamental content rather than form. Egyptian and Libyan armed forces tried to realign basic societal norms and generate the foundations of a new political order.

The scope of these interventions largely depended on two factors: the extent to which value and normative consensus had created a framework within which political institutions were expected to act, and the magnitude of the role assigned to the military. With regard to the first, the more specific the consensus on what political institutions, including the military, could do and, relatedly, the more legitimacy ascribed to the performance of *specifically prescribed functions*, the more limited any overt military intervention in the political process was likely to be. On the other hand, the more repudiation-avoidance motivated the use of coercion, the more activities political leaders tended to assign to the military, thereby increasing the likelihood that when an intervention occurred, it went beyond informal pressure on them.

The interaction of these two factors in integrated societies has been quite different from their interaction in fragmented societies. In well integrated (usually older) nations the "rules of the game" as to what militaries do and how they do it are quite specific. Political leaders generally can rely upon citizens to support their decisions voluntarily, and the armed forces are relegated to the role of defending the nation against external aggression. Disruptions of public order seldom carry sufficient political meaning to polarize a significant antigovernment movement, and conventional police forces are sufficient to secure nonvoluntary compliance should it become necessary. New states, however, tend to be fragmented, and generally the opposite conditions may prevail.

Additionally, in older, more integrated nations the armed forces' involvement in politics usually is limited to lobbying civilian political leaders. They try to maintain or expand their share of the budget and they advise civilian leaders on matters having strategic military implications for foreign policy. Going beyond these activities (e.g., to support a particular political party overtly in a national election or to mediate disputes among civilian leaders) would be regarded as a gross and outrageous violation of the rules of the game.

In contrast, in less integrated new states (and even in some not-so-new states as in Central and South America) the extensive involvement of the military in politics is routine. There is no great outpouring of public wrath if the armed forces intervene to arbitrate a dispute between civilian political leaders or to displace one group of civilian politicians with another. Even if the military assumes total control of government, this will not necessarily generate extensive civil disorder—and for very good reasons, three of which flow from our previous discussion.

First, given the chronic shortage of resources in most new states, the political system cannot possibly meet all system-specific demands, especially since they frequently conflict with the almost inescapable system-general need to create an industrial base for development. Thus, there are almost always large groups of critics of the system. When they cluster in particular geographic areas, they can generate intense regional conflict with the political center. Any serious regional disaffection with leadership can be transformed into outright opposition and resistance. Under such a condition, the disaffected may well support a military intervention.

Second, in most new states the values and norms that underlie specific political organizational and procedural arrangements have not coalesced. The rules of the political game are neither very visible nor broadly supported.[24] Consequently, a military can intervene politically with relative impunity, *particularly if the intervention is rationalized in terms of values and norms for which broad support already has coalesced.* In the name of the fatherland, motherland, representative government, national unity, Islam, socialism, democracy, or whatever, the military can argue it was duty-bound to reorganize a political system or specific political institutions within it in order to "save" them.[25]

Third, most new states live in almost perpetual crisis. So fragile can their political institutions be, so dissimilar from traditional arrangements, and so difficult can they be to operate effectively, that public support for them may be pitifully small while overt opposition can be alarmingly large. Since their political systems also rest on socially fragmented bases, often the best that the leaders of new states can hope for is the indifference of a critical mass of citizens for a period long enough for the system to take root. Unfortunately, time is in extremely short supply in a crisis environment. Small wonder, then, that political leaders rely increasingly on coercion to maintain their positions. Not to do so might well invite immediate repudiation. Since in most instances large increments of coercion generate only marginal immediate changes in unfavorable environmental conditions, the severity of coercive measures tends to increase. But since the leaders of new states lack the technology required to terrorize whole populations,[26] resorting to ever more stringent measures is usually counterproductive. The principal result is to turn nonresisters into active opponents. When the number of active opponents is sufficient, even a minor incident can trigger an intervention and the overthrow of a regime and its leaders.[27] Needless to say, leaders of new states are profoundly aware of the possibility of overthrow if they alienate a critical mass of their population by the overzealous use of force. We may assume, if they had a choice, that the great majority would rather not have to coerce people into going along with them. The problem is how to elicit voluntary support. Enter the representative body.

We already have noted the symbolic value of such a body, whatever its title. Its presence represents the commitment of the political system and its leader to the *idea* of popular government. Although public support is rooted in symbolic attachments and is not under the immediate control of political leaders, representative bodies *are* more or less under their direct control. This is one reason they are incorporated so frequently in the political system of a new state, or are reestablished after a system has been overthrown. The frequent changes in the organization, powers, and procedures of representative bodies in new states may be viewed as attempts by the political center to translate support for the representative institution into support for the leadership itself.[28] Specifically, these changes include actions to: reduce a representative body's power to delay or block the passage of supposedly vital legislation (A. Valenzuela, 1976); encourage legislative members to leave a capital city and spend time in their constituencies monitoring grass roots opinion and "selling" the political system to their constituents (chapter by Hopkins; Barkan, 1976); reduce public bickering and horse-trading by members (Hakes, 1968; Stultz, 1970) and so forth. Some changes are well-intentioned and no doubt appear quite rational to those proposing them. For example, several attempts have been made to discourage members of representative bodies from practicing interest-oriented group politics in countries without norms that support this kind of behavior. Unfortunately, however, these changes may have consequences that were not anticipated. Thus, President Julius Nyerere, troubled by the fact that many Tanzanian MPs seemed to be articulating the parochial interests of their constituencies at the expense of a "national" interest, arranged for a number of representatives of the country's major social groups (e.g., women, farmers, and civil servants) to become "national" members of the Tanzanian Parliament. His assumption was that these new MPs, freed of constituency ties, would aggregate and articulate a national interest. Mr. Nyerere was disappointed to find that the newly created national members, shortly after taking office, began to view themselves and to act as functional representatives of the interests of the social groups of which they were a part (Proctor, 1973).

In addition to generating unintended consequences, fairly frequent and sometimes drastic changes in the power, organization, and procedures of representative bodies are detrimental to the development of the sort of public confidence in government that underlies the legitimacy ascribed to the political systems of older nations. If our analysis is valid, however, political leaders in new states undoubtedly will continue to tinker with them largely because they provide leaders with an institutional device—albeit an imperfect one—for "buying time" during a period when their fledgling political systems are only marginally legitimate and even less effective. Leaders are encouraged to tinker because it is easier to restructure representative bodies than military institutions. When push comes to shove, members of the military can resist change with guns, whereas members of representative bodies can resist only with words.[29]

To recapitulate, most of the changes that have been made in the representative bodies of new states have diminished their autonomy and the scope of their activities. In particular, their participation in the policy process has been carefully limited—at times to evaluative deliberation or surveillance, most often, to perfunctory ratification. Conversely, military institutions in most new states have expanded their activities and aggrandized both the scope and importance of their political roles. In this paper we have tried to suggest reasons why the two institutions have moved in these directions. More specifically, we have tried to show why a shift toward reliance on increasingly authoritarian structures is characteristic of change in most new states, especially those that are socially fragmented societies; and why, despite a special dependency on the military, the leaders of the new states nonetheless exhibit an affinity for the idea if not the reality of representative bodies.

## NOTES

1. Any count of this type is impressionistic in the sense that it varies with what one defines as a military intervention. We define a military intervention as an attempt by the institution labeled "military" to assume or reallocate governmental authority in a country. A general cross-national survey of interventions may be found in Europa Yearbook 1975 (1975:Vol. I, II). Supplementary data have been drawn from a variety of sources including Fred R. von der Mehden (1969), Edward Luttwak (1968), Asian Recorder (1955–75), Africa Research Bulletin (1964–75), Latin America (1967–75), and numerous newspaper references.

2. Although only five countries never have had legislatures, the number of countries with a functioning legislature at any particular time has varied considerably. Blondel notes that the proportion of states with functioning legislatures consistently has been high in the Atlantic and Communist areas of the world (95 percent). In the Middle East it consistently has been low (50 percent to 60 percent). Approximately 80 percent to 90 percent of Latin American and Asian countries usually have had functioning legislatures. In Africa the proportion of countries with legislatures dropped from about 95 percent in the late '50s to about 70 percent in the '60s and early '70s (1973:8).

3. "Political actions," Gerhard Loewenberg has observed (1971b:188), "have instrumental meaning for only a small segment of the population—for most it is a parade of abstractions having only symbolic meaning."

4. The notion of critical mass is somewhat elusive. For a regime to come to power it must have the support of some segment, large or small, of the population. It is this segment that we refer to as the "critical mass." Its size in a given situation will vary with both the type of regime coming to power and the type of regime being replaced. The extent and source of support required for taking power depends upon the structural requisites of the organizations being discarded as well as those being adopted. A "western" popular democracy requires the support of a broad cross-section of both elites and nonelites, whereas a military government can be imposed on a country by a small group of advocates—as long as they are located in crucial branches of government. A political structure also may be toppled by the same critical mass through which it rises, or by a different one that is "critical" at a later time in response to changed conditions.

5. A number of scholars (Kabwegyere, 1974:43–45; Mazrui, 1976:246–272) remind us that not only did colonial powers create potentially new states, they also created new ethnic groups, some of which contributed to the integration problems of new states in the postcolonial period.

6. This distinction between "state" and "nation" is not merely semantic. The state, as a geographical entity, may exist for a time without any unifying values, norms, or organizations that make it and its inhabitants a distinguishable, single unit (i.e., a nation). LaPalombara (1974:34–76) carries this distinction a step further in his discussion of "state," "nation," and "nation-state."

7. This process has been analyzed for Indonesia (Kahane, 1973).

8. Integration has been defined as a "process through which loyalty toward and deference for a society's central institutional arrangements are generated among the several strata of its population. Loyalty and deference are intended to transcend more particularistic loyalties in the population although the latter need not be destroyed in the process" (Kornberg and Hines, 1977). Taking this definition one step further, integration is a process of mutual accommodation among groups in the forging of the bonds that join the community. Community bonds, in turn, must be considered in terms of their values, structure, and performance. System values determine and are determined by the form the political structure takes and the interrelationship of values and structures has behavioral consequences—as suggested in this figure.

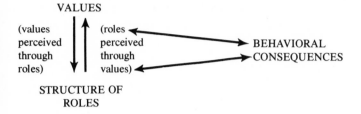

VALUES

(values perceived through roles)

(roles perceived through values)

BEHAVIORAL CONSEQUENCES

STRUCTURE OF ROLES

When the values and role definitions are congruent, the relationship is one of integration. When they conflict, the behavioral consequence may be disintegration leading to a revised set of beliefs (or a revised structure of roles) through which role structures (or values) can be interpreted (Apter, 1971:chaps. 1–3).

9. A case in point was the tripartite division of Nigeria following independence in 1960. The cohesion superimposed on competing tribal groups finally collapsed into civil war (Apter, 1965:119–120, 148, 194).

10. It has been argued that successful national integration ought to facilitate balance and order within a society. By balance is meant a widely shared belief that a new state and its central arrangements will give approximately equal weight to the interests of the several major social, economic, and political groups within a society so the interests of a particular group and region are not overtly and continously sacrificed to those of other groups or regions. By order is meant a condition of social stability that in part reflects a widely shared perception of particularistic interests as more or less equitably balanced by the central institutional arrangements of a state (Kornberg and Hines, 1977).

11. Much has been written about the criteria of political development and the relationship between civilian and military structures in the development process. All too often, however, what is written revolves around an illusory polar dichotomy between "civilian" and "military" rule. Our view is that both military and representative bodies are manifestly political.

12. By way of illustration, Ernest W. Lefever (1970:21) assesses the military's potential as a unifying symbol thus: "A more vivid symbol of sovereignty than the flag, the constitution, or the parliament, the army often evokes more popular sentiment than a political leader."

13. In a thoughtful essay Ali Mazrui has questioned whether in Africa, at least, the current military really is the repository of high level educational and technical skills. He argues that during the colonial period recruits for colonial armed forces, especially in East Africa, were taken disproportionately from the most disadvantaged and rural sectors of society. Since independence many of these men have risen through the ranks and are now senior members of the officer corps. He acknowledges that in West African countries these men were reasonably well educated and trained, but this less often was the case with younger junior officers. Thus, each successive coup in a place like Ghana would bring into prominence more of the less westernized Ghanaian soldiers. "The first Ghanaian coup was more 'Sandhurst and British' than the second. The third, should it take place, would be less 'British' still" (Mazrui, 1976:271).

14. It is not unusual for military defeat to be charged to the government in power, regardless of whether government officials had any immediate control over the success or failure of the military. Syria, with nine successful coups since World War II, provides a classic example of this tendency.

15. The relative success (in comparison with previous conflicts) enjoyed by the Egyptian armed forces in the October, 1973, Arab-Israeli conflict is frequently cited to explain a marked increase in public support for the current political system and President Anwar Sadat.

16. Scholars differ in their evaluations of the military as an instrument of modernization-development. A balanced and succinct assessment of the military's potential in this regard is offered by Mazrui, who says: "It is conceivable that the military can play a critical economic role which speeds up industrialization and accelerates urbanization. There have been military regimes which, because they were less socialist-oriented than the civilian governments they overthrew, and because they were more concerned with bread-and-butter issues than with long-term ideological formulations, have performed better, in economic terms, than their predecessors. The strengthening of new links with the Western world, greater encouragement of investment, and greater promotion of indigenous enterprise have in such cases helped to accelerate both urbanization and industrialization. In this special sense such regimes may be deemed to have contributed to the modernization process. And yet, if part of the effect of these changes is to make the construction of viable and legitimate political institutions more difficult than ever, and to create the potentiality of social and economic restlessness on a wide scale, it could be inferred that the modernizing impact of the military is not necessarily in the direction of consolidating political development" (Mazrui, 1976:248–249).

17. Linz (1975a) discusses the collapse of political systems as a consequence of internal tensions rather than external pressures.

18. Modernization is understood as the "enhanced capacity of a social system to adjust to simultaneous rapid change within its sectors and to events in the outside environment." Three distinct aspects of change seem to be unique referents of modernization: (1) the purposive and systematic articulation and sequencing of political, social, and economic changes; (2) the occurrence and increased acceptance of the view that change is normal and can be of value; and (3) the human psychic transformation away from self-centeredness and toward an expanded world view (Kornberg, Hines, and Smith, 1973:475).

19. New states may make a conscious effort to isolate themselves from the influence of modernized societies. But, as in the case of countries such as Tanzania, Libya, and Saudi Arabia, it is selective isolation to control the potentially disruptive impact of a massive influx of modernizing norms.

20. "Conflicts of interest between different groups and strata—between peasants and land-lords, artisans and merchants, slaves and slave-owners—have existed, of course, in all societies. But it is only in modern societies, with the drawing together of the different groups into the central spheres of society, that these conflicts have become centralized, unifying potentially opposing camps, facilitating their society-wide organization, their becoming symbols of social and political identification, and their making demands on the central political institution" (S. N. Eisenstadt, 1966:22). See also E. Durkheim (1947) and W. Kornhauser (1959).

21. A recent example in the United States was the threatened impeachment and subsequent resignation of Richard Nixon. In citing this example, we are not suggesting that presidential regimes can be distinguished in this regard from parliamentary systems.

22. As Fred R. von der Mehden observes, "it is an obvious fact of political life in the postwar world that it is almost mandatory to profess an ultimate belief in democracy. Definitions of democracy and timing may differ, but the ideologies of almost all countries proclaim some sort of democratic system as the ultimate goal" (1969:118). Also see Eisenstadt (1966:11–15).

23. S. M. Finer has suggested that "instead of asking why the military engages in politics we ought surely to ask why they ever do otherwise" (1962:5).

24. In looking at Latin America, Gino Germani and Kalman Silvert note that the "military will be reduced to their barracks and their professional functions alone only when . . . countries

develop sufficiently complicated power structures and a society sufficiently flexible and integrated . . . when economic and social conflicts have found institutionalized expression within a common framework of shared norms" (1961:62).

25. Colonel Nasser, for example, described the role of the Free Officers Group in the 1952 Egyptian coup in these terms: "The democracy for which we rose in revolt on July 23 is a peaceful, clean democracy. . . . Its purpose is freedom of the individual, freedom of livelihood, true justice—individual freedom, collective freedom, a sound socialist society . . . " (von der Mehden, 1969:120). Similarly, General Gustavo Leigh, a member of the military junta that overthrew President Salvador Allende of Chile in 1973, has declared, "We do not pretend to stay in power in perpetuity, but we will not surrender our command before our profound creative task is concluded. . . . It is an indisputable fact that there exists today no force capable of governing Chile other than the armed forces" (Perera, 1975:82).

26. On the advanced technology required to transform an authoritarian into a totalitarian, coercion-based regime, see Hannah Arendt (1968) and Franz Neumann (1944).

27. A military intervention in Chad provides an almost classic illustration of the situation. The reports of the April 1975 military coup against President Ngarta Tombalbaye casually noted in passing that Chad is one of the poorest and most backward states in the world. Three times the size of California but with a population of only some 3.5 million, it has no railroad, only 150 miles of paved road, is landlocked (more than 1,200 miles away from any seaport) and is virtually in the middle of the Sub-Saharan famine belt that had been hit by a six-year drought. In addition, since 1968 the armed forces, with French support, had been fighting actively a Libyan-backed Moslem rebel group in the Northeast known as Frolinat. Reports from observers at the scene noted that after the fighting at the presidential palace, jubilant troops drove through the streets shouting "We have won, we have won, the tyrant is dead." Tombalbaye had been named provisional president at the time Chad became independent (1960). He was elected president in 1962. By 1969 he had succeeded in so drastically reducing opposition to him he was reelected president for another seven-year term without opposition. Among those who had been arrested for opposing him were the former commander of the armed forces, the former chief of the national police, and the former director of the president's personal military staff. A radio announcement by the leader of the coup, General Noel Odinger, acting commander of the armed forces, said: "Our armed forces have exercised their responsibilities before God and before the nation. I ask all of you to remain calm and not to be worried about your fate . . . " (Associated Press, 1975).

28. Valenzuela's analysis of the Chilean situation in this volume offers a tragic example of how this process can go so far as to trigger an executive-legislative conflict that ultimately invites intervention by the military.

29. If Richard Sisson's speculations are valid, leaders also may be encouraged to change, reorder, and even periodically dispense with representative bodies because the public support that representative bodies do generate tends to be cumulative. A reconstituted or resurrected representative body, according to Sisson, may not have to generate support *de novo* but can take up where it left off in a previous incarnation (1973).

*Chapter 4*

# LEGISLATURES IN ORGANIC STATIST-AUTHORITARIAN REGIMES—THE CASE OF SPAIN

## JUAN J. LINZ

Spain offers the interesting experience of an authoritarian regime (Linz, 1970a, 1975b) that has attempted to institutionalize a system of representation divergent from that of western competitive, pluralist democracies without making the official single party the dominant center of power. The corporativist ideology has served Franco and his supporters in their efforts to create political institutions in the hope that they would outlive their founder. Corporativism is a multifaceted political phenomenon and we find strains of it in a variety of types of political systems, as Philippe Schmitter (1974) has rightly emphasized, but only in a few regimes do we find an effort to institutionalize it at the center of the political system. Corporativism is still perceived as a logical and even attractive alternative to political pluralism expressed through political parties and to the presumably monolithic, ideological, bureaucratic, and privileged single-mass party. The Cortes Españolas since its creation in 1943 was the most long-lived, predominantly corporative legislature in the world. Therefore, a better knowledge of this legislature can help social scientists understand the working in a modern society of a system of representation that contrasts with the system underlying the type of legislature usually studied. Since authoritarian regimes are likely to continue considering some form of corporative representation as an alternative to other forms, it is useful and interesting to analyze the working, composition, and public perception of such a chamber.

The corporativist ideology and certain forms of corporative organization of society and politics are present in many forms in authoritarian and even in democratic political systems. However, no political system known to us has been organized on purely corporative conceptions. Those that have been claimed to be so have only combined institutions and principles derived from corporativism with other structures, particularly those of bureaucratic-military-technocratic and single-party movement regimes. On these grounds we prefer to use the expression "organic statism,"[1] formulated by Alfred Stepan (1978), rather than "corporativism" to identify regimes that include important corporativist elements (Linz, 1975b:306–313).

No political system based on a corporativist ideology has approximated even closely the blueprints of corporativist ideologists. Certainly this applies to the "arrested totalitarianism" of Fascist Italy in view of the role played by the party and the state bureaucracy in conjunction with the personal power of Mussolini. The corporativist elements of the regime never were allowed to develop fully (Aquarone, 1965) and the ideologists and politicians advocating their full institutionalization in the late '20s and early '30s ultimately were frustrated and defeated by a regime that better might be described as "arrested totalitarianism" (Linz, 1975b:322–336). In a like vein, Nazi totalitarianism, after toying briefly with *ständisch*-corporativist ideologies, made the party and its organizations the center of power. It retained the Reichstag as an emasculated legislative body to meet only on ceremonial occasions to approve unanimously the decisions of the Führer and to reconfirm the 1933 Enabling Act that gave him extraordinary powers (Schwarz, 1965:527–528; Schneider, 1968).

The Spanish and Portuguese authoritarian regimes, born in the heyday of the Fascist and Catholic variants of corporativism, have incorporated corporativist elements into the institutional structure of the state to a greater extent than have any other political systems. In addition, the relative weakness of both official single parties, FET y de las JONS in Spain, and the even less significant *União Nacional* in Portugal, particularly as compared with PNF in Italy, makes the corporative element in the Iberian countries appear to be more important than the formal *Stato Corporativo* in Italy to which Italian jurists and ideologists as well as sympathetic foreign observers devoted much attention (Linz, 1975b:306–315; Schmitter, 1974; Aquarone, 1965; Lasswell and Sereno, 1966). Nonetheless, even in Spain and Portugal the corporative institutions are artificial and incomplete. In Spain, at least, the conditions for an inclusionary and consequently successful institutionalized corporativist organic statism (Stepan, 1978) were largely absent.[2] In Portugal, where some of those conditions seem to have been available to Salazar, for reasons that are not clear the effort was not carried as far as could have been expected (particularly in comparison with some Latin American cases like Mexico).

It shall be our task in this chapter to analyze the nature and role of legislatures in the organic statist variant of authoritarian regimes with special emphasis on Franco's Spain. Unfortunately, there have been no behavioral studies of either the Cortes or the Camara Corporativa and the Asamblea Nacional in Portugal (Schmitter, 1975a, 1975b)—only institutional analyses in a formalistic, legal tradition and ideological expositions of the "Spanish way to democracy" conducted by supporters of those regimes (Iglesias Selgas, 1968). While there are some data on the composition of these legislatures, we lack any minimally adequate analysis of what really went on within the chambers, and particularly the committee rooms of either the Cortes or now defunct two chambers of the Salazar regime. However, to avoid any misunderstanding we should stress that those chambers are only components in their regimes and not as important as their rulers and supporters in the executive, the upper levels of the bureaucracies, the parties and the militaries. In authoritarian regimes power ultimately rests in the hands of a leader or small group of persons and those called upon by them to collaborate in governing. In particular, the latter usually include persons co-opted from different social elites, political groups and the bureaucracy. Regardless of their "social representativeness," however, their power is not accountable to the citizens at regular intervals under conditions that permit other aspirants to power to compete with them freely for popular support. Power does not rest in the sovereign people but in an individual or group that has appropriated it to accomplish a "historical mission."

In such a context the power of a legislature is fundamentally derivative, granted by rulers more or less grudgingly and within limits they consider desirable. Legislatures are conceived as bodies collaborating in governing, and the rulers are not ultimately dependent on them. No legislature in an authoritarian regime has either the formal or *de facto* power to question the ultimate authority of a ruler or ruling group. The latter, however, can limit a legislature's power considerably. In no authoritarian regime is either the head of state or the government subject formally to a vote of nonconfidence by the legislature.

The fundamentally subordinate position of legislatures in authoritarian regimes is reflected in some or all of the following characteristics:

1. The power of the authoritarian rulers is established independently of the creation of the legislature and does not need to be ratified by a legislature if one is convened.
2. Legislatures are not usually convened shortly after the instauration of a new regime and their initial powers are likely to be limited severely.
3. The constitution-making process is basically in the hands of the ruling group, which sometimes may seek a plebiscitarian ratification, and the legislature is called to participate in that process with limited authority.
4. The ruler or ruling group reserves to itself the right to make laws, and these the legislature cannot abrogate.
5. As a consequence of these conditions, the rulers are able to shape the legislature so that, even with an expansion of functions or its members' political ambitions, the legislature will be unable to initiate any change in the nature of the regime within the rules of the regime. Moreover, any such change is not likely to originate in the legislature, even though the legislature might act to legitimate it.

Any formal or apparent similarity between legislatures in democracies and authoritarian regimes, or growth in power of the legislatures of authoritarian regimes should not obscure this basic difference.

It is no accident that the constitutional theory of authoritarian regimes and the legal texts on which it is based do not recognize a principle of division of powers between legislative, executive, and judiciary. The Spanish *Ley Orgánica del Estado*, Article 22 explicitly says: "The institutional system of the Spanish state is based on the principles of unity of power and coordination of functions." Article 6 says: "The head of state is the supreme representative of the nation, personifies national sovereignty, exercises supreme political and administrative power, is vested with the national leadership of the Movement . . . guarantees and insures the regular functioning of the high organs of the state and the proper coordination between such organs." Sovereignty is neither vested in the legislature nor even shared by it.

No government in a country with corporative representation has derived its authority from a corporative type of chamber and electorate. No such chamber has freely enacted the constitution of such a country. Instead, ruling groups that have not been legitimized by organic democracy have intervened and applied principles that contradict the ideology. The roles played in the process by regime founders (e.g., Franco, Salazar, Dollfuss) and the recourse to such inorganic principles of democratic legitimization as plebiscitarian referenda (e.g., in the case of Spain) cannot be ignored. Of the authoritarian regimes that have claimed that they seek to apply the theoretical model of corporative democracy, none has abandoned formally the organization or legitimization of political participation by inorganic processes like participation in a non-corporatively organized single party or direct elections without the intervention of corporative-type structures.

## THE LEGISLATURES OF AUTHORITARIAN REGIMES

Authoritarian regimes initially rule through a small junta or cabinet drawn from the ruling group. Some bureaucratic-military regimes, like those of Eastern Europe in the interwar years, are able to work within a formal parliamentary framework with a dominant government party that obtained a majority through corrupt electoral practices, co-optation of some political elites and outlawing or harrassing those that opposed them, and by tolerating a weak and tamed opposition (Janos, 1970). In other cases, the national council of the single party, or the members of the regime's party in an existing legislature and representatives of other parties willing to join them in a *parti unifié*, serve as an advisory or legislative body. However, since the principle of representation has become an essential element of legitimation in contemporary societies, sooner or later new legislative institutions are created.

In forming such bodies, generally two principles are employed to assure control by the ruling group and/or the leader—free appointment and ex-officio membership. Sometimes the free appointment option is disguised as a single slate offered to the electorate in a plebiscitarian election with no opposition. In an authoritarian regime that list (e.g., the famous *listone* in the Fascist Italian elections) is drawn within the inner circle of the ruling group and involves the co-optation of leading figures in the regime-supporting groups (De-Felice, 1968:473–477; 1974:311–313). Whatever authority is associated with the appointment, however, derives not so much from representativeness as from co-optation by the rulers. The alternative—inclusion of office holders in the regime as ex-officio members—is an even more convenient and effective mechanism, for this allows for their substitution at any moment and, consequently, ordinarily justifies presuming a submissive membership. After all, while those who have been co-opted for the length of the legislature might feel independent for that period, office holders who can be dismissed freely are not as likely to feel this way. Even if an electoral principle is introduced later, authoritarian rulers prefer that those elected be office holders so that the legislative mandate will remain dependent on their continuation in office.

Once political pluralism and, with it, political parties have been rejected, and internal democracy in a single party with organized factions competing among party members for support is perceived as too threatening, some alternative has to be found to give some semblance of democratic participation. Here corporativism becomes extremely handy as an ideology. Sincere believers in a corporative organization of society and the state, particularly intellectuals, will offer well-intended blueprints. However, in historically known corporative regimes the evidence points to a manipulative use of the principle for the deliberate purpose of disenfranchising large sectors of the society. Max Weber (1968:I, 297–299) in an insightful discussion of representation by agents of interest groups in *Economy and Society* emphasized this point and stressed how corporativism could be used to disenfranchise either the numerically superior classes or those strata whose power had rested on economic position (as in the case of the Soviets). In theory, as a principle for organizing participation of the people in the political process, organic democracy can serve as an alternative to electing representatives by numerical aggregates of citizens, an invention attributed to Kleisthenes (Simmel, 1950:106–107). In fact, no organic democracy assures an even approximate equal participation of all people and, even aside from all the impurities in its implementation, for structural reasons it introduces gross inequalities in participation. It is inherently unable to articulate and aggregate major policy choices for a large and complex modern society. It cannot be a functional equivalent to political parties in structuring the policy choices for a society.

Paradoxically, in modern extremely complex societies with myriad groupings; with individual freedom to change family status, occupation, and residence; with criss-crossing social circles; with transformation of institutional churches into free religious communities—in short, with the individualization of man—the so-called organic structures are nonexistent because they are either too numerous and specialized or involve only a small part of the personality and life of people (Simmel, 1900;1908;1964:150–154). Therefore, since they do not really exist with the clarity needed to attract and hold the loyalty and identification of people, to a large extent the organic structures to be represented in the political sphere have to be created by those in power. This contrived rather than natural character of the constituent groups of such a state is most apparent in the concept of corporativism offered by Philippe Schmitter, that of "constituent units organized into a limited number of singular, compulsory, noncompetitive, hierarchically ordered and functionally differentiated categories, recognized or licensed (if not created) by the state and granted a deliberate representational monopoly within their respective categories in exchange for observing certain controls on their selection of leaders and articulation of demands and supports" (Schmitter, 1974:93; also see H. J. Wiarda, 1974; Pike, 1974; Diamant, 1960; Voegelin, 1936).

It is no accident that in an advanced society corporative groupings are more artificial than the variety of political parties that emerge when citizens seek to attain power by freely supporting a variety of freely recruiting leaders (Smend, 1955). The organization of representation on the basis of corporative principles offers infinitely more leeway for the rulers to determine the composition of legislatures than does the wide range of electoral manipulation in "inorganic" democracies. The proportion of seats to be assigned to different groups is far from obvious, and the choice of a principle for allocating seats—be it occupational, industrial, or residential—can change the composition of a corporativist chamber radically. Therefore, almost by definition, without resorting to such visible deviations from justice as unequally sized districts or gerrymandering, corporative representation can achieve an allocation of power acceptable to the rulers.

Inevitably, elections to represent corporative groups cannot take place easily in large constituencies that articulate large sectors of opinion. Instead, they are conducted in small units whose representatives elect others among their peers who, in turn, elect those at higher levels. According to the theorists of corporativism, this assures immediacy and personal contact between electors and their representatives. In fact, it deprives citizens of any immediate opportunity to make their representatives accountable to them. The ideology of corporativism also facilitates retention of control of major policy choices by those in power since, in principle, those elected are qualified only to judge, and, presumably, are interested primarily in those matters that most directly affect their narrowly defined constituency. This makes difficult the articulation of broader societywide conflict without the reemergence of political parties. Since the system cannot function without recognizing or licensing groups that are granted representational monopolies, the state's capacity to regulate those groups gives the rulers a decided advantage. Even if the autonomy of those groups were respected by those in power, a minority within a group cannot form or transfer its allegiance to another group easily as can a minority in a political party (albeit with many difficulties). Pure corporativism, in the absence of ideologically structured cleavages cutting through the corporative groups, is not likely to articulate or aggregate large bodies of opinion.

These are some of the principal characteristics of a corporatively organized society that make the principle of corporative representation appealing to authoritarian rulers. In practice, as well as in theory, corporativism is designed to prevent the political articulation of either class cleavages in a Marxist sense, or major sectoral cleavages (e.g., those along rural-urban, regional, religious, or cultural lines). Since the central cleavages in a modern society that lead to major political choices are of these broad rather than specific types, corporativism in principle excludes such broader issues from discussion. As Max Weber wrote (1968:298), "representative bodies of this type [of interest representation] tend to lack effective individual leadership (Führerlosigkeit)," and, therefore, also to lack real political leadership capable of mobilizing large masses of people behind any political alternative. In this sense, corporativism encourages a basic apoliticism of the population and transforms issues into technical decisions and problems of administration. Ultimate political choices either are not made or have to be made by the ruling political group independently of the representatives of the corporative interests, and any opposition is most likely to emerge outside of the corporative framework. The autonomized power of the state—"verselbständigte Staatsgewalt," to use the expression of Marx (1955) in the 18th Brumaire—represented by the ruling group, the bureaucracy, the armed forces, the party, economic oligarchies or a combination of them, is most likely to make the real political choices. Furthermore, as we know from the work of Robert Michels (cf. S.M. Lipset, 1962 and Linz, 1966: cv–cxiii), the narrower the scope of a constituency the greater the apathy and disinterest of the members. Corporative representation therefore, contributes to a complex process of depoliticization and creates the political apathy that characterizes authoritarian regimes with a weak or no single mobilizational party. The great ideological lines of cleavage—basic class conflicts, regional-cultural linguistic conflicts, and religious-cultural divisions—that occur in a modern society have to find expression outside the channels created for representation of the society. Therefore, noninstitutionalized alignments within the regime and a-legal and illegal oppositions (Linz, 1973) sooner or later appear. They will not be reflected even with minimum effectiveness in the halls of the legislature.

Even assuming both a basically inclusionary intent on the part of authoritarian rulers and favorable conditions for the success of their efforts (Stepan, 1978), a legislature based on corporative principles will not be the main arena of political debate unless other representational principles also are introduced. At most, by enacting legislation it will be a useful collaborator with a ruling group in the process of law making, and providing information, technical expertise, a sounding board, a certain publicity, and an additional legitimacy to the political choices actually made by the rulers but submitted to legislators in the form of bills to be considered, and generally approved. Corporative chambers, through amendments to bills, criticism and occasional discussion of government initiatives, exercise of the power to ask questions, and so on, can contribute to the legislative and political process, improve its quality, or serve as a minor obstacle to the initiative of the rulers, but they can not formulate or articulate real political alternatives.

## REPRESENTATIVE INSTITUTIONS IN THE FRANCO REGIME

Since the liberal constitution of 1812 that abolished representation by estates, Spain has had legislatures elected in proportion to population, even when a second chamber was based on other principles. Political instability, civil wars, military interventions, and electoral corruption prevented full institutionalization of a constitutional monarchy until the Restoration in 1875 (Sanchez Agesta, 1964; Sainz de Varanda et al., 1957; Nohlen, 1966, 1969). The dictatorship of

Primo de Rivera (1923–29) interrupted that process and 1927 signaled the first attempt at a corporative chamber—the Asamblea Nacional Consultativa (Sainz de Varanda et al., 1957:536–610; Garcia Canales, 1977:115–168). The fall of the dictatorship and, shortly afterwards, of the monarchy led to the instauration of a democratic Republic (1931–36) with a competitive party system (Linz, 1967) that was eventually overthrown in a bloody civil war (1936–39).

The one discernible common denominator among the different forces that supported Franco in the Civil War was their hostility to the pluralism of political parties and liberal democratic institutions. In fact, early in the Civil War the military formally outlawed *all* political parties even while de facto Falangists and Carlists were organizing party militias to fight shoulder to shoulder with the armed forces. There was the temptation of a state party based on personal loyalty to Franco, a *franquista* party. However, in the second half of the '30s fascism had too great an appeal to youth, as well as a potential for integrating the masses and for foreign support, to be disregarded (Linz, 1970b). Neither could Carlism be ignored—its proponents had contributed some of the most courageous units to the fight and its philosophy represented a significant ideological tradition of the Spanish antiparliamentary, antiliberal right. In view of the impracticality of ignoring these groups, Franco decided in 1937 to create a unified party under his leadership incorporating these forces—Falange Española Tradicionalista y de las JONS (Juntas de Ofensiva Nacional-Sindicalista). Years later this official and privileged single party would be called Movimiento Nacional and until very recently it was the only legal political party in Spain. Only recently has the law of political associations provided for a pluralism of political groups within the framework of that single party, with the promise of legal recognition and activity now a fact for all separate parties but the Communists. In the early stages of the regime the two constituent parts of the new organization—the fascist Falange and the JONS—hoped that it would become the basis for a movement regime, but in the course of the long history of the regime the party lost all its vitality and capacity for mobilization and has become a bureaucratic organization with a paper membership (Linz, 1970b; Martínez Val 1975: 144–167, 197–200).

Franco, in a speech at Salamanca on April 19, 1937, marking the unification of parties, delineated the ideological assumptions under which representative institutions were to be created:

. . . verbalist and formal democracy of the Liberal state, that failed everywhere, with its fictions or parties, electoral laws and votes, . . . that confusing the means and the end, forget the true democratic substance. We, abandoning that doctrinaire concern, oppose [to it] an effective democracy, bringing to the people what really interest them: to see and feel themselves governed in an aspiration of integral justice, in relation to the moral factors as well as the economic-social ones; moral freedom at the service of a patriotic creed and an eternal ideal, and economic freedom, without which political freedom turns into a farce (Franco Bahamonde, 1943:14) (translation mine).

The new single party was to have a national council, Consejo Nacional; a politbureau, the Junta Políticia; and a secretariat that would assist the leader of the party who was also the head of state and Generalísimo of the army. The Consejo Nacional initially was constituted only by certain members appointed by the leader, or ex-officio on the basis of holding certain appointive positions. There were no elected members. Until 1943 the Councils remained relatively small bodies in which were represented the different forces that initially had entered the coalition led by the army. They assured some continuity with the National Councils of the Fascist party of the prewar period before its unification with the Traditionalists. In some respects the institution was modeled after the Gran Consiglio del Fascismo but it was much less homogeneous in composition than that body since its membership was larger and it was not the creation of a charismatic leader of a victorious mass movement.

In 1942 Franco felt that the institutionalization of the regime and the clear distinction of the state from the party required a legislature. The Cortes Españolas were created without, however, disbanding the Consejo Nacional that languished in inactivity for years. The Cortes were to serve " . . . for the expression of contrasting opinions within the unity of the regime, for the expression of aspirations and of accountable and founded criticism, and for intervention in the legislative process," but "continuing in the Head of State the supreme power to dictate legal norms of general character. . . . The organ created will represent, at the same time, a valuable instrument of collaboration in that task, a principle of auto-limitation for a more systematic institutionalization of power." It was to be a corporative chamber rather than one in which political parties would compete for power. It was not to be the collegiate representation of the leadership of a disciplined single party with a single ideology. It was to be a body between a true legislature and a consultative assembly, in theory more independent and powerful than Primo de Rivera's Asamblea Nacional, initially, at least, less independent of the executive and less critical of its actions.

## THE FRANCO CORTES

Legislative bodies, particularly those in developing nations, have been described as institutions dominated by the entrenched powers of the society, and functioning primarily to protect their interests by blocking, slowing, or diverting change and development. For this reason we shall analyze in considerably more detail the mode of qualifying for membership, representativeness, procedural practices, and evolving future of Franco's Cortes.[3]

The Cortes were to be continuous bodies, ex-officio members would stay on and bridge the three-year periods of each sitting. Only in part would membership be renewed formally. The leadership of the legislature, particularly its president, was endowed with great powers and often would continue without reappointment. The president would control the appointment of committee chairmen and other officials of the chamber as well as of legislators to committees. However, practice and some changes in rules over the years eventually reduced his tight control of the legislative process. The president was appointed by Franco rather than elected by the legislators or *procuradores*. After Franco's death he was to be selected by the king from among three persons proposed to him by the Consejo del Reino. The composition of the chamber, despite continuous modifications in detail that expanded its size, remained basically unchanged until 1966 when the new Constitution created 108 seats, two for each province irrespective of population, to be elected directly by heads of families.

The Consejo Nacional del Movimiento has continued to exist as a separate body, even though, since 1948, many of its members also have sat in the Cortes. This creates some confusion, since Spanish commentators sometimes speak of an upper house—the Consejo Nacional—first as an organ of the Falange Española Tradicionalista y de las Juntas de Ofensiva Nacional-Sindicalista (the single party created by fusion on Franco's authority in 1939) and since 1966 as a part of the Movimiento characterizing it as a "political chamber." Since the members of the Consejo Nacional all have been members of the Cortes since 1966 and since the Consejo Nacional also meets separately to discuss both basic political laws and legislation affecting the Movimiento as an organization, it is difficult to say if Spain has a unicameral or bicameral legislature.

Forty appointed *consejeros* occupy very special positions. After Franco's replacement as head of state they were to continue to hold their seats until age 75. Vacancies in these seats were to be filled by co-optation by the Consejo from among three candidates proposed by the remaining members of the initial forty. Thus, all members of the Cortes are not even legally equal to their peers (de Miguel and Linz, 1975b).

The Cortes is a multisector rather than multiparty legislature, though some particularly cohesive sectors may operate like parties. For example, one of the Sindicatos members acts as a whip, and they may tend to vote as a bloc when the secretary-general of Sindicatos is a powerful man who is interested in an issue. Since the appointment, indirect election, or indirect revocation of the mandate of many *procuradores* depends on different ministries (e.g., mayors who often are elected to represent the municipalities of a province can only be legislators as long as they are mayors, and this depends on the minister of the interior or the provincial governor), over time the sectors reflect to some extent the ideological tendencies represented in the cabinet. This reflection is far from precise because of delays in renewing office holders and in balancing the tendencies in each sector. Thus, while it would be possible, with some effort and error, to distinguish *procuradores* by ideological background, it is doubtful if such a "political" classification would be of much use in predicting the positions they take or the votes they cast on most bills. The location of groups by the tracing of personal loyalties and clientele relationships in a sociometric-historical-biographical study of the informal networks through which the *procuradores* have attained their positions and to which their political futures are tied, would be an equally dubious approach to identifying party-like activity blocs. Certainly alignments in a legislature without parties are infinitely less visible than even in a fractionalized and undisciplined party system.

## THE SECTORS IN THE FRANCO CORTES

The sectors are the basic building blocs of the Cortes. We already have noted the special status of the *procuradores* who are also members of the Consejo Nacional del Movimiento—"the collegiate representation of the Movimiento." They include four groups: (1) forty members appointed by the Caudillo; (2) twelve representing three sectors of Cortes members; (3) six appointed by the Council president and the party secretary-general; (4) fifty-five elected by the 13,175 local party council members and 12,078 municipal representatives acting as electors of two *consejeros* per province (irrespective of the number of party members). The latest available figure (1962) on party affiliation was 931,802 men and 294,931 women. In the absence of any real internal party democracy, however, the influence of party members on the selection of the *consejeros* is minimal.

The largest group in the chamber is the 150 Sindicatos representatives. Among them, 84 are chosen in indirect multistage elections to represent employers, workers, and technicians in equal proportions. Their election is five steps removed from the membership of the Sindicatos and four from the 571,000 representatives at the plant or enterprise level. To the 84 may be added 12 *procuradores* for farmers, four for cooperatives, three for commerce, and one for the newspaper guild. Of the remaining 46, 32 are ex-officio members of the Cortes by virtue of their appointed positions in the Sindicatos leadership.

Local governments provide the second largest group of members. The group includes: (1) one representative of each provincial council, elected by members, but actually almost exclusively by the presidents, all of whom are appointed by the government; (2) two representatives elected by the municipalities of each province from among the members of the municipal councils, those elected mostly being mayors (of 53 members, 49 are mayors, 32 from provincial capitals) who, in turn, are appointed by the government; and (3) representatives elected by the municipal councils of the seven cities over 300,000 inhabitants and Ceuta and Melilla. In short, of the local government group of 115 *procuradores*, the appointment and, consequently, dismissal of 110 depends on the government.

Another group of 108 *procuradores* was created by the constitutional reform of 1966 and is elected by the 16,415,139 eligible voters—heads of household and married women—at the rate of two per province (Hermet, 1974; Martinez Cuadrado, 1974). Despite the many difficulties in becoming a candidate, it is not impossible for "nonestablishment" candidates to run and, in some cases, to win. Of the 328 candidates who ran in 1967, 64 percent did so by qualifying as ex-*procuradores*, or by obtaining the endorsement of either five *procuradores* or half of the provincial council members. Only 36 percent qualified by obtaining over one thousand signatures. From this latter group a small faction of independent *procuradores* emerged—deciding to caucus, appeal directly to public opinion, and offer some opposition to the government. Unlike most members of the Cortes, some of them could claim legitimately to speak directly in the name of a large constituency without the mediation of the government (Cuadernos para el Diálogo, 1967).

Another group of members consists of representatives of associations of the bar, medicine, engineering, and other liberal professions. To that group can be added the representatives of the national academies, the National Research Council, and the rectors of the twelve state universities. Finally, the members of the cabinet, high courts, and advisory councils are ex-officio members. In addition, the head of state can appoint 25 *procuradores* freely.

The representativeness of the Cortes and the extent to which it actually implements the corporative ideal promulgated by the regime can be revealed by an analysis of any differential presence of sectoral representatives in the leadership and the rank and file, and of the relation of sectoral representation and leadership position to the social characteristics of the members (as compared with the distribution of these characteristics in the populace and in other assemblies). To identify leaders we took into account the fact that the Law and Reglamento invest the president of the Cortes and the committee chairmen appointed by him with unusual power. Indeed, in the Cortes plenary sessions are even more ceremonial than in most legislatures. Therefore we grouped as "legislative leaders" the president, vice

TABLE 4.1

**PROPORTIONAL REPRESENTATION OF SECTORS AMONG LEADERS AND NONLEADERS IN THE CORTES (1968)**

| Sectors | Leaders | Nonleaders |
| --- | --- | --- |
| Cabinet | 1.3% | 3.6% |
| Appointees of head of state | 5.3 | 4.4 |
| Elected Consejeros Nacionales | 16.0 | 9.1 |
| Appointed Consejeros Nacionales | 22.0 | 5.1 |
| Co-opted Consejeros Nacionales | 4.0 | 0.6 |
| Procuradores for Sindicatos | 22.7 | 27.8 |
| Procuradores for municipalities | 10.7 | 22.6 |
| Professional associations, etc. | 2.7 | 4.4 |
| University rectors and cultural organizations | 5.4 | 2.9 |
| High courts | 1.3 | 0.8 |
| Elected directly by heads of household | 12.0 | 20.9 |
|  | N=74 | N=474 |

The percentages add up to more than one hundred because some *procuradores* hold seats in more than one sector, i.e. are members of Consejo Nacional and cabinet members.

presidents, secretaries of the Cortes; those occupying comparable positions in the Consejo Nacional; and the presidents, vice-presidents and secretaries of the permanent, regular, and special committees, as well as the members of the Comisión Permanente (Standing Committee) of the Consejo Nacional. In the 1967 legislature they constituted a group of 74 leaders and 474 rank and file members. Sectoral representation in the two groups is presented in Table 4.1, and there are clear differences. The appointed *consejeros nacionales* constituted 22 percent of the first group and only 5 percent of the second. On the other hand, local government representatives constituted only 11 percent of the leaders and 23 percent of the rank and file members. Family *procuradores* were also underrepresented in the leadership (12 percent versus 21 percent).

Leaders were more likely to have been born in Madrid or provincial capitals than in other communities, and almost twice as many resided in large cities (mostly in Madrid). As compared with the rank and file, fewer leaders are less than fifty years old (14 percent compared to 23 percent), more had studied in Madrid and abroad, and many more have a law degree (70 percent versus 42 percent). The proportion of civil servants among leaders is 52 percent (they might also exercise other activities) as compared to 27 percent among the nonleaders. Taking only the super-elite *cuerpos* of the administration, the proportions of leaders and rank and file in this group are respectively 41 percent and 14 percent. Even more specifically, among leaders the *abogados del Estado*—the elite corps of the Ministry of Finance—constituted 15 percent of the group as compared to 2 percent of the rank and file.

Only one of the leaders reported a lower middle-class occupation, whereas 7.1 percent of the rank and file *procuradores* reported being engaged in either working class or lower middle-class occupations. This class differentiation is also reflected in the fact that 32 percent of the leaders are listed in the DICODI (1962) directory of corporation and large business leaders—compared to only 16 percent of the rank and file members (Roselló García, 1962). More of the leaders also are members of ASCER (Agrupación Sindical de Contribuyentes Empresarios de Rústica)—the association of large landowners—4 percent versus 0.4 percent among nonleaders. The legislative leaders are also much more likely to occupy or have occupied high political and politico-administrative appointments in the executive branch of the government—37 percent were undersecretaries or director-generals and 21 percent provincial governors, compared to 8 percent and 5 percent respectively among nonleaders. Finally, the leaders in 1968 were well established legislatively, 20 percent having been in the very first legislature and 45 percent having been seated by 1955, as compared to 6 percent and 16 percent among nonleaders. Correspondingly, 14 percent of the former and 39 percent of the latter were freshman *procuradores*.

## WHO ARE THE *PROCURADORES*?

Even the most democratically elected legislature is not a mirror image of the society, but obviously there are different degrees of "representativeness" and the presence or absence of members with certain backgrounds reveals something about the distribution of power. The members of the Cortes, independently of their power or influence, due to the system of recruitment by co-optation, ex-officio memberships, and direct appointment by the head of state, certainly represent the elite of the regime. However, due to the stability and slow renewal of membership we would expect an overrepresentation of older generations and the surviving founders of the regime.

The Cortes has a larger proportion of members over fifty than does the British House of Commons (1945, 1959, and 1964) (58 percent versus an average of 50 percent in the House), but is close to the third, fourth, and fifth German *Bundestag*. The proportion of men under forty also seems to be smaller than in the democracies. The members of the Consejo Nacional are somewhat, but not much older than the remainder of the legislature, and this is accounted for largely by the appointees (56 percent over fifty-five and 72 percent over fifty). Illustrative of the slow renewal of the party elite compared to other sectors of the legislature is the fact that 18 percent of the freshmen legislators, as compared to 9 percent of the members of the Consejo Nacional, are under forty.

With regard to generations, one-third of the legislature's members were adults (twenty-four years old or over) at the outbreak of the Civil War. Another large proportion (23 percent) were of military age (nineteen to twenty-three) at the time. Members from the post-Civil War generations with little or no personal memory of those dramatic days still constitute less than one-fifth of the group. In contrast, almost one-half of the elected members of the Consejo Nacional del Movimiento were between fourteen and twenty-four when the Civil War started in 1936. This is the front generation—the *alféreces provisionales* (the reserve officers who played a decisive role in assuring

Franco's victory)—that also provided 65 percent of the last Franco-appointed cabinet. The appointed *consejeros* came more often from the groups entering the new unified party in 1937 and are from a somewhat older generation, almost one-fifth having been university students during the Republic. The generational experiences of these legislators certainly will not lead them to question the regime.

Only the representatives of the municipalities (25 percent under forty-five) and the newly created sector elected by heads of household (38 percent under forty-five) are distinctly younger. The first datum suggests a relatively rapid renewal of the elite of the regime at the local level, perhaps at a faster rate than at the national level. The great difference in age and, consequently, in generational experiences helps explain the distinct role and degree of self-consciousness of the family sector and why it may constitute, in part, an opposition within the system (Díaz-Nosty, 1972; Hecht, n.d.:26).

With respect to education, occupation, and sector of employment, not surprisingly the Cortes is nonrepresentative, being heavily weighted toward the elite ends of these dimensions. In the absence of working class parties to present candidates, the proportion of members of the Cortes with only primary education is below the 7 percent that sat in the Italian postwar legislature. However, the proportion with higher education is close to the Italian average and slightly larger than that in the Bundestag and the 1959 House of Commons. 46 percent of the members have law degrees, close to the 42 percent among Italian legislators. The number of engineering and architecture degree holders is large considering the small number of graduates of the elite technical schools. The Consejo Nacional has an even larger proportion of members with a legal education, 64 percent, and lawyers are even more dominant among its appointed members, 72 percent. Advocates of corporativism have cried out against the lawyer-politicians dominating democratic parliaments, but even the most political sector of a semicorporative chamber is disproportionately recruited from among law school graduates. The sindical group contains the greatest concentration of members with a middle level academic, technical, or semiprofessional education, 37 percent.

Only 2 percent of the members of the Cortes are manual workers. Indeed, the proportion is only 7.6 percent in the Sindicatos sector, in which according to corporative theory, at least one-fourth should be manual workers. The proportion of manual workers is about one-third of that in the legislatures of the United Kingdom, France, Italy and one-half of that in Germany in 1957. The proportion of those giving farming as an occupation, 8.4 percent, is small for a country that had close to 50 percent of its active population in agriculture when the regime was established, and still has 27 percent in that activity. Even when the regime appealed to the peasantry of northern and central Spain, its elite was significantly less agricultural than that of the German Reichstag and the Nazi party MdRs in the '20s and early '30s. The underrepresentation of persons claiming to be farmers or landowners is characteristic of the corporative chambers of Spain, Portugal, and Italy, and suggests that territorial rather than corporate constituencies may assure a better representation of the countryside.

Spain has been described as a military dictatorship, but in recent years the armed forces have withdrawn more and more to their professional role. Even so, 10.6 percent of the *procuradores* were military officers and the proportion was larger among the Consejeros Nacionales. The clergy is practically absent from the 1968 Cortes and the interests of the church are represented by laymen identified with Catholic organizations. As in other Latin European legislatures professors occupy 5 percent of the seats, less than in the Portuguese Cámara Corporativa, and fewer than the 14 percent in the first legislature of the 1931 Republic. Civil servants, particularly of the elite corps, are well represented, holding more than one out of every five seats. Moreover, they constituted over one-half of the leaders of the legislature. The higher civil servants are one of the key elements in the elite of the regime. Businessmen and managers, including those in the public sector, occupy close to one-fifth of the seats and over one-third of the leadership positions. Perhaps reflecting the recent rapid capitalist development, they constituted a larger proportion than in the 1965–69 Cámara Corporativa of Portugal or in the 1939 Italian Cámera dei Fasci e delle Corporazioni. Spain was still a monarchy without a king in 1968, but its aristocracy occupied only 3 percent of the seats in the Cortes.

Elsewhere (de Miguel and Linz, 1975a) we have analyzed the continuity and change in membership of the nine legislatures since 1943. The data show much continuity in membership and a continuous process of renewal, except for certain periods when major international and other changes (e.g. the end of World War II) necessitated major internal changes. Between 51 percent and 72 percent of the *procuradores* in one legislative period sit in the next, between 40 percent and 50 percent continue for a third period, and between 29 percent and 38 percent meet their fellow legislators nine years later for a fourth time. However, the continuous expansion of membership of the Cortes has assured a higher rate of renewal. Ignoring the problem of mid-term appointment or election, in the nine legislatures 4,587 incumbencies were held by 1,979 persons. As in other legislatures, freshmen *procuradores* are less likely than old timers to hold leadership positions. This continuity, the absence of dramatic shifts in composition, and slow but continuous renewal have been consistent with the stability and slow change of the regime. It did, however, make it more difficult for these men to support the changes that the first government of King Juan Carlos presented for their approval.

The Cortes created by Franco not only broke with both what he called inorganic democracy and the new principles of representation he designated as organic democracy, but also represented an enormous discontinuity in the Spanish political class. Seven years after the last peacetime meeting of the Republican Cortes, only 31 (3.1 percent) of the 992 persons who had been deputies during the Republic returned to the assembly hall on the Carrera de San Jerónimo. Of the 470 elected in 1936, only 26 returned to the Cortes in 1943 or subsequently. At least seventy (15 percent) died violently, having been executed or assassinated by one or the other side in the war, and at least another 172 (37 percent) went into exile abroad. Of the 31 Republican deputies that returned, seven had been elected as Tradicionalistas, three as representing the Bloque Nacional, and seventeen as representing the CEDA. Considering that the CEDA had had some 150 deputies, this is a small proportion compared to the small parties on the extreme right. Only two men who had initiated their political lives under the constitutional monarchy and continued actively in it during the Republic would sit in the Cortes. Few countries have experienced so great a discontinuity (Linz, 1972).

### THE CORTES IN THE EVOLUTION OF THE FRANCO REGIME

The changes undergone by the Cortes—in its organization, activities, and membership—reveal much about political development in a relatively stable authoritarian state. This will be developed in the analysis that follows. Also, Spain's relative if temporary success in managing conflict by adopting a corporative ideology and implementing it in a semicorporative institution would seem to indicate that an assembly had great functional potential for symbolizing the corporate society, co-opting and manipulating the populace, and achieving control by producing an apathetic polity through the tactic of segmentalizing interest groups.

In its first thirty-two years the Cortes has changed from a collaborator of Franco in law making to a legislature in an authoritarian semiconstitutional monarchy. At the least, it has changed, but at a rate slower than the regime has approached a crisis point. Perhaps the reality includes some of both extremes. Since the summer of 1975, the role of the Cortes was to make or to approve constitutional changes that ultimately would lead to its disappearance in that form or to its temporary survival as a second chamber, or to reinforce the institutions created by Franco in opposing the policies of the first government of King Juan Carlos I. In essence, the issue was between a revised, popularly elected constituent assembly whose members represented political parties instituted constitutionally with or without the cooperative participation of the Cortes or the status quo sustained by a Cortes that blocked change. Although the latter stance by the Cortes might have sustained a Franco-style authoritarian regime indefinitely, it was more likely to lead to a sudden, possibly violent crisis. [Postscript. Fortunately in 1977 the Cortes decided to give way to a freely elected constituent assembly.]

Much of the basic information and research needed for a full analysis of the Cortes is unavailable. Except for Manuel Fraga Iribarne's book (1959), a monograph by A. Garrorena Morales (1977), and a series of recent articles[3] that focus on its legal aspects, essentially we have only journalistic accounts of its activities.[4] However, it was not without significance that, after years of neglect, shortly before Franco's death Spanish political scientists turned to a more systematic analysis of the constitutional laws that regulate the institutions of the regime. Since those laws ultimately are linked with the process of Franco's succession, the establishment of a monarchy, and the separation of the prime ministership and the head of state (first Franco and now the king), they provide part of the context in which political change has taken place. Those who wanted fundamental political changes but were not confident that they could or should be provoked by a total breakdown of the regime attempted to achieve them by stretching the meaning and intent of the constitution's provisions so as to facilitate a change of the regime within the regime (de Esteban, Varela, García Fernández, Guerra, and Ruiz, 1973; Ollero, 1974:1441–1466). Obviously, such a change is far from easy and might have proved impossible. Nevertheless, those who were committed to the continuity of the regime but conscious of the need for adaptation to a changing society and European context also were ready to explore more thoroughly, more flexible interpretations of the legal texts (Fernández-Carvajal, 1969). To add to the ambiguity of the likely outcome of those analyses, [at the time of writing in 1975] we know too little about the thinking of the relevant actors—the new king, Juan Carlos; the incumbent prime minister at the time of the transition from Franco to his successor; the actual members of such key bodies as the Consejo del Reino; the president of the Cortes; the legislators themselves; and, not least of all, such key actors outside of the governmental and political institutional arenas as the leadership of the armed forces and of the various alegal to illegal oppositions. We know even less about how they would act within this complex institutional/legal framework.

It is certain, however, that the ideological legitimacy of organic democracy has been eroded seriously, not only in its rejection by those who have always been opposed to it but also by its prior defenders who have shown a growing awareness of its failure to assure the participation of the people in the regime. In a sense, the diehards were right in saying that the *aperturistas* (those who want to open up the political system) were attempting to introduce into the system conceptions of representation that were incompatible with the essence of the regime. The ensuing debate about political associations and legislation to regulate them, the creation or blocking of such associations by different interests within the regime, and the role of such associations in the electoral process from the municipal to the Cortes level reflected the extent to which even the regime's supporters were abandoning a belief in organic democracy. The "associations" might or might not be the functional equivalent of parties, and might or not become parties by another name, but they certainly are based on direct appeals by political leaders to citizens as citizens and not as members of organic groups. They offer vaguely formulated political ideological alternatives within the narrow spectrum of the sectors that support the regime.

It is in this strange context that the semicorporative Cortes has been developing during at least the last decade. In this period it has undergone changes that have made it a more lively and meaningful political arena and, perhaps, a somewhat more influential body. Albeit the context increasingly has been politicized, the Cortes has continued to be fundamentally a law-making body, and even the most political of debates took place and still take place in the context of discussing particular laws and amendments to government proposals.

TABLE 4.2
*PROCURADORES* IN THE CORTES BY SECTOR AND THEIR
PARTICIPATION IN COMMITTEE DEBATES

| Sector | Silent members | Total members of committees |
|---|---|---|
| Cabinet members | 10 | 20 |
| Conserjeros Nacionales | | |
|    Representing provinces | 27 | 53 |
|    Appointed by the head of state | 22 | 40 |
|    Appointed by the prime minister | 2 | 6 |
| Presidents of high bodies (court, council | | |
|    of state, etc.) | 5 | 5 |
| Sindicatos | 57 | 150 |
| Local administration | 66 | 111 |
| Family | 29 | 104 |
| University rectors | 6 | 18 |
| Cultural institutions | 3 | 6 |
| Professional associations and chambers | | |
|    of commerce | 7 | 23 |
| Appointed by the head of state | 15 | 25 |
| Total | 239[a] | 561 |

a. Those *procuradores* holding seats in more than one capacity have been counted in each sector, therefore the total of individuals is not identical to the sum of the detailed groupings.
Source: Aguilar and Martínez (1975). This journalistic but serious analysis focuses on the year following the important speech of February 12th, 1974, by Prime Minister Arias Navarro that symbolizes the "apertura" (opening) of the system after the death of Carrero Blanco.

Other parliamentary processes, (e.g., questions directed to the government) also have become more frequent and more important. In fact, in theory and to a lesser degree in practice, the revitalization and more frequent meetings of the Consejo Nacional have made that body an arena for more strictly political debate. However, except for a minute minority representation of other sectors, the Consejo Nacional consists of the Movimiento representation of the Cortes rather than of either corporative or directly elected family representatives.

Even in the view of those who want to stretch the meaning of the constitutional provisions the government does not need the support of the Cortes except for constitutional changes, and still controls in the long run much of its composition (except the 40 *procuradores* appointed until age seventy-five by Franco). Therefore, despite gains, the Cortes is still limited to its restricted traditional and conventional functions. Limited data which showed enormous differences both

TABLE 4.3

## DISTRIBUTION OF "RUEGOS" PETITIONS AND "PREGUNTAS" QUESTIONS AMONG DIFFERENT SECTORS OF THE CORTES

| Sector | Number of procuradores making request | Number of procuradores in the sector | Percent in sector active | Number of requests presented | Percent of all requests made |
|---|---|---|---|---|---|
| Family | 47 | 104 | 45.2 | 222 | 63.4 |
| Sindicatos | 33 | 150 | 22.0 | 80 | 22.9 |
| Local | 7 | 111 | 6.3 | 8 | 2.3 |
| Consejo Nacional elected members | 9 | 53 | 17.0 | 13 | 3.7 |
| Consejo Nacional appointed members | 2 | 46 | 4.4 | 2 | 0.6 |
| Culture | — | 18 | — | — | — |
| Chambers and professional associations | 8 | 23 | 34.8 | 24 | 6.9 |
| Appointees of Head of State | 1 | 25 | 4.0 | 1 | 0.3 |
| Presidents of institutions | — | 5 | — | — | — |
| Total Cortes | 107 | 535 | 20.0 | 350 | 100.1 |

Source: A. Garrorena Morales (1977:129).

among committees and in rates of participation of different sectors and individual legislators (see Tables 4.2 and 4.3) suggest that the most lively and, perhaps, most influential activity in the Cortes occurs in its committees. Therefore, an analysis of committee chairmanships and seats may be the key to understanding its role as a law-making body. Such an analysis still is likely to support the conclusion that changes in the Cortes have been of less consequence than changes in the political system.

Even without the necessary research we can suggest a few dramatic and symbolic changes in the Cortes. When the Cortes were created, the Boletín Oficial de las Cortes Españolas (the equivalent of the Congressional Record) was available only to its members. The press did not report what was going on in the palace of the Carrera de San Jerónimo. In recent years, however, not only the plenary sessions but also most of the committee meetings have been open, and the press sometimes reports critically on them. Whereas the president of the Cortes previously had been appointed at will by the head of state for an unlimited term, since the Ley Orgánica del Estado (LOE), the president is appointed for a fixed term of six years from a list of three nominees drawn up by the Consejo del Reino. Admittedly, however, the president remains vulnerable to the power of the head of state and his government while retaining control of the agenda and committee appointments of the Cortes.

The most important change in the Cortes, however, has been the introduction of the *procuradores familiares*. Two are elected directly for each province, irrespective of population, by the heads of households and married women. In spite of the efforts of the Movimiento-Organización and of manipulation by the different "political families" in the government, a number of more or less independent *procuradores* have managed to be elected. Conscious of both their democratic legitimacy and the fact that for at least the length of one legislature the government could not deprive them of their seats, a number of these members have acted more like legislators in democratic countries than like the docile *procuradores* of previous sessions. Some of the 108 family *procuradores* who entered the ninth legislature after the 1967 LOE acquired a sort of group consciousness that led them to meet to discuss matters of common interest, not only in the halls of the legislature but also in different cities of Spain. This led a sympathetic, recently liberalized press to call them "las Cortes transhumantes" ( a term referring to merino sheep who move searching for pastures) and to express considerable support for their activities. The number of *procuradores familiares* participating in those efforts to establish contact between the legislators and the people varied. When the government decided in September 1969 to forbid one such meeting, after considerable debate about their legitimacy the holding of meetings outside the Cortes building in Madrid ceased.

Since only some of the members of the family group had participated, this manifestation of independence clearly was a symbolic act of a minority. The same significance can be ascribed to the negative votes of a number of those *procuradores* to the appointment of Prince Juan Carlos as Franco's successor. Ten of the nineteen "no" votes and four of the nine abstentions came from members of this group in a roll call vote that was not televised like the rest of the session. More important, perhaps, than those symbolic acts was the active participation of *procuradores familiares* in committees and in questions addressed to government. In 1968 and 1969, of 122 questions addressed to the government, 63 came from the family *procuradores* and only 34 from the sindical legislators and 14 from all other sectors of the chamber. Their participation changed the pattern from that of the eighth legislature in which only seven such questions in all were asked (Díaz-Nosty, 1972:112; Garrorena Morales, 1977).

If the enormous inequities in representation due to the fact that all provinces have two *procuradores familiares* regardless of electorate size were to end under a principle of direct election, this sector of the chamber, perhaps, could be even more important. At present, however, while one province has one such member for each 975,000 members of its electorate, another has one for approximately each 35,500. Yet even with the correction of such inequities, the relatively small share of the family sector in the total membership of the legislature and the many restrictions in the procedures for their elections (Cuadernos para el Diálogo, 1967:12–14), indicate that they signify change only *in* the Cortes rather than *of* the Cortes.

A similar change of the Cortes also could be effected by making it illegal to be a *procurador* while holding an appointed office or serving as a civil servant. Such a proposal was introduced by the government for *procuradores* who hold the position of undersecretary, director-general, and civil governor of a province, or similar positions in the Movimiento-Organización, or who serve in the administration of justice. It also would have required civil servants and officers to take leave while serving. Such proposals involve major changes, considering the number of higher civil servants in the Cortes (Bañón Martínez, 1974).

Such changes as these by themselves would not weaken other links through which the regime has dominated the Cortes, however. For example, over the years the men in the ministries who have occupied key positions on the borderline between politics and administration (e.g., the undersecretary and director-general) have occupied seats in the Cortes. On the average, over 20 percent of the occupants of such positions have been legislators while or after holding those offices. Relatively few were *procuradores* before assuming their key positions in the executive (Alba, 1975). Similarly, quite a few of the cabinet members had not been *procuradores* in the Cortes before acceding to their positions, but ex-cabinet members have been very likely to remain *procuradores*. On the average, for the years 1943–67, 8.6 percent of the 4,586 positions in the legislature were occupied by men who had served as cabinet members by 1974. It appears that membership in the legislature is not a step in the *cursus honorum* to the most powerful positions in the executive. Rather, those positions assure their incumbents a seat afterwards.

In view of the origins, definition of purpose, organization, and membership of the Cortes, it is not surprising that many of its roles and public perceptions of the body and its members reflect inherent characteristics of a corporative chamber in an authoritarian regime (as well as of any corporative second chamber of either a pluralistic democracy or a mobilizational single-party authoritarian or totalitarian regime). These characteristics include limited public attention to and visibility of the legislature and legislators, a low level of information about members, and low prestige accorded them. It is also no accident that such key political figures as cabinet members are not recruited from the ranks of the legislature, even though ex-cabinet members tend to be assured a seat in the Cortes (de Miguel and Linz, 1975b:116–118). Major political issues, widely debated in the society and articulated in visible alegal or illegal movements of opinion and/or even organizations, find almost no echo in the halls of the Cortes. If they do it is only belatedly or indirectly. In fact, it probably could be shown that even under Franco the cabinet has been more sensitive and responsive to major political changes than has been the legislature. Nor is it an accident that the most politically conscious and articulate, the most independent-minded and critical of the legislators (Díaz-Nosty, 1972:79–104, 143–161, and passim; Garrorena Morales, 1977) have appeared not in any of the sectors of the Cortes elected according to corporative principles, but, rather, among the 108 *procuradores* elected on the basis of inorganic suffrage.

Even the most outspoken defenders of the political status quo and of the tradition of the regime also have not been recruited from the *procuradores* in the corporative sector of the Cortes. Rather, they come from among those appointed by Franco or from the members of the Consejo Nacional del Movimiento.[5] After these many years, the corporative system of representation still has not provided leadership for the regime. The corporative system of representation, as distinct from the Sindicatos bureaucracy and the local government representatives sitting in the Cortes, has not been the breeding ground of the elite, and the Cortes has been reduced to collaborating in the process of law making, representing specific interests more or less effectively, and attempting occasionally to control or at least to criticize some of the decisions of the executive. Inevitably, all the other functions performed by legislatures, particularly in democratic parliamentary regimes, have escaped the Cortes and its members.

## THE CORTES AND PUBLIC OPINION IN CHANGE

How did Spaniards perceive the political system we have described, its possible future evolution, and more specifically the Cortes in that context? Survey research (Centro de Investigaciones Sociológicos, 1977; Gomez-Reino et al., 1976; López Pina and López Aranguren, 1976) allows us to follow in detail the climate of opinion that made the change of regime necessary and possible. When Metra-Seis (1975b) asked Spaniards in the streets of seven of the largest cities: "Do you believe that the maximum of political opening [*apertura*] that our laws allow has already been achieved or that it could be expanded further?" only 16 percent said it had been achieved, while 75 percent said that it could be expanded further. In indicating whether they were "favorable to an evolution of our political system toward a Western style of democracy [France, England, etc.]," 74 percent answered "yes," and only 20 percent "no." On the question of "what is more important in a democratic political system, the maximum respect for the rights and freedoms of individuals, or that the system would produce deep social changes even when those rights and freedom would have to be limited," 67 percent chose the first and only 28 percent the second alternative. While the responses suggest the existence of much potential support for a Western type of democracy, those with opinions also were aware that such a system would require fundamental changes in the institutional structure. In response to the question, "Aside from that, do you believe in the possible evolution of our political system toward a democracy of the style of France, England, etc. without reforming our fundamental laws [Leyes Fundamentales, that is, the constitution]?" 60 percent said "no," and only 28 percent said "yes." Obviously, while these data derive from probably the most politicized and critical sector of the population, it is this urban, metropolitan sector that will be decisive in the transition.[6]

In December 1975, after the formation of the first cabinet of Juan Carlos I, the same organization asked, "Concretely, what do you think will be the political line to be followed by the new government?" Only 19 percent expected that "it will make the necessary changes to make our system equal to the democratic countries of western Europe," though 42 percent personally wished just that. A plurality of 28 percent "expected it to introduce some reforms democratizing the system but without identifying itself with the western democracies," a preference expressed by only 13 percent. Those not wanting any change (13 percent) or wanting liberalization without changing the essence (6 percent) were fewer than those actually expecting the government to pursue such policies (13 percent and 14 percent respectively).[7] Apparently, about one-fourth of the respondents expect to be disappointed. Over the years the polls have revealed a growing interest in politics, a greater willingness to perceive a political crisis, and more criticism of the capacity of those who govern Spain. For instance, in 1973, 54 percent of a national sample still felt that political conditions were good or very good, but by February 1975 that proportion had declined to 32 percent. A significant number of respondents were unable or unwilling to answer some of the questions and a certain number probably disguised their opinions. Even so, the data indicate clearly a latent dissatisfied electorate that has become increasingly more manifest with Juan Carlos' ascension to the throne.

In the Spanish case development seems to have fostered a more critical stance on the part of the public. Political criticism is fuel for an open party system. What do the polls suggest in that regard? Despite the fact that the Cortes excluded political parties, even before the death of Franco Spaniards had started speculating about how they would vote in a free election with parties. Several surveys asked more or less directly for the political preferences of the potential electorate, playing with the ambiguities created by public discussion of the political associations.

The 1973 DATA survey found 50 percent still without an opinion on the issue of parties and associations. Of those with opinions, 13 percent considered associations and parties undesirable, 2 percent considered parties undesirable and were ambivalent toward associations, 3 percent were favorable to associations but not to parties, 12 percent considered both favorably, and 20 percent were aware and concerned but more or less undecided about their desirability. These data suggest that, while opinion was slow in forming, support for creation of a system of associations by the regime was concentrated among those who also favored political parties. Three years later, after the January 1976 programmatic speech by then Prime Minister Arias, Metra-Seis reported that 70 percent were favorable to the

TABLE 4.4
PARTY PREFERENCE IN 1973

| Party preference | Percent of total sample | Percent of those who express a preference | Probable distribution of a vote[a] |
|---|---|---|---|
| Movimiento | 15 | 30 | |
| Falange | 4 | 8 | 13.9 |
| Tradicionalistas | | | |
| Carlistas | { 1 | { 2 | |
| Democracia cristiana | 14 | 28 | 40.5 |
| Regionalistas | 1 | 2 | —[b] |
| Liberales | 3 | 6 | |
| Social-democratas | 6 | 12 | 4.7 |
| Socialistas | 5 | 10 | 40.9 |
| Other | 1 | 2 | |
| | | 100 | 100 |
| None | 7 | | |
| D.K., n.a. | 43 | | |
| | 100 | | |

a. Calculations based on applying Italian voting patterns to Spain. See Linz (1967: 268–271).
b. Not calculated.

legalization of political parties, and 36 percent even favored the legalization of the Communist party.

Before the recent explosion of political activity, DATA asked in 1973, "Assuming that the new law of associations would allow the existence of these groups or political tendencies, for which one would you vote if you could?" and offered a list that excluded the Communists. Table 4.4 summarizes the responses and also contains our calculations of the possible vote for the largest blocs (excluding the regionalist sentiment) derived by applying the patterns of different strata in the Italian electorate to the 1964 Spanish social structure (Linz, 1967:269). These calculations obviously reduce the strength of the alternatives to the right of the Christian Democrats, where the regime supporters were to be found, and reveal considerable potential strength on the left in a regime that does not permit it to reach the large mass of the population. Nonetheless, the Communists have been able to organize their cadres in industrial centers with Comisiones Obreras, the underground but very visible labor organization.

Because DATA also asked questions in that survey about the role of

TABLE 4.5

INTERESTS BELIEVED TO BE PREFERENTIALLY REPRESENTED BY A *PROCURADOR* IN CORTES
BY POLITICAL TENDENCY THE RESPONDENT WOULD VOTE FOR (DATA, 1973)

| | Political tendency of respondent | | | | | | | |
|---|---|---|---|---|---|---|---|---|
| Interests he defends: | Movimiento | Falange | Democracia Cristiana | Social-democratas | Socialistas | Liberales | Tradicionalistas, Carlistas | Regionalistas |
| Those the government indicates to him | 25% | 25% | 32% | 41% | 50% | 35% | 40% | 32% |
| His own | 3 | 9 | 9 | 10 | 7 | 9 | 3 | 8 |
| Those of a particular group | 2 | 4 | 5 | 8 | 5 | 7 | 3 | 16 |
| Those of the upper classes | 3 | 5 | 4 | 9 | 7 | 12 | – | 22 |
| Those of the middle classes | – | – | 1 | 1 | – | 1 | 3 | – |
| Those of the working classes | 3 | 4 | 2 | 1 | – | 1 | – | 8 |
| Those of the province or sector that elected him | 18 | 20 | 20 | 18 | 12 | 18 | 23 | 8 |
| Those of all Spaniards | 27 | 27 | 16 | 7 | 7 | 9 | 17 | 5 |
| D.K., n.a. | 19 | 7 | 11 | 6 | 11 | 7 | 10 | 3 |
| Number of cases | (679) | (177) | (618) | (285) | (220) | (136) | (30) | (37) |

## TABLE 4.6

### INTERESTS THAT A *PROCURADOR* IN CORTES SHOULD REPRESENT BY POLITICAL TENDENCY THE RESPONDENT WOULD VOTE FOR (DATA, 1973)

| Interests he should represent: | Political tendency of respondent | | | | | | | |
|---|---|---|---|---|---|---|---|---|
| | Movimiento | Falange | Democracia Cristiana | Social-democratas | Socialistas | Liberales | Tradicionalistas, Carlistas | Regionalistas |
| Those the government indicates to him | 4% | 3% | 4% | 1% | 3% | 2% | –% | 5% |
| His own | – | – | – | – | – | – | – | – |
| Those of a particular group | – | – | – | – | – | – | – | – |
| Those of the upper classes | – | 1 | – | – | – | – | – | – |
| Those of the middle classes | 1 | 1 | 3 | – | 1 | 1 | – | 3 |
| Those of the working class | 8 | 15 | 8 | 10 | 12 | 18 | 3 | 8 |
| Those of the province or sector that elected him | 18 | 15 | 19 | 26 | 23 | 16 | 23 | 30 |
| Those of all Spaniards | 56 | 60 | 60 | 61 | 54 | 58 | 70 | 54 |
| D.K., n.a. | 13 | 6 | 6 | 2 | 7 | 4 | 3 | 3 |
| Number of cases | (679) | (177) | (618) | (285) | (220) | (136) | (30) | (37) |

the *procurador* in the recent Cortes, it is possible to relate these latent partisan preferences to attitudes toward institutions of the regime (Gomez-Reino et al., 1976). One question that previously had been asked in 1971 revealed that, of those with opinions, the proportion thinking that *procuradores* defend the interests of all Spaniards dropped from 35 percent in 1971 to 24 percent by 1973. The proportion thinking that they should do so rose from 54 percent to 67 percent. By contrast, in 1971, 20 percent said that the *procuradores* were defending interests articulated by the government, but by 1973 the proportion had risen to 35 percent. In both years few (6 percent and 4 percent) believed this should be their task. The polls also revealed the relation of preferences in the latent pluralistic party system to their assessments of the actual performances of the *procuradores* in the Cortes and their feelings about the proper role of a legislator. The data clearly reveal major discrepancies in which certain interests are deemed to be represented much more and others much less than respondents feel they ought to be (see Tables 4.5 and 4.6). These discrepancies allow calculation of an index of dissatisfaction with the performance of the legislature. It is based on the ratio between interests defended and those that should be defended for the responses that specify the interests of the government, of the upper class, of the *procurador* himself, and of a particular group. As would be expected, the lowest level of dissatisfaction is expressed by those who identify with the only legal political organization, the Movimiento. It might be surprising to see that identifiers with other groups of the Franco coalition should have higher indexes of dissatisfaction. However, Falange support is the alternative for fascists who are disappointed with the regime for not fulfilling their hopes for a national syndicalist revolution. This is reflected in the relatively large number of Falange supporters, as compared to Movimiento supporters, who say that *procuradores* should represent the interests of the working class.

## POSTSCRIPT

At this writing (July 1978) in the complex political process by which Spain has been moving from an authoritarian regime to a democracy,[8] a freely elected Cortes is finalizing a new constitution. After considerable hesitation and some false starts under a first government of the monarchy, which did not succeed in opening the road toward democracy, a second government under the leadership of Prime Minister Suárez proposed on September 10, 1976, a Law for the Reform. After going through the steps provided for constitutional reform by the fundamental laws of the Franco regime (Lucas Verdú, 1976), it was approved by the Francoite Cortes and a popular referendum opened the way to a free competitive election on June 15, 1977.

For our purposes the important fact is that the Franco-created and largely appointed Cortes, which had initially appeared to be a potentially major obstacle in the transition to democracy without great discontinuities, recognized the need for change and approved the reform law. This untied the complex institutional structure created by Franco, committing what was called at the time a political hara-kiri. After a lively debate with the defenders of organic democracy, who argued the unconstitutionality of any change in the fundamental principles that underlay the type of legislature described in this chapter, those who advocated letting the people choose between organic and inorganic democracy prevailed. The law was passed on the 18th of November by 425 votes in favor, 59 against, and 13 abstentions. The debate was in reality one between authoritarianism and democracy. The Law for the Reform, formally the eighth fundamental law of the regime, was in fact the provisional constitutional law for the passage to democracy. It permitted a transacted transition within the formal legality of the old regime and prevented the break with the past advocated by the opposition. In the view of unrepentant Francoists, brilliantly represented in the debate by Blas Piñar, who today leads the antidemocratic extreme right, the law was a constitutional change against the spirit of the constitution—what the Germans would call *verfassungswidrige Verfassungsänderung*. It was as opposed to the Franco institutions as the Ermächtigungsgesetz of 1933 was contrary to the Weimar constitution. The difference is that the vote of the Cortes was uncoerced.

In a referencum on December 15, 1976, 77.7 percent of the eligible voters, all adult Spaniards, cast their ballots: 73.2 percent voting "yes," 2.0 percent voting "no," 2.3 percent casting blank ballots, and 0.2 percent void ballots. Only 2.6 percent of those voting favored the existing constitutional system, the organic democracy. The opposition parties of the left had advocated without too much enthusiasm abstention from the referendum, for they did not approve the specific provisions of the law. However, correlations between participation and "yes" voting and the vote for those parties in the June 15 legislative elections show their appeal was largely ignored by the voters. Only in the Basque country, where the regional nationalists also advocated abstention, was there active abstention. It reduced participation in Guipuzcoa province to 44.9 percent and in Vizcaya province to 53.2 percent. Analysis shows that this low participation was due largely to the influence of the Partido Nacionalista Vasco and other Basque parties on the left of the PNV.

A month after the referendum, when Spaniards were asked in a survey by DATA their opinion about the political change, 36 percent saw more positive than negative things in it; 32 percent, an equal proportion of good and bad; and 20 percent saw more negative things. Asked to whom or what this positive sentiment should be mainly attributed, from a list offered 20 percent mentioned Prime Minister Suárez, 20 percent the king, and only 3 percent, the Cortes. When asked who was responsible for any negative sentiments, among the alternatives 11 percent mentioned the Cortes, 2 percent Suárez, and 2 percent the king. Clearly, although the Cortes had played an important role in making the transition possible, it was not perceived as positively as was the king and his prime minister.

The complex process sketched here involved a "backward legitimation" for those who felt bound to the existing legal order, even if not to its ideological assumptions. This was probably also true of a large part of the armed forces. After "forward legitimation" by incorporating into the political system for the first time all those Spaniards who had remained in the opposition to the Franco regime or become alienated from it in the course of the years, including the Communist party legalized in the spring of 1977, finally the way was opened to a parliamentary democracy under a constitutional monarchy with a multiparty system of the western type (Rubio and Aragon, 1977).

On June 15, 1977, Spaniards elected a congress and a senate that would draft a new constitution. In the lower house vote the UCD, a coalition led by Prime Minister Suárez, obtained 34.8 percent of the vote and 167 of the 350 seats; the socialists, 29.4 percent of the vote and 118 of the seats; the communists, 9.3 percent of the vote and 20 seats; and the conservative Alianza Popular, 8.4 percent of the vote and 16 seats, with 20 of the remaining seats going to the regional parties. The extreme right was able to obtain only 0.6 percent of the vote and no seats. Organic democracy had been rejected almost unanimously by the electorate and a new regime was born.

# NOTES

*This is a shortened version of a paper written in July 1975 and revised for publication in January 1976. It therefore does not take into account adequately publications that have appeared after that date, nor the historic events that have led to the dismissal of the Franco authoritarian regime and the instauration of a democracy. The text refers to the institutions before the death of Franco. This chapter was facilitated by the assistance of DATA, Madrid, in collecting and analyzing public opinion poll and biographical data, and the research assistance of Rocío de Terán. The Concilium for International and Area Studies, Yale University, supported the research generously.*

1. "Organic" refers to a vision of the political community in which the component parts of society harmoniously combine to enable the full development of man's potential. "Statist" is used because of the assumption in this tradition that such harmony does not occur spontaneously in the process of historical evolution but requires power, rational choices and decisions, and occasional restructuring of civil society by political elites. This captures the idea that the organic unity of civil society is brought about by the architectonic action of public authorities—hence "organic statism," much in the sense used by Stepan (1978).

2. Two types of corporatism may be distinguished. Inclusionary and exclusionary corporatism are elite responses to perceptions of crises of participation and control and both endeavor to use the power of the state apparatus to forge a new state-society equilibrium. But in inclusionary corporatism, a central aspect of the attempt to forge a new equilibrium is the use of controlled *inclusionary policies* aimed at incorporating new groups into the economic and political model being sought by the state elite. In contrast, in exclusionary corporatism, a central aspect of the attempt to forge a new equilibrium is the reliance upon *exclusionary* policies aimed at excluding or redefining already developed organizations and practices which can challenge the economic and political model being sought by the state elite. The five conditions—summarized only briefly—used by Stepan (1978) to explain a favorable outcome of inclusionary corporativist attempts are: (1) organizational strength and ideological unity among the state elites in favor of controlled inclusion; (2) low levels of noncorporatist sociopolitical organizational density and, consequently few uncommitted groups present; (3) absence of conditions for polarized political mobilization; (4) little social welfare legislation and structural reform before installation; and (5) great economic and symbolic resource capability in relation to effective demand. In the Spanish case (1) was medium low, (2) very low, (3) very low, (4) very low and medium, and (5) low in the crucial post Civil War years and medium high in recent years.

3. There are a number of juristic studies that political scientists or sociologists studying the Cortes should not ignore (Gascon Hernandez, 1945:19–20; Fraile Clivilles, 1974). Since the Cortes is intimately linked with the Consejo del Reino, and the latter collective body has important functions both in arbitrating between the government and the legislature and in the selection of the prime minister (particularly) after the death of Franco, we should refer to Martinez Sospedra (1974:III, 1:1241–1290). He also gives important information on the social and political background of its members. Other major formal studies of political institutions include those of Estrena Cuesta (1974) and Tomás Villarroya (1974). Angel Garrorena Morales' (1977) monograph on the parliamentary control function, in addition to an institutional and descriptive analysis, includes responses of 41 procuradores to a questionnaire on their role in the Cortes. An interesting effort to analyze the functioning of the last Franco legislature (Aguilar, forthcoming) in the absence of significant roll call votes, resorted to measuring the length and intensity of applause.

4. Annual reviews of political and social development generally devote a chapter to the role of the Cortes with information on questions to the government, subjects of sessions, newspaper commentary, etc. An example of this type of analysis is provided in Martinez Cuadrado

(1970:331–362). The 1971 volume complements the collective biography by DATA (1969) for the tenth legislature. For a summary, see Diaz-Nosty (1972:165–184).

5. The leading spokesmen of the hardline of the regime like Blas Pinar, Fernández Cuesta, and Girón, do not hold their seats in the Cortes in the corporative sectors, but by fee appointment or as Consejeros Nacionales.

6. Differences between 100 percent and the total given are accounted for by "no answers" (Metra-Seis, 1975b).

7. The difference from 100 percent is accounted for by "no answers" (Metra-Seis, 1975a).

8. For a critical analysis of the Law for the Reform, see P. Lucas Verdú (1976). For the public opinion response, see Centro de Investigaciones Sociológicas (1977) and a study by DATA, forthcoming.

*Chapter 5*

# PARLIAMENTS IN FRANCOPHONE AFRICA: SOME LESSONS FROM THE DECOLONIZATION PROCESS

## VICTOR T. LE VINE

By mid-1975 there were some forty independent African states, not including South Africa and Rhodesia. With the exceptions of Ethiopia, which experimented briefly with powerless parliaments under its 1931 and 1955 constitutions, Egypt, which has had Parliaments off and on since 1866, and Liberia, whose Congress dates back to 1847, all the rest recently came to independence with a full panoply of legislative institutions. As of June 30, 1975, only nineteen had retained their national legislatures: seven of that number were ex-British colonies (of an original dozen), and nine, ex-French colonies (of an original seventeen). The nineteen, it may be added, represent a reduction (since 1945) by almost half of the number of African legislatures, most of the decline taking place since 1965.[1]

The focus of this paper is the fourteen former French colonies of what was once known as French West and Equatorial Africa, plus the island Malagasy Republic (formerly, Madagascar), also once a French colony. Their common colonial past, as well as a number of other descriptive similarities, make it possible to discuss them as a group[2] and to suggest from their example how and why legislatures have declined both in number and significance throughout the African continent. Moreover, a look at those that remain in the fifteen countries may illuminate the changes that have taken place in legislatures and legislators alike since independence.

The argument to be offered here is relatively simple: parliaments in French-speaking Africa declined—be it by design or circumstance—because they never became significant elements in national decision-making processes. The evidence suggests that, prior to independence, generally between 1946 and 1960, these legislatures operated principally as institutional appendages to electoral systems whose prime function, in turn, was to create a political environment in which the members of the indigenous elite could compete among themselves for control of their common, eventual inheritance: the postcolonial successor state, Legislatures, as one of the chosen instruments of the colonial succession, were also designed to help legitimize the inheritance itself (as well as its inheritors); in the prevailing climate of post-World War II anticolonialism, only democratic legacies were acceptable, and legislatures symbolized independence won through processes of popular, participatory, self-determination. After independence, to be sure, the new ruling elites proceeded either to dismantle or simply emasculate the legislatures that had had so important a role in propelling them to power. They could hardly have been expected to provide similar opportunities to their political enemies or other presumptive elites; moreover, they soon discovered that their legislatures could easily be converted into appendages of neo-partrimonial rule or of the single ruling party.

## CONTEXTS: PARLIAMENTS AND THE COLONIAL SITUATION

Insofar as legislatures purport to perform both general representative and law-making functions, they have been and remain peculiarly European institutions. The point is admittedly trite, but it must be made if we are to understand the delay, then decline of legislatures in much of the non-European world.

In the twentieth-century postcolonial worlds of Africa, Asia, and the Middle East, legislatures never were intended to serve traditional democratic and law-making tasks. To begin with, these had been principally British and French colonial worlds, and as France had produced a prototypical democratic national assembly in 1789, so could Britain glory in the "Mother of Parliaments." The "Mother of Parliaments" was justly renowned for her fecundity; wherever the British flag flew there grew, sooner or later, some version—be it full-fledged or merely embryonic—of the Westminster model. In Africa, the British normally began with appointed councils. Over time, these institutions increased their elected indigenous components until after further metamorphoses, they had changed into full legislatures, complete with speakers, prime ministers, loyal opposi- tions, and rules and procedures à la Erskine May.[3] The French were no less anxious—though admittedly slower and, on occasion, more hesitant—to include *le parlementarisme* in their colonial package. France's *mission civilisatrice* demanded no less.[4]

Before 1946, France had provided highly selective participation in local and metropolitan law making to its colonial dependents. Gover- nors in various colonies were often "advised" by carefully chosen indigenous councillors, and in a very few, very special instances, the inhabitants of colonial territories were granted a modified form of French citizenship, complete with the privileges of organizing local councils and of sending deputies to the National Assembly in Paris. In Africa, the inhabitants of the Senegalese communes of Dakar, Gorée, St. Louis, and Rufisque, as French nationals (though *not* as French citizens), obtained symbolic representation in the French Parliament (one deputy) as early as 1848; however, it was not until 1916 that they were granted the rights of full citizenship. In any case, Senegal was exceptional, since the French had no intention of granting similar concessions elsewhere in its vast African empire, or of providing the franchise en masse. France did not want, after all, to become "the colony of its colonies."[5]

After the Second World War, for reasons that need not detain us here, all this changed. The "second" French Constitution of 1946, in whose drafting a number of Africans had had a hand, created not only enlarged overseas representation in the French parliament, but also a set of local representative assemblies in the colonies and a suprater- ritorial "French Union," complete with its own super-Assembly. In time, the French Union, as well as its successor (in 1958), the Community, collapsed because no one—except perhaps the French themselves—had any illusions that such organizations could perform anything more than purely symbolic functions. The local assemblies, however, grew into full national assemblies, modeled at the time of their independence almost without exception on that of the Fifth Republic.

It goes without saying that the French and British entertained some high hopes for their former wards. (The Belgians, Spanish, and Por- tuguese had fewer illusions; they were much more prepared to let the local political chips fall where they may.) Among these hopes was the expectation—now in retrospect, proved demostrably false—that metropolitan institutions, including legislatures, could somehow survive translation from Paris and London to the far ends of the earth. At least the British had some reasons for so believing, since the parliamentary graft had taken well on Canadian, Australian, New Zealand, and South African soils. The French, with equally myopic optimism, were sustained by the cultural arrogance of the *mission civilisatrice* and its attendant institutional mythology. Aside from the fact that Asians and Africans more often than not found British democratic forms and norms largely irrelevant (if not incomprehensible) when applied to their local circumstances, and French ideals and practice contradictory, what may have been the fatal flaw in French and British intentions was the *institutional* bias with which they operated.

Both the British and the French had, by the end of the nineteenth century, come to take for granted a seemingly inevitable connection between political norms and institutions. Democracy meant, in the political cultures of both countries, *parliamentary* democracy: the sovereign popular will incarnate in a sovereign national legislature. Without belaboring the point, it is clear that this bias was not shared by most of Europe's African wards. Admittedly, the language of preindependence nationalism contained important demands for effective indigenous legislatures in the context of a general advocacy of liberal (i.e., Western) or socialist democracy.[6] But it is also clear that such legislatures were not usually seen as ends in themselves; for example, they were deemed instrumental to the eventual transfer of power from colonial to indigenous elites, or were considered as adjuncts to the processes of popular mobilization (for which the nationalist party had the prime responsibility).[7] Withal, once independence had been attained, not only could some African governments permit their legislatures to lapse into impotence, but increasingly, others came to regard them as dispensable encumbrances.

Finally, it should be stressed that the French and British had almost diametrically different ideas about the processes of colonial political devolution with which both countries became involved after World War II. Neither gave up their colonies with enthusiasm. The British government obviously hoped they would remain members of the Commonwealth, but many somewhat more skeptical Englishmen with colonial experience were prepared for varieties of independence outside the British orbit.[8] In either view the creation of British-style parliamentary institutions represented a highly desirable important condition antecedent to self-government/independence.

The French—at least, French governments until 1958—refused to consider independence for their colonies as a possible goal until very late in the colonial game, and as Ruth Schachter Morgenthau (1964:61–74) has amply documented, they even sought by every means possible to discourage their African wards from opting for it when that became possible in the Constitutional Referendum of September 1958. When Guinea rejected the Constitution of the Fifth Republic and opted for independence (the only African territory to do so), French resistance to the idea, as well as that of most francophone African leaders, finally crumbled.[9] The institutional implications of the French position were clear enough: colonial devolution meant transferring local authority to indigenous elites operating within the framework of essentially French-inspired institutions such as local parliaments. The successor state in French Africa would be an African-run state, but with tight constitutional, political, social, and economic links to France. To be sure, the design broke down after 1958, but by then the institutional mold had been already set.

## PARLIAMENTS AND COLONIAL DEVOLUTION IN FRANCOPHONE AFRICA

We suggested earlier that legislative institutions set up in francophone Africa between 1946 and 1956–57 were important not because they performed significant legislative functions, but because they operated as part of a structure of political devolution. That structure took shape initially in Paris, the result of a variety of internal and international pressures on French colonial policy. Notable among these influences were de Gaulle's insistence on changing the basis of French imperial relationships (heralded by the Brazzaville Conference in January 1944), the postwar renascence of the French political Left (with a strong reformist orientation to colonial questions, especially among the Socialists and Communists), the emergence of an anticolonial consensus at the United Nations (which resulted in writing new sets of rules aimed at self-determination, particularly with respect to the Trusteeship territories), and the examples set by an increasing number of postwar settlements resulting in the independence of former colonies (India, Ceylon, Burma, etc.).[10] The African contribution was provided by *évolué* politicians, mainly from French West Africa, who began to use the new postwar arrangements to demand, and ultimately get, an increasing voice in the shaping of the African territories' future. Their principal weapons were the new institutions themselves—political parties, interterritorial movements, representation in the institutions of the Fifth Republic, and, last but not least, the local assemblies and councils. That story is highly complicated and largely beside the point of this analysis; what is important for our purposes is to focus on the role of the legislatures in the process.

The institutions in question were, in fact, a very mixed bag and must be seen in the context of a flood of other colonial reforms, some connected directly with French constitution making during 1945–46, others not so related or occurring before that activity.[11] Among these reforms, of greatest significance was the creation of a variety of metropolitan and African councils and assemblies providing both voice and representation to African interests. They were of two kinds: those that operated in Paris, and those that did so in Africa. Each set had its own distinct impact on the Africans involved, but both provided (in conjunction with the other reforms) the opportunity for an explosion of political activity in French Africa as Africans responded by becoming candidates for the new offices, forming political parties and trade unions, and organizing electoral campaigns.[12]

Of the two sets of institutions, the ones based in Paris were the only ones with effective decision-making power, a circumstance that seemed both right and natural to both their French and African participants. The real meaning of the new institutions—at least initially for the Africans—lay in their *participation*, in the possibility of influencing decisions, and not necessarily in wielding power per se. Their francophilism, after all, required meaningful involvement in French politics, not (until much later) an independent voice in the disposition of their affairs. The Paris-based institutions, then, groomed a generation of African *parlementaires*, socialized to French political values, and to the intricacies of French political and parliamentary life.[13]

There were nine Black African delegates from French West and Equatorial Africa and Madagascar to the first Constituent Assembly (26 November 1945–19 April 1946) and eleven to the second (11 June–28 September 1946). The two groups included some of francophone Africa's brightest political lights: Amadour Lamine-Guèye, the Senegalese lawyer who had formed the first political party in French West Africa; Léopold Sédar Senghor, poet, politician, and *agrégé*; Felix Houphouet-Boigny (Ivory Coast), Sourou Migan Apithy (Dahomey), Douala Manga Bell (Cameroun), Jean-Félix Tchicaya (Middle Congo), Yacine Diallo (Guinea), Fily Dabo Sissoko (Sudan), and Gabriel Darboussier (Sudan). In the first National Assembly of the Fourth Republic (November 1946), of 618 deputies, 23

TABLE 5.1

**AFRICAN REPRESENTATION IN PARIS, 1945-58**

| Territory | Constit. Ass'y 1945-46 | Constit. Ass'y 1946 | I. Nat'l Ass'y 1946-51 | II. Nat'l Ass'y 1951-55 | III. Nat'l Ass'y 1956-58 | Council of Rep. | Ass'y of Fr. Union |
|---|---|---|---|---|---|---|---|
| Senegal ⎱ | 1:1 | 1:1 | 2 | 2 | 2 | 3 | 3 |
| Mauritania ⎰ | | | 1 | 1 | 1 | 1 | 1 |
| Sudan ⎱ | 1:1 | 1:1 | 3 | 4 | 4 | 4 | 5 |
| Niger ⎰ | | | 1 | 2 | 2 | 2 | 3 |
| Ivory Coast | 1:1 | 1:1 | 3 | 2 | 2 | 3 | 4 |
| Guinea | 1:1 | 1:1 | 2 | 3 | 3 | 2 | 4 |
| Dahomey | 1:1[a] | 1:1[a] | 1 | 2 | 2 | 2 | 2 |
| U. Volta | – | – | (3)[b] | 4 | 4 | 3 | 5 |
| Total, A.O.F. | 5:5 | 5:5 | 13 | 20 | 20 | 20 | 27 |
| Gabon ⎱ | 1:1 | 1:1 | 1:$\frac{1}{1}$ | 1:$\frac{1}{1}$ | 1:$\frac{1}{1}$ | 1:1 | 1 |
| Middle Congo ⎰ | | | | | | 1:1 | 1 |
| Ubangi Shari ⎱ | 1:1 | 1:1 | 1:$\frac{1}{1}$ | 1:$\frac{1}{1}$ | 1:$\frac{1}{1}$ | 1:1 | 2 |
| Chad ⎰ | | | | | | 1:1 | 3 |
| Total, A.E.F. | 2:2 | 2:2 | 2:4 | 2:4 | 2:4 | 4:4 | 7 |
| Cameroun | 1:1 | 1:1 | 1:2 | 1:3 | 1:3 | 1:2 | 5 |
| Togo | – | – | 1 | 1 | 1 | 1 | 1 |
| Madagascar | 1:1 | 1:1 | 2:3 | 2:3 | 2:3 | 2:3 | 7 |

Notes: (1:1 = 1 Rep. from 1st European "collège" and 1 Rep. from 2nd African "collège").

a. Both deputies represented Togo as well.

b. The territory was reconstituted in 1948.

Source: With the exception of the Malagache data, adapted and translated from extratextual Table 5 in Franz Ansprenger, *Politik in Schwarzen Afrika* (Cologne and Opladen: Westdeutscher Verlag, 1961).

were elected from African constituencies. Only 3 of this number were Europeans.[14] Subsequent changes in the electoral law, plus the reconstitution of the Upper Volta territory in 1948, brought that number up to 31 (of which 7 were European) by the Assembly of 1956–58. An equal number (of which 6 were European) sat as Senators in the Council of the Republic (of 315 Senators), and 40 were representatives to the 204-member Assembly of the French Union.[15] Finally, by way of completing the picture, some 8 Africans representing trade unions and economic associations sat in the 169-member Conseil Economique. (Table 5.1 arrays the data summarized above.)

In all, the African presence in Paris was far from negligible; more often than not, however, it was translated into occasional influence rather than continuous impact.[16] In the constituent assemblies it operated to wrest relatively minor concessions from the majority (such as the compromise to permit common roll elections to the French Parliament from the eight Afrique Occidentale Française [A.O.F.] territories, though not for the four in Afrique Equatoriale Française [A.E.F.] or for elections to the territorial assemblies, except in Senegal), and to keep colonial issues from being overlooked or buried. The Africans' most important early accomplishment was the *Loi Lamine Guèye* of 7 May 1946, which granted all inhabitants of the Overseas Territory what amounted to qualified French citizenship: they retained their personal status (and were not obliged to accept the French civil code), but were not given the franchise unless they belonged to certain specified categories. In the National Assembly, the African deputies managed to help in enlarging the overseas franchise, but generally they suffered from (a) the *immobilisme* of that body on colonial questions from 1946 to 1956, (b) fragmentation of their influence (for example, a number affiliated with the Communists, the marginal men of the Assembly), and (c) the preoccupation of the Assembly with other matters, notably Madagascar, Vietnam, Algeria, postwar reconstruction, etc. A few of their number even attained membership in French governments, though again with limited effect (Ansprenger, 1961:76–77). Moreover, the Rue Oudinot, which together with the National Assembly comprised the real nexus of power on overseas affairs, was never headed by an overseas deputy. The Assembly usually provided statutory authority along broad lines and in sweeping terms, but the Ministers for Overseas France could and did legislate by decree and ordinance (as they were often permitted to do by enabling legislation) on a host of important political and administrative matters.

As for the Council of the Republic and the Assembly of the French Union, in neither body did African representation make much difference, though Africans sat in them in slightly greater numbers than they did in the National Assembly. Because of constitutional limitations the Council of the Republic could, at most, only delay legislation passed by the National Assembly, and the Assembly of the French Union could debate overseas matters and advise the government thereon, but little else.

If Africans sitting in the Paris-based "quadrisynodical circle"[17] exerted relatively little influence on the making of policies affecting the African territories, it becomes legitimate to ask what they accomplished by being in Paris, and whether the experience was worthwhile in other respects. The principal commentators on the subject agree that the principal benefit for the African *parlementaires*—as indeed for those from other overseas territories—was educational. They acquired unique political experience: their involvement in French parliamentary affairs socialized them to French politics and political mores (Morgenthau, 1964:20).

Even the delegates to the Assembly of the French Union found similar profit in the activity of that almost purely honorary body: they learned how to confront important colonial issues, and to do so with verve, insight, and on the basis of careful preparation and study. Albert Sarraut, old colonial minister and president of the Assembly of Union, argued that while much of that body's activity was without issue, it was still useful:[18]

> In this Assembly much work is done with great expertise, science, deliberation, and documentation. But we are much like a mill whose millstones grind corn destined never to be baked into bread. Only the National Assembly can make laws. So we pack our meal into sacks and haul them to the Palais Bourbon, where they remain largely unopened.

Further, the *parlementaires*, by their visible presence and articulate participation, helped to educate French politicians to African concerns and became available as a source of concentrated support when French governments sought to enact colonial reforms. The *parlementaires* also learned the rules of party organization and affiliation, and this made possible some important initial liaisons between French and African parties on the African electoral scene. Two other important effects on African party activity and formation must also be noted, the first was probably foreseeable, the other, wholly unanticipated. First, it was perhaps inevitable that the *parlementaires* would come to dominate the African parties in the local assemblies as in the countryside. Second, the conservatism on colonial reforms that marked the second Constituent Assembly (as well as the National Assembly from 1946 to 1955), certainly contributed to the *parlementaires'* decision to build an African-based party rostrum which could voice African concerns and pressure the *métropole* through its local, overseas governments. The activities of the several interterritorial political parties and movements—of which the most important was the Rassemblement Démocratique Africain (RDA)—plus the *parlementaires'* ability to affect occasionally the distribution of power between Africans and the territorial administration (getting governors or administrators reprimanded or replaced, using party majorities in the territorial assemblies as a lever to force concessions, etc.), all served to build a powerful counterweight against the *immobilisme* of the National Assembly and the several governments of the Fourth Republic. To a very large extent, it was this counterweight that eventually persuaded the National Assembly in 1956 to adopt the historic *Loi Cadre*, which created local, African executive councils, gave the territorial assemblies wider legislative powers, and ushered in the period of dyarchy leading directly to independence for all the territories with which we are here concerned.[19]

We turn now to the African legislatures themselves. To begin with, it is clear that despite some encouraging signs to the contrary at the first Constituent Assembly, the French government saw the Grands Conseils and the territorial assemblies mandated in 1946 as little more than training grounds for Africans in the handling of some technical and economic aspects of public affairs. The African *parlementaires* had hoped—and expected—that the new assemblies would develop into embryonic legislatures. It was not to be; the government, patterning its action on a French law dated August 10, 1871 (dealing with the powers of departmental councils), empowered the general councils (as they were called until 1952, when their names were changed to territorial assemblies) to decide on local budgets and the rules for the assessment of taxes, and to elect representatives to the Grands Conseils and the Council of the Republic. They had also to be consulted on a wide variety of other matters—land concessions, mining permits, economic infrastructure, etc., and had final say (subject to review by the French Council of State) on such things as the sale and management of public land, recruitment to the public services, social assistance, scholarships, production loans, and the like. In all, their activity was severely circumscribed; the assemblies could not discuss political matters, were permitted to deliberate only on what the French conceived as narrowly technical matters (guided by the resident French officials), and their ambit of consultation, though fairly broad, remained consultative, that is, the local governor could (if he chose) disregard any advice they gave. In addition, despite vigorous African objections, elections to the assemblies were held on the basis of the dual "collège" system (except in Senegal, because of its unique historic position). Guaranteed seating in the assemblies, the local French citizens were expected to assist in the training of their African confrères and to restrain any tendencies to undue political effervescence. (Table 5.2 summarizes representation on the African assemblies.) The Grands Conseils, in their turn, were designed as larger versions of the Conseils Generaux, with substantial budgetary powers, but little more than advisory functions on matters affecting the operation of the two administrative federations—operations in the charge of the governors-general and their staffs. Delavignette (1962:128) succinctly describes the functions of and the general assumptions behind the new African-based legislatures:

According to the logic of a French Republic (seeking to) integrate Black Africa, a local assembly particular to each territory would be a sort of general council comparable, if not analogous, to the general councils of metropolitan departments. It (the local assembly) would relate to the (territorial) Governor as the departmental general council related to the prefect. Consultative at a first stage, it would gradually awaken to deliberative responsibilities, but (only) to handle well-defined matters of local interest. (Translation mine.)

This narrow, even parsimonious view of the African assemblies' powers and functions was to last until 1956 and the *Loi Cadre*. In the interim, however, the assemblies came to take on some unanticipated functions, the result largely of the African elite's reaction to its unfulfilled expectations[20] and to the extraordinary enlargement of political opportunities of which the assemblies were the institutional centerpieces. Three related sets of developments, then, help to explain why the local assemblies eventually became foci for nationalist agitation, and later, instruments in the African conquest of political power: (a) the new postwar structure of political rules and institutions operated to enlarge the African elite recruitment base as well as (b) to stimulate the growth and proliferation of African political parties, thus ensuring (c) the use of the local assemblies as guaranteed, legal, government-sanctioned forums wherein and wherewith to challenge the colonial system.

One of the major predicates of French post-World War II constitutional reform was, as noted earlier, the measured integration of the colonies with the *métropole*. Thus, at the inception of the process the colonial elite and electorate both were to be small and only slowly to enlarge through mutual accommodation.[21] The first postwar enlargement of the franchise opened the system only to those persons who had already participated in some sort of formal relationship with the colonial regime, be it (at one extreme) because they were *notables évolués*, or (at the other) simply paid taxes regularly.[22] This first

TABLE 5.2

**LEGISLATURES IN FRANCOPHONE AFRICA, 1945-60**

| | Territorial Assemblies | | | | | National Assemblies | |
| | 1946-52 | | 1952-57 | | 1957-58 | 1959 | 1960 |
| | Iᵃ | IIᵃ | I | II | CRᵇ | | |
|---|---|---|---|---|---|---|---|
| Senegal | 50ᶜ | | 50 | | 60 | 80ᵉ | no elections |
| Mauritania | 6 | 14 | 8 | 16 | 34 | 40 | no elections |
| Sudan | 20 | 30 | 20 | 40 | 70 | 80 | no elections |
| Niger | 10 | 20 | 15 | 35 | 60 | 60 | no elections |
| Ivory Coast | 18 | 27 | 18 | 32 | 60 | 100 | 70 |
| Guinea | 16 | 24 | 18 | 32 | 60 | no elections | no elections |
| Dahomey | 12 | 18 | 18 | 32 | 60 | 61 | 60 |
| Upper Volta | (10 | 40)ᵈ | 10 | 40 | 70 | 75 | no elections |
| Total, A.O.F. | 265 | | 384 | | 474 | | |
| Gabon | 12 | 18 | 13 | 24 | 40 | no elections | no elections |
| Middle Congo | 12 | 18 | 13 | 24 | 45 | 61 | no elections |
| Ubangi-Shari | 10 | 15 | 14 | 26 | 50 | 50 | no elections |
| Chad | 10 | 20 | 15 | 30 | 65 | 85 | no elections |
| Total, A.E.F. | 115 | | 159 | | 200 | | |
| Cameroun | 16 | 24 | 18 | 32 | 70ᶠ | no elections | 100 |
| Togo | 6 | 24 | 30ᶜ | | 46ᵍ | no elections | no elections |
| Madagascarʰ | 15 | 21 | 15 | 21 | 107 | 107 | no elections |
| Prov. Assy'sⁱ | 4×(12+18) | | 4×(12+18) | | 6×(40) | 6×(40) | no elections |
| | 1×(14+21) | | 1×(14+21) | | | | |

a. I, II: First (European) and Second (African) electoral rolls (collèges).

b. CR: Common, or single electoral roll; the *Loi Cadre* (1956) abolished the dual roll system in all French territories.

c. All elected on common roll.

d. Territory reconstituted in 1948.

e. Assembly of the Mali Federation: 40.

f. Elections of 23 December 1956.

g. Elections of 27 April 1958.

h. Up to 1957, members of the Representative Assembly were selected from the provincial assemblies on the basis of three from the first "collège," and four from the second, with Tuléare having an extra second "collège" seat. From 1957 on, deputies were chosen by direct popular election, from a single roll. The 107 figure is for the lower (Assembly) house of the bicameral legislature.

i. Up to 1957, there were five provincial assemblies; four had twelve first, and eighteen second "collège" seats. Tuléare had fourteen and twenty-one. From 1957, the six provinces elected forty councilors, each from a common roll.

Sources: Ansprenger (1961: extratextual Table 5), Morgenthau (1964), Republic of France (1953), Pascal (1965), Catroux (1953).

definition of the franchise was, in fact, so narrow that only some 203,000 people—less than 1 percent of the total population of French Africa south of the Sahara (omitting Madagascar) were given the vote. The figure includes, needless to say, nearly all 20,000 or so adult Frenchmen in these territories (Mortimer, 1969:58–59).[23] By 1957, given the changes in franchise qualifications mandated in 1948, 1951, and 1956, the potential electorate for *Afrique Noire* had grown to some fourteen millions, of which more than half (7,449,100) exercised their right to vote in the elections of March of that year.

In the beginning, however, it was an elite electorate—composed mainly of *évolués*, near-*évolués*, and *évoluables*—that sent its elite to Paris and to the territorial assemblies. And that latter elite never relinquished its preeminent position in the years thereafter. A key piece of evidence in support of these propositions is the occupational composition of the territorial assemblies from 1946 to 1958: during this period (in which the assemblies also grew in size) a steady proximate 60 percent of the members fell wholly or partially under the rubric of "government employees". Further, with the exception of the chiefs, the rest were drawn from the French-sponsored "modern" colonial elite. Even the chiefs could be included in either group, since those who sat in the assemblies were either traditional magnates who had made their peace with the colonial administration, or who owed their positions to it.[24]

The gradually growing electorate, the new political rules and institutions not only redrew (to the Africans' benefit) the definitions of the elite, but also stimulated the creation and proliferation of political groups at all levels. In addition to the RDA, which began as a reaction to the African *parlementaires'* relative powerlessness in Paris, over 300 political parties emerged between 1946 and 1958 in the French African territories to contest metropolitan and local legislative seats.[25] Eventually, and particularly after 1956–57, the number of parties diminished significantly through processes of absorption, consolidation, disappearance, or proscription. As we shall note presently, the *Loi Cadre* of 1956 certainly hastened this constriction since it put a high premium on territorially based party organizations and on the move toward single-party systems. In any case, it is clear that in French Africa the institutional structures preceded and then catalyzed—and were *intended* to precede and catalyze—the growth of political parties.

Finally, we come to the relationship between the new elite, their political parties, and the legislatures themselves. As was noted previously, the local assemblies were not expected to be deliberative beyond the narrowest of technical concerns. Their rules of order, based on those of National Assembly in Paris, were intended to promote sobriety and propriety in the performance of assemblies' deliberative and consultative functions. At all events, the assemblies were conceived as classrooms, or at most, as seminars, under the benevolent tutelage of France and its representatives. As it turned out, the francophone African elite took the assemblies along somewhat different paths.

First and most important, the elites, denied effective voice in the Paris institutions, used the assemblies as their principal tribune for critiques of or attacks upon the colonial system. In this the *parlementaires* of the RDA provided a persuasive example. Members by legal right in both the local and Parisian assemblies, clad in parliamentary immunity, invested with an influence that could often check the colonial administration or put it on the defensive, the deputies and senators of the RDA had (in the local assemblies) the use of a rostrum, a secretariat, a legal workshop for their propaganda, and if necessary, a base for popular agitation. Thus, despite the limitations imposed on them, the local assemblies almost from the first converted technical issues into political ones: the budgets became the occasions for heated debate, minor consultative matters were used as opportunities to criticize French officials, and in general, the representatives to the Grands Conseils and the Conseils Généraux

> . . . began using the limited powers to transform these councils into the type of organization they desired. In particular, they used to the utmost the legal means at their disposal to control the local administration. For example, the Assemblies' permanent committees kept a regular watch over the governors' activities between plenary sessions; the Assemblies despatched so many missions of inquiry that the Council of State on several occasions had to warn them that in so doing they were unjustifiably meddling in the affairs of the administration; their requests for additional information sometimes effectively put the administration on the spot; and finally, they often submitted their "observations" on matters of local interest to the governor-general or to the Ministry of Overseas France (Thompson and Adloff, 1958:71–72).[26]

When, as happened frequently, the local administrations began to seek ways to bypass or curtail the assemblies' rights of discussion and control, or when attempts were made to control elections and harass political parties, the Africans reacted vigorously by increasing their pressures. Some of these pressures, it may be added, resulted in local disturbances, as for example in the Ivory Coast 1949–51, Guinea 1954–56, and, of course, Madagascar in 1947, where a full-scale rebellion broke out that was repressed at a cost of perhaps 60,000 Malagasy lives.[27]

Second, the different uses to which the assemblies were being put served to invigorate party competition. The prizes in each territory became not so much legislative power—since that was denied the African elite—as (1) majorities in the assemblies and a protected position from which to wage the struggle with the Parliament and the French government on one front, and with the local administration(s) on the other, (2) identifiable, easily mobilized, and reliable electoral constituencies, and (3) party structures that could effectively capture (1) and build a power base upon (2).

All this lasted until 1956 when the *Loi Cadre* and its related events changed the political—and legislative—rules of the game.

## THE *LOI CADRE*, DYARCHY AND THE LEGISLATURES

Constitutional developments in 1956 and 1958—the *Loi Cadre* (framework law) and its related decrees, plus the coming of the Fifth Republic—radically altered the relationship between France and its African dependencies. These changes permitted the territories an unprecedented degree of self-government, led them to a period of dyarchy, and then propelled them to independence itself, but under circumstances and with connections to France far removed from those they envisioned in 1946. Of particular interest for our purposes is the fact that in the 1957–60 period, local legislatures operated as effective parliaments—for the first, and usually the last times. It should be added that, ironically enough, this efflorescence of legislative effectiveness probably contributed a great deal to the legislatures' decline after independence.

The specific details of the *Loi Cadre* of 1956, of the set of twelve statutory decrees that elaborated its provisions, or of the circumstances that led up to its passage are not germane to our discussion, and need not detain us here.[28] It is important, however, to note that the "African counterweight" played only a small role in persuading the French to undertake what amounted to a basic shift in their colonial policies. As a matter of fact, between 1952 and 1954, partly because of the disturbances in Africa, considerable sentiment had developed in France to reduce the African political role. It was suggested, for example, that the territorial assemblies be reduced to purely advisory functions. Withal, the key elements in the change appear to have been several severe shocks to France's self-esteem (the disastrous Vietnam defeat of 1954, the growing Algerian rebellion, and the inability to prevent early independence for Morocco and Tunisia), recognition that Africa might have sound economic prospects (a view conducive to conciliation with African nationalists), and finally, the new (1955) Statute for Togo, by whose formulas the government hoped to avoid the independence demanded by Togo politicians under the terms of the U.N. Trusteeship arrangements. According to the latter statute, Togo became an "Autonomous Republic," with a legislative assembly having much more power than those in the neighboring territories, and—most important—with an elected African executive including a prime minister.[29]

The Togo Statute marked the first significant step toward the *Loi Cadre*; it was continually cited to back up African claims for genuine legislative and executive powers, and helped to create a climate in which it became possible for those favoring colonial reforms to push their points of view. In the end, the *Loi Cadre* did not go as far as the Togo statute, but it did mandate some notable political changes: the vote became universal and by a single college, the powers of the Grand Conseils were significantly reduced (in favor of the territories), (largely) elected territorial executives were created, the public services were organized into French *and* territorial services, and the powers of the territorial assemblies were greatly enlarged. In effect, through the *Loi Cadre*, France accepted a division of power between the territories and the government in France, but since it retained considerable residual powers, not independence. Further, insofar as the *Loi Cadre* gave the territorial executives and legislatures authority previously reserved to the Grand Conseils, the National Assembly, and the local administrations, the significance of African representation on the Grands Conseils and in Paris declined correspondingly.

Our main point remains, in any case, that from 1957 (when the reforms were put into practice) the local legislatures became involved in a wide range of effective decision making. Debates in the assemblies took on new significance since the stakes had now become much higher, and given a new crop of friendly and cooperative local governors, the African Vice-Presidents de Conseils began acting as if they were in fact the heads of governments. The reforms also had a profound effect on the political parties; since it had now become possible for the assemblies to elect *en bloc* the members of the new government councils (except the governors, who formally presided over them), solid party majorities in the assemblies would become even more important than before. Consequently, the general elections of March 1957 became among the liveliest ever held in French Africa. In several territories (Senegal, Guinea, Ivory Coast, Chad, Mauritania, Upper Volta, Dahomey), notable constriction in the number of political parties occurred through the formation of coalitions, by way of mergers, absorption, or simply disappearance, and in others (such as Upper Volta, Niger, and the other A.E.F. territories) the occasion stimulated opposition groups to make major efforts to win seats.[30] The new rules also hastened the political balkanization of the old A.O.F. and A.E.F. federations, forcing the *filiales* of such interterritorial movements as the RDA to concentrate on local, rather than federal (or Parisian) organization and issues. The effort paid off handsomely for the RDA and its branches: of the total of 474 seats at stake in the eight A.O.F. territorial assemblies, the RDA captured 236, almost four times as many as those won by its nearest rival, the Mouvement Socialiste Africain (MSA). It was less successful in the A.E.F., where it won only 54 out of 200, and these mainly in Chad. However, it had clear majorities in the assemblies of four territories (Guinea, Chad, Ivory Coast, and Sudan), which gave it automatic control of the councils of government. In Upper Volta and Gabon, its leaders became the heads of coalition governments. Most important, the new majorities—except in four territories[31]—signaled a common (and later, after 1958, irreversible) trend toward the creation of single-party regimes. (Table 5.3 arrays the data for the above observations.)

The dramatic events of 1958—the coming of de Gaulle to power in May, the September Referendum on the Constitution of the Fifth Republic—temporarily led the African territories to accept membership in the proposed French Community as autonomous units. However, the defeat of the Constitution in Guinea and Madagascar—which gave them immediate independence—and the special negotiations with the trust territories—which assured Togo and the Cameroons independence in 1960—began the mass conversion of wavering African leaders to the idea of independence.[32] By the end of 1960 all the territories had become independent.

For the legislatures, now led by their own prime ministers, the 1958–60 period represented a period of transition to independence. Most significant for our purposes, however, is the fact that during this period the African executives, as heads both of legislative majorities and (usually) strong political parties, took the opportunity to consolidate their own and their parties' positions. Inasmuch as the 1959 constitutions gave the African governments virtually free rein on local matters, it became possible for them to bring strong—sometimes even shattering—pressures on their opposition. In any case, the other party to the dyarchy, the French, were little disposed to interfere. The legislatures, with few exceptions, became the handmaidens of strong parties and dominant leaders; energies devoted from 1957 to the vigorous business of law making, were now turned to discussions about new constitutions, to the minutiae of the prospective institutional transfer, and to reinforcing their leaders' and parties' hold on power.

## INDEPENDENCE AND THE DECLINE OF THE LEGISLATURES

As was noted at the beginning of this study, the former French territories acceded to independence with a full panoply of legislative institutions. Almost all the new constitutions appeared modeled on

TABLE 5.3

**MAJORITIES/PLURALITIES IN THE A.O.F. AND A.E.F. TERRITORIAL ASSEMBLIES ELECTIONS OF MARCH 1957**

| Territory | Party | Seats won to total seats | Percentage seats won |
|---|---|---|---|
| Senegal | MSA | 47/60 | 78.3 |
| Mauritania | UPM | 34/34 | 100.0 |
| Sudan | US/RDA | 57/70 | 81.4 |
| Niger | MSA | 41/60 | 68.3 |
| Ivory Coast | PDCI/RDA | 58/60 | 96.6 |
| Guinea | PDG/RDA | 58/60 | 96.6 |
| Dahomey | PRD | 35/60 | 58.3 |
| Upper Volta | PDU/RDA | 37/70 | 52.8 |
| Gabon | CA | 18/40 | 45.0 |
| Middle Congo | UDDIA | 21/45 | 46.6 |
| Ubangi-Shari | MESAN | 50/50 | 100.0 |
| Chad | PPT/RDA | 46/65 | 70.7 |

Party Acronyms: MSA–Mouvement Socialiste Africain; UPM–Union Progréssiste Mauritannienne; US–Union Soudanaise; PDCI–Parti Démocratique de la Côte d'Ivoire; PDG–Parti Démocratique de Guinée; PDU–Parti Démocratique Unifié; PRD–Parti Républicain du Dahomey; CA–Convention Africaine; UDDIA–Union Démocratique de Défense des Intérêts Africains; MESAN–Mouvement d'Evolution Sociale D'Afrique Noire; PPT–Parti Progréssiste Tchadien that of the Fifth Republic, establishing what de Lusignan calls "strengthened presidential regimes," in which unicameral legislatures were definitely subordinate to presidents armed with a variety of weapons against their potential recalcitrance: dissolution, the power to call national referenda, the power to demand a second reading, and in extremis, emergency powers "whenever the circumstances warrant it." The exceptions (in 1960) were Mali, Madagascar, and the Cameroons. In Mali the National Assembly was permitted to choose the chief executive/head of state, and could vote nonconfidence in the government. Two ministerial crises in succession led to the automatic dissolution of the Assembly. Madagascar, because of its quasi-federal arrangements, adopted a bicameral legislature, but invested executive power in the president who could, however, be overridden by a vote of censure signed by one-fifth of the members and ratified by an absolute majority. The Cameroons initially established a strong presidential regime and a unicameral legislature, but when in 1961 it federated with the former British Cameroons, a triad of legislatures were created: a federal assembly with guaranteed seating for both states, and two state legislatures. These, in summary, were the main provisions of the first constitutions; all were subsequently amended, revised, rewritten, or simply dropped to reflect later political realities, with legislatures relegated to impotence or, in a number of cases, simply abolished.

Why the heavy French—even Gaullist—flavor in the new constitutions? Albert Mabileau argues (1967:27) that above all the explanation lies in the "weight of the colonial fact" (*le poids du fait colonial*). Consider the new leaders themselves:

> It was the legitimate heirs of the colonizer (*les dauphins du colonisateur*) themselves who had engineered decolonization—something which certainly favored continuity with the colonial past. . . . They were, in effect, all men of French education and culture, who sat in the territorial assemblies or, fewer in number, in the Metropolitan Parliament or the Assembly of the French Union, when they were not ministers of the Republic like F. Houphouet-Boigny. There is nothing astonishing about the fact that they were impregnated with French legalism, attached to democratic formulas—even if that attachment was often simply a formality—and used to functioning in parliamentary institutions. (Translation mine.)

Further, Mabileau argues (1967:28) that time was an important factor. In less than a year—after May 1958—the first new constitutions were elaborated and adopted, and shortly thereafter, those of the independent states:

> The Africans apparently hoped to put at their disposition, and as rapidly as possible, an institutional system that would permit them to "create the State and the nation." No leader had any illusions about the originality of the regime he helped set up. One could (even) speak of institutions "received" from the colonizer; because it was necessary to erect quickly the mechanisms of the new system, the simplest solution was to borrow as much as possible from the colonial regime.

Finally, there is little question but that de Gaulle himself, as well as the highly personal way he resolved constitutional questions about executive power in his favor, had an enormous impact on francophone African leaders. The *regime presidential*, of all French constitutional innovations, seemed most fitted to their circumstances and needs.

In previous sections we noted how the French African legislatures, deprived of real legislative powers except in the narrowest, technical areas, became first extensions of the electoral system in its elite recruitment functions, then protected bases from which to conduct the nationalist struggle, and finally, for a brief period, limited parliaments in their own right. The seeds of their eventual decline had, of course, already been sown, but their fate was nowhere so clearly forseen as in the case of Guinea, considered in 1958 somewhat aberrant for its forceful rejection of de Gaulle's new order. For that reason, and because the Guinean leaders made no bones about what they intended for their new national legislature, the Guinean situation is worth examining in summary detail.

The Guinean Constitution of 1958 is one of the shortest in Africa: it contains a mere 53 articles, very few of which are over a single sentence long. Its major premise was the creation of a "nonparliamentary" government of the "strong presidential" type. The president was given all executive powers, and serves as head of state, government, and the armed forces (Art. 20). A unicameral National Assembly was granted the traditional prerogatives of ordinary legislation, voting on the national budget, and of supremacy over the executive (Arts. 9, 16, and 24, respectively). In practice, notes Bernard Charles (1972:22–23), the Assembly is "singularly limited in its legislative role." Few ordinary laws are introduced by members, proposed budgets are rushed through untouched, and the president's stated responsibility to that body is devoid of meaning (Charles, 1972:23). The key point is that in Guinea it is the party, not the

National Assembly, that matters. In theory, the *Parti Démocratique de Guinée* (PDG) concentrates in its hands "all political, judiciary, administrative, and technical powers." The president of the Republic is its secretary general, and his ministers, whom he names and who are responsible to him, may remain in office only so long as "they serve in conformity with the Party line." In fact, the government "is but an organ that executes the party line in administrative matters."[33] It is hardly surprising, therefore, that simple decisions of the PDG's National Political Bureau were sufficient to change the number of deputies in the Assembly, the way they were nominated and the criteria for their nomination. Parenthetically, it may be added that the governing statute of the PDG contains ninety articles, and is more than twice as long as the Constitution.

To what extent is the Guinean situation representative of the fate of legislatures elsewhere in the other fourteen states in our study? Certainly, insofar as the Guinean National Assembly has little formal legislative power, it has much in common with such legislatures, as have survived in other francophone African countries. In all of this latter group (Senegal, Mauritania, Cameroun, Ivory Coast, Gabon) the executive holds almost all the legislative cards, and even what limited powers remain to the deputies (ordinary legislation, budgetary approval, ratification of international accords) can usually be overridden or bypassed through (the president's) use of referendum, dissolution of the legislature, and executive decrees. As in Guinea, in all these countries (as well as in Niger, Chad, and Mali before their military coups) the single (or dominant) party has—at least theoretically—been designated as the supreme repository of power, above—again, at least theoretically—the presidency, the national legislature, the judiciary, and the bureaucracy. Statements to that effect sound much like Sékou Touré's dicta on the subject (Gonidec, 1968:26):

*Senegal (Senghor):*
The party's role is thus one of conception, direction, organization, and control. That is to say, it has primacy over the other organs—political, economic, social, and cultural—whose role is essentially that of research, draftsmanship, and management [étude, élaboration, et gestion]. These (organs) give form to and put into practice the doctrine and program of the party. (Translation mine.)

*Chad (Tombalbaye):*
I recall here the primacy of the party over the governmental and legislative organs, a primacy defined by its power to create and control all economic,

social, and cultural policy in our country (Gonidec, 1971:31). (Translation mine.)

The reality of any of the ruling parties' "primacy" is, of course, an empirical question; what is not in doubt is the legislatures' subordination to other centers or arenas of power.

The People's Republic of the Congo (Brazzaville) went Guinea, and the other states, one better: its 1970 Constitution simply contained no provision for a legislature; all political power was vested in the 30-member Central Committee of the Congolese Labor party (Parti Congolais Travailliste—PCT) and the Council of State. The party Congress presumably retained the right to override decisions of the Central Committee and the Council of State (as it retained the right to revise the Constitution), but there is no evidence that that body ever questions anything put before it by the government.[34] The Constitution of 1973, approved by a referendum that year, appears to have formalized the relationships created in 1970, but only the party Congress has now been complemented by a Peoples' National Assembly of 115 members. The party continues supreme, however, and the new Assembly has been cast in a subordinate, supporting role.

Before returning to the surviving legislatures and the questions posed by their relative powerlessness, a few words about the eight French-speaking states without legislatures are in order. In all eight military men who took power by coups d'etat now rule by decree, having dissolved or dismissed existing legislatures at the time of their coup (Central African Republic, Chad, Dahomey, Madagascar, Mali, Niger, Togo, Upper Volta). Two of the eight military regimes have instituted mixed military-civilian advisory councils (Togo, Dahomey), and in one—Upper Volta—the regime experimented with a brief revival of parliamentary activity (January 1971 to February 1974). It should be added that the Upper Volta revival meant little in substance; the Assembly met for only three weeks during the year, and its activities remained under the close supervision of General Laminzana, the president, who kept the last word on most matters. To complete the record, it must also be added that the military also took power in Congo/Brazzaville in 1966, and the top men in the government are still mostly soldiers. Creation of what at least looks like a parliament—the Peoples' National Assembly—puts the country among the very few in tropical Africa where military rulers have chosen to set up their own legislatures (Upper Volta, Somalia, Zaire, and Ghana—from 1969 to 1972). (See Table 5.4.)

It is certainly no mystery why those who engineer successful military coups more often than not prefer to dissolve, abolish, or suspend the legislatures associated with their predecessors in power. Not only are those legislatures likely to contain a substantial number of the former ruling elite, but, being composed of civilians, are usually damned (in retrospect) for having been wasteful, corrupt, unresponsive to popular needs, unrepresentative, too manipulable, oppressive, and, above all, useless to the system. The general political housecleaning—or purge—that normally follows on the heels of a successful coup tends to sweep legislatures out of existence, if only to permit the new rulers a freer hand in making their decisions. However, it is much less clear why legislatures survive in those political systems where, as in the seven francophone states, they exercise little or no legislative powers. If indeed, as we have suggested, the real political action and the locus of political power lies elsewhere in the system, why not simply do away with them, as have the military men once in power?

One superficial set of answers accompanies the proposition that the surviving legislatures continue to perform some sort of useful function(s) in the system, be it to (a) provide a continuing symbol of the democratic legitimacy of the regime, where such legitimation remains an important aspect of the political culture;[35] (b) offer an alternative channel for elite recruitment and/or co-optation; (c) provide, when

**TABLE 5.4**

**STATUS OF LEGISLATURES IN FRANCOPHONE AFRICA, 1 JULY 1975**

| Country | Legislature | No. members & parties |
|---------|-------------|----------------------|
| Cameroun | National Assembly | 120 all Cam. Nat'l Union (UNC) |
| Congo/Brazzaville | Peoples' Natl'l Assy | 115 all Congo. Labor Party (PCT) |
| Gabon | National Assembly | 70 all Gabon Demo. Party (PDG) |
| Guinea | National Assembly | 75 all Guinea Demo. Party (PDG) |
| Ivory Coast | National Assembly | 100 all Demo. Party of I.C. (PDCI) |
| Mauritania | National Assembly | 50 all Maurit. Popular Party (PPM) |
| Senegal | National Assembly | 100 all Union Progréssiste Sénégalaise (UPS) |
| Central Afr. Rep. | dissolved; Rule by decree since Jan., 1965 | |
| Chad | dissolved; Rule by decree since April, 1975 | |
| Dahomey | dissolved; Rule by decree since Oct., 1972 | |
| Madagascar | dissolved; Rule by decree since May, 1972 | |
| Mali | dissolved; Rule by decree since Nov., 1968 | |
| Niger | dissolved; Rule by decree since April, 1974 | |
| Togo | dissolved; Rule by decree since Jan., 1967 | |
| Upper Volta | dissolved; Rule by decree since Feb., 1974 | |

needed, an alternative echo chamber or a sounding board for the government's policies; (d) provide status and prebendiary pasturage for superannuated or second-rank politicians; (e) provide symbolic regional, ethnic, or minority-group representation; or (f) provide an available pool of people to serve as agents, "communicators," or mass mobilizers on behalf of the regime, or any combination of the above.[36] The above list of functions is probably incomplete; withal, it certainly applies to the francophone states and generally to other African countries with surviving legislatures, whether those countries are ruled by soldiers or civilians, or by combinations of the two. It may also apply to single-party states and to other states that have "adopted the authoritarian strategy," as Linz suggests in the preceding chapter. As a set of answers, however, the above begs the deeper question of why such functions should, in fact, be required of the surviving legislatures. Answers to these questions, it is submitted, emerge from theoretical perspectives about the nature of the postcolonial state.

Sheldon Gellar (1973:403–409) has persuasively argued that "the postcolonial African states resemble those of patrimonial regimes" of precolonial Africa. He uses the term "neo-patrimonial" to distinguish them from the older models, arguing that they share with their prototypes such common features as small governmental centers with limited resources, legitimacy constrained by powerful local forces at the periphery, extensive bureaucratization, the wide use of force, all of which resulted in inherently unstable centers. In addition, they (neo-patrimonial regimes) share with their prototypes certain political features such as the personalized conduct of authority, a tendency to monarchical style, the development of relationships based on clientelistic reciprocities, and recruitment to the elite based on demonstrable loyalty, acts of fealty, or the ability of individuals to gain the confidence of the rulers. Gellar then uses the example of Senegal to demonstrate the applicability of the neo-patrimonial model to Africa. We shall not reproduce either his argument or his evidence here; it appears very well-founded and most useful for our discussion, but with one emendation. Gellar is only one of several commentators on postcolonial Africa to note the extent to which the successor states have come to resemble their predecessors, the colonial state. In fact, it is possible to argue that Gellar's neo-patrimonial regime also resembles, with few modifications, the colonial state, much of whose style, institutions, and predicates were classically patrimonial.[37]

Viewed in this perspective, the first set of answers to the earlier question takes on increased significance.

We noted earlier that in French-speaking Africa the nexus of power and decision making lay outside the legislatures' precincts. Formally, at least, the nexus was defined as the dominant or single party in the seven states not now ruled by decree from the top. In fact, all appear at present to have witnessed a decline in the power of the party in favor of a situation in which the party, as well as the mechanisms of the state, have become ancillary to rule by self-perpetuating political oligarchies.[38] Thus, effective decision making in the system has come to be monopolized by a two-tier combination of the men at the top and the state/party bureaucracy. Political mobilization—in which the party and to a lesser degree now, the legislatures, have been intimately involved—has taken a subordinate place to the necessities of staying in power and finding technical solutions to economic, social, and political problems. The effects of this trend upon the bureaucracy are noted by Gellar (1973:399):

> The relative influence of the state bureaucracy increased and after a few short years of independence came to resemble the colonial state bureaucracy that it had succeeded and that placed a high value on efficiency, order and economic development as opposed to political mobilization. These trends were most evident in moderate Francophone West African states like Senegal, the Ivory Coast, and Upper Volta as well as Ghana after the fall of Nkrumah in 1966.

That the successor bureaucracies themselves often failed to become orderly and efficient is beside the point;[39] the effect of the process as a whole upon the legislatures was to help impose upon them the functions enumerated earlier. What mobilization continues to be carried on, notes Nelson Kasfir (1974:3–25), takes place on fairly low levels: the emphasis is more on "departicipation" than on widespread, mobilized participation in the system.

In many respects, the example of the Ivory Coast epitomizes the trends whose outlines were sketched above. To begin with, as is the case in the other francophone states, the legislature has little effective power. Control rests, as elsewhere, with the president and the party (PDCI) oligarchs. Potholm (1970:242) notes that the National Assembly does fulfill some necessary functions in the political system:

> Its very existence helps to legitimize the system's democratic pretensions by giving "popular" approval to the laws of the land. . . . More impor-

tantly, the National Assembly serves as a patronage mechanism to co-opt would-be counterelites and ensure loyalty to the leaders of the system. . . . The National Assembly also acts as a channel of communication whereby the major decisions of the government are passed on to the ethnic and interest groups that its members "represent.". . . [T]his representation is more symbolic than real but it does provide a flow of information outward from the party-government center, and serves to legitimize the action of the government.

In the Ivory Coast, as elsewhere, the patronage function looms exceptionally large. Along with various party regulars already members of the Assembly, some thirty-seven new deputies were inducted into the legislature at the 1965 elections, and another twenty-three at the 1970 elections. It appears that a goodly number of those entering in 1970 were younger people who had become prominent during the so-called "Dialogue" in 1969, when the leadership undertook verbal confrontation with its most articulate younger critics. The National Assembly became, once again, an instrument of co-optation and patronage, and apparently a good one. Of the new Dialogue-related deputies, Michael A. Cohen (1974:180–181) noted that "in the ten months between the Dialogue and the nominations, they had received administrative favors, a fact which suggests that by the time they were nominated, they might already have been 'bought and paid for.'"

To be sure, there are significant differences in regime style, party cohesion and organization, ability of the regime to deal with national problems, etc., among the francophone states, but Potholm's description of the Ivoirien National Assembly and its role in the system could apply (with a few modifications) to all those with surviving legislatures. Again, but without straining the analogy, the resemblance of the postcolonial francophone state to the French colonial state is striking. The colonial state in French Africa sought to limit participation, and did so by restricting access to both positions of authority and the ballot box. The postcolonial state has achieved the same end by limiting access to positions of power to its establishmentarians[40] and by making the vote meaningless. The colonial state operated to maintain the European elite in power and to control the components of the system through a variety—however liberal its premises—of bureaucratic despotism. The postcolonial state operates to keep a new privileged elite in power, and does so through various mixtures of party and government bureaucracies. The legislatures of the colonial period were not—at least initially—supposed to be involved in politically sensitive areas of decision making, operating rather as schoolhouses for the training of the native elite. The postcolonial legislatures appear to have even less power, and are everywhere used for other purposes than legislation or the training of potential leaders. There are, of course, some perfectly valid reasons for these developments, not the least of which is the influence of the colonial inheritance itself. It may be that African states will evolve unique, perhaps even original ways to solve the problems of effective decision making, but this much is certain, that the legislature *à l'occident* is not one of them.

There remains one unanswered question: given the decline or disappearance of measurable effects on national decision making by surviving legislatures, will they have any role to play in national development? Again, the answer must be an ambiguous one: it depends. It depends, first and self-evidently on the ability of the surviving legislatures to survive; once a legislature becomes simply another instrument of the ruling elite, it can easily be cast aside when it ceases to be useful. It also depends on the disposition of those who control the legislature; if they wish the legislature to perform some useful tasks, or contribute to development, or mobilize popular sentiment, it will survive, and might even entrench itself to some degree. Overall, however, it is fair to say that in most political systems with dependent or emasculated legislatures—certainly those in francophone Africa are representative—apart from unanticipated or unobstrusive functions, these bodies' contributions to development are likely to be pretty much circumscribed by the wishes of their political masters. Under what circumstances could such legislatures regain some autonomous role in the development process? Aside from the obvious but unlikely event that a genuinely democratic regime comes to power and restores the "old liberties," or that those in power give back what legislative powers they—or their predecessors—took away, it is possible that continued, visible progress toward developmental goals might stimulate a legislative revival. Given an approach to development that emphasizes, for example, sectoral growth, or one that recognizes ethnic pluralism, demand patterns based on visible constituencies could generate considerable pressure for articulation within some sort of national forum. In such a set of circumstances, an existing legislature, however impotent, could become the logical institutional framework both for their expression and their containment.

In francophone Africa, the Ivory Coast, Gabon, and Cameroun

have had the most consistent growth rates, as well as demonstrating a capacity for widely felt sectoral growth. There is, obviously, no way to predict what will happen to their legislatures, but if these bodies manage to survive, and if the regimes in the three countries can sustain present rates of economic development, they may well experience a revival of the kind suggested above.

# NOTES

1. In 1971 some 70 percent of African countries still had legislatures, a percentage that then seemed to Jean Blondel both "natural" and "apparently stable." The 1975 proportion, 51 percent, is very close to that in the combined North African-Middle East area. For additional details, see Blondel (1973:8–9).

2. Not the least of these is found in remarkably homologous elite political cultures which I have examined (Le Vine, 1971:1–17).

3. For discussions of some of the West African institutional steps in that development, see Wight (1947, 1945) and Wheare (1950).

4. Two of the better treatments of the whole problem of the policy implications of the *mission civilisatrice* are by Brunschwig (1966) and Marshall (1973).

5. The phrase is of unclear origins, but it reflects a disillusion with the costs of colonialism later associated with the journalist R. Cartier.

6. "The new form of independent African state which the 'national liberation movement' seeks to bring into being will be 'democratic'—in the sense, particularly, that its government will be responsible to a popular assembly elected on the principle of 'one man, one vote'; and 'socialist,' in the sense that it will develop a planned economy, in the interests of the 'masses'" (Hodgkin, 1961:24). For a stinging attack on European political biases, see Chinweizu (1975:234–246).

7. For a discussion of these issues, see Rosberg (1964:23–53). At p. 338, Rosberg cites former Ghanian President Nkrumah on the proposition that representation in the party is of far greater significance than parliamentary representation: "Members of Parliament must remember at all times that they are representatives of their constituencies only by reason of their Party membership and that on no account should they regard constituency representation as belonging to them in their own right. In other words, constituencies are not the property of Members of Parliament. It is the Party that sends them and fights for them to become Members of Parliament." ("Text of an Address Broadcast from Accra, 8 April 1961," supplement to *Ghana Today*, 19 July 1961, p.3.)

8. See for example, Robinson (1965); Cohen (1959:30).

9. The point is well documented by Crowder (1965).

10. For details, see Mortimer (1969). See also Viard (1963).

11. For details, see Morgenthau (1964:32–45), Thompson and Adloff (1958:29–82), and Robinson (1955:157–168; 1958:45–69).

12. The Paris-based institutions included the Constituent Assemblies of 21 October 1945 and 2 June 1946, the Fourth Republic's Executive and Parliament (National Assembly and Council of the Republic, formed in November, 1946, and renewed in 1951 and 1956), the High Council and Assembly of the French Union (1946–58), and the Senate of the French Community (1959–60). The African-based institutions included the Grands Conseils of the West and Equatorial Federations (1947–58); and territorial Conseils Généraux (1946–52), territorial assemblies (1952–57, 1957–58), plus the several legislatures in the UN Trust Territories of Cameroun and Togo (representative assemblies, territorial assemblies, legislative assemblies), and the special

central-plus-satellite legislatures in Madagascar (1946: a representative assembly and five provincial assemblies; 1957: a legislative assembly and six provincial assemblies). The Senate of the Community is worthy of special note because it distinguished itself by being utterly powerless and meeting only twice (July 1959 and June 1960). Georges Bidault's epigrammatic gibe is to the point: "Il s'est reuni deux fois, pour la naissance et pour l'enterrement." (It has met twice, once to be born, and once to be buried.) Quoted by Mortimer (1969).

13. The best coverage of this subject is in Morgenthau (1964:75–124).

14. Two of the black deputies were of West Indian origin.

15. The Europeans were elected from the European "collège" of the dual electoral rolls mandated for elections to the National Assembly held in the Equatorial African territories (Gabon, Middle Congo, Ubangi-Shari, and Chad) and the Trust Territory of Cameroun. Togo and the West African Territories (Senegal, Mauritania, Sudan, Niger, Ivory Coast, Guinea, Dahomey, and Upper Volta) elected deputies to the National Assembly from common rolls. Representatives to the Assembly of the French Union and Senators to the Council of the Republic were chosen by the local assemblies.

16. In the National Assembly of the Fourth Republic, 14 percent of the deputies were from overseas constituencies; 22 percent of the senators in the Council of the Republic were from overseas.

17. The four constitutional assemblies of the Fourth Republic—so designated by Robert Delavignette (1962) (*la cercle d'une quadrisynodie*).

18. Ansprenger (1961:75) citing Albert Sarrault "L'Assemblée de l'Union Francaise," Cette Semaine, Dec. 26, 1951. The translation is mine, unfortunately thirdhand from Ansprenger's translation into German of the French original, which I was unable to obtain.

19. Robert Delavignette has argued that the African counterweight, operating through the *parlementaires*—both in Paris and Africa—had a crucial role in bringing about the post-1955 changes. He (1962:122) cites a resolution passed by the Third Congress of the RDA in 1957: "The Congress salutes the great victories which, during the past eleven years, have opened the way to the political, economic, social, and cultural emancipation of the populations of Black Africa. . . . The Congress considers that *a determinant factor in these victories has been the participation of Black Africa's elected representatives in the sovereign organs of the French Republic.*" The italics are Delavignette's; the translation is mine.

20. During the second Constituent Assembly (June-October, 1946), African delegates became quite resentful, and sometimes even embittered, at the unwillingness of their French colleagues to take the matter of local assemblies seriously. The Assembly's Constitutional Committee (which included the most important African representatives) had proposed, for example, that the local assemblies be consulted when the organic laws that determined the administrative system of the overseas territories were adopted. The French government rejected the proposal. Toward the end of the Assembly, to the anger of the overseas delegates, the French government announced that it would not support the Local Assemblies Bill—which would have permitted the creation of the local assemblies before the Constitution itself came into effect. Finally, under considerable pressure, the government created the local assemblies by decree, thus enabling local input to the Council of the Republic and the election of France's first postwar president. It all left a sour taste in the African leaders' mouths, and a sense of great expectations (raised by de Gaulle, Brazzaville, and the first Constituante) callously betrayed. For an insightful discussion of these matters, see Marshall (1973:287–311).

21. "Assimilation" and "association" represented the two horns of an old French political dilemma. The principles of the Revolution appeared to demand complete social and political integration of colonial peoples to/with the growing influence of colonial conservatives, and permitted the evolution of the argument that, while "assimilation" was a worthy goal, its achievement was likely to be very long in coming, given the enormous differences in culture, economics, and politics between the *métropole* and its colonies. What was needed, therefore, was a long period of civic apprenticeship by the subject peoples' "association." By 1946–47, most members of the African elite considered themselves sufficiently French to be part of

France, but on their own terms. The "assimilation"–"association" dilemma is explored in detail by Betts (1961) and Marshall (1973).

22. The law of October 5, 1946, later amended by that of July 13, 1948 conferred the franchise on some twelve categories of *citoyens de statut local*. The operative parts of the law are included in Le Vine (1968:377).

23. Exact registration figures are provided by Morgenthau (1964:396–397) and rounded-off figures for both A.E.F. and A.O.F., plus Cameroun and Togo, are given in Ansprenger (1961: extratextual Table 2).

24. I have provided a detailed summary elsewhere (1968:376–382).

25. The figure is probably a low estimate, since no complete tally exists. Morgenthau, who dealt only with French West Africa, lists about 200. I (1964) counted 44 parties in Cameroun; add another 50 or so for the A.E.F. territories, plus another 7 for Togo, plus 12 for Madagascar, and the grand total comes close to 320.

26. The activities of the West African assemblies and its members are well described in Thompson and Adloff (1958:54–82).

27. The Malagache revolt is assessed by Raymond Kent (1962); the Ivory Coast disturbances are discussed in Zolberg (1964); and the Guinean incidents are covered in Morgenthau (1964:219–254).

28. The full background to and particulars of the *Loi Cadre* may be found in Morgenthau (1964:62–74); Mortimer (1969:233–241); Ansprenger (1961:241–252); Luchaire (1958); and Robinson (1956:179–185).

29. For details, see Coleman (1956); S. Alcande (1957); and Ansprenger (1961:209–216).

30. The literature on elections in French Africa during the 1946–60 period is particularly sparse. A notable exception is Robinson (1960:281–390). Such detail as is available on other elections may be found in the general works by Morgenthau, Ansprenger, Mortimer, and others cited previously, and in monographs on particular countries and territories.

31. In Mauritania the UPM (Union Progréssiste Mauritanienne) and in Ubangi-Shari MESAN (Mouvement d'Evolution Sociale d'Afrique Noire) had been for some time the only major parties. In neither the Middle Congo, nor in Gabon, had the situation permitted large minority parties to emerge.

32. For texts and commentary on the 1958–60 constitutions, see Sécretariat Général du Gouvernement (1963); Lavroff and Pieser (1961); and Lampue (1961).

33. The quotations are from Sékou Touré (1958–70) Action Politique du PDG, XI:38, 96, Conakry:Imprimerie Nationale (Charles, 1972:25).

34. The best treatment of the role of the PCT in Congo/Brazzaville is Thompson (1973:172–231).

35 See, for example, Allan Kornberg and Kennieth Pittman's contribution to this collection. They argue that a representative body—parliament, congress, assembly, or council—by "its presence represents the commitment of the political system and its leader to the *idea* of popular government" (Kornberg and Pittman, p. 82).

36. Points (b), (c), (d), and (f) are discussed by Stultz (1968:479–494).

37. See Gellar's (1973:423–424) notes #98–108 for appropriate definitional citations. The point is also made throughout Dumont's (1969) classic with respect to the French ex-colonies.

38. On the blurring of distinctions between the party and the state, see Zolberg (1966:122–127). On the decline of the single-party system see Mahiou (1969); Government and Opposition (1967). For a contrary view that arguments about the demise of the single-party system are ill-founded and premature, see Neuberger (1974:173–178).

39. Bretton (1973:199–131) makes this point forcefully.

40. I have documented this proposition with respect to francophone Africa (Le Vine 1975:22–42).

*Chapter 6*

# THE INFLUENCE OF THE LEGISLATURE ON DEVELOPMENT STRATEGY: THE CASE OF KENYA AND TANZANIA

RAYMOND F. HOPKINS

> "We are so poor that we have nothing to earn respect but our principles." *Julius Nyerere, 1967*[1]

> "The full riches of our land will be ours if we guard our national unity, plan our resources carefully, and work hard." *Jomo Kenyatta, 1968*

Kenya and Tanzania, in spite of much common heritage, have adopted quite different development strategies.[2] The flavor of these differences is captured in the contrasting quotations above by the presidents of these two countries. Kenya, with buoyant optimism, has relied upon private ownership and initiative combined with foreign aid and investment in its strategy of a "mixed" economy—the basic outlines of which were laid out in the *Sessional Paper No. 10 of 1965* prepared by Tom Mboya (Republic of Kenya, 1974).[3] Tanzania, with a certain pragmatic pessimism, has adopted a much more socialist route, following the principle of "self-reliance" enunciated by Julius Nyerere in 1967 in the *Arusha Declaration*. All large enterprises and land have been nationalized, and the rural populace has been exhorted to socialize through the formation of cooperative *Ujamaa* villages (see Nyerere, 1968a).

In their respective legislatures, laws and development plans have been approved that formalize these alternative philosophies of development. But these legislatures have few differences in formal structure; both continue to reflect a mutual legacy of "Westminster" norms in the roles and activities of legislators and both operate within a one-party framework. What then accounts for the alternative strategies of the two countries? And to what extent is the legislature important in shaping these development choices? In order to respond to these two questions this chapter will review the alternative strategies of the two countries, analyze in broad terms the role the legislature plays in each country,[4] and offer the conclusion that informal and indirect functions of legislators in the two countries partly account for differences in legislative roles in development, that the legislators of each country play personal roles appropriate to the contrasting capitalist and socialist development strategies of their respective countries.

In both Kenya and Tanzania the legislatures to a large extent have reflected rather basic political activities, usually activities foreign to the Western-style representational system (see Bienen, 1974). Developmental outcomes in each country attributable directly to the legislature are most often by-products of the activities of individual legislators pursuing essentially non-law-making tasks. Particularly in Kenya, the impact of legislators on development has been largely unintentional; that is, the purposes and motivations of legislators' activities affecting development were not aimed at development policy, at least not in the first instance. In both countries the respective development strategies, although different, are advanced, not hindered, by the existence and activities of the legislature. In general, this happens because legislators promote political support for the government's programs in Kenya and Tanzania, and, in some cases, they symbolically and practically contribute to the implementation of policies through individual actions within their constituency. This need not be the case with all legislatures, as Morell (chapter 13 in this volume) makes clear.

Legislative activity may affect development *directly* by influencing the content of policies or *indirectly* through its more diffuse effects on society. Development effects may occur also through the *individual* actions of MPs. Each of these effects differs in its importance, depending on (1) the particular aspect of development affected and (2) the political process in that country. In general, Kenya's legislature has more autonomy of action in its role as a collective body than does Tanzania's. It is less subject to party discipline and more important as an avenue of recruitment for leadership and as a legitimizer of policy.

In Tanzania these functions are performed to a greater extent by the party.

The effect of the legislature and legislators on development policy, while not great in either country, is probably larger in Kenya. Certainly the societal effect of individual MPs' activities is very important in Kenya, as there is greater room for individual initiative by Kenyan than by Tanzanian MPs. In the latter country, MPs who are active locally work much more closely with and under local party, labor, and government officials in pursuing personal, family, or leadership activities. In Table 6.1 the comparative strength of the legislature's influence on development is broadly summarized. The description and analysis in the rest of this paper aim to justify these admittedly gross judgments.

## ALTERNATIVE DEVELOPMENT PATHS AND THEIR IMPACT

As nation-states Kenya and Tanzania have a great deal in common. Both were former British colonies for over forty years, had a Westminster model of government imposed at independence (in 1963 and 1961 respectively), became one-party presidential states headed by strong popular leaders within a short time, and have an economy heavily engaged in agriculture and dependent on foreign currency earned from a sizeable tourist and entrepôt business. For many years their major services—phones, post offices, railways, income tax collections, airlines, and harbors—have been run by a single common bureaucracy. Even their climate, population size (Tanzania 15 million and Kenya 13 million approximately), and geography are similar. Nevertheless, Tanzania has opted in choice after choice for a quite

TABLE 6.1
PATHS OF INFLUENCE OF THE LEGISLATURE ON DEVELOPMENT

| Type of influence | Mode and importance of influence | |
| --- | --- | --- |
| | Collective body | Individual MP's actions |
| Direct (on policy content) | Kenya—some Tanzania—little | Kenya—modest Tanzania—almost none |
| Indirect (on societal constraints) | Kenya—modest Tanzania—modest | Kenya—considerable Tanzania—meager |

different set of development strategies than has Kenya. "Kenya has chosen a mixed economy" (Republic of Kenya, 1974:8), while Tanzania has sought its own socialist system—*Ujamaa* (roughly "familyhood" in Swahili). With respect to these choices the differences and their impact can be seen in terms of: (1) national goals, (2) nationalization of major industries, (3) capital formation, (4) income distribution, (5) rural developments and land ownership, and (6) educational goals.

## NATIONAL GOALS

Although widely circulated statements of national goals often reflect more rhetoric than reality, and can easily exaggerate differences if taken at face value, the contrasts between statements by Kenya and Tanzania are striking. Though both countries have welcomed African socialism and nonalignment, only Tanzania has pursued socialist goals.

For Tanzania, socialism is the goal. Its essence is "the practical acceptance of human equality." That is to say, every man's equal right to a decent life before any individual has a surplus above his needs; his equal right to participate in government; and his equal responsibility to work and contribute to the society to the limit of his ability" (Nyerere, 1968b:103).

To fulfill this goal Nyerere argues that Tanzania must pursue "self-reliance," remaining free from the dominant influence of any foreign country or group of individuals. This fundamental objective shapes policies of nonalignment that include conscious efforts to balance trade and aid from Western and Eastern donors, to resist foreign cultural penetration, and to rely little on private foreign capital. A further implication of self-reliance, according to Nyerere, is an emphasis upon development of agriculture as the key sector in Tanzania's economy. In urban society, state ownership of the organs of production through various state and parastatal corporations is the means to create the socialist society, a state where everyone is either a worker or a peasant. Nyerere has called for a step-by-step transformation of Tanzanian society to implement the goals he has outlined. He envisages telescoping the change processes experienced in countries such as Great Britain, but warns Tanzanians not to expect the process to be a short one, measured in a few months or years (Nyerere, 1968b:132–135).

Kenya's primary goals are rapid economic growth and rapid Africanization of posts in the monetary economy. Kenyan leaders seek to control their economy by means of placing Africans in key positions as directors, heads of agencies and bureaus, professionals, and entrepreneurs. Africans have been urged to make something of themselves, to work diligently toward becoming "successful." This economic growth and upward mobility are to be secured by preserving political order through loyalty and strong state rule. Kenya has expanded government investment and participation in the economy, but still relies heavily on the private sector (Republic of Kenya, 1974: 6–10).

Both countries have committed themselves to the expression of popular will through elections and the achievement of greater equality of wealth. However, Kenya has done little to limit the accumulation of wealth, especially by politicians, while Tanzania has adopted a stiff leadership code which forbids government and political leaders from receiving income from more than one job, from serving on corporate boards, or from other "capitalist" practices. One result of these alternative goals is the greater importance of foreign economic interests in Kenya, a central tenet in Colin Leys' recent critique of Kenya—*The Underdevelopment of Kenya* (1975).

### NATIONALIZATION

In 1967, a few months after the Arusha Declaration, the Tanzanian Bunge (National Assembly) enthusiastically passed legislation permitting nationalization of all major economic enterprises. Banks, insurance companies, food processors, manufacturers, and import-export businesses were reorganized under various government management forms. Compensation to foreign investors followed a tough round of negotiations. The transition to government ownership went smoothly, surprisingly so, in many cases, but fitfully and disastrously in others. The State Trading Corporation, the National Development Corporation, and a host of parastatal firms in particular sectors took over responsibility for these nationalized businesses. One important effect was greater government control over planning, personnel, and individual compensation in the economy.

Kenya has nationalized no businesses and has promised tax and other incentives to prospective new foreign investors. It has, however, pressured businesses to Africanize, and has forced some to sell out to Africans. The government has moved to influence the economy through pricing and marketing policies in agriculture, state bank and financing institutions, and various state corporations. Nevertheless, the private sector "plays a predominant role in manufacturing, commerce, tourism, housing and mining" (Repulic of Kenya, 1974:6). In a survey of urban Kenyans in 1971, nationalization was favored by 62 percent (and opposed by 26 percent), but only 44 percent thought it likely that the government would decide to nationalize major industries. And the proportion expecting such action from Parliament or the cabinet declined somewhat among the better educated.[5] Popular support for nationalization does not mean much, given the heavy stakes the current elite has in the established economic institutions, including many foreign subsidiaries. Kenyanization, the transfer of economic and social assets to citizens, remains the key strategy— along with the affirmation of private property and entrepreneurship.

### CAPITAL FORMATION

While both Kenya and Tanzania have sought foreign aid to finance their development, and both have planned for more aid than was received, Kenya received more foreign capital per capita until recently and has enjoyed a higher economic growth rate. In Tanzania the aim has been to increase capital formation from domestic sources, principally from nationalized industries and taxed export earnings, while Kenya has expected her largest increases in capital formation from private sector and foreign sources.[6] Trend data, however, contradict these aspired goals (IBRD, 1974:vol. 5, app. 6, table 8), as Tanzania has rapidly expanded her foreign debt, especially owing to the building of the new railroad from Dar-es-Salaam on the coast into landlocked Zambia.

Investment in agriculture in both countries has been given a high priority, even more so in Tanzania, while Kenya has given greater encouragement to her more rapidly growing industry—tourism. In the 1960s, during the first two development plans of each country, Kenya achieved a higher average annual growth rate, 6.8 percent, than Tanzania's 5.58 percent.[7] Real growth in both countries is being rapidly eroded by rising population growth; in Kenya the population was increasing at 3.5 percent in 1974, up from 2.5 percent in 1951, and in Tanzania it was growing more than 3 percent, up from an estimated 1.8 percent in 1961.

In spite of Tanzania's goal to reduce foreign dependence, in 1974 Tanzania was listed by the United Nations as among the thirty-two nations "most severely affected" by the world rise in food and energy prices; it had to make a special plea for food aid from the United States. Capital formation was adversely affected in both countries in 1974–75. Their differences in policy with respect to investment, while ideologically quite real, could be explained practically by a nonideological factor: Kenya inherited a far stronger economy from the British and is more able to attract private investors who reap external economies from previous investments and development in Kenya.

## INCOME DISTRIBUTION

While both countries have aimed at more equitable income distribution, only Tanzania has taken direct political action toward achieving this goal.[8] Up to 1967 wages in the nonagricultural sector had grown more rapidly in Tanzania than in Kenya—15 percent compared to 10 percent (Jackson, 1971:356). Since 1967 salaries in Tanzania have been below those in Kenya and Uganda for comparable positions. Pressure from labor movements, the rising cost of living, and the expansion of Africanization to include highly skilled and highly paid positions were all factors in the rising inequality in both Kenya and Tanzania during the period following independence (Jackson, 1971). While the income gap in Tanzania has been reduced somewhat since 1967, it has continued to grow in Kenya. A study of its public service reported that the number of Kenyans receiving a high wage income was growing rapidly, along with growing inequalities in remuneration among employees. Specifically, employees in small firms (with low wages and insecure employment) and the peasantry, do not share proportionately in the growth of the economy (Ndegwa, 1971:30–34). Nevertheless, in 1972 large salary increases for government employees were approved. Indeed, Kenyan politicians have demonstrated some insensitivity to the problem of unemployment and income inequity. The National Assembly in December 1970 voted itself substantial wage increases during a period in which a major government agreement was in effect with unions and private industry to freeze wages in order to expand employment.[9] And the report of the Kenyan legislature's select committee to study unemployment resulted in no direct action.

Following recommendations by the ILO and the World Bank, Kenya's 1974–78 Development Plan called for efforts at redistribution from urban to rural areas. It found average modern-sector wage earners in 1972 received $804 compared to $67 earned by small farmers and those on settlement schemes. In Tanzania, regional average income ranges from about $110 in Arusha to $55 in Ruvumu, a much smaller disparity than in Kenya's provinces. Although the Kenyan government claims to have provided some benefits to the poor through land schemes and remission of school and health fees, high unemployment (significantly above Tanzania in urban areas) remains a critical problem in Kenya, and seems related in part to large income differentials (see IBRD, 1973:67; Republic of Kenya, 1974:42–43; Johnson, 1971).

### RURAL DEVELOPMENT

In Kenya, the pattern of rural development has emphasized opportunities for Africans to acquire land in new settlement areas or on farms acquired from European settlers. Various schemes have aimed at rationalizing the rural productivity through private ownership. Such small holder operations can create a rural class with a stake in the present system (Leys, 1970:8–19). This strategy is an extension of the Swynnerton Plan begun during the Mau-Mau insurrection to rationalize and stabilize the rural areas (for continued colonial rule).

In Tanzania private ownership has been abandoned in favor of communal, cooperative schemes. As Aaron Segal (1967:47) draws the contrast:

> The first glance at a Tanzanian village settlement and a Kenyan land settlement scheme reveals the essential difference: there are no fences in Tanzania separating individual plots. Tanzanian villages are cooperatively owned and producing villages; Kenyan land settlement schemes are made up of individually owned farms which may or may not market cooperatively. The income of Tanzanian villagers represents equal shares of the total income of the group, with its allocation decided by a majority vote of the members; the income of a farmer in Kenyan settlement schemes depends on his own efforts.

However, a World Bank Study in 1973 found that the collective ownership of *Ujamaa* villages was "not working" (IBRD, 1973). Nevertheless, coercive measures were used in 1973–75 to force more rural Tanzanians into these new villages. In general, the legislature has played no major role in the *Ujamaa* program. Individually some legislators have balked, unsuccessfully, at the villagization program, while others, such as Millinga, a once critical backbencher who sought rural reform, have assumed responsibility for the program.

Kenya's policies clearly aim to build a nation of prosperous and individualistic peasant farmers, emulating on a smaller scale the patterns of agriculture introduced by European farmers. However, in practice many elements of traditional agrarian economic life remain in both countries. The sharp contrast between the communally owned cooperative village in Tanzania and the petty capitalist farmer in Kenya is often chimera since real change in peasant life comes far slower than changes in national rhetoric.

Moreover, each country's policy has had mixed results. In 1968 it was estimated there were only 350 *Ujamaa* villages in Tanzania, by 1970 about 1,000, with a population of perhaps half a million, but over half of these were located in one region—Mtwara. In 1972, 5,556 villages were recorded, with an average size of 657 people (IBRD, 1974:vol. 2, p. 5). Few villages fit the "ideal" pattern. And David Feldman is pessimistic about the achievement of *Ujamaa* goals in the Tanzanian countryside, his investigations suggesting that developing commercialism in Tanzanian agriculture undermines communal features of traditional life and encourages individualism. Technological innovation seems to discourage cooperative work as the exigencies of farmers' independent decisions make traditional communal values less salient (Feldman, 1969).

The Tanzanian goal of greater economic equality is structurally related to alternatives for economic growth so that "natural" patterns of change are inimical to *Ujamaa* ideals. One sympathetic observer's conclusion is that whatever success collectives in Tanzania have achieved has been despite TANU, not because of it (Helleiner, 1972).

In contrast, Kenyan land policies have aided rather than attacked entrenched interests. Many leading personalities have acquired large land holdings, while many poor rural families remain landless. Harbeson concludes from his study of land reform and politics through 1970: ". . . that those without land have few economic means, and the landed and landless alike have few political avenues for political identification with the new Kenya nation" (Harbeson, 1971:251).[10]

## EDUCATION

Both Kenya and Tanzania aim toward complete literacy. Policy initiatives in Tanzania have been most advanced concerning the *content* of education, while in Kenya the expansion of exposure to education and certification has been paramount. In 1970, for instance, Tanzania declared a year of adult political education marked by a drive to educate outside formal schools. An emphasis on self-improvement and opportunities for adults to undertake literacy courses under the general guidance of the party, TANU, have marked Tanzania's approach.

Formal education is more available and more competitive in Kenya. Enrollment in primary schools in Tanzania is approximately 45 percent of those eligible, while in Kenya it is about 60 percent. Large regional differences exist in both countries, but are perhaps more pronounced in Kenya where Rothchild points out primary school enrollment in Nairobi was 131 percent of the eligible population (age 7 to 13), but only 2 percent in the northeastern province of Kenya. Nairobi's schools thus even accommodated influxes from other provinces. In Tanzania, first grade enrollment as a percentage of those eligible (7–8) also varied by region, but to a far smaller amount: 81 percent at the coast to 31 percent in Shinyanga (Rothchild, 1969:692 and IBRD, 1973:vol. 1, p. 67). Extreme pressure exists in Kenya for educational opportunities and the government has set a goal of universal primary education by 1980. Each year tens of thousands of Kenyan youngsters take their primary school certificate exam with high anticipation of being offered entrance to secondary school, although there are places for less than 20 percent. Since education is regarded as the major avenue for social and economic advancement, competition has become intense (see Prewitt, 1971).

In Tanzania, Nyerere proposed in March 1967 his "Education for Self-Reliance." He called for a transformation of the inherited education system to one that would give more education to children generally and less instruction to those few who would eventually emerge from the top of the school pyramid. He wanted education to plan for the far larger number who would *not* go on for further education, particularly after primary school. His scheme called for a reemphasis on agricultural education and for cooperative economic activity among teachers and pupils to promote self-reliance in contrast to British standards, with their emphasis on classical subjects (Nyerere, 1968b:44–75). These proposals met lukewarm response to outright opposition from teachers and parents. Although all schools have taken steps to implement these proposals, those schools associated with *Ujamaa* villages have perhaps gone furthest. By altering the school curriculum and raising the age for school entrance, pressure on the economy from the number of young school leavers with high expectations of either earnings or further education should be reduced.[11] The major impact of these revised educational policies has not been fully implemented or realized in Tanzania. Although Kenya has moved away from British practice and standards to some extent, the emphasis on terminal exams, rote learning, and classical subjects continues there even more markedly.

In Kenya, education is such a valued means to advancement that private schools have become important commercial investments. Some legislators earn income from ownership of secondary and correspondence schools, while others have furthered their careers through sponsorship of *Harambee* schools, local self-help endeavors to expand educational opportunities. In addition, technical schools, the first now open at Kiambu, have been formed by local initiative in response to the demand for education. In general, MPs and local politicians have taken the lead in raising funds for such schools. There is no comparable activity in Tanzania. Nor has there been any publicly available study in Tanzania since 1967 to allow more recent comparisons with Kenya (Koff and Von der Muhll, 1971).

In the six domains outlined: goals, nationalization, capital formation, income distribution, rural development, and education, Kenya and Tanzania have quite different development strategies. The rhetoric, public mood, and even life style in the two countries have diverged slowly but increasingly over the last decade. Such changes reflect the impact of political leadership. A brief review of some major features of the political systems of the two countries will be helpful, therefore.

## THE PATTERN OF POLITICS AND THE ROLE OF LEGISLATORS

In both Kenya and Tanzania similar historical patterns of authority are found. At independence, traditional tribal legacies were blended with principles and techniques developed in the nationalist movements and with constitutionally prescribed Western participatory institutions, such as elections and parliaments. The amalgams of these authority patterns emerged somewhat differently in each country and have continued to diverge. Within each country, the roles of the national assemblies and individual legislators also have diverged. This change reflects the impact of more deeply anchored norms for governing and making authoritative decisions than those prescriptions, norms, and role expectations that British parliamentary custom gave to each state. This section will outline some of the major features of each political system with special attention to the way the respective legislators carry out their activities.

KENYA

Of the various participatory structures created at independence in Kenya to meet popular expectations and the British preference for democratic institutions, the National Assembly (which grew out of the Colonial Legislative Council) is the most important. Parties and elections, while functionally related to the Assembly, are, I believe, largely derivative from the accepted existence of such legislative bodies. In countries where parliament was a "transferred" institution, analogous to Kenya, but where these authority structures were ended by military intervention, such as in Ghana, Nigeria, and Uganda, elections and parties have also been eliminated. This argues that the existence of a legislature in Africa promotes elections and parties, or at least factions, more than the reverse (cf. Le Vine, chapter 5 in this volume).

The Kenyan Assembly performs a variety of functions for the political system as a whole, and its current activities can tell us a fair amount about what patterns of authority have emerged. In particular it makes plain the importance of traditional authority patterns and the continuing political dominance of the government bureaucracy, a feature of the colonial system.

Policy-making and law-making functions in Kenya are less important for the legislature than the constitutional formula suggests; but this is almost universally true (see Loewenberg, 1971a, and Packenham, 1970). Functions other than these "formal" tasks generally are more important in Kenya. These include identifying and training political leaders, facilitating communication between the government and populace, articulating constituent and special interest demands, interpreting governmental responses, and legitimizing decisions that are effectively made outside the legislature. If the Kenyan legislature were to disappear, the effects of its absence would be greater for these functions than for its impact on what laws or rules were made.

Law making was never the exclusive prerogative of the legislature (cf. Sisson and Snowiss, chapter 2 in this volume). The cabinet, drawn from the legislature, was always thought to have a central responsibility. But any influence on legislation, including government policy, that the Assembly does have has declined since the immediate postindependence period. During 1963–65 the legislature was able to block several government procedural initiatives and force revisions in others. In the subsequent period 1965–75, such discretionary influence has declined. This same pattern ensued in Tanzania. It is rather different from the pattern Le Vine reports for West Africa, where legislatures were most assertive in the preindependence period and declined as party leaders took over government posts (see Le Vine, *supra*). Initiatives by legislators in 1964 to promote the East African Federation and reduce economic inequalities forced ministers to respond publicly to criticism and highlighted controversies on these issues, though they did not substantially alter the government's position. Increasingly since then, the executive has assumed that the legislature would accept its policies. Even changes in political boundaries in the late 1960s, which required Assembly approval, were made in several cases well before the Assembly was consulted. This indicates the ease of control over the Assembly exerted by Kenyatta and his key officials. Following the 1969 and 1974 elections, which resulted in substantial turnover among MPs (over half in both elections), the legislature has initially—formally or informally—far fewer proposals or private bills.

On most issues there is no independent legislative review or analysis, although in a few instances the Assembly's most important assertions have come through efforts of select committees. For instance, the select committee on unemployment (1971) focused attention on this issue and mobilized support for greater government efforts to ease the problem. In 1975 the select committee investigating the assassination of J. M. Kariuki (a prominent Kikuyu politician) dramatically asserted legislative power by implicating a cabinet member and high police official close to President Kenyatta. By a vote of 62 to 59, a rare vote actually recorded by individual, a government motion to censor the committee's report was defeated (*New York Times*, 1975). This was the first loss by the government since mid-1964 and marked a period of growing frustration and a resurgence of demands for loyalty to the government. But it was followed by repressive steps: first, ministers and assistant ministers who voted against the government were dismissed; then two MPs generally critical were arrested in October 1975. The day after the MPs were arrested at gunpoint in the Assembly, Kenyatta warned a closed legislative session: "the hawk was always in the sky ready to swoop on the chickens" (*New York Times*, Oct. 17, 1975). The next day he received a unanimous vote of personal support.

In spite of instances in which groups of MPs fail to endorse government proposals, such as with the 1970 Succession Bill, influence of the legislature over the course of government action remains slim. Even the recommendations of the special committee investigating

Kariuki's assassination that passed in the legislature were ignored by the government. Presidential prerogatives and the practice of ministries of ignoring parliamentary supremacy (merely a constitutional claim), notably with regard to spending money, saps much of the legislature's potential for influence. Nevertheless, it has retained a tradition of criticism, and populist and radical rhetoric occasionally enlivens Assembly debate. But the consequences of Assembly discussions have diminished for the law-making function. Major policies are made by the executive, either in bureaucratic deliberations or by consultations among a few key people including the president. And, on occasion, President Kenyatta has taken decisions precipitously, even capriciously. There have been instances when, in response to a direct appeal, he would alter a tax measure or announce that a government action would be taken. These occurred without prior preparation, consultation with the relevant ministers or bureaucracies, or consideration of whether legislative consent would be needed.[12] The discretionary power of Kenyatta over policy is more analogous to that of a king than a president, and has reduced the legislature largely to a consultative body on development issues, available on request. Although popular demands are pressed through legislators' activities, demands are not met by legislative decision. However, the use of select parliamentary committees in 1975 as a way to focus attention and pressure the government counters the trend of declining legislative assertiveness from 1965 to 1974.

MPs perform other than law-influencing functions individually and collectively within the political system. The most important of these is to legitimate government actions, which in turn promotes regime support. It is unfortunate that the decline in legislative autonomy vis-à-vis the executive has diminished the capacity of the legislature to affect legitimacy and induced criticisms from more frustrated members. Moreover, the ability of legislators to withdraw support from government leaders can and has become dangerous to leaders. Kenyan leaders have sought to limit such action, for instance, by banning speeches, firing cabinet ministers, and generally condemning critics vociferously.[13] In these ways the Kenyan legislator's autonomous influence has been limited; and the preventive detention powers of the president as well as other prerogatives have been used against selected MPs.

In addition to its direct impact on support, the role of the legislature in recruiting leaders and other functions can and does affect the way the overall system works and thus indirectly the process of building or destroying support. Citizen perceptions usually see government as a monolith; few people see the legislature or any part of government as distinctive (though citizens did have specific views about legislature activity). One conclusion seems to be that the failure of the legislature will not destroy legitimacy, although its success in fulfilling expectations could enhance it (Hopkins, 1975a).

Individual legislators—acting within or outside the assembly—perform a number of important functions: brokerage, recruitment, representation, and promotion. The most important is interest brokerage, which MPs perform in diverse ways. Their role in the Assembly itself in communicating political interests is highly visible, especially during the question hour. And non-Assembly public addresses by MPs abound with enunciations of local demands and aspirations, bringing such claims directly to the attention of the bureaucracy. This function is important in providing an "upward" transmission of demands (see Barkan, chapter 10 in this volume). Alternatively, the interests of the cabinet members and President Kenyatta, such as the enhancement of loyalty among the populace, are promoted by MPs when they make the rather ritualized statements of fealty required in public meetings (by current norms, not legally). In Kenya, interest articulation by the legislators is particularly salient since their "lobbying" through formal Assembly speeches, public addresses, or before the president as the head of a group granted an audience, is the principal method by which MPs can hope to convert electoral promises into policy.

Individually many MPs become patrons for the "clients" in their constituency; and they can expect to be supported so long as they play this role well. Candidates in 1969 and 1974, in vying for public support, frequently promoted themselves in terms of their ability to secure benefits for constituents. Education or close relationships with high officials were cited as attributes that would make them more effective advocates of constituency interests. National policy issues played but a small role in campaign discussions, though more than in Tanzania, where no serious divisions are made public.

As a result of the local appeals, some MPs have been overwhelmed with particularistic demands from constituents. These range from requests for government action in large matters such as increasing the farm land available for African small holders to the petty task of shepherding local constituents through one or another bureaucratic maze. Just as Morell (chapter 13, this volume) found in Thailand, the most important jobs cited by constituents for a Kenyan MP were to "tell government what constituents want" and "obtain development projects for the district" (Barkan and Okumu, 1974).

While local leaders and clans who assist an MP in his election tend to expect special attention, the role of the MP as a personal agent-patron is expected by all constituents. One strategy to limit requests is for an MP to remain away from home, either in Nairobi or abroad.[14] The illusion of some villagers that a problem can be solved if only it can be presented to the MP is not challengeable if it cannot be refuted. But MPs who are available and do see their constituents are the most popular (Barkan and Okumu, 1974:18–20), though usually not part of the major leadership network.

A second, less public mode for communicating interests exists in inter-elite discussions. The patron-client relationship of leaders with their constituents, common to elites, leads to mutual collaboration among leaders on issues that threaten the clientist structure. The oathing in 1969, for instance, was an affirmation of social solidarity. Kikuyu leaders brought virtually all adult Kikuyus to Kenyatta's estate at Gatundu to pledge "to keep the flag [government] in the house of Mumbi [Kikuyu hands]" (Leys, 1975:236). This ritual was designed to inspire allegiance and trust and exact reciprocal promises. Most networks of elites, not only those among the Kikuyu, recognize the need for mutual support; and reciprocal exchanges occur, therefore, among elites on a nationwide basis. In the last several years delegations of local notables led by an MP have arrived at President Kenyatta's farm at Gatundu to pledge their loyalty and plead for one or another particular need. The face-to-face contacts, ritualized format, and acknowledgement of reciprocal obligations of these weekly encounters parallel on a national scale the patron-client transactions between MPs and their local supporters. Kenyatta, at least symbolically, is a national patron, with MPs as his intermediaries.

The other structure for communicating interests is more direct and less flamboyant. Executive officials with discretionary authority (of whom Kenyatta is the most visible and potent) are approached in a suppliant manner and urged to recognize pressing problems. Contacts with ministers and influential civil servants vary considerably among MPs. Often local officials such as town clerks will expect the local MP to press for important budgetary allocations within the relevant ministries.[15] Satisfying local officials on this score may be more important than keeping campaign promises. Although breaking promises may disappoint some constituents, it does not cut an MP's links with local elites. A study in Nyeri district, for example, found occupants of local leadership roles (headmen, cooperative and party officers, etc.) economically better off than random landowners, more conservative on issues, and both more in agreement with the government and favorable toward MPs than average constituents (Stockton, 1971). Success at the center is, therefore, different for local elites than for the average peasant or urban workers. Overall, the brokerage function is important as a link between the periphery and the center, but it is not easy to perform.

A second latent function the legislature performs is political recruitment. Since KANU is largely moribund as a party, the initial selection of national leaders is controlled by local voters. Election to the Assembly identifies potential recruits for government posts. Once elected, however, the rewards available to a local notable arriving in Nairobi as an MP may induce him to conform to existing norms promoting elite cooperation and dampening agitation over dissatisfactions. In this respect, popular local leaders tend to be "system seduced," trading local loyalties for access to privilege.

In many one-party or dominant party systems recruitment of political leadership is carefully controlled. In the Soviet Union a long period of party apprenticeship is normal. In Tanzania a careful review of candidates at local and national levels insures their acceptability for existing leaders and helps to maintain the strength of local party officials. In Kenya the party has used few screening controls, and service in the party has been unimportant in recruitment of leaders. In general the party has been discarded as an instrument of rule as well as of recruitment. Loyalty pledges in 1975 usually dropped reference to KANU, typical from 1969–74; loyalty is declared to Kenyatta and his government.

Elite recruitment occurs in the KANU primary. In 1969 seats were contested in 148 of 158 constituencies; and in 106 locales three or more officials ran for election. The pattern of competition was just as high in 1974. The qualification procedures for election include making a 1,000-shilling "non-returnable deposit" (*sic*) to KANU and passing a language test in English (which less than half seem to have passed). Requirements such as these screen out aspirants with less education and wealth. They are justified on the grounds that debate in Parliament may be in English, though Swahili has been endorsed for use as an official language. They also are to insure a degree of seriousness. Six months of party membership plus these "objective" requirements were the only real hurdles faced by most aspirants. Although the KANU Executive Committee has final approval in principle, it rejects few nominees.[16]

Although the 1969 and 1974 election results led to major influxes of new MPs replacing and rejuvenating some of the leadership at the center, the key cabinet ministers, with one exception, were retained. As Ghai and McAuslan concluded after the 1969 elections: these "were not to provide for a new government; President Kenyatta was to continue as head of government, though individual ministers might lose" (1970:522–23). This pattern was repeated in 1974.

The very existence of the legislature has required procedures for selection of local leaders to form a national leadership pool. In turn, recruitment of new ministers, assistant ministers, and other leaders after the parliamentary election involved a mutual process of selection between the central executive and local areas. Since party controls before and after selection have remained virtually nonexistent, the president and his chief advisors, working through the administrative apparatus, have become the principal force for imposing cohesion and discipline on MPs. Because of the weak party organization, the structure of opportunities offered to new leaders and the induction of new recruits into the elite of the center has become largely controlled by the presidency. Excluding some popular but uncontrollable leaders from the government, such as J. M. Kariuki, is a way to further this control. Kariuki's exclusion may be the reason why rumors that Kenyatta was responsible for Kariuki's murder in March 1975 were so widely accepted; national popularity (as opposed to local popularity) independent of Kenyatta has been enjoyed by few men; perhaps only Odinga, Mboya, and Kariuki. As such they were threats, prior to their removal from politics, to the national clientist structure's chief patron, and perhaps the structure itself.

A third function of the Assembly is to promote a sense of participation and equitable representation. Leaders of the various regions and tribes of Kenya have consistently demanded a fair share of the dividends from independence and economic growth. A central feature of such demands has been equal or balanced representation in the central institutions of society. Since population and geography are the principal criteria for establishing constituencies, such balance is assured. Moreover, the legislature itself not only avoids resentment arising from discriminatory representation, but also provides an important example of equity in contrast to other government bodies. A disproportionately large number of Kikuyu hold administrative posts, and they also enjoy greater educational, industrial, and commercial opportunities. Although criteria of merit, economy, or profit may justify this situation, this has not allayed antagonisms by others. Moreover, a widely held view, confirmed by investment patterns, that development projects are distributed inequitably by region creates further resentment.[17]

The "balance" in the legislature is more symbolic than effective. Though its membership meets a general demand for equity and condemns by implication unrepresentative political institutions, these consequences have not altered the consolidation of Kikuyu power. President Kenyatta's cabinet, by far the most powerful group, though it seldom meets, contains an overrepresentation of Kikuyus. The tribal composition of MPs in the government is more balanced when the thirty-odd assistant ministers are added to the twenty-one cabinet members. Although the post of assistant minister requires few skills and offers a bare modicum of influence, its prestige and financial rewards are attractive. Such positions provide useful patronage posts for the president. They can reward the "faithful" from peripheral areas, bolster the appearance of an equitable balance in government, and co-opt about one-third of the Assembly to an obligation to support, or at least not oppose, government policy.

A fourth function of the legislature is to commit key political leaders to programs or policies designed by the bureaucracy.[18] At the cabinet level this is a consequence of the legislature's internal organization for debate. Because they are called on to answer questions and defend government policy (notably during the budgetary review of proposed expenditures), ministers and assistant ministers usually depend on the cabinet or the president for major policy decisions and on civil servants for minor policy clarifications. Regardless of their personal view (if any) or those of their constituents, their responses to parliamentary questions are expected to conform to "instructions"; and since MPs usually lack staff resources to investigate problems or survey alternative policies, and since special committees have to rely on ministry officials who are volunteered by the government, programs devised by the bureaucracy tend to be accepted and subsequently lauded by political leaders.

Legislative functions must be seen in the broader context of the effective authority structures that held sway in Kenya in the 1971–75 period, about a decade after formal independence. Those patterns reflected not only British norms from which the Assembly's authority derives, but traditional and colonial ones as well.[19] The legislature's role in development has been circumscribed by these two other authority patterns. The most important structure of authority has been the partially traditional clientist system. The system operated in the style of a "court" system, with audiences held at Kenyatta's Gatundu home and at presidential houses in Nairobi, Nakuru, or Mombasa. Petitioners arrived, were screened by personal aides or ministers, and were received by Kenyatta, as chief patron, with traditional ritual; with presentation of gifts, singing, and dancing groups for entertainment; and, finally with exhortations and granting of favors (Leys, 1975:246–248).

A second feature was the bureaucracy. It operated much as it did before independence with functional ministries (education, health, agriculture, etc.) organized by "rational" criteria and with their general bias toward the urban or more bourgeois citizen clientele, a bias continuous from the colonial period (although the European settlers were a more important beneficiary then). The "neo-colonial" character of the bureaucracy was also reflected in the recruitment patterns and activities of the provincial administration, police, and military. Political administration was largely handled by these organizations.

Finally, the legislature, as the major participatory structure, has been sustained in Kenya (in contrast to neighboring Uganda for instance) because it has served to build unity. This "democratic" organ helped to satisfy principles of legitimate government and contributed positively to regime support. But the Assembly functioned essentially neither as a powerful arm of government, as in the United States, nor as the public arena for government business under a pattern of party rule, as in the United Kingdom, nor in noncompetitive ways, as in neighboring Tanzania. Rather the legislature's functions have been shaped by the other structures of authority, traditional, tribal, and clientist alliances, and powerful bureaucratic management systems that control law and order, economic activity, and public services. Though it has assisted in the legitimation and operation of these other structures, its direct role in modifying policy has been through the transmission of demands, operating largely under the license of these other more powerful authority structures.

## TANZANIA

The role of the National Assembly in Tanzania differs from that in Kenya primarily because of differences in leadership style and party strength between the two countries. There are few differences in the organization of elections, patterns of organized activity within the Assemblies, or types of legal authority given to the law-making body. The National Assembly Members in Tanzania are clearly subordinate to the party, TANU, in making national policy and in carrying out "service" responsibilities in local areas for constituents. The same is true, perhaps more so, in Zanzibar, where, after the 1964 "revolution," the Afro-Shirazi party (ASP) leaders succeeded to control of the center. Unlike Kenya, traditional and colonial authority patterns have been largely superseded by the party-state machinery typical in a one-party closed system.[20]

The average income in Tanzania is about 50 percent lower than in Kenya. Consequently the incentives for MPs, while considerably less than Kenya (due to smaller salaries and the leadership code which has been applied to force out party leaders, including legislators, who acquired wealth in a "capitalist" fashion),[21] are still adequate to stimulate vigorous competition for office. In general, "rules" for "successful" behavior by MPs have emerged in Tanzania. These rules are generally understood by both legislators and the highest national leaders who have both articulated and reinforced them (see Hopkins, 1970). Those who have followed them have often done well in Tanzanian politics; of the very highest scorers among MPs in role congruence in 1966, one later became the minister of defense and the other the head of the *Ujamaa* villagization program (see Hopkins, 1975c).

The role of the Tanzanian MP is to work within the intellectual bounds laid out by Nyerere and other nationalist spokesmen and the organizational space defined by party and government machinery. In the case of party-state organization, the relation of the MP to development policy is clear; he is to be consulted as a member of formal bodies, but not accorded much real influence in comparison with American, British, or even Kenyan legislators. For example, under the decentralized efforts to develop, MPs are assigned to serve on local development committees in which they are expected to participate when the Bunge is not in session. But, key party organs in which MPs are often not members—the district and regional executive committees of TANU—review the plans of these groups with power to revise proposals. And these same party committees also have a role in implementation of district and regional development plans, thus firmly controlling what legislators can do in shaping the decentralized portions of development policy (see IBRD, 1974:vol. 3).

The set of "rules" guiding MPs' actions that emerged since independence generally have become accepted. Nyerere summarized these several years ago; he argued that a Member of Parliament has three tasks: "(1) To act as a bridge . . . between people and government for transmission of ideas; (2) to deliberate on new legislation; (3) to keep the government actively devoted to the people's interests by intelligent criticisms" (Nyerere, 1965). This definition leaves out a task earlier (1960–65) left to MPs, namely, the right to criticize government policy at public or private meetings in his constituency (Tordoff, 1965).

Tanzanian MPs have been criticized by national leaders for failing to play their role effectively. The principal criticism has been that many failed to keep in touch with their constituencies, to find out what their problems were, and to help people to understand what was being done and why (Nyerere, 1965). This failure has often been an explanation for subsequent defeat. The other criticism directed toward members, but with decreasing frequency, has been their failure to make more than minimal use of their prerogative to criticize in the Assembly. As in Kenya, criticism has declined, but even more completely.[22] Critics have been silenced or expelled from the party (and hence the legislature). Although according to Nyerere's early conception, questions of detail, timing, and priority should be openly discussed and debated in a one-party state (Nyerere, 1963), by 1967 no serious or broad opposition to the National Executive of the Party was permitted. Public opposition to NEC policy was the basis for expulsion from the party and the legislature in October of that year. More recently (1975), even behavior reflecting nonsocialist personal practices has been used to expel party officials and by implication is applicable to legislators.

Legislators' own role expectations were close to "official" expectations as to their limited prerogatives. Fifty-eight MPs sampled in 1966 were asked to describe their responsibilities as members of the National Assembly.[23] The most frequently mentioned task was work within the constituency, volunteered by 77 percent. Bringing constituency needs and demands before the government was the second most frequently mentioned role task. Two other aspects of the legislator's role, as lawmaker and as critic of the government, were mentioned rather infrequently by only 21 percent and 17 percent respectively. The different frequencies with which these four tasks are mentioned indicate the emphasis which the political system tends to place on these duties. Participating in the legislative process or being a gadfly of the government is seldom a part of even the legislators' own conceptions of their role. Much more important is their work in the constituency, explaining government policy, encouraging and helping in nation-building activities, and carrying problems and complaints from constituents to the government. The role that has emerged for an MP in Tanzania emphasizes his function as a communicator rather than either a deliberator or lawmaker.

In Kenya, which is comparatively more open as a political system, controversial questions and policies may be subject to widespread debate and criticism. There is a public character to discussion, debate, and political differences. Discussion of corruption or internecine feuding frequently takes place in parliamentary debates, during which the principal critics are able to appeal for support for their views or findings. In Tanzanian politics, recently generated norms based on the dominance of party rule and presidential dominance prescribe more stringent boundaries within which the legislator may pursue his own or his constituents' interests. The extent to which a legislator is expected to voice opposition publicly, to denounce instances of corruption, and to feel capable, in a controversy with TANU leaders, to carry the disagreement into broader national arenas, is indicated by the legislators' responses to the question: "If the government introduces a measure before the legislature which you are personally against and which you feel your constituents would not like, what would you do?" A typical response in 1966 was: "He should go to see the Minister concerned and talk with him. Possibly he hasn't seen the measure correctly or perhaps people at home have concocted a story to give people fear. In this case he must explain it to them." One brash young MP who gave a more assertive response, "I would try to stop it by convincing other MPs. Then raise hell in the Parliament if I have to," was expelled from the party and legislature within two years.

A legislator must also support a policy passed in the Assembly, even if it has not been a subject of party formulation. Much like Lenin's "democratic centralism," this rule encompasses the many bills whose details have been drawn up by the government, and not by the NEC. For instance, in 1974 the third five-year Development Plan was drawn up and printed as a document before the NEC had a chance to review it. In this case bureaucratic planners dominated choices, but they had to be sensitive to NEC expectations and previous decisions. Legislators can affect development planning, if not the plan itself, in two ways. First, as in Kenya (and most other countries, e.g., Thailand, Mexico) they can press for government assistance directly with ministries and provide information to relevant local officials about possible benefits available from government ministries. Second, unlike Kenya, they can have a voice in allocating local funds delegated from the "center" under the decentralization scheme begun in 1971–72. Their formal positions on local and regional planning committees, while controllable by the party, at least provide opportunities for asserting their views. When voicing ideas, however, if an MP explicitly disagrees with a decision he is expected not to say so publicly—a decided restriction. Secrecy about political disunity is an important norm for members of the elite (Hopkins, 1970), and is a clear contrast between Kenya and Tanzania. If there is an almost irrational quality to the prescriptions for a closed politics in Tanzania, in Kenya there is a ritualized obsession with declaring oneself in favor of unity, when clearly Kenya lacks it.

Another contrast to Kenya is that Tanzanian MPs who are not members of the government must consider constituency work their most important obligation. Many members from constituencies take this dictum seriously. When Parliament is not in session, a typical Tanzanian MP spends two to three weeks each month traveling in his constituency. Since the Arusha Declaration, MPs are prohibited from holding other jobs to occupy their time. Some have joined *Ujamaa* villages, though this is usually symbolic. In general, local activity by legislators is a far cry from the entrepreneurial activity of many Kenyan MPs and is principally a service function.

The MP who is not a member of government is above all else a communication link, a popularizer, and legitimizer for the party and the government. Other functions, such as brokering in clientist fashion or recruiting new leadership, are sometimes served—but to a far less extent than in Kenya. The role of the Assembly has been principally that of legitimization of government and party decisions within a constitutional framework which gives Parliament supremacy over legislation. However, in spite of "rules of the game," which foster closed politics, the National Assembly is not anachronistic or a mere showcase for propaganda purposes. MPs have been important links between the government and the countryside, and their criticisms in the Assembly have affected some policies. Moreover, their heel-dragging on some economic reform issues has been an acceptable price to pay for the benefits of the Assembly, for its ties to the countryside have enhanced the ability of the Tanzanian government to remain "responsive," especially on serious rural problems.

Expanding the role of the MP, however, would not necessarily promote more "development" in Tanzania. Many MPs were reluctant to see leadership conditions imposed. Most are the social equivalents of these upwardly mobile Kenyans who now enjoy markedly greater privilege. As a result there is good reason to believe that greater pork-barrel legislation, corruption, and pressure to weaken socialist or egalitarian policies would ensue. In short, it is leadership by Nyerere and those who control the party that has made possible the austere approach to development by the elite. Given Tanzania's present strategy, the legislature and legislators could be a force countering efforts at *Ujamaa*, though possibly a more representative force for expressing reluctance among the more "advanced" parts of Tanzania to follow Nyerere's strategy (see the IBRD Report, 1974:vol. 2, appendix 7).

## THE INFLUENCE OF THE LEGISLATURES

The influence of legislatures and legislators on the major development strategies of Kenya and Tanzania, as outlined earlier, is varied, usually not extensive, never decisive in either country, and in general difficult to assess with any precision. This, nevertheless, is the topic of this concluding section.

In situations where legislative activity has been a noticeable factor, it has been principally in clarifying goals, promoting alternatives, or reinforcing implementation, not in formulating specific choices or appraising their effectiveness. The legislator's contribution has been to call attention to problems, e.g., limited educational opportunities, flagrant elite privileges, unemployment, and land pressure, thereby implicitly helping to set priorities. In addition, activities in local constituencies, such as raising funds for schools or clinics or living in an *Ujamaa* village, contributed both substantially and symbolically to each country's alternative development strategy.

National goals were confirmed but not set by the legislature. In each country strong leadership from the key political figures was the determinative factor. In Tanzania the Arusha Declaration goals in 1967 were worked out among the party elite, reviewed by national party and bureaucratic organs (controlled to some degree by President Nyerere) and only then presented to the legislature, basically as a fait accompli. Similarly in Kenya, arguments over land settlement schemes and the degree of accommodation to be afforded departing colonists were fought out by the leading strategists in 1963–66—

Kenyatta, Odinga, Mboya—and then the comparative strength of these leaders was confirmed by increasingly decisive Assembly votes backing government recommendations. In Tanzania, however, MP sniping at elite political privileges—denouncing the new "WaBenzi," the tribe that drives Mercedes—was influential in fostering government restrictions on such privileges. Similar complaints in Kenya often resulted in the extension of privileges to those who complained, and never to any serious curbs on privilege.

In both countries *nationalization* was promoted in speeches by individual MPs during the early years after independence. By the 1970s this goal was not an issue; it had been clearly resolved, though, in opposite ways, in the two states. And these decisions, while discussed in the two Assemblies, were not determined by them. The important role for each country's Assembly and for individual legislators has been in legitimizing these goals through collective action on relevant legislation and through individual acceptance of the goals, at least by implication, in speeches and the example of personal lifestyle in home areas. National control in Tanzania has not expanded patronage opportunities for MPs, by and large, while the localization policies pursued in Kenya have helped reinforce clientist networks and have been popular symbolically as well. Especially the *embourgeoisment* of individual Kenyan MPs has been important in permitting the colonial authority patterns to be sustained as much as they have been. This is one of the important societal (indirect) impacts of the Kenyan legislature.

Capital formation is a major problem for both countries. Raising capital locally through taxation, a stock market for investors (in Kenya, but not Tanzania), development levies, government lotteries, etc. have been influenced only modestly by the legislatures. They have generally supported their respective governments' philosophies about foreign investment. The considerable resentment among intellectuals in Kenya to the continued prominence of European management has not been echoed by Kenyan MPs, except in the case of minor government posts.

In Tanzania unemployment has received far less public attention than it has in Kenya for several reasons. First, the trade unions in Tanzania are effectively controlled by the party and government bureaucracy—President Nyerere appoints the Minister of Labor, who is also the head of the National Union, NUTA. In Kenya, the nation-wide trade union (COTU) has had hard-fought elections, has threatened and carried out brief strikes, and is largely independent of the government but not immune to pressure or intimidation. Second, unemployment is more severe in Kenya and, with its larger urban population, more noticeable. Finally, on this issue the Kenyan Assembly was able to take some initiative by setting up a select committee whose report was widely publicized. This legitimated and promoted further government action on this problem. Unemployment is exacerbated in Kenya by the large "school leaver" corps, many of whom have aspirations for wealth and position far higher than the economy can provide. The fairly important role that Kenyan MPs play in promoting the intense demand for educational opportunity leads naturally to pressure being conveyed by MPs to find places for those who pass through the educational system.

Income distribution is one area of important legislative impact on development policy. As described earlier, parliamentary pressures in 1966–67 in Tanzania helped promote a commitment to redistribution, while Assembly criticisms in Kenya pushed the government toward declaring a policy favoring greater equality in the 1974 Development Plan.[24]

Perhaps the indirect actions of legislators have been most important in shaping development strategies concerning land ownership and education. In Kenya, MPs have acquired land and generally prospered. To play their role as "patrons" discretionary wealth has been important. Kenyan legislators have also promoted educational opportunities by raising funds for and helping organize *Harambee* schools (see pp. 165; 281–282), village polytechnics and provincial technical institutes (nonacademic high schools). They have lobbied hard for educational opportunities for their constituents, amplifying already strong demands. In Tanzania, MPs have played a much less forceful role, acting within party and education ministry guidelines in promoting school functions, accepting the emphasis on agricultural, cooperative (nonacademic) education. Generally they have also had to forego opportunities for advancing personal wealth, particularly through the accumulation of land holdings, the taking over of former European farms, or the establishment of private business enterprises. The public life-styles and promotional activities (and personal resources) of legislators have been important as models whose demonstration effect has helped consolidate acceptance of the alternative development strategies of the two countries.

The influence of legislators and the legislature should be considered in a context with a number of other forces that have influenced national development strategy in each country. Some broad factors such as greater tribal rivalry, natural resource endowment, and in-dustrialization in Kenya (including capital-intensive farming) have been important influences; in Kenya these have favored the frag-mented, more laissez faire pattern of political authority that has emerged. Weaker ethnic rivalry and more unified use of Swahili are examples of broad factors in Tanzania that have promoted the stronger party rule found there.

In addition to such broad factors, six specific groups or actors can be listed as having influence upon development: the chief executive, the bureaucracy, the private business community, foreign investors, the political party, and the legislature. In Table 6.2 I propose some crude judgments regarding the relative impact that these have had. In general, the contrasting orientations of the chief executive (the presi-dent and his key advisors) have been very important in both coun-tries, and the comparative strength of the party in Tanzania has been another important source for shaping policies there. In Kenya, the private sector rather than the party is influential. And in both coun-tries the legislature has only a modest role, though as argued before, somewhat greater in Kenya.

In the lower part of Table 6.2 the influence of the assembly is disaggregated into six activities of legislators. For each the relative

TABLE 6.2

**INFLUENCES ON DEVELOPMENT STRATEGY IN KENYA AND TANZANIA**
**(1965–75)**

| | Scope and weight of effects | |
| --- | --- | --- |
| Sources of influence | Kenya | Tanzania |
| Chief Executive | High | High |
| Government Bureaucracy | High | Medium |
| Party | None | High |
| Private Business | Medium | Low |
| Foreign Investors and Advisors | Medium | Low |
| National Assembly: | | |
| A. In the legislature | | |
| 1. committees | Medium | Medium/Low |
| 2. speeches | Medium | Medium/Low |
| 3. voting | Low | None |
| B. Outside the legislature | | |
| 1. as brokers (communicators) | High | Medium |
| 2. as entrepreneurs | Medium | Low |
| 3. as members of local government units | Low | Medium |

influence is proposed. These crude distinctions of high, medium and low summarize the contrasting impact of the two assemblies on development as described earlier. In Kenya, the most important impact has been through the legislators' role as a broker in the system. Next, speeches and committee actions of the Assembly, along with the entrepreneurial model they set in their private lives, have been important. In many respects the loose clientist network of Kenya performs the political functions of promoting unity, steering government action, and expanding central authority that the party performs in Tanzania. The influence on development of MPs in Tanzania, at least those neither appointed by the president nor members of the government (with ministerial posts) is slim. Their ambitions and opportunities for personal wealth are subject to fairly stringent party control and system norms. Both in and outside the legislature their most influential activity is as a communicator of problems and local interests, and occasionally as the author of a suggestion or proposal that will require ratification by others.

## CONCLUSION

The legislatures in Kenya and Tanzania, like those elsewhere, are formalized consultative systems used to legitimize rule, build a coalition of support for policy (by binding local leaders to it), and correct errors that key leaders or the bureaucracy may make. The alternative development policies of each country can be accounted for partially by the role and functions played by their respective national assemblies.

In both countries legislators pursue personal ambition and reelection. In Kenya such motivations have served to build a national clientist structure for allocating values and a visible, privileged elite which includes most legislators. Their open, mixed economy strategy of development is supported by almost all legislators. The weakness in Kenya is the coalition of clientist structures based on the Assembly. With a weak party, strong ethnic discord, and economic conflict that can be amplified readily given the absence of strong political controls, the Assembly and political structure are vulnerable to the ambitions of other groups, notably the military, particularly in a succession "crisis" after Kenyatta.

In Tanzania, the party and political arrangements are less vulnerable than in Kenya if only because personal ambition has been channeled so successfully thus far into patterns dictated by the needs of rather austere socialist development. This development strategy has been shaped for the most part by Nyerere and TANU. That development strategy itself, however, is likely to erode without Nyerere's leadership and the strong oversight of a vital party apparatus, for the same "traditional" and "neo-colonial" views of land ownership and authority patterns that have been important in Kenya are part of the legacy of Tanzania. The Assembly might exercise more influence in a post-Nyerere era, and would likely then be a force for increasing stratification in society, especially through indirect example, rather than for continuation of socialist experimentation.

In Kenya, the absence of purposive discipline makes the entire consultative-brokerage system vulnerable, but probably not the development strategy it has fostered. In Tanzania there are enormous problems in the attempt to create a socialist state efficiently and effectively. To reshape the beliefs, aspirations, and work habits of the populace is a great task. So the enterprise remains a doubtful, yet intriguing example of development strategy for a poor, newly independent state. The Tanzanian party, bureaucracy, and legislature, facing fewer pressures from regional or ethnic antagonisms and having greater internal discipline, seem more likely to survive the loss of Nyerere's political leadership than do his development policies. Domestic pressures in both countries operating through their respective legislatures are important potential sources for change; in Kenya by challenging the political formula, in Tanzania by challenging the development formula.

## NOTES

*I wish to acknowledge with gratitude support from Swarthmore College, the Woodrow Wilson International Center for Scholars, and the Guggenheim Foundation that enabled me to complete this chapter.*

1. Quoted in Martin Minoque and Judith Malloy (1974:1).
2. The term *development* carries an enormous burden of ambiguous and potentially misleading meanings. In general I have accepted the justifications and meanings given the term by Joel Smith and Lloyd Musolf in their chapter, "Some Observations on Legislatures and Development," the Introduction to this volume. I use "development strategy" to refer to government actions or policies that affect the production or distribution of goods, services, or other values in the society.
3. According to Republic of Kenya (1974:Part I, 1), the 1965 Sessional paper outlined the basic development objectives and the 3rd plan is "a continuation of our country's efforts to achieve these objectives."
4. These reviews are drawn in part from several earlier essays: Hopkins, 1970, 1972, and 1975b.

5. Based on a survey completed in June–August, 1971, in Nairobi and Mombasa. Results are more fully reported in an unpublished manuscript on Kenya (1975b).

6. See Republic of Kenya (1969:17, 146, 308–9). See also United Republic of Tanzania (1969 and 1970:6ff, 20–52). Agriculture is important to both countries but Tanzania is giving relatively greater weight to this sector.

7. The Kenya figure is from Republic of Kenya (1969:43) and the Tanzanian figure is calculated from figures for the years 1964–72 in Green (1972:17).

8. One of the basic tenets of the Arusha Declaration was a commitment to narrow the income gap between the urban and rural sectors and between a small, privileged elite and the mass of the population. Even before this, however, in 1966 steps were taken to reduce salaries of cabinet members and high-level civil servants.

9. The Tri-Partite Agreement of June 1970 had called for a 10 percent increase in employment to attack what appeared to be a serious unemployment situation. However, its major effect seems to be to have induced increased unemployment. It encouraged many more people to seek jobs—but made available posts only at low skill, low income levels, and most firms failed to replace workers who resigned, thereby reducing the effect of a 10 percent increase that was the goal of the agreement.

10. Harbeson (1971) argues that the essential aim of the Swynnerton plan of the 1950s is to structure land settlement of Africans to create a middle class rural population politically loyal to a conservative rather than radical regime and that it has been pursued by the Kenyan government, at least unofficially.

11. The annual plan for 1971 states: "Although it is still too early to assess its effects on the movement to towns and cities of primary graduates, it (education for self-reliance) has certainly made many primary schools self-reliant in food and funds. In 1969 only 12 percent of those who completed primary education found places in secondary schools in Tanzania (slightly over 7,000)" (United Republic of Tanzania, 1971:84). For discussion of the philosophy underlying the new education policy, see Resnick, 1968.

12. For an instance involving a change in wage scales, see *New York Times*, May 2, 1975.

13. A good example of such rhetoric comes from Kenyatta's Labor Day (May 1) speech of 1975 referring vaguely to his critics (some of them MPs): "We know there are those who are seduced like prostitutes to spoil our noble government. We know them. What would you like us to do with them? [Response from the audience: "They should be hanged."] How should they be hanged? [Response: "By a rope."] Where should the rope be placed? [Response: "About their necks."]"

14. As early as 1964 Kenyatta admonished MPs for their tendency to remain in Nairobi when the Assembly was not in session. If they wanted to "sleep in Nairobi . . . run around and see the sights," their membership in Parliament would "have no value." Cited in Stultz (1970:332).

15. In an interview with one town clerk I was told that local MPs were most effective when they engaged in personal lobbying with ministers or high bureaucrats. Their approach in these encounters tended to be more earnest, he thought; and bargains could be more readily struck. He suggested that noise, threats, and obstreperousness in the Assembly could even be counter-productive.

16. Nominees cannot be civil servants (unless they resigned) or occupants of an elected post such as local councillor. See Ghai and McAuslen (1970:522–523).

17. Nearly all of the elite interviewed in Nairobi and Kisumu in 1971 and 1973 mentioned inequities in allocation as an issue creating resentment in disadvantaged regions.

18. Professor Colin Leys suggested this function to me.

19. For a discussion of authority patterns and structures and their relationship to one another in a society and to prevailing social norms, legitimizing principles, and governmental capacity, see Eckstein, 1973.

20. See this "type" as described by Zolberg, and the volume on authoritarian regimes edited by Huntington and Moore (1971).

21. As recently as June 1975, three party leaders were expelled for deviating from the code of conduct.

22. The Report by the commission that studied the one-party state (United Republic of Tanzania, 1965) blamed practices inherited from the British more appropriate to a two-party system for the lack of vigor in Assembly debates. In the British party system, private party caucuses and party whips to enforce discipline were generally accepted as essential to maintain the unity upon which the party in power depended for its control of the legislative process. Thus the TPP and the National Executive Committee provided private forums for prior discussions of policy and legislative matters. These prior discussions, the report concluded, inevitably have "inhibited subsequent discussion on the floor of the house." See United Republic of Tanzania (1965:20–21).

23. This research, which was carried out in 1966, is supported by similar findings by a Dar-es-Salaam based researcher, Kjeshus, in the early 1970s. Moreover, based on my brief research visits to Tanzania in 1971 and 1973 and general attention to events there, I believe these patterns of expectations continue largely unaltered.

24. There are marked problems for both countries in implementing plans, maintaining efficiency in cooperative movement or rural agriculture schemes. But Tanzania has had chronic inefficiencies in this regard, from the failure of the State Trading Corporation to the lack of fiscal regularity and inspection in cooperative enterprises. The food supply has been disrupted by parastatal inefficiency.

# PART II
# LEGISLATURES AND DEVELOPMENT

*Chapter 7*

PRESIDENTIAL POLITICS AND THE DECLINE OF THE
CHILEAN CONGRESS

ARTURO VALENZUELA
ALEXANDER WILDE

On September 21, 1973, ten days after it overthrew the government of Salvador Allende in a bloody military coup, the Chilean armed forces closed the Congress for an indefinite period. Decree Law 27, of that date, argued that the reestablishment of the nation's institutions required expeditious compliance with the directives of the Junta de Gobierno and therefore necessitated the dissolution of the legislature (Republic of Chile, Junta de Gobierno, 1973a:62–63). Not since a brief period in 1932 were the activities of Latin America's most powerful legislature curtailed by military intervention; and before that, only on two other occasions in 1891 and 1924, was the functioning of Congress disrupted by force of arms and then for intervals of less than a year.[1] The military action was a sharp break in a constitutional tradition dating back to 1830.

In justifying its actions, the military Junta has repeatedly cited a resolution, adopted by the opposition majority in the Chamber of Deputies in August 1973, which claimed that the Popular Unity government had violated the Constitution. And yet, once in office, the military proclaimed that the very act of assuming power rendered the Constitution obsolete.[2] Much to the chagrin of opposition congressmen, the Junta, in the name of Chile's institutions, proceeded systematically to dismantle them. Indeed, the military leaders soon made it clear that they did not only hold Chile's Marxist parties responsible, but blamed Chile's "traditional democracy" for the "systematic destruction of the [nation's] being." [3] Political parties and the legislature were thus dispensable in the long term task of training Chileans in "healthier civic habits." Only with a new generation could Chileans be entrusted with democracy—and then within a different institutional system. In the meantime the Junta, appealing to "natural law" took over not only the executive, but also the legislative and constitutional functions previously exercised by Congress (Rieles, 1974:128).

In Chile's highly "legal" political system, this change was made with surprising ease. The prestigious Contraloría General de la República, charged with judging the constitutionality and legality of government decrees, and advising on the constitutionality of laws, continued to function as usual, with the same loyal personnel. As the head of the key Department of Toma de Razón told the authors, "Everything the Junta has done has been perfectly legal. We have disapproved of several decrees because they did not conform fully to the Constitution and previous laws." [4] That department's task was made much easier when the Junta adopted a decree law stating that all past and future decree laws which did not conform to the constitution, automatically modified it, even if not explicitly stated.

Contraloría officials not only thought that the closing of the legislature presented few problems with respect to law making, they argued that without the legislature the country would now be able to make some progress. This sentiment was also echoed by other career officials who escaped being fired in the Offices of National Planning and in the Ministry of Finance. Now it would be possible to proceed with national programs without the hindrance of a legislature "distorted" by political criteria. "There is no politics in Chile. Now, we will finally be able to plan," was a typical reaction. Even the head of the Office of Information of the Senate, historically the most sophisticated agency of its kind in Latin America, told the authors that "nothing has changed here. We now do our legislative reference work directly for the Junta. Some of the staff had to be dismissed, but the majority is still with us." [5] He also noted the unique opportunity which the country now had with the politicians gone. Similar sentiments were expressed by staff members in CONARA (Comisión Nacional de Reforma Administrativa), the high-level administrative and planning body appointed to reorganize the public sector and propose basic changes to the four-man Junta. Drawing on a membership of "techni-

cal" experts from various ministries, as well as university departments which had not been closed down, CONARA in effect became
the "nonpolitical" legislature of the Junta de Gobierno. For them the
legislature was also clearly dispensable.[6]

The purpose of this chapter is to explain how Chile came to this
pass; how a legislature which was arguably the most highly institutionalized in the entire underdeveloped world came to be
abolished. The Chilean Congress exercised real and important functions in the competitive, civilian political system that had existed for
over 100 years. It was a significant way station in the policy process; it
was an important arena of accommodation for political elites; it was a
critical institutional linchpin holding together the centrifugal forces of
social conflict. The Chilean Congress, in short, performed admirably
essential tasks we assign to legislatures among political institutions.
Its destruction leaves an enormous gap in the fundamental processes
of politics.

For reasons that differ from those of the apologists for the Junta,
and as we shall explain, it is our thesis that the Chilean Congress was
not destroyed simply by the power of the gun, any more than Allende
was. Both were victims of a much larger historical process. In trying
to understand this process, it is impossible to ignore the spectacular
interplay of great structural factors—of opposing ideologies and war-
ring social classes, of mobilized masses, polarized political forces,
and intervening foreign actors (Valenzuela, 1975, 1978). But it would
be wrong—particularly in a system as highly institutionalized as
Chile—to overlook the conflict that existed in and between manifestly political institutions. In the last instance, it is the failure of these
institutions—the failure of politics and politicians—which permits
the more direct and naked interplay of social forces.[7]

In Chile the institutional decline of Congress significantly contributed to the breakdown of democracy. This decline of the legislature in
its institutional functions antedated the historic socialist experiment
of the Unidad Popular (1970–73) and is traceable to the rise of a
"rational" planning mentality in the executive and an important shift
in the party system, located above all in the government of Christian
Democrat Eduardo Frei (1964–70).

The functions of Congress were shaped above all by its relationships to the executive and to the party system. These relationships
were defined by formal rules, the most important of which, for our
purposes, were those concerning authority over elections and over
budgets. Beyond these formal rules, which established certain in-

stitutional parameters, lay a host of more informal "understandings" among the different parts of Chile's political elite—which were what made the system work as it did for 30 odd years before the mid–1960s.

The first part of this chapter describes the emergence of a legislature with significant institutional autonomy, during the so-called "Parliamentary Republic" (1891–1924). The corruption and immobility of this legislature-dominated period, however, led to a reaction, which, from 1924 to 1932, gave the executive considerably more authority. As the second part of this chapter shows, this shift still left the Congress with significant functions vis-à-vis the executive. Largely because of the competitiveness of the party system, Congress remained an important arena for legislation, including budgets. Individual legislators performed a genuinely representative function, intervening on behalf of local constituents in the processes of making legislation and then later, in the bureaucracy, of administering it.

These eminently "political" and particularistic tasks were challenged, successfully, by the Christian Democrats from 1964 to 1970. The result, accelerated by the attempt by the Popular Unity (1970–73) to by-pass the Congress and rule by executive action, was the decline and fall of the legislative institution. Wtih the decline of particularism, ideology came to the fore in the parties. With the decline of the legislature, congressional elites within the parties lost ground to extraparliamentary forces. The third part of this chapter analyzes in more detail how this process occurred and its significance. The final section concludes with some reflections on the costs of trying to exclude particularistic "politics" in favor of executive "effectiveness."

## FOUNDATIONS OF CONGRESSIONAL AUTONOMY

Even in the nineteenth century, the age of *caudillos* in most of Latin America, the Chilean Congress was a significant institution. Under the 1833 Constitution, often erroneously interpreted as autocratic and presidentialist, it retained authority over taxing and spending through "periodic laws," which required congressional approval every eighteen months.[8] It became by mid-century an arena capable of sustaining legitimate opposition, a redoubt from which it could launch electoral campaigns and defeat the government. Thus, it was the locus for the expression of dissent and of opposition to presidential authority and also a viable forum for disparate elements to learn how to compromise and work with one another. Its attempts to restrict the president and cabinet, particularly in the electoral process,[9] reached a climax in 1891 when its majority of conservative and Radical forces literally declared war on the presidency. With the support of the more traditional navy, the Congress defeated the president supported by the army.[10]

The subsequent Parliamentary Republic (1891–1924) saw the development of the essential functions which characterized Congress until the 1960s. During the Parliamentary Republic Congress was the central focus of the political system. The most decisive change, in terms of its later effects, resulted from Congress's removing suffrage mechanisms from presidential agents and placing them in the hands of local officials.[11] This shaped the whole subsequent development of the party system, with its strong center-local linkages based on particularistic exchanges. The existence of locally organized, competitive parties in turn strengthened the status of the legislature and greatly influenced its institutional relationships with the executive.

With the shift of electoral control away from executive officials to the municipality, legislators were forced to structure alliances with local leaders and notables in order to survive politically. This accounts for both the greater "localism" (e.g., in the 1876–79 and 1879–82 Congresses, of 26 deputies sampled, 45 percent served in predominantly one and 47 percent in separate constituencies; in the 1918–20 Congress the comparable figures for 24 deputies were 80 percent and 20 percent) and the increased importance of the legal and agricultural occupations as opposed to official ones (e.g., for the same Congresses and samples the proportions in "official" occupations were 31 percent vs. 4 percent respectively, for law 23 percent vs. 42 percent, and for agriculture 4 percent vs. 9 percent) in the Parliamentary Republic (Valenzuela, 1977:appendix 4). Local leaders found it convenient to rely on their national brokers for resources, thus avoiding the onerous task of instituting local taxation for local needs. The system was made possible by the vast wealth of northern nitrate fields, which produced large customs revenues. In fact, during this period other forms of taxation declined dramatically, as the country came to rely exclusively on the export bonanza (Edwards, 1917; Philippi, 1916).

Programmatic considerations contributed in part to the further consolidation of party cliques in the legislature itself, but it was the new pattern of center-local linkages which encouraged the development of party structures outside the congressional arena. Gradually, local notables were replaced by local organizations, particularly in urban areas, as congressmen sought to stabilize local support. The rising cost of campaigns, generated by the increasing need to bribe voters, was a further incentive to structuring local organizations and electoral alliances with other legislators. The middle-class Radical party was particularly successful in working to gain control of municipal offices as a base for launching campaigns to become the dominant party in the Chamber of Deputies (Rivas Vicuña, 1964:115). By 1920 the stability of political parties was quite pronounced. The correlation between voting in municipal and congressional elections was highest for the small, regional Socialist party, but both the Democrats and the Radicals had also achieved considerable stability of electoral support. The personalistic liberal factions had the least consistent support (A. Valenzuela, 1977:chap. 8).

In a good example of what Merton called the "unanticipated consequences of purposeful social action," the goal of nineteenth-century Conservatives and local notables to achieve complete independence from the center led to the emergence of alternative networks of center-local linkages which increasingly slipped out of their hands. And yet, the development of parties outside the legislative arena provided the system with mechanisms for political representation as well as for control. Though in isolated nitrate fields and among transient transport workers incipient antisystem movements gained strength, the parties which extended out of the Congress were clearly prosystem organizations cutting across potential and actual social cleavages.

In Chile, a viable party system, originating in the legislature and relying on legislative log-rolling for goods and resources, emerged prior to the establishment of a powerful national bureaucracy. This had a profound effect on future development. It meant that even with the development of bureaucratic agencies designed to foster economic development and redistribute wealth, political parties with legislative linkages continued to be the principal political networks of the system. Though legislators increasingly would be limited in their ability to generate resources in the Congress itself, they would continue to be the key brokers between constituents and the bureaucracy.[12] By implication, this reinforced the viability of representative institutions. Where a strong bureaucracy emerged prior to a strong party system, as in Brazil and Argentina, the prospect for the development of informal or officially sponsored linkage networks without popular representation was much greater. Under such circumstances the chances of maintaining or fostering democratic institutions was severely undermined.

These positive contributions of the Parliamentary Republic to later competitive politics—the creation of a significant, autonomous legislative institution—were possible because of the subordination of the executive. Its atrophied role, however, became less tolerable as the times changed. By the 1920s Chile was facing serious economic and social problems, related particularly to the collapse of nitrate exports and more generally to the processes of industrialization. Lacking stable majorities for responsible policy making, caught up in a politics of particularistic favors and local interest, the congressionally dominated government was incapable of confronting the new national issues.

The instability of the executive was extraordinary. Cabinets could fall through unfavorable action in *either* house of the legislature, and ministers and cabinets came and went at a dizzying pace. Not counting the first cabinet appointed by each president, 489 ministerial positions were vacated and filled between 1891 and 1925. The average cabinet remained in office only 133 days. While there were 31 full ministerial changes between 1830 and 1891, between 1891 and 1924 there were 93.[13] Almost half of the members of the Chamber of Deputies for the Congress of 1912 had served or would serve in a ministerial post during their congressional careers.[14]

The policy immobility of the Parliamentary Republic was also a product of the congressional penchant for particularism. The bureaucracy created by legislative patronage had no particular merit or esprit de corps, no capacity for intelligent initiative. The Congress dallied endlessly over executive budgets, and when they finally passed, months late, they were a hodgepodge of special favors and particularistic payoffs. An average of only 126 laws per year were enacted during this period—compared with an average of 300 in the period 1925–68 (when in addition the executive was also active in legislating by decree—Tapia Valdés [1966:25, 46]).

It was these qualities of the Parliamentary Republic—its "irresponsibility" and "corruption," as they were seen by the reformers of the 1920s (Urzúa Valenzuela and Barzelatto, 1971:37–52; Bicheno, 1972)—that eventually produced a swing back toward greater executive strength. This change can be seen in the Constitution of 1925 and in a period between 1925 and 1932 of strong presidents who used broad powers under decree laws to reorganize and strengthen the bureaucracy. The Constitution of 1925 barred congressmen from holding cabinet posts and suppressed the "periodic laws" requiring regular renewal by the legislature. It delivered control of elections to an independent tribunal. It attempted to restrict Congress from using the budget laws to extract political concessions from the executive. If the budget law were not approved four months after its submission to Congress, the executive proposal would automatically become law. Furthermore, the Congress could no longer increase budgetary appropriations; it could only approve or reject the executive initiatives. The executive was empowered to designate legislation "urgent," requiring expeditious action on the part of the Congress, and he could also call a special session in which the legislature could consider only his agenda.

Despite this reaction to the excesses and weaknesses of congressional government, the slate was by no means wiped clean. Congress continued to exercise significant functions inherited from the earlier period—now modified and checked by a stronger executive. It is this legacy which makes the usual characterizations of the Parliamentary Republic misleading. Students of Chilean politics customarily decry—in their best liberal-reformist tones—the instability and immobility of the system, qualifying it as an "unimportant" interlude before the advent of modern politics in the 1920s (Pike, 1967:87). It is true that the unstable parliamentary coalitions were unable to address themselves to the growing social crisis of a rapidly changing society. And yet, it would be a serious error to ignore the important place of the period for Chilean institutional development. Competitive politics developed, and the role of the legislature was strengthened significantly. Practices such as ministerial questioning and accountability became part of the political tradition. But, even more importantly, this political system, revolving around a log-rolling legislature, encouraged the development of Chile's unique party system and opened the door for increased participation in the nation's political life.

## THE CRITICAL FUNCTIONS OF CONGRESS IN THE SYSTEM

The formal rules of the system, as rewritten between 1925 and 1932, did give executives resources whose significance was greater relative to those of the legislature. But there was little chance that the executive would be able to assert its dominance as it had before the Parliamentary Republic. An important new dimension had been added to Chilean politics—the party system. Any analysis of the role of legislatures in a political system in which parties are more than legislative factions must take the party system into account. In Chile, the party networks which developed during the parliamentary period were so competitive that no single party was able to elect the president on its own, or capture a majority position in the Congress. Data tabulated at the Dirección del Registro Electoral in Santiago confirm that with the exception of the Christian Democrats in 1965—an important exception which we discuss below—no single party ever held a majority of the seats in either chamber. (See Table 7.1.)

Since 1932 successful presidential candidates generally have come from center parties supported by groups of the left or the right. If coalitions failed to crystallize before the election, no candidate could receive an absolute majority of the vote. Coalitions then had to be put together in Congress to select the president from the two front runners. Presidents, in turn, faced a legislature with a multiplicity of parties. Quite frequently the coalition of parties responsible for the election of the president would disintegrate soon after (in large measure because the president could not succeed himself). Parties rapidly realized that they could maximize their future presidential prospects by disassociating themselves from incumbents, who were seldom able to deliver on their campaign promises. Only rarely did a president have majority support even in one house; none had it in both (Cortes and Fuentes, 1967). (See Table 7.2.)

The competitiveness of the party system made the legislature an institution with which the executive had to reckon. Presidents were forced to bargain with coalitions of parties in order to obtain their legislative programs. Since coalitions would disintegrate, the president was forced repeatedly to structure new ones. This meant shifting cabinets to reflect new alliances, disrupting the continuity of initial policy objectives. As a result there were numerous complete and partial cabinet changes under the various presidents since 1932.[15] Cabinet instability was lowest in the governments of Eduardo Frei and Jorge Alessandri, who had the good fortune to have a party majority and a coalition majority respectively in the Chamber of Deputies. It was highest during the Allende years, as original coalitions crumbled and politics slipped out of political institutions and onto the streets.

On major policy issues, the president would bargain with congressional party leaders to try to secure a compromise. The Radical party, with a generally pragmatic policy orientation, stood at the center of compromises that shifted to the right or left, depending on electoral

**TABLE 7.1**

**DISTRIBUTION OF SEATS IN THE SENATE AND CHAMBER OF DEPUTIES BY PARTY FROM 1945 TO 1973**

| | Chamber of deputies | | | | | | | Senate | | | | | |
|---|---|---|---|---|---|---|---|---|---|---|---|---|---|
| | 1945 | 1949 | 1953 | 1957 | 1961 | 1965 | 1969 | 1949 | 1953 | 1957 | 1961 | 1965 | 1969 |
| | 1949 | 1953 | 1957 | 1961 | 1965 | 1969 | 1973 | 1953 | 1957 | 1961 | 1965 | 1969 | 1973 |
| Liberal | 31 | 33 | 23 | 30 | 28 | 6 | – | 12 | 11 | 9 | 9 | 5 | – |
| Conservative[a] | 36 | 33 | 18 | 23 | 17 | 3 | – | 8 | 7 | 6 | 4 | 2 | – |
| National[b] | | | | | | | 33 | | | | | | 9 |
| Radical[c] | 39 | 42 | 21 | 36 | 39 | 20 | 24 | 13 | 10 | 10 | 13 | 10 | 9 |
| Christian Democrat[d] | 3 | 3 | 3 | 17 | 23 | 82 | 56 | 1 | 1 | 1 | 4 | 13 | 22 |
| Socialist[e] | 9 | 12 | 29 | 12 | 12 | 15 | 15 | 3 | 5 | 9 | 7 | 7 | 6 |
| Communist[f] | 15 | – | – | 10 | 16 | 18 | 22 | 4 | – | – | 4 | 6 | 6 |
| Agrarian[g] | 3 | 14 | 35 | | | | – | 3 | 8 | 10 | – | – | – |
| Others | 11 | 10 | 18 | 19 | 12 | 3 | – | 1 | 3 | – | 4 | 2 | 2 |
| Total | 147 | 147 | 147 | 147 | 147 | 147 | 150 | 45 | 45 | 45 | 45 | 45 | 45 |

a. Includes Conservador Unido and Conservador Tradicionalista.

b. Nationals formed in 1965 with union of Conservatives and Liberals.

c. Includes Radical Democrático and Radical Doctrinario.

d. Before 1957—the Falange Nacional.

e. Includes Socialista de Chile, Socialista Popular and Socialista Auténtico.

f. Includes Progresista Nacional.

g. Includes Agrario Laborista and Ibañista.

Source: Table calculated from data available in the Dirección del Registro Electoral, Santiago, Chile. The figures for the Senate of 1957 could not be checked adequately. They are approximate.

## TABLE 7.2
## RECENT CHILEAN PRESIDENTS AND APPROXIMATE STATUS OF CONGRESSIONAL SUPPORT

| President | Years | Presidential coalition parties | Majority/minority status | Core support |
|---|---|---|---|---|
| G. Gonzalez Videla 1946–1952 | 1946–1949 | Radical<br>Communist<br>Falange Nacional | Minority | Radical |
| | 1949–1952 | Traditional Conservatives<br>Liberal<br>Radical | | Radical |
| Carlos Ibanez 1952–1958 | 1952–1955 | Agrarian-Labor<br>Popular Socialist<br>Other left & right fragments | Minority | Agrarian-Labor |
| | 1955–1958 | Agrarian-Labor<br>Other shifting support | Minority | Agrarian-Labor |
| Jorge Alessandri 1958–1964 | 1958–1960 | Liberal (informally)<br>Conservative (informally)<br>Independent | Minority | |
| | 1961–1963 | Radical<br>Liberal<br>Conservative | *Majority* in Chamber<br>*Majority* in Senate | Liberal<br>Conservative |
| | 1963–1964 | Conservative<br>Liberal | Minority in Chamber<br>Minority in Senate | Liberal<br>Conservative |
| Eduardo Frei 1964–1970 | 1964–1965 | Christian Democrat | Minority | Christian Democrat |
| | 1965–1969 | Christian Democrat | Minority in Senate<br>*Majority* in Chamber | Christian Democrat |
| | 1969–1970 | Christian Democrat | Minority | Christian Democrat |
| Salvador Allende 1970–1973 | 1969–1973 | Socialist<br>Communist<br>Radical | Minority | Socialist<br>Communist |

Source: The most useful source in compiling this table was Lia Cortés and Jordi Fuentes, *Diccionario Político de Chile* (Santiago: Editorial Orbe, 1967). Many other secondary works were also consulted. It should be noted that the table is only approximate. It does not include more complex yearly variations or variations on specific issues.

trends. In the late forties the shift in the presidential coalition from center-left to center-right, after the strong showing of the Communists in the 1947 municipal elections, led to the banning of the Communist party. In the late fifties, a switch in the opposite direction, from center-right to center-left, led to the party's relegalization. The large number of "long termers" in Congress—approximately 20 percent to 30 percent from 1950 on (calculated by us from information available at the Office of Information of the Chilean Senate) as compared to 15 percent or less in preceding chambers (Valencia Avaría, 1951:vol. 2)—schooled in the norms and folkways of the institution, facilitated such shifts.

As Weston Agor has noted in his study of the Chilean Senate, the Congress was not merely a convenient forum in which compromises devised by party groups were ratified; it also provided an arena for the kinds of accommodation later accepted by party organizations. Particularly on middle-level issues, congressional committees were significant institutional forums for bargains and compromises between congressional factions and between those factions and the executive. In exchange for support on a particular policy proposal, the executive would either withdraw another proposal or, occasionally, seek a proposal desired by opposition elements (Agor, 1971a). That Congress played this sort of role vis-à-vis the executive strengthened the hand of the congressional elites within the parties and reinforced the pragmatic, as compared with the ideological functions of the party system.

The institutional significance of the legislature also manifested itself in the careers and activities of congressional politicians. Although the bureaucracy and executive branch grew to the point where, in the 1960s, the public sector represented almost 50 percent of the Gross National Product,[16] congressmen retained their traditional role as the key brokers in the center for small favors. They continued to represent the demands of their geographically defined constituencies in the larger government process, both in making legislation and administering it.

"Casework," in the sense used for U.S. congressmen, was a central part of the job of Chilean legislators. Interviews with a sample of them in a five-province area revealed that they spent over 50 percent of their time in the late 1960s on matters such as obtaining public employment, school admission, or a pension (particularly from the complex and overburdened social security system) for individuals commended to them by local politicians and cronies.[17] Sometimes these activities took the form of intervention with bureaucrats in an administrative agency, sometimes the form of actual legislation. Private laws providing pensions and other dispensations for individuals were an important part of legislative activity. Jorge Tapia Valdés notes that, between 1938 and 1958, over 55 percent of all laws dealt with *asuntos de gracia* (Tapia Valdés, 1966:47). This proportion fluctuated considerably from 1958 to 1968, rising to over 70 percent in 1964 and 1965, declining drastically in the middle years of the Frei government to 35 percent and 17 percent, and rising again to 52 percent with the approach of the 1970 elections (Hughes, 1971). In Chile, as in the United States, such particularistic representation built support for the system by making it more responsive.

The capacity of congressmen to perform these tasks was based, above all, on their continuing influence within the budgetary process. The Constitution of 1925 had attempted to end various abuses of legislative budgeting and give primary initiative and authority in this area to the executive. In the two decades that followed, however, both Congress and the executive tried to by-pass the limitations imposed by the other and to finance their own pet projects (cf., Morell, this volume). As a result, the Constitution was amended in 1943, setting the formal rules which governed the legislative-executive relationship in budgeting until the 1960s. Congress was definitely restrained from adding appropriations to executive proposals (Article 45); the executive, on the other hand, had "emergency" spending made on his authority alone limited to no more than 2 percent of the total of the general Budgetary Law (Article 72, para. 10) (Evans de la Cuadra, 1973:19, 40–41, 195–243).

Congressmen were able to amend the budget law on behalf of local interests both on the floor and in the conference committee (*comisión mixta*) that hammered out the final compromises. Although they were prohibited from increasing expenditures, they could try to have the money allotted for a particular line in the budget destined to their own particular projects. They could specify, for example, the particular roads upon which the Public Works ministry should spend a given item in its budget.[18] The president had a line veto and might strike such provisions. But for most of the period before the 1960s, without majority support even in one chamber, presidents accepted many such amendments as political necessity. Such practices provided for considerable give and take across party lines. The heat of general partisan debate was dissipated somewhat in the face of this homely task of satisfying mundane political needs.

Legislators also intervened actively with bureaucrats in the administration of the law. Historically this happened at the stage that each ministry, once the budget was approved, was drawing up its programs in conformity with the law. The most important ministry dealing with divisible, local services was Public Works. Local representatives of the ministry (known as *ingenieros zonales*) would report to the various bureaus the basic needs of the region over which they had jurisdiction. The line agencies in charge of particular programs would then go about setting priorities with the general approval of the minister—and participation of active congressmen.

For much of this period, bureaucrats did not resist this intervention strongly; indeed, in many ways they welcomed it. This was due in part to the influence of congressmen over the hiring and promotion of civil servants. One influential deputy, when asked, "How do you approach a functionary?" (in a particular ministry), replied: "I believe that it is a good policy to be very cordial with functionaries and always maintain good relations. I, for one, never imply that I would or would not support a functionary for a higher post, and they never ask me to. We both know that when the opportunity arises, I will remember them as competent civil servants" (A. Valenzuela, 1977:153). One study of an agency in the Housing ministry showed that bureaucrats within the agency believed congressmen second only to the executive committee of the agency in influence over hiring (Valenzuela, 1977:154).

Perhaps a more fundamental reason for the cooperativeness of bureaucrats with congressional politicians was that they welcomed their representation of local interests (and the support implied in satisfying them). Though stressing that the intervention of politicians did not conform to the best administrative standards, line bureaucrats in particular believed that *parlamentarios* could be very useful in bringing the needs of various localities to the attention of administrators. The director of the Bureau of Obras Sanitarias of Public Works, in charge of water supplies and sewer systems for local governments, went so far as to say: "I think that in the final analysis, it is not necessary to have detailed planning, since people make noises about what they need. They know what they need for their towns more than we do" (Valenzuela, 1977:149).

In a situation of very scarce resources many administrators found that they appreciated learning about the problems of different communities across the nation from knowledgeable individuals. Plans, on the other hand, might be elaborated completely in a vacuum, with faulty information and unrealistic goals. If communities were able to make their needs known in an intelligible manner, agencies were often in a better position to make concrete and rational decisions for expenditure of resources. Invariably, bureaucrats recognized that some communities might be left out if they did not have effective help from *parlamentarios* in Santiago, and administrators often repeated in interviews the expression "guagua que no llora no mama" (a baby that does not cry does not get fed), or "si no hay piteo no se alimenta" (if there is no whistling, it is not fed), indicating that pressure and complaints are expected if something is to be done for local communities.

The magnitude of the requests received from the congressmen can be illustrated by the fact that when the director of the Bureau of Obras Sanitarias of the Public Works ministry was interviewed, his office had received thirty *oficios* (official memos) from legislators in two days. A full-time staff member was employed just to answer the various communications that came in. In this office the director had two separate charts. One had the original plans and priorities drawn up by the planning office of the Dirección, while the other had actual and projected plans which he had finally decided on. These were based on the needs of his office and on information he had received from outside—including information given by *parlamentarios*. He freely admitted that one of the main influences in changing the original priorities was that of deputies and senators.[19]

Chilean congressmen, then, were quite effective in intervening on behalf of their localities in the various administrative agencies. This occurred not only in the face of severely limited governmental resources—but also *because* resources were so scarce. Because there was not enough to go around, some criterion had to be used for assigning priorities. The effective representation of demands—the intervention of politicians—was an important decision rule for bureaucrats making hard choices.

In Chile's highly ideological political system, particularistic transactions played an important role. While each individual transaction was insignificant, the aggregate of all of these transactions had a significant impact on the system (Blondel, 1973:14–15). For analytical purposes, one can argue that Chilean politics were divided into two arenas: a center arena and a local arena.[20] In the center arena, which predominated in the capital city, ideological and programmatic considerations were paramount. Disciplined parties sought to enact measures which would conform to their vision of society. The Congress was the key arena for compromise of divergent views.

However, the Congress, through individual legislators, was also a vital link in the politics of the local arena. Acting as national brokers at the top of networks of face-to-face relations, they attempted to extract vital resources for individual clients or groups of clients. Dating back to the Parliamentary Republic, congressmen of all parties could bargain with minority presidents to obtain support for these initiatives. This radically different style of politics reinforced the norms of accommodations and compromise and helped to diffuse the often bitter ideological disputes on major issues. By structuring working relationships on minor issues, the politics of the local arena contributed to strengthening the norm of accommodation on major issues. This style of politics precluded the possibility that a given party's conception of what society should be like would become reality. In that sense major transformations were not possible. On the other hand, it was also impossible to stay wedded to the status quo. The output or lack of output of the legislature was dependent on the ability of competitive forces to structure compromise. In the absence of a legislative arena, one of those disparate visions of society, in order to succeed, would have had to impose itself by force at the expense of the others. With the demise of Chilean democracy and its legislature this reality has become painfully true.

## EXECUTIVE ACTION AND THE DECLINE OF CONGRESS

During the government of Popular Unity (1970–73), conflict between the executive and the opposition majorities in the legislature reached severe levels, and the legislature underwent a clear and public decline as an institution. For the first time in Chilean history a coalition dominated by the left, rather than the center or right, succeeded in electing a candidate to the presidency. Allende was determined to implement his program through bold executive action including administrative reinterpretation of existing legislation, implementation of ignored provisions on the books and use of *resquicios* or loopholes in the legal structure.[21] But his broad executive initiative was due not only to an unwillingness to sacrifice his far-reaching program but also to the fact that after 1970 it was no longer as important for presidents to structure compromises with the legislature.[22] Congress had been dealt a severe blow by constitutional reforms adopted before Allende's election in the closing days of the Frei administration. These reforms culminated an institutional decline which had begun earlier and was well advanced by the time Allende took office.

Antiparliamentary themes have a long tradition in Chile (Bicheno, 1972), but the most severe reduction of Congress's role can be traced to the rise of modern technocratic planning in the early 1960s and more particularly in the administration of Eduardo Frei (1964–70). Congressmen reacted strongly against these trends, and opposition legislators were particularly bitter.[23] They felt that in previous governments all congressmen benefited from log-rolling on pork-barrel and particularistic matters but that under Frei they were simply locked out of many benefits.

The Christian Democratic government did represent a fundamental change in Chilean politics. For the first time in the twentieth century, the center of the political arena was occupied neither by an essentially pragmatic party, such as the Radicals, nor by a diverse political movement with a vast range of political tendencies, such as the Agrarian-Labor party. Christian Democrats blamed the incrementalist traditional politics for the stagnating Chilean economy plagued by high levels of inflation. To break out of the cycle of sluggish growth and at the same time incorporate marginal sectors into the mainstream of Chilean society, they proposed a bold strategy of centralized planning and the institutionalization of innovative programs of social mobilization.[24] The give and take of Chilean politics would have to be replaced by a "modern" conception of statecraft. The absolute majority of the votes which they received in the 1964 presidential election gave the Christian Democrats confidence that they would be able to abandon coalition politics; and the 1965 congressional elections, in which they won a majority of the seats in the Chamber of Deputies, reinforced that conviction.

But, the Christian Democrats did not become, in Giovanni Sartori's terms, a dominant "center tendency" (Sartori, 1966). They continued to be merely a "center pole" drawing support from elements on both sides of Chile's highly polarized system. In particular, Frei's success in 1964 was due to the strong support of the right and was not the result of the emergence of a new majority force in Chilean politics. In office, the Christian Democrats ignored the "coalition" nature of the election, and attempted to rule, for the first time in modern Chilean history as a single party (*partido único*). The few Christian Democrats who argued for a less ideological style and for an effort to achieve a more pragmatic center consensus, particularly with the old

Radicals, were simply overruled by majority sentiment within the top leadership. With the strength of the executive office on their side, the party sought to overcome its minority position by challenging traditional understandings. Eventually this challenge led to a change in the formal rules governing the executive-legislative relationship itself, and contributed in part to a breakdown of consensus which would lead to the breakdown of the regime.[25]

The Christian Democratic effort to institute central planning was thwarted from the outset by bitter opposition in the Senate. This meant that much of the modernization effort was channeled through the Ministry of Finance (*Hacienda*). A key tool in this process was the Office of the Budget. The transformation of this bureau from an office of accountants into an instrument of planning, begun in the mid-1950s, had delivered to the executive a new tool of great potential—not so powerful as the planners imagined in ordering and rationalizing the actual processes of change, but certainly powerful enough to upset the delicate balance in the budgetary process that had existed theretofore between executive and legislature.

The legal cornerstone in the transformation of Budget was DFL 47 of 1959, a Decree-with-Force-of-Law made under broad legislative authority delegated to President Jorge Alessandri. Before DFL 47, the Budget Bureau had been a kind of service agency among the ministries. DFL 47 gave the agency the skilled personnel of its own to begin thinking of the budget in a new way—not just as the record of how government operations should be financed but the key executive instrument for guiding policy priorities. In instituting program budgeting, the new agency reorganized the format of the budget document and, more fundamentally, attempted to reshape the way that budgets were made. The first stage of budgeting within a ministry was no longer to be gathering together the needs of its various local representatives but, rather, planning in conformity with presidentially established priorities.

Even as the initial Budget Bureau reorganization was just beginning there was congressional apprehension about its implications. Legislators argued that the decrees went beyond anything they had authorized the executive to undertake. With the substitution of program for line budgeting, it became almost impossible for them to influence particular items. The effect was to remove almost entirely the possibilities of meaningful bargaining over the budget in the legislature—or more particularly, in the formerly critical arena of the *comisión mixta* conference committee.

There was a continuing effort to expand executive discretion in administering budgets, chipping away little by little at any practices which allowed congressional influence. In 1965, when they controlled the Chamber of Deputies, the Christian Democrats passed a budgetary amendment allowing the executive to transfer funds freely between different items. There is evidence that at least some deputies saw clearly the implications of this amendment for Congress's whole role in budgeting (Republic of Chile, Congreso, 1965:2514).

It is worth noting briefly some of the specific tactics used by the Frei government to eliminate traditional forms of legislative influence. Perhaps the most important was not tolerating amendments introduced by congressmen to divide the funds for a particular budgetary item. Only on rare occasions would opposition legislators find that their amendments were not item-vetoed by the executive, though influential Christian Democratic congressmen, particularly close to the 1970 presidential election, were allowed to keep their amendments (Hughes, 1971). The control which the Christian Democrats had of the Chamber of Deputies made it possible for them to stand fast. Sergio Molina, the Finance Minister, managed to obtain almost perfect party discipline from the large number of newcomers to electoral politics. Many amendments simply never were approved by the Chamber majority—or what happened more often, Christian Democrat congressmen voted for opposition amendments with the knowledge that the executive would veto them, then refuse to override the veto.

Government planners responded to the outcry from Congress by arguing that amendments could not be presented without prior study of the projects in the ministries. However, even when opposition congressmen obtained those studies and introduced amendments based on them, the executive still used its veto. As Sergio Molina told the authors, "We resisted to the end. They argued that they knew the reality of their provinces, but we had to protect our national plan." [26] This was the whole thrust of the Frei government: to do away with particularistic considerations in order to rationalize national planning.

Another tactic successfully used by the Frei government for this end was to present the Budget Supplement Law (which might amount to one-quarter of the total budget) only in extraordinary sessions called by the president. In these sessions, by constitutional limitation, Congress could act only on the president's agenda. Breaking with tradition, the executive insisted that this meant that no amendments could be offered and no items supplemented. The party discipline of the majority Christian Democrats insured that his position would be upheld.

Still another specific area in which the Christian Democrats struck at congressional patronage was that of subsidies to various "worthy causes" in local districts. Traditionally, legislative politicians log-rolled among themselves to divide up small amounts of public funds for the benefit of particular hospitals, convents, sports clubs, orphanages, and the like, within their constituencies. The total sum never amounted to much, a fraction of one percent of the budget. Acting on principle, against all particularism—and on the grounds that this portion of the budget, the reading of which took the better part of a day, wasted the time of valuable administrators—the government tried repeatedly to eliminate this item altogether.[27] The reaction was so severe that legislators (including even some Christian Democrats) voted to cut major portions of the budget. Subsidies were never eliminated but the government created a level of acrimony quite disproportionate to the importance of the planner's principle.

These executive measures undermined the informal mechanisms for compromise within the legislature. Conflicts between the two chambers over approval of the Budget Law clearly increased with the advent of the Christian Democrats. Table 7.3 lists the numbers of sessions required to approve this measure, the number of official memoranda sent back and forth to the executive, and the number of

TABLE 7.3
DELAYS IN APPROVING THE BUDGET LAW
IN SUCCESSIVE ADMINISTRATIONS

| President | Years | No. of sessions required to approve law | Average no. of days over deadline until last session | No. of trámites or "shuttles" | No. of official memoranda |
|---|---|---|---|---|---|
| Ibáñez | 1953–1955 | 16 | 12.3 | 7 | 9 |
|  | 1956–1958 | 25 | 3.0 | 8 | 18 |
| Alessandri | 1959–1961 | 19 | 16.3 | 8 | 11 |
|  | 1962–1964 | 29 | 78.3 | 10 | 19 |
| Frei | 1965–1967 | 37 | 19.0 | 14 | 24 |
|  | 1968–1970 | 55 | 113.3 | 14 | 22 |
| Allende | 1971–1972 | 60 | 167.3 | 11 | 25 |

Source: Drawn from the *Boletines de Sesiones del Parlamento* (1952–73).

*trámites*, or steps, in the "shuttle" between both houses required to agree on the same bill.[28] The increase in the number of sessions and the growing use of the "shuttle" system rather than the traditional Conference Committee to resolve differences between the two houses were indications of a breakdown of previous norms and mechanisms of accommodation.

The presidentialist impetus of the Christian Democrat government culminated in the successful passage at the end of 1969 of a series of far-reaching constitutional amendments. The "Great Reform" was not a simple thing, but its overall thrust was clear: to reduce still further the functions historically exercised by Congress. Frei had introduced the proposals originally in 1964 but they had died for lack of parliamentary support. When the Christian Democrats promised to support a constitutional change which would take effect in the next presidential term, the conservative National party decided to support the initiative. (Ironically, in light of the subsequent victory of the socialist Allende, the Nationals supported the reform because they believed their candidate, Alessandri, was sure to become the next president and would need increased executive powers to deal with a leftist-dominated legislature.)

The government proposal included four major provisions.[29] The first provided mechanisms to resolve an impasse between the two branches, or more clearly stated, a situation where the legislature rejected a presidential initiative. With the constitutional amendment the president would be able to dissolve Congress and call for new elections, or turn directly to the people for approval of a measure through plebiscite, or submit a dispute to a new Constitutional Tribunal for arbitration. In its second provision the constitutional reforms contemplated several measures to accelerate the legislative process. Amendments extraneous to the *idea matriz* (central concept) of the bill would be barred. In addition, the president could declare certain legislation as "urgent," meaning that it could become law within thirty days unless the Congress acted on it. Finally, legislative committees would be empowered to work out the details of a law after general approval from the chamber in question, without the measure having to go back to the full body.

The third provision was equally far-reaching. It barred congressional initiative not only in budget matters and in public patronage, but in *all* matters—social security, salary adjustments, pensions, any compensation, in the private as well as the public sector—which comprised the heart and soul of particularistic exchanges. Congress was to be reduced to approving or disapproving executive proposals. Finally, the reforms were to give constitutional sanction to "Program Laws." During the first six months of a presidential term the president would submit his general program to Congress. On approval of this general outline, the president would be empowered to institute most of his program through executive decrees. Thus, many of the measures implemented by the administration, with its strong majority, as well as several others, would be enshrined by constitutional provision—marking the most severe limitation on congressional power in the country's history.

The proposed constitutional amendments generated great controversy. Exclusive executive jurisdiction over economic and welfare matters was strongly criticized by the country's labor federation, and the provision calling for dissolution of the Congress met enormous resistance within the government party itself. In fact, the refusal of several Christian Democratic congressmen to vote on that provision led to the suspension of eight of their number. Even so, that proposal was finally defeated. The "Program Law" and the "emergency" provisions were accepted in weakened form. With the strong opposition of Communists, Socialists, and Radicals, the government succeeded in adopting all of the other major proposals.

## PRESIDENTIALISM AND THE "POLITICS" OF LEGISLATURES

There is in any democratic politics an inherent tension between the needs for representation and for effectiveness. All representative systems periodically seem to suffer a kind of policy immobility—the incapacity of "politics" to deal with pressing problems. Then the cry arises for more effective government which, in modern conditions, means more power to the president. This is one way of understanding what happened in Chile in the 1960s: that Eduardo Frei and the Christian Democrats were not blinded by some simple rapacity or lust for power; but that they were blind in the way that men are always blind in history, caught up in a partial vision all the effects of which they could neither understand nor dominate.

The overriding imperatives of Chilean society in the 1960s—agreed by all, the Christian Democrats only headed the consensus—were economic development and administrative efficiency. From this it seemed to follow irresistibly that the president had to be master and the legislature brought to heel. The president was the promoter of development, its chief engine (Evans de la Cuadra, 1970:84; Eduardo Frei, 1970:40).[30] But there was more to this presidentialist thrust than the desire to achieve these goals. There was a deeper gaullist undertone which deprecated the legislature per se and its whole practice of "politics," meaning representation of particularistic interests, bargaining and compromising and log-rolling. Only the executive could really *govern*. Frei ruled much more by executive action than did his predecessor, by-passing the encumbrances of the Congress by from two to five times his predecessors' rates (Hughes, 1971). Ratios of executive to legislative outputs were at levels of 15, 24, and 38 to 1, as compared to earlier ratios in the 5 to 9 to 1 ranges. The volume was also at least 20 percent greater. This shift reflected the Christian Democrats' belief that the presidency was more free institutionally to make hard choices, less captured and compromised by the forces of "politics" (Evans de la Cuadra, 1970:58).

It is not our purpose to say that the Christian Democrats were wrong, nor that the particularism of Congress did not have real costs, nor that the problems faced by Chile in the 1960s did not cry out for urgent solutions (as they do even more today). The problem with the Christian Democrat critique was not that it was wrong, as far as it went, but that it was too partial and too narrow. They understood well the costs of underdevelopment, and the way that legislative politics contributed to them. But what they did not understand was that the price to be paid for eliminating that politics was very high—all out of proportion with any gains that would accrue through executive efficiency. The Christian Democrats, if they had not been so ideologically motivated, might easily have tolerated the small luxury of congressional particularism. The cement of small favors was never more than a tiny portion of the national budget, and no previous president had ever presided over budgets the size of those of Eduardo Frei. Thanks largely to his own significant tax reforms, government resources more than doubled between 1964 and 1970 when they reached the astounding level of 50 percent of Chile's Gross National Product (Republic of Chile, Ministerio de Hacienda, 1973:35).

It would be a serious oversimplification to argue that the reduction of the role of Congress led to the breakdown of Chilean democracy during the Allende years. And yet, the rise of a planning ideology, with its strong antipolitics bias, contributed significantly to the erosion of the traditional Chilean politics of compromise and accommodation. In particular, the effort to cut back on the role of Congress as the key arena for compromise on issues of national importance as well as on the myriad of critical, but small, issues vital for electoral politics, led to a reduction of communication among political elites of divergent factions and made more difficult the center consensus necessary for preserving the regime.

During the Allende government Congress had no other choice than to be either an acquiescent body or a negative center of opposition. Had the legislature continued to have a say over basic, though secondary, matters such as wage increases for groups of the private sector, the range of negotiable issues would have been much greater. As Chile's leading legislative expert has argued, "by giving the executive sole jurisdiction over such matters, the reforms effectively precluded the possibility that the opposition would have any real chance of acting as a loyal opposition." [31] Elements on the left, who earlier had opposed weakening the legislature, took advantage of the new governmental prerogatives now that they controlled the executive. Elements on the right (and gradually on the center) reacted by using the remaining powers of a weakened legislature to harass the president.[32] Politics moved outside of institutional channels—out of the hands of politicians—into the streets—and eventually into the hands of the military. As a staff member of the Senate, who had served for nearly twenty years within that institution, told the authors while reflecting on the 1970 constitutional reforms:

> those provisions marked the final demise of the legislature as an arena for accommodation and compromise. From then on, and by definition, it would become a negative body, pitted in an adversary relationship against the president. . . . Increasingly senators and congressmen who had worked closely together for years, despite policy agreements on party-defined issues, began to drift apart.[33]

Tapia Valdés agrees. "When Congress ceased to be the center of conciliation—that center did not move elsewhere—it simply disappeared giving final impetus to the politics of confrontation." [34]

The tragedy of Chile has roots not only in the polarization of vast social forces but also in the demise of small particular exchanges. Particularism, the greasing of political wheels that squealed, was peculiarly the province of the legislature. When it lost that province, the other element of politics with which it had so long existed in delicate counterbalance—ideology—came to dominate the exchanges in the institution. When congressional politicians lost the capacity to deliver concrete favors, they lost ground within the party organizations to other elites who traded in more symbolic currencies.

When Congress lost its particularistic functions, the territorial cleavages that cut across the system lost salience and were overwhelmed by those along more economic lines, above all the cleavages of class.

## NOTES

1. For a general chronology of Chilean politics in English see Gil (1966). On the Chilean military the best single volume is Joxe (1970).

2. See Rieles (1974). The declaration of the Chamber of Deputies is reprinted in the same volume and in Echeverría and Frei (1974:vol. 3). The sort of logic involved is discussed more generally by Kornberg and Pittman in chapter 3 of this volume.

3. For this attitude see Republic of Chile, Junta de Gobierno (1973a:66). For similar sentiments the reader is referred to many of the recent books published in Chile such as Silva (1974). For a review essay of the literature since the coup see Valenzuela and Valenzuela (1975).

4. Interviews were conducted by the authors in Santiago, Chile, in July and August of 1974. At Contraloría every department head, as well as several departmental aides, the secretary-general, the chief counsel, and the acting comptroller-general were interviewed. In other agencies interviewing was less systematic, though important policy makers were questioned. The authors are engaged in a large scale study of the Chilean budgetary process supported by the Social Science Research Council.

5. The authors spoke to most of the staff members still working for the Senate as well as several dismissed staff members.

6. Most interviews with CONARA personnel were conducted by Arturo Valenzuela in October and November of 1974.

7. Both authors have been much influenced in this emphasis on political factors (in addition to social forces and economic structures) by Linz (1978). See also, Huntington (1967:chap. 1).

8. For this argument, which takes issue with the standard interpretation that Diego Portales was the founder of Chilean institutions, see Valenzuela (1977:chap. 8).

9. For a thorough study of the background and effects of this law, see Valenzuela (1972).

10. There are three major trends in the literature on the conflict. The first group of works are partisan treatments defending the president (e.g., Bañados Espinosa [1894]) or the Congress (e.g., Rodriguez Bravo [1921 and 1926]). These works emphasize ideological differences and personal differences between major actors. The second group of works stresses more the institutional cleavages which developed between the two institutions, particularly over the problem of electoral intervention. In this group one finds historical treatments such as Encina (1942), and Amunátegui Solar (1946). The third interpretation is that of Ramirez Necochea (1951). He argues that foreign nitrate interests were being hurt by Balmaceda and that in alliance with local elements which were bought off they overthrew the president. A good review of the historiography of the civil war is that of Blakemore (1964).

11. A good comparative discussion of the 1891 law and the laws of 1854 and 1887 is Moya Figueroa (1901). The best and most comprehensive analysis of the 1891 law is Correa Bravo (1914). For a more detailed discussion of the argument in this and subsequent paragraphs, see Valenzuela (1977).

12. Cf. the argument of Daalder (1966:60).

13. These figures were calculated from the compilation of ministers in Valencia Avaría (1951:354–400).

14. Biographical information was obtained from Valderrama (1915). Information was cross-checked with the listing of deputies in Valencia Avaría (1951).

15. Based on tabulations by the authors from various compendia. Alessandri and Frei had totals of 20 and 22 ministers, respectively, Allende had 65. For the former two the average length

of cabinets were two years, five months, and two years, seven months. For Allende it was slightly under six months. He also had 9 interior ministers as compared to the 2 for Alessandri and 3 for Frei. The Allende pattern was quite like those of cabinets of presidents from 1932 to 1946.

16. The dominant role of the state in the Chilean economy is documented in Republic of Chile, ODEPLAN (1971:7, 170–76, 373, 383).

17. Interviews were conducted by Arturo Valenzuela in 1969 for a larger study of local government in Chile. A sample of 14 municipalities in a five-province region was chosen for intensive study. It became very clear in pretests of the structured questionnaire with local officials that local and other community leaders relied heavily on congressmen to obtain benefits for individuals and groups. The study of local communities was thus supplemented by a study of the role of congressmen. Congressmen from the five-province area were interviewed over a period of three months, and their activities closely monitored. In addition to congressmen, all of the Department heads in the Ministries of Public Works and Housing, as well as officials from the Ministry of Finance and the Contraloría, were interviewed. The discussion in this section is based on the larger study. See Valenzuela (1977).

18. See for example, Republic of Chile, Ministerio de Hacienda (1968:67).

19. On the weakness of ODEPLAN and planning in Chile from a planner's perspective, see Contreras Strauch (1971). This author relies extensively on the excellent work of Osvaldo Sunkel. For an English version of Sunkel's views, see Boeninger and Sunkel (1972).

20. For an elaboration of this distinction and a more detailed discussion of its importance in understanding Chilean politics, see Valenzuela (1977:chap. 7).

21. A major exception to this generalization was the Allende government's nationalization of copper, which received unanimous support in Congress.

22. Decree laws—laws simply promulgated by the executive, without meeting the constitutional requisites for legislative process—were prominent between 1924 and 1932. Many of these decree laws were later accepted as legal; indeed, Allende employed several during his government. More commonly, Congress delegated very broad powers to the president from time to time to make Decrees-with-Force-of-Law (DFLs). This occurred eleven times between 1927 and 1954, and another ten between 1955 and 1964. See Evans de la Cuadra (1973:57). A definitive discussion of the broader topic of "irregular legislation" is to be found in Silva Cimma, (1968:168–207).

23. This characterization of congressional attitudes is drawn from interviews by Valenzuela in 1969 and by both authors in 1974. Among our many generous and acute informants, we are especially grateful to Iván Auger Labarca, whose acerbic sagacity is the product of nearly 20 years as congressional staff, chief counsel to several committees, and founding member of the Office of Information in the Senate. Valenzuela was fortunate enough, more recently, to be able to interview about these same themes Jorge Tapia Valdés, also a long-time staff member of the Senate and twice a minister in the Allende government.

24. For data on inflation and economic growth, see Republic of Chile, ODEPLAN (1971).

25. It should be stressed that had Salvador Allende won in 1964 with a similar majority, it is likely that his coalition would have embarked on a similar strategy. The point is not that other forces within Chilean politics were not also concerned about transcending the old rules, but that the disappearance of a pragmatic center made it possible to undermine those rules. The precarious balance of Chilean politics had depended on the pragmatic center. The rise of Christian Democracy marked the end of that center and of the precarious balance.

26. Both Sergio Molina, the prime mover in this change, and Humberto Vega, Subdirector of the Budget under Allende, were extremely helpful and generous with their time in long interviews with the authors in 1974.

27. Molina interview.

28. The "shuttle" was similar to the *navette* system of the French Third Republic. See Williams (1964:282–84).

29. See the excellent study of Piedrabuena Richards (1970). This is a detailed analysis of every step of the legislative history of the amendments.

30. Evans' whole discussion of the "rationalization" of the legislative process is a revealing statement of the presidentialist persuasion. See Evans de la Cuadra (1970:39–45).

31. Interview with Jorge Tapia Valdés.

32. Allende's cabinet ministers were subject to a continued succession of impeachments which were often clearly political. In addition, the Congress adopted constitutional reform legislation by a majority vote—and claimed that a two-thirds majority was not needed to override the presidential veto. This issue became one of the most critical and divisive of the Allende presidency. For a discussion of these questions see Valenzuela (1975, 1978).

33. Ivan Auger, personal interview.

34. Jorge Tapia, personal interview.

*Chapter 8*

## THE ROLE OF THE INDIAN PARLIAMENT IN ECONOMIC PLANNING

### R . B . J A I N

This chapter deals with the impact of the Indian Parliament upon the intricate processes of national economic planning. In a democratic society—which India set out to be upon independence—no plan can succeed without adequate public involvement and the assent of those involved in its execution. Although national economic planning is both technically complex and politically exacting, such planning often has been undertaken in developing countries, where governments generally have assumed responsibility for coordinating human and material resources.

In all countries national economic planning has been largely an activity of the executive branch whereas the place of the legislature in the process is generally not well known. This chapter will try to remedy this deficiency by tracing legislative actions relating to planning in a major country whose devotion to planning has been great. Before examining and evaluating the performance of the Parliament, however, it will be helpful to set forth briefly the background and nature of national economic planning in India.

### GENESIS OF PLANNING IN INDIA

Even though there had been a variety of preliminary efforts at planning in the decade before independence, effective planning on an all-India basis could not start until India became free in 1947 and the major problems of partition and the unification of the native Indian states were partially resolved. Since then, the central theme of public policy and philosophy of national planning has been to promote balanced economic growth to increase opportunities for gainful employment, equality in incomes and wealth, and improved living standards and working conditions for the masses. The Constitution of India includes "social and economic planning" in the concurrent list of powers, i.e., as a power given both to the federal government and the states (Constitution of India II:34;35b,c). The legal basis for a national plan was provided through a parlimantary statute on the subject in 1949. The discussion in Parliament had envisaged the establishment of a Planning Commission and a National Economic Council to work as organs of intergovernmental cooperation in the economic and social fields. In pursuance of recommendations of the Advisory Planning Board of 1946, the Planning Commission was established by a cabinet resolution of 15 March 1950.[1] The National Development Council was constituted in 1952.

Since its inception, the Planning Commission has formulated and implemented five Five Year Plans. The First Five Year Plan, launched in 1951, basically prepared the ground for a more systematic mobilization of the nation's resources. The emphasis on agriculture, especially food production, paid off with the achievement of an 18 percent increase in agricultural production during the plan period. Food production rose by 50 million tons by the end of the first plan. Industrial output rose 5.8 percent, mainly by greater utilization of existing capacities.

The Second Five Year Plan emphasized basic and capital goods industries. The allocation to industries was increased from 5.8 percent in the First Plan to 20 percent of the total plan outlay, the emphasis being given to increases in steel output, machine building, heavy engineering and chemical industries and to essential intermediate products like cement and fertilizers. The revised target of foodgrains production was 80.5 million tons annually, an annual increase more than 15 million tons over the highest annual output during the first plan. Another shift in planning strategy was the stress laid on fulfillment of physical targets. Deficit financing to the extent of Rs 1,200 million for the whole plan period was resorted to for the first time. This was the primary cause of a price increase of abut 30 percent (wholesale index) during the five years. Food shortages resulted in imports for the first time in the decade. However, the massive industrial investment nearly doubled industrial output (a 94 percent increase since 1951). Agricultual output rose 16 percent during the second plan.

The first two Five Year Plans also saw the nationalization of two major industries and the Imperial Bank of India. Civil aviation was nationalized and two airlines, Air India International and Indian Airlines Corporation, established in 1953. The life insurance business also was brought under the newly formed Life Insurance Corporation. The premier commercial bank of the country, the Imperial Bank of India, was brought under government ownership in 1955 and renamed the State Bank of India. Imports of foodgrains under the US PL-480 program started in 1956.

The Third Five Year Plan laid greater emphasis on agriculture, including irrigation, on heavy industries, and on certain social services like technical education. The priority given defense production, however, resulted in a nearly 35 percent increase in money allocated to industries. Partly because of the effects of successive wars, the planning process received a setback during this period. For the first time there were wide gaps between targets and achievements in all major areas of output. Food production was only 73 million tons in 1956–66 against the plan target of 100 million tons. Industrial production increased slightly more than 7 percent against the target of 11 percent growth. The debate on the planning process, which started after the third plan, led to a three-year postponement of the Fourth Five Year Plan. Meanwhile, in June 1966 the rupee was devalued by 36.5 percent.

With the start of the fourth plan (1969–74), several major economic measures were adopted. Fourteen commercial banks were nationalized in 1969. Coal mines and general insurance were taken over two years later. The major economic event during the period was a government takeover of wholesale trading in wheat in 1973, as a first step to a state monopoly in foodgrains distribution. The measure was reversed the next year. The Fifth Five Year Plan, which started in 1974, included the assurance of a minimum standard of living to the bottom 30 percent of the population in the economic ladder (Link, 1975).

## THE PLAN FORMULATION PROCESS

From one perspective, the integrative needs of social and economic planning can be combined with democratic control only if the planning bodies accept participation as a vital part of the planning process. In this view, a plan must consider the needs and opinions of those affected by it even if these do not always agree with the rational or aesthetic view of the planners, and planning authorities need to promote discussion of both the plan's objectives and the various ways in which these objectives may be achieved (Hampton, 1970–71:346).

The planning procedure that has evolved in India over twenty-five years is designed to achieve such objectives. It now has become essentially a backward and forward process—"an exercise in successive approximation and successive coordination and a combination, on the one hand, of perspective planning, five-year planning and annual planning, and on the other, of national planning, sectoral planning and regional planning" (Sen, 1974:53–58).

The formulation of a five year plan is a time-consuming and complex process. The National Development Council,[2] the Planning Commission, together with its working groups and advisory panels, the ministers of the central government, state governments, and Parliament are all involved. Participation of the private sector is secured through various development councils and representatives of commerce and industry.

The process has four stages. During the first stage, which begins about three years before the commencement of the new plan, studies examine the state of the economy and identify the principal social, economic, and institutional shortcomings. The tentative conclusions of these studies help formulate the general approaches to the next five year plan. These are submitted by the Commission to the central cabinet. They are placed before the National Development Council, which indicates the rate of growth and the broad priorities to be assumed in the preparation of the plan. In its final report on the reorganization of the planning machinery, the Administrative Reforms Commission (ARC) suggested that the Planning Commission, when seeking guidelines from the National Development Council for the formulation of the national plan, should give a tentative framework of the plan considered feasible by it and also indicate other alternative approaches calling for different degrees of effort. Such basic factors as the rate of growth, resources required, and sacrifices involved should be brought out clearly. Detailed work on the formulation of the plan should proceed in the light of the guidelines given by the National Development Council (Republic of India, Administrative Reforms Commission, 1968:9). The formulation of the Fifth Five Year Plan has followed the procedure recommended by the ARC.

In the second stage, the Planning Commission works out the general dimensions of the plan in the light of the tentative rate of growth indicated by the National Development Council. This stage ends with the preparation of a draft memorandum which outlines the main features of the plan under formulation.

The third stage is directed toward the preparation of a draft outline of the plan in light of the observations made on the draft memorandum by the National Development Council. The draft memorandum also is commented upon by the states and the central ministries and, after approval by the Council is circulated for public discussion. It is then considered by an informal consultative committee of members of Parliament, and by Parliament as a whole.

The fourth stage concerns the preparation of the final report on the plan. The Planning Commission, in association with the concerned central ministries holds detailed discussions with the state governments regarding their plans. Discussions are also held with representatives of major organized industries in the private sector through various development councils as well as chambers of commerce and industry.

In the light of the points raised in these discussions, the Planning Commission prepares a paper bringing together the principal features of the plan, the policy directives to be stressed, and the issues which may require further consideration before the plan is finally drawn up. The paper is submitted to the central cabinet and the National Development Council. The final report on the plan is based on the conclusions reached on this paper. A draft of the final report is considered by the central ministries and the state governments and is then submitted for approval to the cabinet and the National Development Council. Thereafter, it is presented to Parliament for discussion and approval (Republic of India, Administrative Reforms Commission, 1968:45).

## PARLIAMENT AND THE PLANNING PROCESS

The Indian Parliament is involved in the processes of planning at two different stages: first, when the Draft Five Year Plans prepared by the Planning Commission are submitted to it for a general discussion; and, second, at the time of adopting the plan proposals before they are implemented. While the first stage gives an opportunity for wider discussions, the second is merely a formality.

## PARLIAMENTARY COMMITTEES AND THE DRAFT FIVE YEAR PLANS

The legislature as a body, however constituted, cannot scrutinize the details of the voluminous plan documents effectively, based as they are on extensive data, research, and analyses by national and international specialists. It has neither the time nor the expertise for a thorough scrutiny of the varied and complex details—only the broad principles and policies of the plans can possibly be considered. The Indian Parliament, therefore, has evolved a process of discussing the draft plan documents through different types of parliamentary committees.

The committee system is said to have the advantage of saving considerable floor time of the House. Policies inherent in the plan documents can be examined on their merits and possibly on nonparty lines. Further, members serving on these committees may be able to develop some degree of expertise and make special contributions in areas of particular interest to them. It even affords backbenchers an opportunity to express their views freely and to feel a sense of participation. The views expressed in the discussions in these committees can be utilized suitably by the Planning Commission and the government in finalizing the plans.

The first type of committee is an informal consultative committee, first created in 1954 to associate the members of Parliament with the processes of administration. As in the case of the various central ministries, it became the practice to constitute an informal consultative committee of members of Parliament for the Planning Commission. The informal consultative committee appointed during the tenure of the Third Lok Sabha consisted of 101 members. From 1964 to 1966, the committee met 22 times, the highest attendance during this period being 34 and the lowest 3. As a rule, the committees hold their meetings during the session of Parliament, and the ministers concerned preside. The average duration of each meeting is one-and-a-half hours (Republic of India, Department of Parliamentary Affairs, 1958–59:4). Poor attendance of members at committee meetings and failure to assign them any statutory functions contribute to their ineffectiveness. They do not make decisions or even vote on any matters. A minister has absolute discretion over what he should disclose in the meetings. These committees are obviously intended to be informally consultative and advisory, and nothing is referred to them officially and kept pending until they consider it. One study of the working of such committees points out, "their functioning seems to suggest that these are bodies, bereaved of any real power, which have not lived up to the optimism one detects in the official references to them" (Maheshwari, 1972:234).

The second type of committee stemmed from prime ministerial initiative. In December 1958 the then Prime Minister Jawaharlal Nehru appointed a committee consisting of some members of Parliament to discuss the plan. The committee was reconstituted in November 1965, with the prime minister, five other ministers, and eight members of Parliament. Attendance at the meetings of this committee has been better than at those of the informal consultative committees, though data that indicate the impact of these committees on plan proposals are lacking.

The third type of committee that has contributed substantially to the discussion of the economic planning program of the government is one specially constituted from among the members of Parliament (of both houses) to discuss documents relating to various plan proposals. This device was first adopted in the formulation of the Second Five Year Plan. On a report of the Business Advisory Committee, the Lok Sabha on 11 May 1956 approved the formation of four committees of the House to discuss the Second Five Year Plan. Each committee was to discuss a separate group of subjects (Republic of India, Lok Sabha, 1956:cols. 7986–7993). No number of members was fixed,but it was hoped that each committee would consist of members eager or at least willing to participate in the discussion of the subjects allotted to that committee. The chairmen of the committees were to be appointed by the Speaker out of those constituting them. Only a brief summary of the verbatim record was to be submitted to the Parliament for its consideration. An approved report of the Business Advisory Committee (Republic of India, 1956:n.13, cols. 7989–90) suggesting that the Planning Commission assign officers to assist the committees in their deliberation had attached to it a rider that committees thus formed were to arrive at no decisions and pass no resolutions. They were only to express their views, which then would be made available to all the members. Thus, from their very inception the scope of operation of the committees was quite restricted, reflecting the government's uncertainty as to the possible impact they might have on the modification of the plan documents. As the then Speaker Sardar Hukam Singh said, they were only "making an experiment" (Republic of India, Lok Sabha, 1956:col. 7990).

Since 1956, plan committees have been constituted regularly at the time of the discussion of the Draft Second, Third, Fourth, and Fifth Plan documents. With the exception of the Second Five Year Plan, which was discussed under four groups of subjects, the next three plans were broken into five different groups of subjects allotted to committees 'A,' 'B,' 'C,' 'D,' and 'E' respectively. The slightly varied group of subjects from plan to plan indicate shifts in the scope of the discussions of the various committees. As is observed from Chart 8.1, the only consistency in subject allocation has been in respect of committee 'C,' concerned with agricultural and rural economy.

The size of plan committees has varied from plan to plan and from committee to committee. As is clear from Table 8.1, the number of members was largest in the Fifth Five Year Plan and lowest during the Fourth. The latter partly reflected a rather uncertain economic situation that led members to be skeptical about its success. This skepticism ultimately led to a three-year plan holiday, 1967–69.

The membership of the plan committees has been drawn from the full spectrum of political parties. The 393 members (250 from Lok Sabha and 143 from Rajya Sabha) who offered themselves for membership on the various committees included 204 from the ruling party and 189 scattered among all opposition parties. Undoubtedly, the opposition parties have had a stronger interest in participating in the deliberations of the committees, their representation being 48.1 percent, against 32.7 percent of the total membership of Parliament.

The occupational profile of the members of plan committees does not depart drastically from that of the entire Lok Sabha. For the fifth Lok Sabha, political and social workers together with journalists and writers were most clearly overrepresented (45 percent vs. 25 percent) and lawyers and teachers and industrialists underrepresented (14 percent vs. 27 percent) on the plan committees. Data for the current plan indicate that only a small proportion of the MPs who volunteered for the plan committees have actually attended meetings (Table 8.2) or participated in their discussions when present (Table 8.3). Nor have the plan committees spent much time in meetings compared to that spent by financial committees of the Lok Sabha. Committee meetings for the third plan consumed approximately seven-and-a-half hours, for the fourth plan approximately eight-and-a-half hours, and for the fifth plan approximately ten hours. In contrast, in 1967–68 the Estimates Committee met 95 times for a total sitting time of 200 hours.[3] The Public Accounts Committee met 95 times in 1965–66, with 278 hours spent in deliberations.[4] The comments made by mem-

CHART 8.1
ALLOTMENT OF SUBJECTS OF THE VARIOUS PARLIAMENTARY PLAN COMMITTEES

| Committees | II Plan | III Plan | IV Plan | V Plan |
|---|---|---|---|---|
| 'A' | Plan, policy outlay and allocation | Policy, resources and allocation | Policy, resources and allocation | Policy, resources and allocation |
| 'B' | Industries, minerals, transport and communications | Industry, power and transport | Industry, power and transport | Industry, power, transport, and scientific and technological research |
| 'C' | Agriculture and rural economy | Agriculture and rural economy | Agriculture and rural economy | Agriculture and rural economy |
| 'D' | Social service and labor policy | Social services | Social services | Social services, education, manpower, planning and population policies |
| 'E' | — | Technical manpower and scientific research | Education and manpower planning | Implementation and public cooperation |

## TABLE 8.1
## MEMBERSHIP OF THE PLAN COMMITTEES CONSTITUTED FOR THE SECOND, THIRD, FOURTH, AND FIFTH PLANS

| | Second Plan | | | Third Plan | | | Fourth Plan | | | Fifth Plan | | |
|---|---|---|---|---|---|---|---|---|---|---|---|---|
| | Lok Sabha | Rajya Sabha | Total | Lok Sabha | Rajya Sabha | Total | Lok Sabha | Rajya Sabha | Total | Lok Sabha | Rajya Sabha | Total |
| 'A' | 60 | 22 | 82 | 63 | 44 | 107 | 50 | 30 | 80 | 92 | 63 | 155 |
| 'B' | 77 | 37 | 114 | 86 | 50 | 136 | 42 | 34 | 76 | 116 | 67 | 183 |
| 'C' | 66 | 25 | 91 | 105 | 53 | 158 | 68 | 30 | 98 | 126 | 69 | 195 |
| 'D' | 47 | 32 | 79 | 48 | 37 | 85 | 27 | 21 | 48 | 111 | 54 | 165 |
| 'E'a | – | – | – | 20 | 14 | 34 | 40 | 24 | 64 | 78 | 39 | 117 |

a. Committee 'E' was not formed during the discussion on the second plan.

TABLE 8.2

FREQUENCY OF ATTENDANCE OF MEMBERS AT THE SITTINGS OF THE PLAN COMMITTEES (V PLAN)

Members attendance in plan committees

| Committee | Members | | | One sitting | | | Two sittings | | | Three sittings | | | Four sittings | | |
|---|---|---|---|---|---|---|---|---|---|---|---|---|---|---|---|
| | L.S. | R.S. | Total | L.S. | R.S. | Total | L.S. | R.S. | Total | L.S. | R.S. | Total | L.S. | R.S. | Total |
| 'A' | 92 | 63 | 155 | 15 | 11 | 26 | 10 | 5 | 15 | 6 | 5 | 11 | 8 | 3 | 11 |
| 'B' | 116 | 67 | 188 | 20 | 10 | 30 | 22 | 8 | 30 | 10 | 4 | 14 | 14 | 3 | 17 |
| 'C' | 126 | 69 | 195 | 19 | 9 | 28 | 14 | 11 | 25 | 11 | 6 | 17 | 13 | 3 | 16 |
| 'D'a | 111 | 54 | 165 | 15 | 5 | 20 | 15 | 5 | 20 | 5 | 5 | 10 | 4 | 1 | 5 |
| 'E'a | 78 | 39 | 117 | 11 | 3 | 14 | 5 | 9 | 14 | 5 | 1 | 6 | 3 | 1 | 4 |

a. Committees 'D' and 'E' had only four sittings each.

| Committee | Five sittings | | | Members remaining absent | | | Absentees— maximum % of total members |
|---|---|---|---|---|---|---|---|
| | L.S. | R.S. | Total | L.S. | R.S. | Total | |
| 'A' | 5 | 7 | 12 | 48 | 32 | 80 | 51.6 |
| 'B' | 16 | 11 | 27 | 34 | 31 | 65 | 35.5 |
| 'C' | 10 | 4 | 14 | 59 | 36 | 95 | 48.7 |
| 'D'a | – | – | – | 72 | 38 | 110 | 66.7 |
| 'E'a | – | – | – | 54 | 25 | 79 | 67.5 |

## TABLE 8.3

## PARTICIPATION OF ATTENDING MEMBERS AT THE SITTINGS OF THE PLAN COMMITTEES

| Committees | Members participating in the discussions in the plan committee | | | | | | | | | |
|---|---|---|---|---|---|---|---|---|---|---|
| | First sitting | Second sitting | Third sitting | Fourth sitting | Fifth sitting | Sixth sitting | Seventh sitting | Eighth sitting | Ninth sitting | Tenth sitting |
| | **Third plan** | | | | | | | | | |
| 'A' | 13 | 9 | 11 | 19 | 12 | 8 | 2 | – | – | – |
| 'B' | 11 | 13 | 15 | 13 | 22 | 24 | – | – | – | – |
| 'C' | 12 | 13 | 19 | 11 | 27 | – | – | – | – | – |
| 'D' | 12 | 10 | 12 | 12 | – | – | – | – | – | – |
| 'E' | 8 | 5 | 7 | 9 | 9 | – | – | – | – | – |
| | **Fourth plan** | | | | | | | | | |
| 'A' | 9 | 6 | 7 | 6 | 1 | 4 | 5 | 7 | 9 | – |
| 'B' | N.A. | N.A. | N.A. | N.A. | – | – | – | – | – | – |
| 'C' | 10 | 7 | 16 | 14 | 2 | 13 | – | – | – | – |
| 'D' | 7 | 10 | 10 | 5 | – | – | – | – | – | – |
| 'E' | 10 | 2 | 10 | – | – | – | – | – | – | – |
| | **Fifth plan** | | | | | | | | | |
| 'A' | 1 | 9 | 6 | 8 | 11 | 12 | – | – | – | – |
| 'B' | 6 | 7 | 1 | 11 | 15 | 9 | 18 | 24 | 7 | 11 |
| 'C' | 14 | 1 | 14 | 17 | 12 | 15 | – | – | – | – |
| 'D' | 20 | 1 | 14 | 10 | – | – | – | – | – | – |
| 'E' | 10 | 1 | 10 | 8 | – | – | – | – | – | – |

bers of the plan committees in their meetings suggest that their low participation reflects the uncertainty they felt about the attention that government planners would give to their recommendations.

A careful perusal of the proceedings of the plan committees that reviewed the Third and Fifth Five Year Plans suggests that committees frequently have tended to question the adequacy of the principles underlying the planning programs. The tone has often been general. Planners have been reminded of the goal of social justice, of the need to organize adequately to accomplish goals, and of the importance of securing the cooperation of the public in implementing programs. There have been highly specific recommendations as well, including references to the kinds of taxes that ought to be levied in specific situations, the adequancy of resources from current revenue and public enterprise earnings, and the order of priorities in allocation of specific funds. Several plan committees have expressed doubt as to their influence on the planners, and have urged a revised procedure whereby they would have an earlier input. Despite such suggestions, the procedure basically has remained unchanged through the fifth plan.

### DISCUSSIONS OF PLANS ON THE FLOOR

In addition to the committee work, both houses consider these documents in their regular sittings, and give final approval before the plan is put into operation. The number of days devoted to plan documents in the Lok Sabha were 5, 3, 20, 9, and 4, and in the Rajya Sabha were 3, 4, 13, 14, and 6, for plans 1 through 5 respectively. This is not much time for discussing a subject of such importance. Even for the third plan, to which Parliament devoted more days than the others (the record on the fifth plan is not yet complete because of its recency), discussion time amounted to only about 2 percent of the sitting time of a Parliament during its five-year term.

A sample analysis of the discussion on the Fifth Five Year Plan indicates that the time allotted to different political parties in the discussion is very much in proportion to their relative strength in the House. The debates reveal that the members of Parliament take considerable interest in this highly technical and complex subject. Although it cannot be ascertained whether they have had time to go through the voluminous plan documents in all their ramifications and to have scrutinized them fully, the many alternate and substitute motions customarily offered by members of the various political parties suggest that they tend to take their work seriously. Of course, many of the criticisms and comments are made on a purely partisan basis.

It is difficult to measure the impact of the debates in the House on the final plan programs, policies, and priorities. Since the appraisal of the plan programs is not like that of a law that has to be either supported or rejected on a majority principle on party lines, it is possible that the entire purpose of involving the MPs in discussions of the plan perspectives and approaches is only to acquaint them with the broader economic and social policy outlines of the government on a long-term basis, to learn their reactions, and to discern whether sufficient dissatisfaction exists to require some modification in how a plan is put into effect.

Prime Minister Gandhi's views of Parliament's role in the discussion of the Plan documents are contained in a statement to the Lok Sabha in 1969:

> . . . [I]t is through these discussions that we can secure the commitment of the people to the goals envisaged in the Plan and evoke the necessary enthusiasm and the hard and sustained effort, without which no plan, however well-conceived or technically good, can possibly produce results. Government, therefore, attaches great importance to Parliament's part in shaping public opinion and in mobilizing the support of the people for the success of the Plan.[5]

After submission to Parliament for general approval, the plan in effect comes before the members again in the form of yearly approval of the budget. In practice the members do not make an easy connection between the overall plan and the detailed annual budget estimates. However, they have an opportunity to consider the impact of budget items upon the plan and to ask for a reappraisal of unfulfilled plan targets.

## IMPLEMENTATION OF PLANS

The crucial question of how a plan is administered has only recently received much attention from Parliament. This has come via the plan committees. Aside from a few stray remarks, it was not until the fifth plan that plan committees dealt with defects in the execution of the plan and suggested remedies.[6] Committee 'A', for example, asserted that policies dealing with curbs on deficit financing, disincentives to investments in nonessentials, construction of public distribution systems, land reforms, and the reduction of conspicuous consumption were not being implemented adequately. The committee (Republic of India, Lok Sabha 1969:col. 183) also believed that "Peoples' involvement in all the plan process is a must if the plan is to succeed. Effective participation of all the beneficiaries concerned should, therefore, be ensured in the implementation." Committee 'E' similarly observed that the performance of economic planning in India had not inspired popular confidence or elicited the support of the masses. It suggested that there was an urgent need for reorienting the existing administrative machinery at the center as well as in the states, and that it was necessary to have similar monitoring and evaluation cells at the district and block levels to supervise the execution of local plan schemes (Republic of India, Lok Sabha, 1974a:xii and xiii).

Involving Parliament in more systematic periodic evaluation of a plan during its life has been proposed in various quarters. Committee 'E' mentioned above, recommended that the Planning Commission make an annual report to Parliament on implementation and that this be discussed in depth by a special parliamentary committee. A similar recommendation was made in 1968 by the Administrative Reforms Commission (ARC) appointed by the government of India to report on a series of administrative reforms in different fields. In its final report on the "Machinery for Planning," it recommended that the Planning Commission place before the Parliament annual progress reports on plan performance, as well as its evaluation report, for discussion in the House. The ARC observed that it would be helpful if a special committee of Parliament (consisting of about 25 MPs and including leaders or deputy leaders in the various political parties as well as a few independent members) were to be constituted to go into these reports in detail and make necessary recommendations. A similar practice also was recommended for the state legislatures.[7]

The plan committees have not been very successful as vehicles for an effective parliamentary scrutiny of the five year plans. Such a scrutiny has to be continuing and concurrent, based on adequate study, assimilation of information, analysis of data, and operational research in performance evaluation. The plan committees had little standing. They were not constituted by the houses of Parliament on a specific motion or for any specific purpose and ceased to function as soon as the synopsis of their proceedings was laid on the table of both houses. Constituted on no specific criteria or relative background of members, and with no expectation of their making decisions or recommendations, they were in the very nature of things not capable of any detailed scrutiny of the plan in its various ramifications.

It is against this background that the ARC made its strong recommendations (Republic of India, Administrative Reforms Commission, 1968:55). The success of the ARC's recommended parliamentary committee would depend upon: (a) its members taking a great interest in committee work and developing necessary expertise; (b) the Planning Commission and the government cooperating with the committee by providing it with full and timely information; (c) the staff providing the necessary expert research and professional assistance; and (d) the committee aiming at becoming an effective instrument for making management-type inquiries into plan implementation, backed by adequate information, data, and supporting materials, and leading to an internal performance or efficiency-scrutiny harnessed to the needs of both the Parliament and the government (Shakdher, 1974:531–533).

Creation of such a committee, it was further argued, would vindicate the principle that planning is a nonparty national endeavor. It would also establish a principle that in this system of government, Parliament and the government of the day are not competing centers of power in socioeconomic planning but inseparable partners. The planning process from formulation to implementation is a joint cooperative venture of the Planning Commission, the central government, the state governments, and the Parliament. In a committee discussion, it would be far easier for members to make, and for the government to accept, constructive suggestions, thereby putting to effective use a great deal of varied experience, expertise, and ability available within and outside the Parliament (Shakdher, 1974:533).

In the last analysis, the close involvement of members of Parliament in the planning process, the annual report from the Planning Commission to Parliament, and the reports that might be made from time to time by the proposed Parliamentary Committee on Plan Implementation together could involve the public at large in the plans and create a healthy public awareness of them. The reports of the plan committee might also bring to light any unremedied shortcomings and educate public opinion in the operational mechanics of the process of planning. If so, the committee would have the effect of strengthening the mechanism of accountability to Parliament and the people in the field of planning. Furthermore, the committee reports might provide considerable feedback to the House for discussion there of the annual plan for the next year (Shakdher, 1974:532).

## PARLIAMENT AND PLANNING IN PERSPECTIVE

Despite the deficiencies noted in Parliament's review of the formulation and implementation of five year plans, the process at least has provided an opportunity for a better understanding of national economic planning, intricate as it is. The members of Parliament have had the opportunity to learn and to criticize. The planners have had a chance to take account of feedback from the elected representatives. To an extent, therefore, Parliament has served a legitimizing function as well as a publicizing one. The undoubted paucity of substantive changes in the plans as a result of legislative comments and recommendations must be balanced against the complexity of planning in a federal system. The planning process in India basically rests on a proper evaluation of the requirements of various state governments and the union territories as well as on a systematic coordination and balancing of the often conflicting demands and priorities emanating from various sources. There is a statutory duty to consult local interests, local authorities, and the people at large. Such coordination cannot be achieved either on the floor of the House or in the deliberations of the committees. Nothing can be imposed on the states from above. They are autonomous in their developmental activities, and it is only through their consent and involvement in both formulation and implementation that planning can be achieved in the respective regions. It is against this background that the role of the National Developmental Council, composed of the elected representatives of various states, assumes greater significance and importance in the planning process. However, this is not to suggest that the legislative role in the planning process cannot be improved along the lines of the recommendations already discussed.

That the legislature could play, but has neither seriously sought nor played, a significant role in plan formulation and plan implementation and, thereby, in socioeconomic development, perhaps may be interpreted as indicating the irrelevance of legislatures in general to socioeconomic development. However, the above evidence of the role of Lok Sabha in economic planning should dispel such notions and emphasize that legislatures are not inherently irrelevant in the processes. Past and present practice does not mean that under changed conditions it would not play such a role. To enable parliaments to perform effectively their role as public planning bodies, one of the important alternative suggestions made by David Apter (1973) is that legislatures become forums of open debate on planning, participate in priority setting through legislative decision making, and serve as agents of popular and technical review and revision. This would counteract technocrats' unawareness of political needs. Without going into the details of his proposal (p. 13), it is sufficient to note that Apter recognizes no present legislatures fit the requirements he outlines. The role of Parliament, particularly that of the lower house, would certainly have to deemphasize debate and approval of general priority programs and enabling legislation and emphasize specific reform bills and, ultimately, the amendment of bills in response to public reactions. Only in this manner would a popularly elected house like the Lok Sabha be able to strengthen the relationship between governmental planning and the public needs and to coordinate and possibly to harmonize the different needs and demands people might have in an increasingly complicated world.

Because we have considered Parliament and planning rather narrowly, to provide a somewhat broader picture it would be helpful to place parliamentary action against an admittedly sketchy backdrop of constituency, party, and recent events in India.

## CONSTITUENTS' INPUT INTO THE PLANNING PROCESS

Although MPs provide a basic strand in the politics of planning in India, they receive little, if any, input into the planning process from their constituents for two main reasons. The first concerns the organized process of planning. The federal structure of the government and the inclusion of "economic and social planning" in the concurrent list of powers relegates the formulation of state plans incorporating regional and local interests to the state level. In actual practice, however, the planning initiative comes from the center and the state governments become mainly instruments through which developmental efforts are pushed. The Planning Commission and the center generally endeavor to induce development in the states by offering them assistance. Since there is no equivalent to the Planning Commission at the state level (although in some cases a state planning board which is no more than a committee of department officials does exist), the main links between the center and the state level planning systems tend to be specialized along subject lines—for instance, a transport working group at the center may be associated with transport working groups in the states. The state inputs thus can be overlaid by sector rivalries rather than the regional ones, and in determining these the technical-professional officials almost always have the upper hand over the elected members.

Second, even at the level of the states, the state minister has official dealings with the appropriate minister at the center. Some, of course, are more effective than others in pressing their claims. But in most states the chief minister is the key figure in relations with the center, and the states' developmental plans, practically speaking, are finalized at the National Development Council (NDC), where compromises are settled between the conflicting and rival claims of state governments. The MPs get the opportunity to discuss and approve the plan in the House only after its tacit approval by the NDC. In such circumstances the MPs are hardly in a position to press any regional or local claims. As our analysis has shown, both parliamentary and committee deliberations are dominated by sectoral interests rather than the regional interests of the constituents of the MPs, although a state bloc of MPs may carry some influence at some points. These features of the process explain why there is hardly any constituent input via MPs in the planning process.

However, this is not to suggest that the constituents have no role at all in the planning process. They can provide such inputs through the members of the State Legislative Assemblies (MLAs), who at times might press these claims successfully at the more rudimentary MLA committees in states. The introduction of the Panchayati Raj (PR) system, designed to introduce self-government at the district, block, and village levels, with specific responsibilities in development fields, has not only expanded democratic participation in rural areas but also has ensured the development of closer links between the MLA and rural India. The voters expect the MLA to be the broker between the masses and the elite. The MLA must ensure effective contact with the masses in his constituency in order to guarantee a solid base of electoral support. Thus, he has to act as a mediator, assisting his constituents to acquire developmental benefits and helping them to solve problems in dealing with the state bureaucracy. The special regional and local claims of a district and the area within its jurisdiction are formulated at the level of the district development councils (popularly known as *Zila Parishads*, the highest structure of the PR system), of which the MLAs and MPs from that area are important members. It is here that the constituents of a particular area may contribute to the planning process. Since they have greater and more frequent access to their MLAs, they naturally first approach them rather than the MPs. In turn, they and the leaders of the ruling party in the PR institutions tend to help their supporters procure developmental benefits through the village development council and, subsequently, in the state assembly. The MP's role in such meetings is minimal—to help arrange compromises between the rival claims of the MLAs and the party leaders.[8]

Relatedly, it is quite difficult for an MP in India to have close direct relations with his constituents. There can be, as Professor Morris-Jones (1971:203) puts it, "no equivalent of the week-end exodus from Westminister; neither as political educator nor as welfare agent does the MP appear regularly before his constituency." The distances and the length of parliamentary sessions make it necessary for him to rely on intermediaries, and the key intermediaries are the MLAs of the party whose assembly constituencies are contained in his own larger Lok Sabha constituency and who may well have been instrumental in his own electoral success. An MLA "will be more region-bound than the MP, but even in his case 'constituency party' does not yet exist in the British sense of the term" (Morris-Jones, 1971:204).

## PARTY DISCIPLINE IN ECONOMIC PLANNING

Political parties in India have all the organizational characteristics of "Western" party systems. They have "platforms," individual members, hierarchies of committees, paid officials, voluntary workers, and representatives in central and state legislatures. Their leaders use familiar political language and present themselves as proponents of policies which ought to command the support of a majority of public-spirited citizens. Most of their pronouncements on the ideology and programs of social and economic planning come through their manifestoes and through their party resolutions in their annual sessions. Through their members in the legislative bodies they seek to follow up these programs in the government. Through the various structures of their organization inside and outside the Parliament they exercise control and direction over their professed policies.

Economic planning in India has largely been the product of the thinking within the Congress party (The Indian National Congress) before and after independence. The Planning Commission itself came into being as a result of the earlier commitment of the Congress party to a program of planned development.[9] Only after the Commission's establishment in 1950 did Congress begin to seek the basic principles on which planning was to proceed. By the very force of circumstances, the First Five Year Plan could be only a modest attempt at the rehabilitation of a partitioned economy. The economic processes did not then feel the impact, for planning was still in an experimental stage.

Once economic planning had gained some momentum, the Congress attempted to spell out its ideology in 1955 at the end of the first plan. The famous Avadi Resolution of the Congress in January 1955 declared that in furtherance of the objectives set forth in the Preamble and the directive principles of state policy of the Constitution, planning should take place to further establishment of a "socialistic pattern of society" with the principal means of production under social ownership and control and an equitable distribution of national wealth. In subsequent years, Congress resolutions specified support for various means and goals in the plans, and reiterated the general urgency of the need for planning and its rapid acceptance.

Other political parties made similar pronouncements on economic planning. For instance, the Communist Party Congress in 1958 expressed its support for the "progressive features" of the plan and attributed the difficulties that had arisen to "unwarranted and harmful concessions" to big business, executive reliance on foreign capital, iniquitous taxation of the common people, deficit financing, and "dependence on the bureaucratic machinery." The Praja Socialist party agreed only with the last point. At its Fourth Annual Conference in 1958, it accused Congress of weaknesses in organization, maladministration, corruption, and an "inability to comprehend and communicate to the people the stubborn difficulties inherent in the rapid social and economic transformation of society." All these views were reflected subsequently in the speeches of the members of the respective political parties in the Lok Sabha debates on the Second Five Year Plan between 10 February and 9 May 1958, during which only 18 of no fewer than 63 questions about the plan reflected the usual localized interests. In the course of the budget debates, the plan was subject to 12 varied cut motions based on earlier party commitments of the members raising them.

In the beginning the rightist parties in the country (the Jana Sangh and the Swatantra) seemed completely opposed to the concept of planning. The general secretary of the Jana Sangh was skeptical of the whole idea of planning and the government's declaration that it would achieve socialism through democratic means. According to the party ideology, " . . . in theory, it [socialism] implied authoritarianism, and in practice it had everywhere resulted in totalitarian governments" (Upadhyaya, 1958:187–88). Later, however, both the Jana Sangh and the Swatantra parties did seem to recognize the need for planned economic development of the country, but they remained ardent critics of the whole Congress philosophy that underlay the planning system as well as of the manner in which it was carried on by that party and its leaders, and of the economic philosophy and specific proposals embodied in the plans (Jhangiani, 1967:78–79). Similarly the Swatantra party rejected the current pattern of "centralized and top-heavy planning of the Soviet type." It was in favor of having planning carried out within the limits of the freedom guaranteed by the Constitution, to develop the growth of conditions in which the people's enterprise will find full and unfettered scope (Swatantra Party, 1962:11). Like Jana Sangh, the Swatantra party also was critical of the composition and functioning of the Planning Commission.

Such pronouncements and postures of various political parties on economic planning give their MPs a kind of mandate to adopt a particular party line in the parliamentary proceedings on the subject. They invariably carry this out faithfully not only in the parliamentary committee meetings but also on the floor of the House.[11] MPs of different political parties, including the ruling one, hardly ever differ from the already announced party approaches. The members are so party-bound on these issues that the occasion for taking any disciplinary action against them rarely arises. There have been occasions when the leadership in a political party was split in its basic ideology concerning economic and social goals. In such cases matters came to a head within the party organization outside the legislature, and these quarrrels invariably have resulted in the resignation of one or the other group from the party membership.[12]

The Congress party being the ruling party at the center and in the majority of states, has had to face a special problem in coordinating and disciplining the various state party units and their interests in the planning process. Like the distribution of the power system within the government, the authority structure of the Congress party has changed substantially over the past two decades. The formal structure of authority as it is spelled out in the Congress Constitution provides for a highly centralized party. The working committee, parliamentary board, and central election committees are given vast powers over the party organization, the coordination of party-government relations, and candidate selection. As chief executive of the party, the working committee has the power to superintend, direct, and control all subordinate Congress committees, and it is this organ which also invokes sanctions for breaches of party discipline and takes all actions it sees fit to further the interest of the Congress party.

Because of its growth as a centralized political organization, the central leadership of the Congress party has always felt that many political areas required some degree of national uniformity. After independence, the party considered it convenient for the working committee to attempt to establish national policy on planning which could be used as a model by the states. As the working committee was also the chief executive of the party at the national level, Congress discipline could be invoked whenever necessary to persuade the state Congress ministries to take action in general accord with the all-India policy agreed upon by the central government and the chief ministers in the working committee. Party discipline could also be invoked to control insurgence by a member of the mass organization. Although the working committee's policy-coordinating role has not solved all the difficulties of center-state relations, the handling of such pivotal decisions as those involved in planning and language policies leaves little doubt that coordination would have been even more difficult had it not been for the working committee.[13]

As a coordinator of center-state relations, the working committee came to handle both planning and nonplanning issues. Its role in these areas has varied considerably over the past two decades. During the early years following independence, the working committee was the sole arena in which center and state leaders could discuss policy objectives. In course of time it also became a significant center for coordination. In drawing up the First Five Year Plan, Jawaharlal Nehru relied extensively on the working committee to develop all-India policies for those matters under the constitutional jurisdiction of the states, such as land reform. But with its creation, the National Development Council largely has acquired the responsibility for coordinating center-state relations in planning. The working committee, however, still supplements the newly created machinery in performing a role it once had monopolized. Its role in coordinating center-state relations and establishing an all-India policy cannot be minimized.

To dominate the working committee within the Congress party structure is, therefore, to control the mass organization. For, although the formal structure of power recognizes the working committee as simply the executive arm of the Congress party, charged with carrying out the program laid down by the All India Congress Committee and the Annual Sessions, the informal and actual structure of power is quite the reverse (Kochanek, 1968a:433). It is the working committee which makes policy for the mass organization. The "official resolutions" submitted for ratification to the AICC and Annual Sessions are seldom modified or rejected. When serious challenges do occur at such meetings, they are usually manifestations of divisions within the dominant elite, and they involve attempts to mobilize support by and for antagonistic points of view within the leadership. Through the working committee, therefore, the parliamentary leadership is in a strategic position to control the mass organization and ensure party-government coordination. "The issue of party-government relations is more often than not a matter of intra-party factionalism, in which the dialogue of competition for ultimate power in the parliamentary wing disguises itself as the problem of coordinating parliamentary and organizational wings" (Kochanek, 1968a:433).

Most other political parties have modeled their internal organization on the pattern of the Congress party, with some differences among them in their manner of working and the character of their internal mechanisms for arriving at decisions and policies. Party discipline is invoked in more or less the same way and through the same type of party organs by these other political parties, although perhaps not with the same effectiveness.

THE EMERGENCY AND THE PLANNING PROCESS

Events in India after the declaration of emergency on 27 June 1975 raised speculation as to the future of parliamentary processes, but we were concerned only with changes in the planning process that might have resulted from these developments. Under the Constitution, a declaration of emergency does not by itself automatically set aside parliamentary procedures or dissolve any duly constituted parliamentary committees in existence. Parliament, however, may on its own through a resolution suspend any of its regular procedures or rules of business and modify its timetable to facilitate consideration of more urgent issues. This is precisely what happened in the monsoon session of the Indian Parliament, which took place after the declaration of emergency from 21 July to 10 August 1975. Some of the regular features of the parliamentary session, like the question hour, and some other provisions of the rules of business of the Lok Sabha were temporarily suspended by the Parliament through its own resolution. None of the duly constitued committees of the Parliament were either dissolved or altered in composition. All continued to function, with an emphasis on consideration of the issues in the changed environment of an emergency. In the second session of the Parliament after the emergency, beginning on 5 January 1976, none of the existing provisions for parliamentary business were suspended, and parliamentary procedures were adhered to as usual.

There were, however, substantial changes in the issues being discussed before the Parliament, those arising out of the declaration of emergency coming before the Parliament and others being relegated to the background. The economic policies embodied in the Five Year Plans were replaced by the issue of the success of the 20-point economic program formulated and implemented by the government after the declaration of emergency. However, the ultimate objectives of the two programs did not differ substantially. Efforts to revise proposals for the Fifth Plan because of the changed circumstances still had to be reconsidered by the plan committees of the Parliament. Neither the emergency nor the subsequent election of a non-Congress government has given rise to changes in the planning procedure that have not been initiated through the Parliament's own resolution. Changes made in this fashion have always been possible irrespective of emergencies, governments in office, or parties in power. One might, of course, find a radical change in the tone, the ideas, the temper, and the different approaches of the members in the course of committee and parliamentary debates on these questions of planning.

## NOTES

1. For a text of the Cabinet Resolution No. T–P(c)/50 dated 15 March 1950 and the term of reference of the Planning Commission, see Republic of India, Estimates Committee (1958:24–36). Also see Republic of India, Administration Reforms Commission (1967:34–37).

2. The National Development Council (NDC) is a central high-level organization for coordinating policies and programs of central and state governments. It is comprised of the prime minister as the chairman, and the chief ministers of the state government. From a strictly legal point of view, the NDC like the Planning Commission is essentially an advisory body. However, since it is comprised of the highest political authorities in the country, it has, by convention, acquired a unique position and its recommendations are treated with the greatest deference by the central ministries and the state governments.

The meetings of the National Development Council are held at least twice a year, its standing committee meets frequently, and various specialized committees may also be formed. Thus, for example, formulating the Fourth Plan, the council set up five committees to deal with (1) industry, (2) social services, (3) development of hill areas, (4) agriculture and irrigation, and (5) industry, power, and transport. The Council has evolved into an administrative agency to achieve the fullest cooperation and coordination in planning between the central and the state governments and to ensure uniformity of approach and unanimity in the working of the national plan. The main functions of the Council are: (1) to prescribe guidelines for the formulation of the national plan, including the assessment of resources for plans; (2) to consider the national plan as formulated by the Planning Commission; (3) to consider important questions of social and economic policy affecting national development; and (4) to review the working of the plan from time to time and recommend such measures as are necessary for achieving the aims and targets set out in the national plan. The NDC gives its advice at various stages of the formulation of the plan and it is only after its approval has been obtained that a plan is presented to Parliament for consideration. The Council has been largely responsible for giving Indian Plans a truly national character and for ensuring a national unanimity in approach and uniformity in working.

3. Adapted from Shakdher (1974:518).

4. See Jain (1975).

5. Adapted from Shakdher (1974:515).

6. See, for example, Mr. M. R. Masani's motion on the Draft Fifth Five Year Plan (Republic of India, Lok Sabha, 1969:cols. 202–207).

7. For details see Republic of India, Lok Sabha (1974b:xi).

8. For an empirical analysis of the decision-making process at the level of Panchayati Raj institutions, see Dubey (1975:75–84).

9. For details see Hanson (1966:27–28).

10. See Republic of India, Lok Sabha (Second) (1958:vol. 15, cols. 10007–84, 10096–126, 10208–91, 10296–332, 10333, 10342, 10343–50, 10432–546; vol. 13, cols. 5891–92, 5894–957, 5969–86, 8115–203, 8569–613, 8616, 8617–87). Also quoted by Hanson (1966:157).

11. See my analysis of the discussion of the Third Five Year Plan in the parliamentary committees and in the House earlier in the chapter.

12. This happened at the Bangalore session of the Congress party in 1969 on the question of nationalization of banks between Mrs. Indira Gandhi and Mr. Morarji Desai (the prime minister and the deputy prime minister at the time and the top party leaders), which resulted in the ultimate resignation of Mr. Morarji Desai from the party and the party split. Similarly Professor Balraj Madhok, an influential member of the Jana Sangh and its MP, had to resign from his party when he differed sharply from the party ideology in 1973. He later joined a newly established party Bhartiya Lok Dal.

13. For details see Kochanek (1968a:188–189).

*Chapter 9*

## LEGISLATURES AND POPULATION POLICY IN THE THIRD WORLD

TERRY L. McCOY

In the 1960s rapid population growth was seen increasingly as a serious obstacle threatening the development of Asia, Africa, and Latin America. Pressures grew on national governments in these areas to adopt measures designed to decrease the rate of demographic expansion. Concern for the "population explosion" sweeping the Third World culminated in Bucharest, Rumania, where representatives of the world's nations gathered in August of 1974, World Population Year, to attend the World Population Conference. If we assume uncontrolled population growth to be an urgent problem in need of solution—and there are those who do not share this assumption— then the extent of legislative involvement in contributing to its resolution is an indication of both the way and extent to which legislatures may be positive forces for modernization. The purpose of this chapter is to assess the role of national legislative institutions in the making and implementation of Third World population policies. It reviews the causes of and possible means of controlling rapid population growth, analyzes the participation of national legislatures in the population policy process up to this point, and seeks to interpret the findings of this case study in terms of the broader theme of legislatures and development, or more specifically the consequences of the former for the latter (Packenham, 1970).

[242]

## THE PROBLEM AND GOVERNMENT INTERVENTION

Most experts define population policy objectives to include controlling composition and distribution along with size and growth (Eldridge, 1968:381–382). By this definition few if any of the world's nations, developed or underdeveloped, have population policies per se. Rather they have policies or programs that affect—directly or indirectly, intentionally or unintentionally—one or two of the principal demographic variables. Developed countries, for example, tend to be concerned with population distribution while less developed countries are increasingly turning their attention to size and growth, perhaps at the expense of distributional and compositional problems that might in the long run prove to be just as troublesome. In this chapter population policy encompasses only those government activities relevant to the rate of growth of a nation's population. To be precise we are concerned with what might best be called "fertility control measures," commonly called "family planning programs," though we shall refer to them as population policies.

The size and rate of growth of national populations are the products of the balance between emigration and immigration and the balance between mortality and fertility. Although historically important in the settlement of some Third World countries (e.g., Argentina, Brazil, Rhodesia), immigration is no longer a significant source of national growth. And, despite the fact that emigration continues to act as a demographic escape valve for some densely populated regions, such as the Caribbean islands (Ebanks et al., 1975), it cannot do so indefinitely. The decline in migration as a growth factor is in large part due to the relative ease with which it could be regulated by the state (for a proposal to tighten up United States immigration, especially from Latin America, see United States Domestic Council Committee on Illegal Aliens, 1976). Moreover, migration can be only a factor in the growth and decline of national or specific populations, not of the world population because migration involves only redistribution and not a change in numbers. Discounting migration, then, we are left with mortality and fertility, or more precisely an imbalance between the two, as the cause of the current population explosion.

Until the nineteenth century, long-term population growth rates throughout the world were at very low levels due to conditions of high mortality that balanced correspondingly high fertility. Then, as industrialization occurred in Europe and North America, death rates began to decline, producing a temporary acceleration in the overall growth rate which lasted until birth rates also declined for a variety of reasons, the details of which are subject to some dispute among demographers. On entering the latter half of the twentieth century, fertility was back in balance with mortality in developed countries of the world, and their growth rates were under one percent per year and approaching zero. The irony of the demographic transition in the industrial world, and the reason for lingering uncertainty as to the causes of fertility decline, is that it occurred without any social intervention let alone government policy.

As with other aspects of modernization, the demographic transition was delayed in Asia, Africa, and Latin America. It began in the early part of this century and has yet to be completed, which is what the population explosion is all about. With the transfer of modern techniques of death control—public sanitation, epidemiology, nutrition—from the developed countries to their colonies and economic dependencies, death rates, particularly infant mortality, dropped precipitously. The decline was so steep and so quick that it left fertility out of balance, and overall growth rates shot up from between 1 and 2 percent to over 3 percent per year (Hauser in *Rapid Population Growth*, 1971:103–122). Consequently, it is not uncommon to find countries in the Third World whose populations are doubling every 20 to 25 years. Understandably, such a prospect is viewed with great alarm by most observers. In addition to the Malthusian spectre of famine, an image brought alive in the 1970s by developments in Bangladesh and the Sahel region of Africa, experts point out that a rapidly growing population diverts scarce resources from direct productive investments into social infrastructure and public welfare. Continuation of such allocation patterns would eventually bring economic development to a halt and, by implication, produce widespread sociopolitical unrest.

With the exception of a dwindling number of countries, such as Saudi Arabia, which refused to participate in the World Population Conference, and Argentina, which recently adopted a set of pronatalist measures, there is growing consensus that for the Third World continued high fertility constitutes a genuine problem on which governments must act. One scholar goes so far as to argue that "no other index divides the world so sharply into 'developed' and 'underdeveloped' as does fertility" (Daly, 1970:567). Beyond recognizing that fertility is a problem, there is uncertainty over how to lower it, an uncertainty in turn reflected in disagreement over the appropriate role of government.

It is possible to identify three positions on the question of fertility control. First, there are the "developmentalists," those specialists who argue that fertility will decline when, and only when, the society experiences general socioeconomic development. According to this view, popular in the Third World (Mauldin et al., 1974), measures aimed at controlling births and planning families are doomed to failure unless the environment is conducive to smaller families. In economic terms the problem is not one of insufficient supply but lack of demand for contraceptive services. Government must, therefore, focus its efforts on general development and not be diverted by population-control measures. To buttress their case, proponents of the developmentalist position point to the historical experience of the developed countries as proof that the transition to low fertility will occur only as a result of larger societal changes. At the other extreme from the developmentalist are the "population planners." They begin with the assumption that development will *not* occur without *first* lowering fertility. Given the fact that lower fertility is the key to development, population measures are central to any development strategy, and no effort should be spared in slowing the growth rate. In essence, demographic developments are too crucial to be left to voluntary decisions but must be planned and strictly regulated. In its pure form this position has few adherents because of its coercive implications; however, the experience of centrally planned societies like China and the realization that voluntary efforts have real limitations may increase the attractiveness of population planning for the Third World (see Berelson, 1970:9). Finally, the "family planners" argue that, if supplied with the information and means, individual couples will voluntarily limit their offspring and national fertility rates will drop.

Occupying the middle ground between waiting for development and coercing behavior, the family planning approach currently dominates world population policies. Its popularity also reflects the pressures and financial support of a network of developed nations and international organizations which has vigorously promoted family planning in the Third World over the last decade (see McCoy, 1974). The heart of a national policy based on family planning is a system of clinics, offering contraceptive services, which is typically administered by the ministry of health (maternal and child health section— MCH). The clinics may also be supplemented with educational and communications components.

In analyzing the contribution of legislative bodies to population policies, we shall therefore focus on legislative participation in the evolution of a national system of family planning activities. It is appropriate, however, to point out that in the last few years several Third World governments have begun to experiment with "beyond family planning" measures such as antinatalist incentives and institutional reforms (McCoy, 1975). This trend, which can be expected to continue, represents the beginning of reconciliation among the developmentalist, population planning, and family planning approaches to fertility control (Rich, 1973; Teitlebaum, 1974). We shall consider the implication of this trend for legislature and population policy making in the concluding section.

## LEGISLATURES AND POPULATION POLICY

The objective of this section is to map out what roles national legislative bodies have played in the making of population policies up to this time. We will consider: (1) an aggregate comparison of 107 less developed countries; and (2) available case study materials.

### CROSS NATIONAL PATTERNS

A summary of the raw data for this comparative inquiry, data covering virtually the entire current universe of less developed countries, is found in the Appendix at the end of this chapter. In order to compare such a large number of cases, substantial data reduction was necessary; therefore, a few words about the coding are appropriate even though the Appendix contains a more detailed explanation. In classifying national policies we relied on Nortman (1974) who distinguishes among countries with "no policy to reduce the growth rate and no support of family planning activities" (coded 0, None), those with "official support of family planning activities for other than demographic reasons" (coded 1, Family Planning Activities), and countries with an "official policy to reduce the population growth rate" (coded 2, Antinatalist). The countries in the first category tend to have pronatalist policies while the essential difference between the latter two categories is intent. Countries where the government is on record favoring population reduction go in 2 while those with family planning activities but no demographic objectives are coded 1. To a certain extent it is valid to think of those in category 2 as having stronger, more antinatalist policies than those in 1 although there are some important exceptions, such as Cuba in Latin America.

Likewise, countries in category 2 are more likely to have gone beyond family planning to change fertility.

In classifying national legislative bodies, the distinction was made among those countries where none existed (0, None), those with a legislature of no significant power (1, Nominal), and countries with an independent, influential legislative body (2, Significant). Countries with appointed legislatures, one-party regimes, or under military rule were put in the nominal category unless there was evidence to the contrary; whereas those with what Sisson and Snowiss (chapter 2, this volume) refer to as "law-affecting" legislatures fall in the last category. In searching for a legislature's specific participation in population policy making (as opposed to its general policy-making role), the author examined a wide variety of sources looking for any reference to legislative intervention. Given the nature of the data generated, the findings of this exercise must be considered preliminary. They should, however, establish a basis for subsequent inquiry.

By mid-1975, almost two-thirds of the governments in the Third World had initiated some kind of fertility control effort (see Table 9.1). Regionally, certain Asian nations moved first and furthest. Although the Latin Americans got a later start, all but two of these countries had abandoned traditional policies by 1975. Clearly lagging behind, Africa is still moving in the same direction. There is every reason to expect that the shift toward fertility control will continue. In fact, it is not inconceivable that in another decade virtually all less developed countries will have undertaken family planning activities and that most of these activities will be openly justified in terms of decreasing population growth.[1] What does the cross-national ecological analysis indicate about the role of national legislative bodies in this movement toward fertility control?

Of the seventy decisions to initiate or strengthen a control policy, 83 percent occurred in regimes with legislatures. So there is preliminary evidence that legislatures could be instrumental in effective population policy development (see Table 9.2). But in only slightly over one-fourth (18) could they generally be considered significant participants in public policy making. Therefore, the analysis thus far is inconclusive, for although the presence of legislatures is associated with policy development, the power of legislatures in policy development is highly questionable. Regionally, legislatures are most closely associated with the emergence of antinatalist policies in Asia and Latin America.

TABLE 9.1

THIRD WORLD POPULATION POLICIES BY REGION

| Policy | Region | | | |
|---|---|---|---|---|
| | Africa | Asia | Latin America | All |
| | (44) | (38) | (25) | (107) |
| None (0) | 50% | 42% | 8% | 37% |
| Family Planning Activities (1) | 34 | 13 | 72 | 36 |
| Antinatalist (2) | 16 | 45 | 20 | 27 |
| | 100% | 100% | 100% | 100% |

Source: See the Appendix.

TABLE 9.2

STATUS OF NATIONAL LEGISLATURE DURING YEAR OF POPULATION POLICY ADOPTION

| Legislature | Region | | | |
|---|---|---|---|---|
| | Africa[a] | Asia[b] | Latin America[c] | All |
| | (22) | (24) | (24) | (70) |
| None (0) | 27% | 8% | 17% | 17% |
| Nominal (1) | 55 | 71 | 46 | 57 |
| Significant (2) | 18 | 21 | 37 | 26 |
| | 100% | 100% | 100% | 100% |

a. Ghana classified as nominal.
b. Sri Lanka classified as nominal. China and Taiwan classified twice because of two fundamental policy decisions.
c. Grenada classified as nominal. Mexico classified twice.
Source: See the Appendix.

In considering future prospects for legislative intervention in population policy making, we must first note the general decline of legislative institutions in the Third World. Table 9.3 shows that only 66 percent of the 107 less developed countries had legislatures as of 1975, and of these, only 17 percent could be considered of serious law-affecting capacity. During the several months of 1975 when the author was working on this project, the national assemblies of two important countries—Bangladesh and India—were respectively eliminated and downgraded. Clearly, only a few Third World coun-

### TABLE 9.3
### STATUS OF NATIONAL LEGISLATURE, 1975

|  | Region | | | |
|---|---|---|---|---|
| **Status** | **Africa**[a] | **Asia**[b] | **Latin America**[c] | **All** |
|  | (44) | (38) | (25) | (107) |
| None (0) | 43% | 26% | 32% | 34% |
| Nominal (1) | 48 | 58 | 36 | 49 |
| Significant (2) | 9 | 16 | 32 | 17 |
|  | 100% | 100% | 100% | 100% |

a. Guinea Bissau classified as nominal.
b. Laos classified as none, United Arab Emirates as nominal.
c. Grenada classified as nominal.
Source: See the Appendix.

### TABLE 9.4
### LEGISLATURES AND POPULATION POLICIES

|  | Legislature (1 or 2) | No legislature (0) |
|---|---|---|
|  | (85)[a] | (25) |
| Policy (1 or 2) | 68% | 48% |
| No policy (0) | 32 | 52 |
|  | 100% | 100% |

a. China, Taiwan, and Mexico counted twice.
Source: See the Appendix, pages 257–261.

tries even have legislatures with the potential of revising existing policies or initiating new ones. Of the 57 countries with legislatures at the time they settled on a national population policy, 14 either eliminated or downgraded (a trend most pronounced in Latin America) these bodies completely (albeit six of the 67 with policies either gained a legislature or had the existing one strengthened). Thirteen of the 40 countries with no policy have no legislature; in only three can it be considered significant.

Table 9.4 summarizes the relationship between legislatures and population policies derived from the aggregate data on 107 less developed countries. Since it documents a positive correlation ($Q = .40$) between the existence of a legislative body and the adoption of fertility control measures, we cannot exclude the possibility that legislatures do participate in population policy making even though we have also encountered evidence challenging such a conclusion.[2] Consequently, we must now look behind these highly aggregated associations for information on specific legislature inputs.

## POLICY SPECIFIC PARTICIPATION

Legislatures cannot assist in the effort to control population growth if they do not exist. Yet despite the unmistakable Third World drift away from democratic parliamentary regimes, in a significant minority of countries legislatures survive as independent, visible participants in policy making. Moreover, even a majority of those countries which have opted for authoritarianism choose not to eliminate the legislature completely (see Linz, chapter 4 in this volume). In this section we go beyond the mere presence or absence of legislative bodies in search of what specific roles they have played in the elaboration and execution of population policies. The findings for each country are briefly summarized in the last column of the Appendix. When, after searching through all available country materials, we could find no reference to legislative participation in population policy making, we entered a notation of "n.e." (no evidence of any role), indicating that in our judgment the legislature played no role. The underlying assumption operating here is that no mention of the legislature implies that its role in the policy process was at most secondary. This would have to be the most common finding of the exercise, and from it we are forced to conclude that the presence of a legislature, even a relatively strong one, does not guarantee significant intervention in population policy making. Nor, according to our findings, does legislative participation always contribute to the evolution of strong, effective policy. As we now elaborate on these conclusions, it is prudent to bear in mind the tentative nature of the evidence.

One would hardly expect the initiative for government intervention to control fertility to come from the legislature in countries with a tradition of executive dominance. Even in the United States where the three branches of government are constitutionally coequal, responsibility for policy initiation has traditionally fallen on the president. Although there are rare references to members introducing family planning bills in parliament (e.g., Brazil: Johnson, 1970:26–28) in defiance of traditional policy, the initiation of successful changes in population policy has almost universally come from the executive branch. Third World legislators have not sought to convert the latent support of women for family planning (elicited in KAP—Knowledge,

Attitudes, and Practice—surveys) into official policy. Quite to the contrary, male-dominated legislatures often oppose family planning in spite of the apparent reservoir of public support. Interestingly, in Guatemala it was a woman deputy who submitted a bill to strengthen the family planning program (Watson and Lapham, 1975:273). Even when *legislators* strongly support family planning and population control, such as in El Salvador, the *legislature* has not pushed for policies reflecting these views (Verner, 1975 and 1977). Not only do population policies usually not originate in the legislature, in many cases they come into existence without legislative authorization. Although there are exceptions, like India and Barbados, where a legislative commission first recommended action be taken to deal with excessive growth (UNICA, 1976), most current policies got their start through administrative orders (from the minister of health expanding MCH to include family planning) and/or executive decrees (from the president's establishing a national population council). For instance, the policies of Chile and Costa Rica, which at the time had the strongest legislatures in Latin America (along with Uruguay; Astiz, 1973:115), began without congressional approval. In countries with comprehensive implementing legislation, congressional authorization is many times a pro forma approval of executive action (Mexico, Iran, and Taiwan for example).

National legislatures usually have not served to represent popular will, nor even special interests, in either initiating policy consideration or legislating policy decisions. They have been largely uninvolved in either of the two aforementioned direct "law-affecting" activities. They have, nevertheless, played other, albeit less important, roles in the making of population policy.

Even in the absence of major legislation, there is often evidence of parliamentary debates being conducted on government population policy. Not infrequently these feature the opponents of population control casting the issue in an unfavorable, polemical light. Two of the most common critiques raised are those of the nationalist, attacking family planning programs as a foreign plot to keep less developed countries weak, and the Marxist, which rejects such services as an attempt to divert popular pressure for more fundamental change (see Stycos, 1974:5–14). It seems safe to assume that parliamentary debates which highlight these views have an inhibiting effect on government action. The same has been true of congressional investigations of population-related programs. The Brazilian Congress, for instance, focused public attention on the family planning services of foreign missionaries in the Amazon basin by branding them as "genocide" in an official investigation (Daly, 1970:556). Such legislative publicity no doubt reinforced official opposition to population control in Brazil. However, in those countries where the executive branch is committed to a population policy (now including Brazil), congressional debate and hearings provide a semblance of popular participation and freedom to oppose, but there is little evidence of substantive impact on official policy. In Mexico an opposition deputy in the heat of debate linked the president's comprehensive population bill to United States imperialism, but the measure subsequently became law by unanimous consent (Turner, 1974:7). Likewise political controversy emerged in the debate on Morocco's policy but once again without apparently deleterious effects.

The one aspect of policy making which has experienced significant participation by legislative assemblies is appropriations. Even where authorized by executive decree, the legislature can exert influence on population activities through its budgetary powers. Although these vary from nation to nation, there are documented instances of legislatures refusing to grant appropriations or to increase them. The Venezuelan Congress initially approved granting public funds to the private family association but then refused to sanction any expansion in public financing until recently (I. S. Wiarda, 1974:337; Gonzalez Cerrutti and Kar, 1975:7–8). On the other hand, no instances of a legislature appropriating more funds than requested, or even pushing for more funds, were discovered. Presumably legislatures could exert similar control over population programs through their participation in reviewing and approving national development plans, though there is no evidence of their having done so.

Review of available country materials tends to strengthen the view that legislatures have taken a back seat to executives and bureaucracies in the shaping of national population policies. In very few countries do we find the legislature centrally involved in initiating, formulating, legislating, and revising public efforts to bring population growth under control. Where there has been legislative intervention, it has come often in the form of either symbolic legitimization of executive proposals or occasionally obstructionist opposition to standard policy measures. As Third World population policies have evolved thus far there is little to support the proposition that legislatures contribute to the battle against rapid population growth. On occasion they appear to have detracted from it.

## CONCLUSIONS

Three factors help explain the marginal, sometimes negative role played by legislative institutions and put the findings of this case study into broader perspective. The first is the simple fact that many less developed countries have no legislature to participate in policy making. The second and third factors concern the nature of those legislative bodies which do exist and the special character of the policy in question. The institutional and environmental attributes which constrict the influence of Third World legislatures in general unquestionably limit their role in population policy making. The absence of adequate staff support and weakness, or nonexistence, of standing committees make it difficult for the legislature to build and maintain the technical expertise required for informed participation in population policy making. The very instability and discontinuity of Third World legislatures render it even more unlikely that they can acquire individual or collective mastery of the matter. Their unrepresentativeness, particularly of lower class and female viewpoints, often combines with a weak identification of the legislator with his constituency (sometimes reinforced by the absence of residency requirements) to insulate lawmakers from domestic support, albeit largely latent, for public family planning services. Ironically the individual legislator may be growing closer to his constituents as the legislature's power as an institution declines (see Barkan in this volume). This development is not likely to increase the legislature's law-affecting powers in population matters, although it may involve legislators as intermediaries between the people and the family planning bureaucracy. Finally, constitutional and political conditions combined with tradition usually give the executive a preponderance of power, thus relegating the congress, parliament, or national assembly to reactive, symbolic roles. Provisions for states of siege, legislating by executive decree, and item vetos are common in most Third World constitutions. Under them, the legislature can either oppose or go along with little positive power to create policy. Its powers are typically negative in character. Through control of the purse strings (often quite attenuated) a congress could refuse to fund the president's family planning program, but it would be hard put to generate alternatives. Behind such constitutional arrangements increasingly lies the concentration of political power in executive hands, through miliary rule and/or the one-party state.

Thus far we have focused on the general characteristics of legislatures in search of possible explanations for the weakness of their intervention in population policy making. However, despite these constraints, it would be a mistake to generalize from this case study to legislative participation in other policies. There is evidence in the other contributions to this volume, and the author is personally convinced through previous research on agrarian reform, that Third World legislative bodies do play more significant roles than they have thus far in the making of this particular policy. Consequently, we are led to population policy as a variable helping to explain legislative performance.

Over the last decade, one of the most alarming aspects of the population question for Western observers is the apparent casualness with which it is taken in most Third World countries. Although more and more governments in Asia, Africa, and Latin America are adopting fertility control measures, there is still a pronounced discrepancy in the urgency assigned population control by the developed Western (but not Eastern) nations and those in the Third World. This gap was evident at the 1974 World Population Conference in Bucharest (Mauldin et al., 1974). Instead of acting on population growth as a top national priority, most Third World governments have given it marginal consideration. Instead of integrating population policy into their overall development strategy, it is buried in a minor division of a secondary ministry, MCH in the ministry of health. Instead of educating their people in the urgency of fertility control, most governments have chosen to frame their newly initiated family planning services in other than antinatalist terms. To be sure there are exceptions to these generalizations. There are a few countries, most notably in South and East Asia, with strong, increasingly comprehensive population control policies. They are still exceptions, however, for most less developed countries do not have genuine antinatalist policies. What they have are isolated family planning programs with indirect or no demographic objectives.

It is hardly surprising that national legislatures have not devoted much time or attention to minor programs in the ministry of health for which there is little active public support or political payoff. What often attracts their consideration is not the substance of current family planning efforts but their foreign support. Once again, with some notable exceptions such as India, China, and Cuba, the most enthusiastic proponents of population control in the Third World have been outsiders. It is precisely the persistence of outside pressure and existence of massive foreign assistance for population control that have been points of contention in many legislative assemblies. The issue becomes one of nationalism and outside intervention in domestic politics. No Third World government wants to appear as though it has caved in to foreign pressures for anything, much less demands that it control national population growth. Consequently, the common strategy has been to avoid confrontation in the legislative and public arenas by quietly grafting family planning services on to existing health programs. Demographic objectives are played down, if not denied altogether, in favor of maternal and child health care rationales.

The international family planning establishment, dominated by such organizations as the International Planned Parenthood Federation, Population Council, and United States Agency for International Development (the major donor of population-related assistance), has supported the low visibility strategy as a means of getting a foot in the door, which they assume then can be opened wide at some subsequent point for a more frontal attack on rapid population growth. It seems clear, however, that a policy of serious antinatalist intent has two requirements—a series of comprehensive measures beyond family planning and the commitment of internal resources—that entail controversy and national debate. The decision to move from a policy based on largely foreign-financed voluntary birth control services to one encompassing a wide range of measures (liberalized abortion and sterilization, direct incentives to limit family size, societal reforms to provide women alternative roles, expanded social security coverage) integrated into the overall national development effort is unlikely to go unnoticed. Rather it would probably take on the dimensions of a full-fledged policy debate in which all important national groups and institutions intervene. Therefore, as Third World governments shift from foreign-backed family planning approaches to comprehensive domestic attempts to control population growth, their legislative bodies may become more centrally involved in policy making. Among countries with legislative bodies evidence of this possibility comes from the current experiences of South Korea, Singapore, and Sri Lanka (Watson and Lapham, 1975:226, 236, and 258). History indicates that initial legislative intervention may not necessarily be functional to policy development in the direction desired by foreign observers and lending agencies, but where legislative approval is finally achieved national policy is likely to reflect a more committed, complete, and integrated attack on the problem.

By way of summary, this study of 107 less developed countries has found that, although there is an ecological correlation between antinatalist population policies and the existence of legislatures, these institutions have not been at the forefront of the drive to slow population growth in Asia, Africa, and Latin America. In part this is due to the absence of or pronounced subordination of Third World legislatures, but it also reflects the nature of population policies, which in fact are usually not policies but merely foreign-induced family planning programs. If population control efforts involve other than family planning programs in the future, we expect the participation of existing legislative bodies to increase, while still maintaining relative inferiority to the executive branch. If these conclusions are valid—and the necessity of subjecting them to more intensive, systematic testing must be reiterated—they would coincide with the arguments of experts like Rich (1973), Teitelbaum (1974), and Berelson (1970) as well as the preference of many Third World governments (Mauldin et al., 1974) to abandon family planning in favor of a more integrated developmental approach bringing rapid population growth under control. While such a strategy might tax the patience of international lending agencies, initially its long-run demographic results should be greater than those promised by current population control programs. Finally, our study suggests that in analyzing the consequences of legislatures for development one must carefully consider the policy or issue involved as a variable explaining legislative behavior. In general, it seems safe to conclude that the more important the issue, the more likely the legislature is to be involved, although seldom if ever, in a position of leadership.

## NOTES

*The author acknowledges the assistance of both the Center for Latin American Studies at the University of Florida and the Mershon Center at the Ohio State University.*

1. Although comparatively rare, a few countries have moved in the opposite direction, most notably Argentina in 1973. More recently the government of Uruguay imposed a new tax on contraceptives "in an attempt to get the birth rate up," according to *Latin America*, October 3, 1975, p. 307. Both countries have low fertility and growth rates.

2. The value of Yule's Q (a measure of association for $2 \times 2$ tables) actually increases to .62 when the "Nominal" legislative category is combined with the "None" category rather than with the "Significant" category.

APPENDIX

## INDICATORS OF LEGISLATIVE PARTICIPATION IN THE POPULATION POLICY MAKING OF 107 THIRD WORLD COUNTRIES

| Country | Policy[a] | Year adopted[b] | National Legislature[c] adoption year | National Legislature[c] 1975 | Legislative role in population policy[d] |
|---|---|---|---|---|---|
| **Africa** | | | | | |
| Algeria | 1 | 1971 | 0 | 0 | — |
| Botswana | 2 | 1970 | 2 | 2 | Population in development plan |
| Burundi | 0 | — | — | 0 | — |
| Cameroun | 0 | — | — | 1 | n.e. |
| Central African Republic | | — | — | 0 | — |
| Chad | 0 | — | — | 0 | n.e. |
| Congo | 0 | — | 0 | 1 | n.e. |
| Dahomey | 1 | 1969 | 1 | 0 | |
| Egypt | 2 | 1965 | | 1 | Established by executive decree |
| Equatorial Guinea | 0 | — | — | 1 | n.e. |
| Ethiopia | 0 | — | — | 0 | Statistics legislation |
| Gabon | 0 | — | — | 1 | n.e. |
| Gambia | 1 | 1969 | 2 | 2 | n.e. |
| Ghana | 2 | 1969 | 0→1 | 0 | Possible role, 1969–1971 |
| Guinea | 0 | — | — | 1 | n.e. |
| Guinea Bissau | 0 | — | — | (?) | — |
| Ivory Coast | 0 | — | — | 1 | Pronatalist legislation |
| Kenya | 2 | 1966 | 1 | 1 | Probably debated by parliament |
| Lesotho | 1 | 1972 | 0 | 0 | — |
| Liberia | 1 | 1973 | 1 | 1 | n.e. |
| Libya | 0 | — | — | 0 | — |

APPENDIX, *continued*

| Country | Policy[a] | Year adopted[b] | National Legislature[c] adoption year | National Legislature[c] 1975 | Legislative role in population policy[d] |
|---|---|---|---|---|---|
| Malagasy Republic | 0 | — | — | 0 | — |
| Malawi | 0 | — | — | 1 | n.e. |
| Mali | 0 | — | — | 0 | — |
| Mauritania | 0 | — | — | 1 | n.e. |
| Mauritius | 2 | 1968 | 2 | 2 | Legislative debate, probably more |
| Morocco | 2 | 1968 | 1 | 1 | Evidence of political controversy |
| Niger | 0 | — | — | 0 | — |
| Nigeria | 1 | 1970 | 0 | 0 | — |
| Rhodesia | 1 | 1968 | 1 | 1 | n.e. |
| Rwanda | 0 | — | — | 0 | — |
| Senegal | 0 | — | — | 1 | n.e. |
| Sierra Leone | 1 | 1973 | 2 | 2 | n.e. |
| Somalia | 0 | — | — | 0 | — |
| South Africa | 1 | 1966 | 1 | 1 | n.e. |
| Sudan | 1 | 1970 | 0 | 0 | — |
| Swaziland | 1 | 1970 | 1 | 0 | n.e. |
| Tanzania | 1 | 1970 | 1 | 1 | n.e. |
| Togo | 0 | — | — | 0 | — |
| Tunisia | 2 | 1964 | 1 | 1 | Wide range of legislation |
| Uganda | 1 | 1972 | 0 | 0 | — |
| Upper Volta | 0 | — | — | 1 | n.e. |
| Zaire | 1 | 1973 | 1 | 1 | n.e. |
| Zambia | 1 | 1973 | 1 | 1 | n.e. |

**Asia**

| Country | | | | | |
|---|---|---|---|---|---|
| Afghanistan | 1 | 1970 | 1 | 0 | Evidence of limited role |
| Bahrain | 0 | – | – | 1 | n.e. |
| Bangladesh | 2 | 1971 | 1 | 0 | Probable role |
| Bhutan | 0 | – | – | 1 | n.e. |
| Burma | 0 | – | 1 | 1 | n.e. |
| China | 2 | 1957 (1) / 1962 (2) | 1 / 1 | 1 | Discussed by People's Congress |
| Fiji | 2 | 1970 | 2 | 2 | n.e. |
| India | 2 | 1952 | 2 | 1 | Apparently active role |
| Indonesia | 2 | 1968 | 1 | 1 | n.e. |
| Iran | 2 | 1967 | 1 | 1 | Parliamentary approval of programs |
| Iraq | 1 | 1972 | 0 | 0 (?) | — |
| Jordan | 0 | – | – | 1 | n.e. |
| Khmer Republic | 1 | 1973 | 1 | 0 | n.e. |
| North Korea | 0 | – | – | 1 | n.e. |
| South Korea | 2 | 1961 | 0 | 1 | Budgetary role and debate |
| Kuwait | 0 | – | – | 1 | n.e. |
| Lebanon | 0 | – | – | 2 | n.e. |
| Laos | 2 | 1972 | 1 | (?) 2 | n.e. |
| Malaysia | 2 | 1966 | 2 | 2 | Active role |
| Maldive Islands | 0 (?) | – | – | 1 | n.e. |
| Mongolia | 0 | – | – | 1 | n.e. |
| Nepal | 2 | 1966 | 1 | 1 | n.e. |
| Oman | 0 | – | – | 0 | — |
| Pakistan | 2 | 1960 | 1 | 1 | Possible role |
| Philippines | 2 | 1970 | 2 | 0 | Evidence of opposition |
| Qatar | 0 | – | – | 0 | n.e. |
| Saudi Arabia | 0 | – | – | 0 | — |
| Singapore | 2 | 1965 | 2 | 1 | Significant debate and legislation |
| Sri Lanka | 2 | 1965 | (?) | 2 | n.e. |
| Syria | 0 | – | – | 1 | n.e. |

APPENDIX, *continued*

| Country | Policy^a | Year adopted^b | National Legislature^c adoption year | National Legislature^c 1975 | Legislative role in population policy^d |
|---|---|---|---|---|---|
| Taiwan | 2 | 1959 (1) 1968 (2) | 1 | 1 | Legislative approval |
| Thailand | 2 | 1970 | 1 | 2 | n.e. |
| Turkey | 2 | 1965 | 1 | 2 | Two key laws |
| United Arab Emirates | 0 | – | – | (?) | — |
| N. Vietnam | 1 | 1962 | 1 | 1 | n.e. |
| S. Vietnam | 1 | 1971 | 1 | 0 | n.e. |
| Southern Yemen | 0 | – | – | 1 | — |
| Yemen | 0 | – | – | 1 | n.e. |
| **Latin America** | | | | | |
| Argentina | 0 | – | – | 2 | Recent pronatalist legislation |
| Bahamas | 1 | 1968 | 2 | 2 | n.e. |
| Bolivia | 1 | 1968 | 1 | 0 | n.e. |
| Brazil | 1 | 1974 | 1 | 1 | Debate, bills, investigation |
| Chile | 1 | 1966 | 2 | 0 | Apparently very limited |
| Colombia | 2 | 1970 | 2 | 2 | Significant debate and legislation |
| Costa Rica | 1 | 1968 | 2 | 2 | Legislated by executive decree |
| Cuba | 1 | 1962 | 0 | 0 | — |
| Dominican Republic | 2 | 1968 | 2 | 2 | Legislated by executive decree |
| Ecuador | 1 | 1968 | 2 | 0 | n.e. |
| El Salvador | 1→2 | 1968 | 1 | 1 | Presidential address to congress |
| Grenada | 1 | 1974 | (?) | (?) | n.e. |
| Guatemala | 1 | 1969 | 1 | 1 | Some pressure from congress |

| Country | [a] | [b] | [c] | [c] | [d] |
|---|---|---|---|---|---|
| Guyana | 0 | — | 0 | 2 | n.e. |
| Haiti | 1 | 1971 | 1 | 1 | n.e. |
| Honduras | 1 | 1966 | 1 | 0 | n.e. |
| Jamaica | 2 | 1966 | 2 | 2 | Significant legislation |
| Mexico | 2 | 1972 (1) 1974 (2) | 1 | 1 | Debate but unanimous support of executive proposals |
| Nicaragua | 1 | 1967 | 1 | 1 | n.e. |
| Panama | 1 | 1969 | 0 | 0 | — |
| Paraguay | 1 | 1972 | 1 | 1 | Seminars for legislators |
| Peru | 1 | 1975 | 0 | 0 | — |
| Trinidad Tobago | 2 | 1967 | 2 (?) | 1 | n.e. |
| Uruguay | 1→0 | 1974 | 0 | 0 | Recent pronatalist measures |
| Venezuela | 1 | 1968 | 2 | 2 | Opposition to funding |

a. Policy classification from Nortman, 1974. Coded as follows: 0 = no antinatalist policy nor government support for family planning activities (N=40); 1 = government support for family planning activities but not for population control reason (N=38); 2 = officially antinatalist policy and government support for family planning activities (N=29). Countries not classified in Nortman were classified using information in International Planned Parenthood Federation, 1974.

b. From Nortman, 1974, and International Planned Parenthood Federation, 1974.

c. Information in these two columns concerns the existence of some kind of national legislative body. The first refers to existence of such an institution during the year (see previous column) the policy was adopted. Coded as follows: 0 = no national legislative body; 1 = a nominal legislative body dominated by the executive branch and of little substantive influence; 2 = independent, representative, and influential national legislature. A dash (—) indicates not relevant; that is, no present population policy. In coding each country, the author consulted a variety of sources, such as Needler, 1970; Ismael, 1970; Rubin and Weinstein, 1974; Badgley, 1971; The Statesman's Yearbook 1974–1975, 1974; The Statesman's Yearbook 1975–1976, 1975; The International Year Book and Statesman's Who's Who, 1974; Deadline Data in World Affairs, n.d., and Stebbins and Amoia, 1973.

d. This column briefly summarizes evidence on the role of the national legislature in population policy making; n.e. indicates that there is no evidence of any legislative involvement. Information derived from a variety of sources, including Nortman, 1974; International Planned Parenthood Federation, 1974; United States Agency for International Development, 1974; Population Council, New York, 1969—; American Universities Field Staff, 1972–74; Watson and Lapham, 1975; and miscellaneous other case studies and reports.

# PART III
# LEGISLATORS AND DEVELOPMENT

*Chapter 10*

# BRINGING HOME THE PORK: LEGISLATOR BEHAVIOR, RURAL DEVELOPMENT, AND POLITICAL CHANGE IN EAST AFRICA

## JOEL D. BARKAN

A discussion of the role of the legislature in the developmental process of an agricultural society can well consider the question of whether and how legislatures contribute to rural development. Indeed, rural development, or the lack of it, constitutes the core of the crisis of underdevelopment which plagues most Third World states. Despite the green revolution, the rural areas, particularly in Africa, have experienced the lowest, often negative rates of economic growth during the last decade.[1] They have suffered the most from famine, population growth, and disease and have received the least in terms of income distribution[2] and government services. And, not surprisingly, it is in rural areas that the seeds of revolt and revolution have found the most fertile soil in which to grow.[3]

The problems of rural development constitute a serious challenge and a great opportunity for legislatures of Third World countries, for it is with respect to these problems that the significance of the legislature in the developmental equation and its utility as an institution ultimately will be assessed. Legislatures which contribute to overcoming the obstacles to rural development, or at least to mitigating the hardship of underdevelopment, are likely to become valued institutions. Legislatures which fail in this task may cease to exist—through disuse, military coup, revolution, or some combination of the three.

The future of legislatures in the less developed countries (LDCs) is tied to the rate of rural development as a consequence of three conditions which are the subjects of this chapter. First, and most obvious, legislatures by definition are representative institutions, the members of which are elected to serve not only the national interest, but the interests of subnational, territorial, or group constituencies. Legislatures may make decisions collectively, but the positions taken by individual legislators, especially in developing countries, are invariably perceived in terms of their impact on the constituents they represent.

Second, most citizens in the rural sector of the LDCs are not politically inert nor significantly less interested in matters of public policy than their brethren in the urban and "modern" sectors, though they may perceive and evaluate these issues in more parochial terms. Indeed, data recently gathered in rural Kenya by the writer suggest that most peasants are not situated beyond the boundaries of the national political system, as is often supposed, but are very much insiders. They have a reasonably clear idea of what they want from government and the institutions, procedures, and officials through which they can best obtain it. They also are prepared and able to hold accountable those decision makers who do not respond to their demands.

Third, because of the nature of their activities, the source of their authority, and the role expectations which most residents of the rural areas ascribe to their jobs, legislators are able to contribute to the process of rural development in a way that civil servants and party officials cannot. As representatives of the rural population, legislators are not primarily concerned with extending central government authority and programs into the periphery of the political system, but rather are interested in articulating the demands of the people they represent at the center.

In such a capacity, legislators can play a unique and often critical role in the process of rural development—a role which on the one hand may increase the rate of development in the rural areas, but which may also frustrate the prospects of managed and coordinated change, at least from the perspective of central government planners. Similarly, the contribution legislators make to rural development is likely to raise the level of public support for national institutions (i.e., central government) and the legislature in particular, in the short run, but may lead also to increased political instability over the long term.

## PERSPECTIVES ON LEGISLATIVE BEHAVIOR
## RESEARCH IN LDCS

Before exploring the three conditions outlined above, several preliminary remarks are in order about the assumptions underlying an
inquiry into the relationship between legislative behavior and development, and about a fruitful perspective to take in such an inquiry.
What follows is a brief exposition of the guidelines the author followed during the Kenya field study reported below, and by colleagues
engaged in parallel investigations in Korea and Turkey.[4]

In chapter 1, Smith and Musolf discuss three related perspectives
on the relationship between legislative behavior and development
which have dominated the literature on this problem, but which need
some modification for our purposes: first, as the authors point out,
there has been an emphasis on the collective and institutional role of
the legisla*ture* rather than a concern with the activities of individual
legislat*ors*; second, studies in the past tend to have taken a relatively
narrow view of the legislative process which stresses how legislatures
contribute to the making of public policy—either through the actual
passage of legislation and/or the modification or ratification of executive decisions—rather than looking at other activities and functions
their members perform; third, interest has focused on how legislatures contribute to a central government's attempt to manage the
developmental process through collective decisions which allocate
resources, rather than through individual efforts to *distribute* resources already allocated to various sectors of society.

While highly relevant to the study of legislative behavior in countries where the legislature is already an institutionalized part of the
political system, these perspectives may lead us up several blind
alleys when investigating legislative behavior in the LDCs. This is
particularly true with respect to the role played by African legislators
in the process of rural development. Where they continue to function,
African legislatures are extremely weak institutions vis-à-vis the
executive branch (cf. Le Vine, chapter 5, and Hopkins, chapter 6; this
volume). MPs are invariably members of the ruling party with the
result that even where party discipline is low, and parliamentary
debate sharp, as in Kenya, legislators do not challenge the government over fundamental policy decisions, but rather over the implementation of these decisions. Conflicts between MPs, and between the government and backbenchers rarely arise from ideological

differences, or differences in the overall conception of how development ought to proceed, or which sectors should be given priority in the developmental equation. Nor are they usually a function of major group and corporate interests, because such interests are either insignificant or, where present, concentrate their efforts on the executive branch. Because African legislators primarily represent rural populations which have similar needs, conflict within the legislature tends to be of a highly personal nature and drawn along sectional and ethnic lines. Such divisions, consequently, are highly fluid and make it difficult to view the legislative process either as bargaining between relatively stable and identifiable groups for the purpose of creating public policy or as a systematic debate over alternative conceptions of what development should entail. When defined narrowly in terms of the collective activity within the legislative chamber, the legislative process is little more than a sounding board for public opinion and an instrument for questioning and overseeing the operations of the executive branch.

Important as these activities may be, conceptions of the legislative process which orient research toward such collective activity are likely to yield fewer insights into both the general and developmental role and significance of legislative behavior in Sub-Sahara Africa than a broader perspective encompassing the activites of individual legislators which occur outside the legislative chamber. These activities consist mainly of various forms of constituency service and are of great importance because they constitute the substance of one of the few linkages that exist between the largely rural and sedentary populations of these societies and the central government. These activities integrate rural populations into the political system, and integration is a precondition (though obviously not a guarantee) for both public support of central government institutions and of government policies designed to foster development in the rural areas. Activities not usually regarded as the corpus of legislative behavior in the strict sense but performed only by "legislators" (or more appropriately, political brokers whose legal status and authority are derived from membership in a national representative assembly) are reasonably regarded as "legislative" behavior for the purpose of our discussion.

## LINKAGE BEHAVIOR AND RURAL DEVELOPMENT

The contribution made by African legislators to rural development is almost totally a function of their attempts to establish linkages between their constituencies and agencies of the central government rather than of their efforts at law making or parliamentary debate. These linkages, which we shall define simply as stable and valued networks for communication and exchanging resources between the center and periphery of the political system, are critical to both the political and economic development of the rural areas, on the one hand, and the development of viable and valued national political institutions, on the other. As first discussed by J. H. Boeke (1963) and Edward Shils (1961), and subsequently others (LaPalombara, 1971), developing countries are dual societies consisting of a core of national and "modern" institutions located in one or two central cities, and an underdeveloped hinterland (periphery). These two sectors are distinct in both the activities and values of their respective residents and their spatial relationship to one another. Given the dualistic nature of less developed societies, political and economic integration depends on the level of penetration and interaction between the two.

One characteristic of developing societies, however, is that integrative agents are rare and create few linkages. In Sub-Sahara Africa the most numerous by far are those civil servants of the central administration posted to the rural areas. It is for this reason that much of the recent literature on rural development in Africa has focused exclusively on this group and neglected legislators and what they do. Civil servants are charged with penetrating the periphery. The same is true of party officials, but party organizations in most African countries still under civilian rule have declined to the point that they are usually referred to as "nonparty" states and, accordingly, party cadres serve as links in only a handful of countries. Even where party organizations are strong, as in Tanzania, party cadres at the periphery are more often than not members of the local milieu rather than agents from the center.

In contrast, legislators constitute the only group of political actors whose explicit task, both formally and informally, is to link the periphery and center by representing the periphery at the center and by mediating the respective demands of each. While civil servants posted to the rural areas provide substantial feedback to the center on the needs of these areas, the primary purpose of such feedback obviously is not to facilitate demands by the periphery on the center but to enhance the success of central government programs and reinforce central control at the local level. As a result of administrative policy not to post civil servants to their home areas, and because of periodic transfers, civil servants are also invariably strangers in the areas they serve. By contrast, most legislators in Sub-Sahara Africa are permanent or semipermanent members of the local community at the time of their election, and must maintain close ties with the local community if they wish to remain in office. They are thus not only in a position to create different and autonomous linkages between center and periphery but also may be more successful in the linkages they forge. As agents of the periphery, they are linkers whom residents of the rural areas are likely to accord higher trust than they do civil servants and others trying to penetrate these areas from the outside.

A related, salient feature of developing societies too often neglected by social scientists concerned with the development of national political institutions and macroeconomic change is that politics in these societies are often highly decentralized. As already noted and to be explored further, residents of the rural areas are not politically inert. For most of these people, however, the arena of political action is not at the center, but on the periphery, and, consequently, it is on the periphery where the most significant contestants at the center must develop their political base. This is particularly true in Africa where party organizations have atrophied and do not offer aspiring politicians a mechanism through which to advance their fortunes. In the absence of party organizations, political brokers must concentrate their efforts on the electoral unit, in most cases the parliamentary constituency. Consequently, national politics in most African countries still under civilian rule is a contest between local political bosses from the periphery operating in their capacity as links to the center where they compete for "the national cake." To understand the role of legislators in the process of rural development therefore, one must examine the activities of legislators at the periphery, and from the "bottom up" as well as from the "top" of the political system down.

Viewed in this manner the role of a legislator in the process of rural development in Sub-Sahara Africa is basically that of an entrepreneur whose dual functions are to mobilize the resources of his constituency for community development projects, on the one hand, and to extract resources from the central government for these projects on the other. Projects of this type are usually small to medium in scale, costing between $50,000 and $100,000. Organized on the principle of self-help, they run the gamut from schools, health centers, cattle dips, and irrigation works to feeder roads, crop and settlement schemes, and various forms of cottage industries. Despite their limited size, projects of this type have a tangible effect on the lives of the rural population, are highly visible, and constitute the substance of most demands made by the people for government assistance to their development efforts.

It is this persistent demand for projects that comprises the challenge and opportunity rural development offers the "legislative" process. MPs who are capable of responding to the challenge and who are permitted to do so—an opportunity which varies considerably across the continent—obtain considerable political payoffs while serving the rural population. When organized adroitly, community development projects provide a natural base for creating extensive constituency machines and patronage systems. Energetic MPs, or would-be MPs for that matter, are thus in a position to use local projects as personal vehicles for their own advancement; sometimes by organizing projects on their own and sometimes simply by persuading and organizing existing local organizations (e.g., clan welfare societies, school associations, churches, or cooperatives) to embark on new ventures. When this entrepreneurial activity occurs in a constituency without party organization, and particularly central party control, some MPs are capable of tying together a series of projects into such an elaborate network of patron/client relationships that they become undisputed bosses of their constituencies.

In Kenya, MPs who are particularly successful at developing such networks often attempt to extend their depth and range of influence. In their constituencies they offer support to associates in local town and county council elections, and in neighboring districts they support promising parliamentary candidates. MPs who are successful in the latter invariably are recognized as national leaders at the center, a status that often is confirmed formally by elevation to a ministerial post.

In addition to providing a basis for local political machines, legislators' efforts at initiating community development projects are among the most important activities, indeed often *the* most important activity, on which they are judged by their constituents on election day. Peasant evaluations of the performance of MPs in obtaining resources from the center for community development correlate highly with the proportion of the vote MPs receive when standing for reelection. More important, such evaluations are excellent predictors of the number of candidates who will challenge the incumbent, those with successful records in community development being confronted by fewer challengers. It is no wonder, therefore, that both MPs and other local notables who consider challenging them for their seats devote substantial time and resources to organizing such projects and other forms of service to individual constituents.

When given the opportunity, voters in rural Africa are highly rational. All things being equal, i.e., the tribal and/or clan background of the contestants, rural populations will judge the performance of their MP and vote their self-interest—perhaps more than voters in industrialized societies where party identification limits the extent to which the electorate will switch allegiances. As a result, most parliamentary elections in Africa are essentially referenda on the incumbent legislator's performance on the rural development issue (Hyden and Leys, 1972; Barkan, 1976).

That MPs are expected to play an active role in the rural development of their constituencies, and that they recognize these expectations and their political payoffs is amply confirmed by our Kenyan data. The opportunities for meeting these expectations, however, vary considerably as a result of four factors: (1) the availability of resources at the center for distribution to the periphery, and/or the existence of alternative resources on which legislators can draw; (2) the role of the national political party, the extent and nature of its organization, and the ideological goals to which it is committed; (3) the posture of the civil service towards legislators; and (4) the nature of the electoral process.

Given the limited resources African governments have that are not earmarked for recurrent budget expenditure or tied to major development schemes (as in the case of projects being assisted by foreign aid), it is not surprising that there is a substantial gap between the pleas for assistance to MP-initiated community development projects and what is available for them to obtain. However, because most projects require relatively small initial capital investments as distinct from recurrent expenditure, the challenge to the MP is not so much the existence of resources as access to them.

Such access is a function both of the rules of the game and, of course, of the MP's standing with those senior decision makers, usually ministers, who release the available funds. With respect to the former, it matters much whether the national leadership and official ideology encourage and permit MPs to organize community development projects and to seek government aid in bringing them to fruition. Thus in Kenya, where these activities have the official and well-publicized blessing of President Jomo Kenyatta, an increasingly specific and semicodified set of procedures has evolved over the last decade by which legislators initiate and obtain a variety of matching grants from the government to sustain projects. In this instance, positive sanctions are accorded to the explicitly entrepreneurial roles MPs play on the periphery. Considerable latitude is given to individuals operating on the periphery on the assumption that their success will produce both benefits for the rural population and increased support for the regime—all, it might be added, at a relatively low cost to the center.

Under this system, MPs make direct claims on the ministers and assistant ministers in charge of the ministries most relevant to their projects. The result, of course, is that ministers use a significant portion of their budgets as patronage and end up playing a role vis-à-vis individual MPs similar to the role that MPs themselves play vis-à-vis residents of their districts. Where implemented, especially if done on a regular basis, such exchanges of resources for support establish viable links between center and periphery. The legislator as linker has fulfilled his mission and, no doubt, furthered his career. Moreover, he does this *by never entering the legislature* or engaging in conventional collective "legislative" activity with fellow MPs.

MPs also seek resources by approaching prominent civil servants, both at the center, where they seek to establish working relationships with permanent secretaries, assistant secretaries, etc, and on the periphery, where they work with provincial and district commissioners, the district heads of central ministries' field staffs, and such provincial and district development councils and planning bodies as exist. As might be expected, legislators who succeed in obtaining administrative backing at the district level stand a better chance of getting what they want when they lobby at the center.

Finally, like political entrepreneurs the world over, African legislators are not unaware of the principle that "money is the mothers' milk of politics," for, as a class, they invariably seek to accumulate sufficient personal resources to finance or at least to provide seed money for the projects in which they are involved. Opportunities for accumulation by individual legislators and legislators as a group, however, vary markedly from one country to the next. In Kenya, where legislator-initiated efforts at community development are actively encouraged and where the national political party has ceased to function, legislators are permitted to engage freely in private business ventures. More often than not they are favored over their fellow citizens when it comes to obtaining bank loans for their schemes. Many Kenyan MPs also sit on government regulatory boards from which they derive a second salary. By contrast, Tanzanian, and to a lesser extent Zambian legislators are subject to strict party control and are forbidden by their nations' leadership codes from receiving any income over and above official emoluments for legislative duties.

The existence or absence of viable party organization, particularly at the grass roots, is a second major variable affecting the extent to which legislators engage in entrepreneurial activity to promote rural development projects, create personal political machines, and establish linkages from the periphery to the center. Where party organization is well developed, legislators are often restricted in their efforts because the party is simultaneously an instrument of central control, as in Tanzania or Guinea, and an instrument for broadening the base of political participation on the periphery. Given these functions, parties encroach on the linkage activities of both civil servants and legislators. Because decision making within party organs is often a collective activity, legislators, no matter how prominent their position, cannot control the organization to the extent possible where they manage their own personal machines. Moreover, in the few African countries where parties are viable institutions, virtually all resources available for small-scale development projects and patronage are controlled by the party organization and/or by party-state development committees. Legislators are not given the opportunity to lobby directly and individually at the center for financial assistance but must channel such requests up the party hierarchy. The deep commitment to socialist principles by virtually all strong parties in Africa also restricts entrepreneurial activity by individual legislators as noted above.

The third significant variable affecting the opportunities for legislators to promote rural development is the competence and posture of the civil service. Where the civil service, whether via central government ministries, the provincial administration, or parastatal agencies, seeks to monopolize all community efforts at developing the rural areas, the opportunities for legislators obviously are limited. This has been the historical pattern in most African states and dates back to the colonial period when the civil service was usually the sole authority charged with and capable of promoting rural development. Given the absence of private institutions, state agencies have always been preeminent in this area. It is only in recent years that legislators and party organizations have begun to challenge their supremacy. Because of its proclaimed expertise and the relatively higher education of its personnel, the civil service often has been reluctant to share authority for rural development with those playing political roles. Legislators are invariably perceived as opportunistic, unsophisticated, and disruptive by civil servants, especially by recent college graduates who man most of the key posts in the rural administration (Barkan, 1975:165).

Thus, the latitude and support legislators receive from the administrative state in most African countries, and the extent to which legislators are brought into the local planning and distribution process, depends in large part on the tolerance of the civil servants who control the rural administration and the general posture set by the national leadership. In a few countries, most notably Kenya, it would appear that such tolerance is on the rise, for civil servants and legislators increasingly have become aware of the distinctions between the different linkage roles they play. On the one hand, civil servants have come to realize (as their colonial predecessors did before them) the need to work through the local notables of the areas in which they serve if they are to obtain the cooperation of the rural population. As noted above, civil servants invariably are strangers in the rural areas in which they serve. They must make extensive use of chiefs and other grass roots elites to communicate government policy to the general population, and are beginning to recognize that legislators also may be an asset in this regard. On the other hand, despite the general suspicion which legislators have of civil servants because civil servants so often ignore them and attempt to limit their actitivies, legislators are quick to cooperate with civil servants when given the opportunity because civil servants can provide the resources needed to make legislators' efforts at promoting community development a success. Put differently, both groups of linkers need each other to succeed in carrying out their respective duties.

The fourth, and perhaps most important determinant of the extent to which African legislators promote rural development is the electoral process. Though elections in most African countries have not taken place on a regular basis, their effect on the behavior of individual legislators has been significant. In Kenya, Tanzania, and Zambia, incumbent MPs have learned very quickly that they must deliver the goods to their constituents and make frequent visits back to their districts if they are to maintain public support. Because African elections are almost always one-party affairs and all candidates are members of the most numerous ethnic group and/or clan in each constituency, ascriptive criteria seem to be relatively poor predictors of election outcomes even though they are important factors in the voters' minds. Voter loyalty to individual candidates, including in-cumbents, is consequently low. As noted above, parliamentary elections are essentially referenda on the incumbent's performance, a situation which usually results in the defeat of more than half of the MPs seeking reelection.[5]

Consequently the impact of periodic elections on the legislative process in African states has been considerable in the decade and a half since most of these countires gained self-rule. Compared to their predecessors, the present generation of legislators seems to spend considerably more time in community development work, both in the constituency and in the capital, and less time in legislative debate. Simply stated, political careers are not built in Parliament. Even where the proceedings of the National Assembly are reported thor-oughly in the press and over the radio, as in Kenya, the typical rural voter has limited access to the media, especially newspapers, where coverage of parliamentary activities is most extensive. Attendance at parliamentary sessions is normally low.[6] Nor are legislators involved with committee work. Few committees exist and those that do meet irregularly. Rather, MPs in the capital city attending parliamentary sessions spend much of their time lobbying at central government ministries on their constituents' behalf since that is where "the ac-tion" lies.

Under these circumstances, the electoral process has tended to produce a form of what Scott (1972:111–112) termed "inflationary patron-client democracy" in discussing the situation in Southeast Asia. With each passing election the demands for development by residents of the rural areas rise. As a result, more aggressive, more educated, and on the whole more competent MPs replace those who are defeated seeking reelection. The ultimate result of this circulation, however, may be an overload of demands for resources that cannot be provided to the periphery by the central government, or can be provided only at a cost to central government programs and plans for coordinating the development process. Escalating demands on legis-lators, and in turn the escalation of their demands at the center, also will result eventually in more intense conflict among MPs than there is at present. While such conflict ultimately may give rise to more organized forms of bargaining among MPs, perhaps in the form of collective legislative activity within the legislature itself, it also may result in zero-sum forms of political conflict that will undermine the stability of the entire system. Though it certainly stimulates legis-lators to greater efforts in promoting rural development in their constituencies and raises the quality of legislative personnel, the holding of regular parliamentary elections in Africa has a variety of impacts whose net significance is not yet clear.

In the last few pages we have discussed in broad outline the roles legislators in African states play as linkers from the periphery to the center, the relationship of this role to the process of rural development, and the major factors that determine the variations this role often takes in African political systems still under civilian rule. Let us now turn to a more specific analysis of legislator behavior and rural development in Kenya and Tanzania.

## LEGISLATORS AND RURAL DEVELOPMENT
## IN KENYA AND TANZANIA

Because Kenya and Tanzania differ so markedly in their ideological and organizational approaches to their development (see Hopkins, chapter 6 in this volume), the two countries present an almost ideal pair for research assessing the range of conditions under which African legislators involve themselves in rural development. Yet in each country the popular expectations of what legislators should do is roughly the same. As suggested above, the significance of the legislators in African political systems is to be found in linkage rather than parliamentary activities. It is therefore interesting to note that while most Africans living in the rural areas do not have a clear notion of what transpires within the National Assembly, they nonetheless have a very clear conception of what the legislator's role should entail. This becomes immediately apparent when considering the findings from our surveys of the adult population in thirteen Kenyan constituencies[7] (see Table 10.1). When asked to state which of seven activities they felt were most important for Kenyan MPs to engage in, linkage activities, particularly those concerned with articulating local demands at the center and obtaining resources for community development efforts, were repeatedly stressed.

The degree to which MPs are perceived as servants of the locality at the center is illustrated further by responses to questions about whose opinions an MP should regard as most important when facing a controversial issue. The responses, which appear in Table 10.2, suggest that most Kenyan adults believe the MP should be an instructed delegate, sensitive to party ideals but should keep the wishes of his constituents preeminent in his mind—especially when considering their opinions in conjunction with his own.

## TABLE 10.1
### MOST IMPORTANT ACTIVITIES ON WHICH KENYAN MPs SHOULD SPEND THEIR TIME

| | Kilifi South | Embu South | Mbooni | Kirinyaga West | Githunguri | Laikipia West | Kadjiado North |
|---|---|---|---|---|---|---|---|
| **Linkage Activities** | | | | | | | |
| Explain government policies to constituents | 11% | 4% | 4% | 15% | 10% | 17% | 9% |
| Tell government what people want in district | 36 | 45 | 40 | 35 | 27 | 33 | 38 |
| Obtain projects and benefits for the district | 31 | 25 | 35 | 40 | 25 | 10 | 19 |
| Visit district frequently | 8 | 19 | 7 | 3 | 4 | 25 | 10 |
| **Nonlinkage Activities** | | | | | | | |
| Take active part in the debates of the national assembly and pass bills | 9 | 1 | 3 | 4 | 27 | 8 | 4 |
| Help constituents with their personal problems | 3 | 3 | 6 | 3 | 6 | 4 | 15 |
| Help solve conflicts in the community | 3 | 2 | 4 | 1 | – | 3 | 6 |
| Total Linkage | 86% | 93% | 86% | 93% | 66% | 85% | 76% |
| Total Nonlinkage | 15 | 6 | 13 | 8 | 33 | 15 | 25 |
| N = | (269) | (126) | (190) | (210) | (49) | (169) | (284) |

| | Kerichio | Ikolomani | Busia East | Nyakach | Mbita | Kitutu East |
|---|---|---|---|---|---|---|
| **Linkage Activities** | | | | | | |
| Explain government policies to constituents | 9% | 9% | 4% | 6% | 4% | 6% |
| Tell government what people want in district | 19 | 29 | 34 | 25 | 61 | 21 |
| Obtain projects and benefits for the district | 32 | 20 | 14 | 34 | 21 | 56 |
| Visit district frequently | 23 | 20 | 22 | 13 | 5 | 11 |
| **Nonlinkage Activities** | | | | | | |
| Take active part in the debates of the national assembly and pass bills | 6 | 7 | 6 | 9 | 5 | 3 |
| Help constituents with their personal problems | 5 | 10 | 15 | 10 | 2 | 3 |
| Help solve conflicts in the community | 5 | 4 | 6 | 4 | 2 | 1 |
| Total Linkage | 83% | 78% | 74% | 78% | 91% | 94% |
| Total Nonlinkage | 16 | 21 | 27 | 23 | 9 | 7 |
| N = | (254) | (277) | (244) | (282) | (242) | (276) |

Similar conceptions of legislators' roles have been found in Tanzania, though the evidence is more fragmentary. Jon Moris (1974: 349–50), reporting the findings from thirty community surveys (as distinct from constituency-wide surveys) conducted prior to the 1970 elections, noted that an overwhelming percentage of respondents expected their MPs to follow their wishes when confronted by a controversial issue in the National Assembly.

Given these highly parochial conceptions of what the legislative role should entail, it is not surprising that most incumbent legislators in both Kenya and Tanzania have adjusted their own role expectations to be roughly congruent with those of their constituents. Both Jeffrey James (1972) and this author (Barkan and Okumu, 1974), via separate surveys, have found Kenyan legislators preoccupied with constituency service and noted that legislators report spending more time seeking government resources for community development projects than in any other activity.

As is to be expected, Kenyan MPs do not define their roles as primarily those of delegates, something on which the electorate largely concurs, for they perceive one of their main tasks to be assisting the relatively unsophisticated populations they represent in articulating their needs. Neither, however, do they see themselves as trustees whose first concern is serving the national interest. As a result, few of the legislators interviewed by this writer felt that one of their prime duties was to explain government policies to their constituents, or otherwise serve as agents of the center. Indeed, this task was explicitly viewed, especially by backbenchers, as a duty of civil

TABLE 10.2

**VIEWS KENYAN CONSTITUENTS FEEL THEIR MPs SHOULD REGARD MOST IMPORTANT WHEN DECIDING A CONTROVERSIAL ISSUE**

|  | Constituents | Party | Civil servants | Interest groups | Advisors and friends | His own beliefs |
|---|---|---|---|---|---|---|
| Very important | 83% | 52% | 42% | 45% | 27% | 30% |
| Somewhat important | 14 | 35 | 42 | 39 | 39 | 36 |
| Not important | 3 | 13 | 16 | 16 | 34 | 34 |
| N = | (3,852) | (3,815) | (3,797) | (3,804) | (3,800) | (3,801) |
| Group whose views are most important: | 56% | 12% | 8% | 8% | 4% | 8% |

servants posted to the rural areas. However, because MPs are officially expected to be agents of both the center and the periphery, and
because they need to maintain good relations with the national leadership to obtain the resources they and their constituents need, it is not
surprising that the intensity of MP feeling on this point is rarely
articulated in public. Tanzanian MPs are especially prone to role
conflict in this regard because of the supremacy of the Tanganyika
African National Union (TANU), the national party, in Tanzanian
political life and the variety of effective control mechanisms it does
not hesitate to bring to bear on legislators seeking to establish an
independent base.

Having discussed the parochial orientation of East African legislators, and noted that this orientation is enhanced periodically by the
ability of their constituents to hold them accountable at the polls, it
behooves us to describe what legislators' involvement in rural development projects usually entails, and how the developmental activities of Kenyan and Tanzanian MPs differ in light of the different
conditions existing in the two countries. Though popular expectations
of what legislators behavior should entail appear to be similar in the
two countries, the actual behavior of MPs is highly dissimilar because
of the vastly different nature of the national political parties in each
system and the ideological goals they are committed to achieve. From
its inception the Kenyan African National Union (KANU) has been
little more than a confederation of local machines with little cohesion
at the national level other than that supplied by its leader, Mzee Jomo
Kenyatta. The highly factional nature of the party also has increased
during the first decade of independence as machines organized along
ethnic lines and across administrative districts in the late 1950s and
early 1960s have been replaced steadily by a multitude of smaller
organizations at the constituency level. Because Kenyatta and his
close associates have never been able to establish and control a highly
disciplined party organization, they have preferred instead to let the
local factions multiply and the national party organization fall into
disuse. This situation has been highly conducive to the entrepreneurial instincts of would-be political leaders seeking to establish small
bases of power on the periphery. Kenyatta has also encouraged this
situation for the purpose of undercutting the base of major ethnic
leaders, such as Oginga-Odinga and Paul Ngei, who were capable of
posing a threat to his rule.

Consistent with these developments has been the repeated bless-
ings Kenyatta and the national leadership have given to *Harambee*,

the national movement of rural development through self-help under whose banner most projects are organized. Though *Harambee* means "pull together" in Swahili, the ethic propounded by the slogan—which is also Kenya's national motto—has been entrepreneurial as well as collective in significance. The *Harambee* ethic thus has legitimized officially the entrepreneurial efforts of legislators and their rivals by bringing them into the fold of collective self-help. What might otherwise be regarded as a manifestation of opportunistic individualism is now perceived by all as an important feature of "building the nation" (Godfrey and Mutiso, 1974).

In this context legislators are given a virtual free reign to organize whatever development projects they like, and then seek financial resources from the government once the projects have been deemed viable. A typical project might be the building and organization of a secondary school or the building of a feeder road. Once planned by the MP together with a critical number of local notables a public meeting will be held to announce and discuss the project with the general public, the *wananchi*. After a round of speeches, a collection will be taken and several hundred dollars raised. Local notables, and especially the MP, are expected to make substantial contributions themselves at these events and often match the funds donated by the general citizenry.

Once sufficient funds are collected—often after a series of such meetings over the course of several months—construction on the school or road will begin and government assistance be sought. The amount and type of assistance varies from project to project depending on the influence of the MP with both the provincial administration and the center, and the project's worth as evaluated by the relevant government ministry. Over the past decade about a thousand primary and secondary schools have been built in Kenya through *Harambee* efforts. Because of the magnitude of this effort and the wide range in quality of the schools set up, the Ministry of Education has developed an increasingly specific and stringent set of standards which must be met before the government will provide assistance. This has also been done to conserve ministry funds and limit the surplus of semieducated manpower these schools have produced. While *Harambee* schools provide an excellent example of the extent to which legislators can promote rural development and reap short-term political benefits, they are also an example of the uncoordinated nature of locally induced change. Projects of this type may not yield lasting benefits to the rural populations, and, indeed, may give rise to severe dislocations—both economic and political—over the long run, unless they are initiated within the framework of a national development plan. Such a framework, however, is often ignored and/or forgotten by MPs when embarking on their efforts. For this reason specific guidelines must be laid down by all government agencies that are likely to be approached for assistance to such efforts if the total product is to be of lasting value. As one might expect, such guidelines—where they have been specified—are frequently the subject of political pressure and debate.

It is important to note, moreover, that of the MPs rated highly on an evaluation index in my research, all had achieved significant success on various *Harambee* efforts. Two are worth mentioning here. Both are energetic young men in their mid-thirties who are frequently regarded as rising stars on the Kenyan political scene. The first is a graduate (in political science!) of a prestigious American college who represents a constituency near Nairobi. This man makes frequent visits to his constituency, holding open meetings three times a week at the district officer's headquarters to discuss the problems of whomever wishes to see him. On any one day this MP will speak with thirty to fifty constituents and then return to Nairobi to oversee a fledgling construction business. This man attends parliamentary sessions only sporadically and, when he does, rarely speaks. Because of his high visibility in his constituency, however, he has been highly successful in raising funds for *Harambee* road projects. He contributes heavily to these projects. Needless to say, his company has won a significant share of the contracts let by the Ministry of Works to build them. In the election of October 1974, he was reelected with 77 percent of the vote and was subsequently appointed an assistant minister.

The second represents a district one hundred miles west of Nairobi that was once a significant area of European settlement. Since independence more than twenty thousand people have migrated into the area in the hope of obtaining land vacated by the departing colonial farmers. These hopes usually go unfilfilled, however, because the farms being sold by their European owners are invariably too large for the typical African farmer to buy. Despite a variety of government programs to purchase such land for small-scale African settlement, most has been bought up by wealthy Africans, leaving many people landless. To help alleviate this problem, this legislator has created a private cooperative which over the last few years has purchased 103,000 acres and divided the property among roughly 5,000 families.

In the election of 1974 he was reelected with 58 percent of the vote in a three-man contest. Like our first example, this man rarely speaks in the National Assembly because, as he puts it, "one can be more effective by not shouting." It is important to note, however, that part of his success stems from the fact that he is one of two assistant ministers for Lands and Settlement, a post he retained in the reshuffle of the government which followed the election.

While some observers might regard these two examples as involving conflicts of interest, most, having perhaps read *Plunkett*, would view them as "honest graft." These legislators certainly see themselves as operating clearly within the rules of the game of Kenyan politics and, no doubt, are regarded in a similar vein by the general public. Indeed, it is precisely because these MPs have engaged in such activities that they received high marks from their constituents in our surveys and were reelected by wide margins in an election that sent 58 percent of their colleagues down to defeat.

In contrast, members of the Tanzanian National Assembly are not allowed to engage in such free-wheeling forms of constituency service, and it is perhaps for this reason why these legislators and the National Assembly are of declining importance in that country. As already noted, Tanzanian legislators labor under a stringent leadership code and must operate within the confines of an extensive party organization that reaches down to the grass roots. Though politics is to a great extent an inherently entrepreneurial activity, Tanzanian MPs explicitly are required to forsake such activity in order to be consistent with TANU's socialist ideology and collectivist norms of how public policy ought to be made. Tanzanian legislators thus have few if any independent means or resources to foster rural development in the manner of their Kenyan counterparts. Indeed, their only significant role in the rural development effort is as members of the regional and district development committees.[8]

The role of Tanzanian legislators in these committees, however, is at best marginal. With more than forty members, the committees are chaired respectively by the regional and district chairman of the party. The vice-chairmen are the regional and area commissioners, the senior civil servants in the rural administration, and the secretaries are the regional and district development directors, the civil servants charged with overseeing all development efforts in the rural areas. These bodies are basically executive planning and budget request agencies for the rural areas. Their geographic jurisdiction usually encompasses several parliamentary constituencies with the result that the MPs who are members of the committees must focus their attention beyond the areas they represent. The committees consider recommendations from the divisional and ward development committees which are dominated entirely by party officials, and on which MPs do not sit, and are in turn responsible to Maendeleo, the Ministry of Rural Development, and the president. Under this system, MPs are given virtually no opportunity to initiate programs for their constituencies though obviously they attempt to articulate the needs of the people they represent. Nor do they have the opportunity to modify the national plan for rural development significantly when ultimately it is brought before the National Assembly at a later date. While it is perhaps possible to conceive of the regional and district development committees as subnational legislatures, the subordination of the MPs to party personnel and civil servants is such that the impact of the individual MP is difficult to discern.

Given this situation, Tanzanian MPs are not in a position to develop autonomous and institutionalized linkages from the periphery to the center, linkages on which the viability of the National Assembly ultimately depends. Nor, however, are they in a position to frustrate a national approach to the process of rural development as are their counterparts north of the border. The marginal role played by Tanzanian MPs is a function of the fundamental nature of the Tanzanian political system. As a result of the supremacy of TANU—supremacy which has recently been recognized formally by a constitutional amendment placing it above the National Assembly as the nation's foremost law-making body—and the party's commitment to socialist development, it is little wonder that questions occasionally arise as to what function the national legislature or its members play. It is perhaps for this reason that the number of parliamentary constituencies were reduced and their boundaries made coterminous with the country's administrative districts and party divisions before parliamentary elections were held later in 1975. Whether this change has breathed new life into the legislative process or whether it will accelerate the decline of the legislator and the National Assembly still remains to be seen.

## SUMMARY AND CONCLUSION

We began this chapter with the suggestion that the most fruitful place to consider legislative behavior and rural development was to turn our attention away from the collective activities of the legislature to the individual efforts through which legislators attempt to establish linkages between the periphery and the center. This change in perspective requires a broadening of the concept of what constitutes the "legislative process." It is necessary because, while they do not affect the allocation of public resources significantly, given the right conditions, the members of most Third World legislatures can and do affect their distribution. In conclusion, therefore, we offer the following generalizations regarding the significance of linkage behavior for both rural development and the overall process of political change. These may be divided with respect to their significance in the short or long term.

### SHORT TERM EFFECTS

1. Where legislators are free from party control and its attendant ideological constraints to function as individual entrepreneurs, and where elections are held on a regular basis, legislators will spend a substantial amount of their time promoting rural development in their constituencies because it is in their interest to do so.

2. By engaging in entrepreneurial activities to foster rural development in their constituencies, legislators create linkages between the center and periphery of the political system that are qualitatively different and autonomous from the linkages created by other potential linkers, notably civil servants. The establishment and, particularly, the maintenance and institutionalization of such linkages increase the level of vertical integration in these societies. When this occurs, popular knowledge and expectations of the activities and procedures of central government personnel, and perhaps central government institutions as well—including the legislature—rise. In short, Third World legislatures might be relatively unimportant institutions, but their members engage in activities which are essential prerequisites for the growth, influence, and autonomy of those bodies.

3. Where legislators engage in entrepreneurial activities to foster rural development, progress can be achieved. On the one hand, community development efforts raise the social welfare of the populations concerned, or at least mitigate the hardship of underdevelopment. On the other, rural populations become more receptive to other government-initiated efforts at changing their condition. The net result is that rural development is likely to proceed at a faster rate than if guided by civil servants alone.

## LONG TERM EFFECTS

1. The more vertical integration in Third World political systems results from legislator-initiated attempts to create linkages between the center and periphery, the higher the level of popular demand for government outputs, and the greater the intensity of conflict among MPs to obtain such outputs for their constituents. Thus, increased vertical integration may be a precursor of increased horizontal disintegration, a possibility which cannot be ignored in plural societies where ethnic and religious cleavages run deep. Legislator-initiated change in the rural areas consequently may raise the prospects for political stability in the short term but lower the prospects over the long haul. Given the fragile nature of many Third World political systems, however, particularly in Africa, the luxury of planning for some future crisis may not be feasible, for the future is now.

2. The more effective legislators are in initiating economic development through small-scale autonomous efforts at the grass roots, the less likely that economic change can be coordinated effectively across the entire society. Thus, legislator initiated development is likely to be unbalanced development—development which probably will occur at a more rapid pace than balanced development, but which produces dislocations and serious inequities in the process.

The net desirability of legislator involvement in the process of rural development thus depends in part on where one's values lie. For those who seek more rapid change in the rural areas, and the creation of representative political institutions at the center, the choice is clear.

## NOTES

1. Between 1963 and 1972 per capita agricultural production fell in Latin America and the Far East, increased approximately 1 percent per year in the Middle East, and remained unchanged in Africa. By contrast, industrial production in the Third World increased at a rate of roughly 10 percent per year while labor productivity in the industrial sector rose by about 4 percent annually (United Nations, 1974:24, 28, 44).

2. Upon considering income distribution in 43 developing countries, Adelman and Morris report that on the average the poorest 60 percent of the population, virtually all of whom reside in the rural areas, receive only 26 percent of the national income. Income inequality increases, moreover, with a rise in national income, for such an increase is almost exclusively a result of growth in the modern, and invariably urban sector. See Adelman and Morris (1973:141–185).

3. One need only be reminded that since the end of World War II, most revolts and revolutions in the Third World have been rurally based, e.g., Cambodia, China, Ethiopia, Kenya, Guinea-Bissau, Malaya, Mozambique, the Philippines, Vietnam, Zaire.

4. In 1973 and 1974 members of the Comparative Legislative Research Center of the University of Iowa, together with colleagues at the Universities of Dar-es-Salaam, Istanbul, and

Seoul conducted three field studies on the nature of the relationships between members of the national legislature and their constituents. In each country a sample of 150–300 adults was surveyed in each of twelve to fourteen parliamentary constituencies to determine mass perceptions of the legislative process, and the level of contact between ordinary citizens and their MP. In addition to the mass surveys, a sample of local elites was interviewed in each constituency. Interviews were also conducted with roughly thirty to one hundred members of the national legislature, including those representing the districts which constituted the research sites for the study. Data from these surveys are now being analyzed. A comparative volume on legislative behavior and development in the three countries is planned.

5. In 1969, 54 percent of the MPs seeking reelection in Kenya were defeated, while 58 percent lost their seats in 1974. Only 34 percent of the incumbent MPs were defeated in Tanzania in 1970, but 44 percent of the incumbents did not seek or were barred from seeking reelection by TANU, the ruling party.

6. In 1974 average attendance in the Kenya National Assembly was between thirty and fifty MPs, or no more than one-third of the House. Quorums were frequently not achieved, a situation which led President Kenyatta to castigate the members publicly as "lazy" public servants who were not doing their jobs.

7. The Kenyan surveys of adult citizens were conducted in fourteen constituencies of which thirteen were rural. Constituencies selected as research sites were chosen on the basis of geographical distribution, ethnicity, and level of development to reflect the country as a whole. Only the findings from the rural constituences are presented in this chapter.

8. All decisions regarding specific rural development projects in Tanzania are made by a hierarchy of ward, division, district and regional development committees, chaired at all levels by the party secretary of the geographical unit over which they have jurisdiction. MPs are only members of development committees at district and regional levels. These committees are usually composed of 10 to 15 members of which only one or two are legislators. In all cases the majority of members are party officials and senior civil servants.

# Chapter 11

# THE PARLIAMENT OF MALAYSIA AND ECONOMIC
# DEVELOPMENT: POLICY MAKING AND THE MP

## LLOYD D. MUSOLF
## J. FRED SPRINGER

Legislatures in developing countries have long been criticized for their weakness in making policy. This criticism has been so effective that scholars currently investigating these legislatures have all but abandoned the analysis of their impact on policy and gone in search of alternative functions which are only minimally related to the shaping of public policy. In this chapter we propose a limited reassessment of the minimal legislature's role in policy making. Our argument is, briefly, the following:

1. There is ample evidence that legislatures in developing countries are not central to policy making. However, important peripheral influences in this regard may have been ignored because of (a) a restricted view of the policy-making process, (b) a focus on the activities of legislatures as collective decision-making bodies, and (c) a failure to consider the relation of non-rule-making legislative functions to the policy process broadly defined. Case studies, such as this one on Malaysia, are necessary to clarify this assertion.
2. Economic development has been a major policy preoccupation of the new nations and has central importance in the politics of Malaysia.
3. When the Malaysian Parliament is analyzed as a collective

policy-making body, our survey of MPs confirms the argument for minimal influence on economic policy.

4. When the individual activities of Malaysian MPs are framed by an expanded conception of policy making, the MPs' involvement in economic policy making, particularly through linkage activities, is indicated.

5. In conclusion, the activities reported by Malaysian legislators resemble recent observations on the functioning of minimal legislatures elsewhere and indicate the need for renewed examination of the policy-making role of legislatures in the developing nations.

These assertions organize the present paper, and are elaborated below.

1. *There is ample evidence that legislatures in developing countries are not central to policy making. However, important peripheral influences in this regard may have been ignored because of (a) a restricted view of the policy-making process, (b) a focus on the activities of legislatures as collective decision-making bodies, and (c) a failure to consider the relation of non-rule-making legislative functions to the policy process broadly defined.*

It is not the purpose of this chapter to resurrect the notion of the centrality of legislative rule making. It is apparent that legislators as lawmakers find themselves facing difficult conditions, not merely in developing countries but even in those that pride themselves on their democratic vitality. There is much to be said for Raymond Hopkins's view in chapter 6 that legislatures everywhere "are formalized consultative systems used to legitimize rule, build a coalition of support for policy (by binding local leaders to it), and correct errors that key leaders or the bureaucracy may make." Nor should our focus be taken as a denial of the existence of other legislative functions that are, in fact, of great importance. Far from derogating these non-rule-making activities, our intent is to place them more clearly in relation to policy making.[1]

Legislatures that are "ultimately subordinate to other elements in the political system"—and these are typical of developing countries—have been called (Mezey, 1972:686) "minimal legislatures." It is desirable to base such a designation upon a broad understanding of what affects the policy process. This involves more than passing a statute. Indeed, the utility of an expanded view of policy making is not restricted to the minimal legislature but is of value in the most esteemed of legislative settings. Speaking of the Mother of Parliaments, Bernard Crick (1970:52) has observed its tendency to move away from a fixation on crucial policy decisions and to "take a wider view of legislation." Unable to control the shaping of crucial legislation, the House of Commons began to interest itself "more in the formulation of policy at the pre-legislative stage and in the scrutiny of legislation at the post-legislative stage."

Crick's comment suggests the utility of breaking policy making into stages and evaluating the place of the legislature in each. The breakdown could be as elaborate as that provided by Groth, R. J. Lieber, and N. I. Lieber (1976:9–18): initiation, deliberation, approval, application, adjudication and enforcement, auditing and monitoring of policy, and termination and amendment. For present purposes, however, a simpler scheme should serve equally well. Mezey (1974) has conceived of policy making in three stages: formulation, decision making, and implementation. Legislators participate in formulation through consulting privately with government representatives or by formally introducing a bill. Legislative participation in decision making involves deliberating and acting (familiar components, one may note, of the rule-making function). Legislators may be involved in implementation either as overseers of administrative actions or as advocates of the government's policies. The legislature's place in each of these stages would be gauged not merely by the extent of the participation of its members but also by whether or not the activities account for any of the variance in the final shape of the policies. The present case study focuses on participation and relates it to economic policy making and political necessities. There is a need for other case studies which can determine the precise effects of participation on policy content.

A virtue of Mezey's broad view of policy making is that it can enfold both the collective and individual activities of legislators. If the collective policy making of legislatures is generally weak in developing countries, as is generally conceded, it is especially appropriate to examine the individual activities of legislators for their policy-making implications. Our analysis will examine both collective and individual activities in a specific case setting, and will refer to legislative activities not generally associated with deliberating on bills and enacting them into law.

2. *Economic development has been a major policy preoccupation of the new nations and has central political importance in Malaysia.*

In the immediate postwar period, economic development tended to be defined as a long-term, sustained increase in per capita real product (Kuznets, 1959:14). More recently, there has been a decided emphasis on the additional goals of economic redistribution (Adelman and Morris, 1973). As we shall see, Malaysia has reflected this changed emphasis by increasing its redistribution efforts since independence. Malaysia has been noted for its devotion to formal development programs and, unlike most other Southeast Asian countries, has made sustained efforts to implement them (Ness, 1967:240).

Malaysia came into being through a nonviolent separation from the British colonial masters, a lengthy process which also produced a complex jockeying for influence among emergent political groups (see Means, 1970). Peninsular Malaysia—then known as Malaya—received its independence in 1957, and the Federation of Malaysia was formed in 1963 out of Malaya, Singapore, and the North Borneo states of Sabah and Sarawak.[2] Singapore withdrew in 1965, leaving the eleven states of Peninsular Malaysia and the two eastern states to continue in the Federation. The national government is headed by a constitutional monarch who is elected for five years by his colleagues among the hereditary rulers of the nine Malay states.[3] The king occupies approximately the same position in relation to the rest of the government as does the British head of state. Following the British parliamentary tradition, the prime minister selects his cabinet from members of either house of Parliament. Although the second house in a federal system could serve an important function, the Dewan Negara (Senate) has been a rubber stamp for the Dewan Rakyat (House of Representatives).[4] The Dewan Rakyat now consists of 154 members who are elected from constituencies drawn to favor rural areas.

In seeking to create a viable government, Malaysia has had the advantage of more natural wealth than most developing countries. Malaysia is relatively underpopulated, and its exports of rubber, tin, and palm oil provide it with a per capita income that is exceeded in Southeast Asia only by Singapore (United Nations, 1975:13). Against these decided advantages must be posed disadvantages of geography and ethnicity. Sabah and Sarawak are not only separated from the rest of Malaysia by several hundred miles of ocean, they are considerably less developed. To bring them into the Federation, they were granted special constitutional concessions which have been the source of some friction. Communal rivalries are exacerbated by the cultural, religious, and economic diversity of the leading ethnic groups. Essentially, the conflict is over the claim of the Malays to special status as the leading indigenous group and the urging of the somewhat less numerous Chinese and the much smaller group of Indians and Pakistanis that all residents be treated simply as Malaysians; this situation is complicated further by an uneven racial distribution between the eastern and western parts of Malaysia.[5] In Sabah and Sarawak, non-Malay indigenous groups have sometimes claimed that their status is not recognized adequately by the dominant indigenes. Despite communal conflicts, however, the substantial size of the various ethnic groups, none of which has a majority, creates a mutual interest in finding a modus vivendi.

Ethnic politics is further complicated by economics. The corporate sector of the economy is dominated by foreign corporations, but, of the two-fifths that are domestically owned, the Chinese have about 60 percent (Chopra, 1974:200). Chinese economic power is offset by Malay political dominance. Much of the impetus for the extensive programs of economic development comes from the Malay-dominated government's drive to elevate the economic position of the Malay masses.

In view of the tensions generated by communal differences, Malaysia has experienced remarkably little violence in its twenty-year history. In the 1960s, the credit for keeping the government on an even keel has generally been given to the Alliance, a coalition of communally based parties. The leaders of these parties tended to operate quietly behind the scenes in reaching understandings, thereby disarming potential communal conflict. This method of reconciliation received a decided shock in the parliamentary election of May 1969. The jubilation of opposition parties at the reduced Alliance majority in the new Parliament produced counterreactions which quickly turned into bloody communal riots. Parliament was suspended and the country was ruled by a Malay-dominated National Operations Council. When Parliament was reconvened in 1971, the ruling coalition forced through restrictive constitutional amendments. Public discussion, even in Parliament itself, of certain sensitive issues—the special positions of the Malays, the sovereignty of the hereditary rulers, the place of the Malay language, and non-Malay citizenship provisions—was forbidden. At the same time, the political leaders put all communities on notice that rights, freedoms, and political activities were to be narrower than in the past so as to prevent new racial confrontations. In looking ahead to the 1974 parliamentary elections,

Prime Minister Tun Abdul Razak forged a political coalition more broadly based than in the past called the National Front. Thus, with a somewhat different mix, Malaysian democracy has returned to a coalition of communal representatives (though some components of the Front are multiethnic in theory if not in actual membership).

The future stability of government in Malaysia may, however, be based less on skillful coalition-building than upon an expanding economy. So long as economic development is perceived as a non-zero-sum game, substantial economic programs can be regarded as benefiting national unity even though one communal group benefits more than others.

Overcoming rural poverty was a concern in Malaysia even under the British (Ness, 1967:125); efforts have been intensified greatly since colonial times. In explaining the high priority given rural development by the creation of the Ministry of Rural Development in 1959 under then Deputy Prime Minister Tun Abdul Razak, Gayl Ness (1967:241) has pointed out: ". . . the ethnic balance of political power made it imperative that something be done in rural areas. The rural Malays were overrepresented in the legislature and the position of the Malays was protected constitutionally." The 1969 riots led the government to incorporate into the Second Malaysia Plan (1971–75) the "New Economic Policy," which proclaimed two goals: eliminating poverty and ending racial economic imbalance.

3. *When the Malaysian Parliament is analyzed as a collective decision-making body, our survey of MPs confirms the argument for minimal influence on economic policy.*

Our investigation of Parliament's role in Malaysian economic policy making relies largely on data gathered from a sample of Malaysian MPs. Interviews with nearly a third of the members of the newly elected Fourth Parliament were conducted in March–April 1975. Elections to the Dewan Rakyat had occurred in August 1974, and respondents were asked about their perceptions of events during their first meeting, i.e., the budget meeting of November–December 1974.[6] The interview schedule was adapted from one that the University of Iowa had employed in Korea, Turkey, and Kenya.[7]

The fifty respondents may be said to constitute a stratified sample modified chiefly by accessibility. The single stratification variable used was membership in the National Front or in the opposition parties. As the latter MPs were far more eager for interviews, they are overrepresented in the sample despite the best efforts of interviewers.[8] Though the sample was not deliberately purposive in other respects, it is representative with respect to party and ethnic composition.

Fall 1974 was a period of great world-wide uncertainty in the wake of the Arab oil embargo and price increase coupled with the spread of international recession. Economic concerns dominated the agenda of the fall 1974 meeting of the Dewan Rakyat. "Inflation/stagflation" was most frequently perceived by MPs as an important problem raised in the legislature (26 percent),[9] with unemployment and associated problems of economic growth (32 percent) receiving the next most frequent mention. These expressions of concern for the overall health of the Malaysian economy were seen as important by many more MPs than any other problem mentioned.

Though no other problem approached the level of concern expressed for these macroeconomic issues, economic difficulties also characterized a number of the less pressing issues of Malaysian politics in the fall of 1974. The Malaysian economy depends heavily on the export of agricultural and mineral production, and this dependence can be threatening in the face of international economic instability. Hence there was worry over the price of primary products (14 percent). Governmental ineffectiveness in addressing longstanding economic problems provided another focus of criticism by MPs. "Land and housing" (14 percent) is a shorthand reference to a range of chronic problems associated with illegal squatters, slow progress in constructing low-income housing, and similar matters receiving periodic attention in Parliament. Concerns for "implementing development" (14 percent) refer to slower-than-desired progress in achieving elemental economic objectives and distributing the benefits of development to lower economic groups. "Poverty" (10 percent) is another problem associated with the inadequate distribution of developmental benefits. Thus the bulk of the remaining problems mentioned by our respondents are associated with failure in implementation and/or distribution within economic development programs.

Economic development in specific sectors of the economy provides further cause for concern among some MPs. The Green Book plan is a government proposal to spur the production of foodstuffs. (The plan will be examined in greater detail in a subsequent section of this chapter.) Even the student demonstrations of December 1974, which received some attention in the legislature, were spurred by rural economic difficulties. The focus of the disturbances was the allegation of starvation in the countryside (*New Straits Times*, Dec. 12,

1974)—a claim that was indignantly denied by the government. Though the extent of preoccupation with economic issues may be attributable partly to the worldwide recession and its inevitable repercussions in the Malaysian economy, the sensitivity of the Malaysian MP to economic problems is evident.

The MPs' awareness of economic policy as an important matter for legislative discussion argues for the appropriateness of our substantive area of inquiry, but it does not address the central questions of our analysis directly. Does the legislators' interest in and sense of urgency about economic questions translate into major legislative involvement? Utilizing Mezey's elaboration of the policy-making process, we turn to an investigation of Parliament's collective role in its various stages.

Under the parliamentary system, we would expect little or no formal involvement of legislators in policy formulation, the first stage of policy making as described by Mezey. Or, to state the matter more precisely, one would expect minimal participation of the legislature in framing bills, even though individual legislators might have influence on the initiation of policy changes. The former expectation is borne out in the Malaysian case. The sweeping New Economic Policy, for instance, was developed by an economic task group of civil servant officials at a time when Parliament was prorogued (Elyas, 1974: 41–43). Individual development programs have frequently originated from within the civil service, from whose ranks Tun Abdul Razak rose. In brief, an examination of initiatives in Malaysian economic policy reveals almost no formal participation by the Parliament or its committees.

In the second, or decision-making stage of the policy process, the evidence is that the Dewan Rakyat plays only a peripheral role. Observers of Malaysian politics have noted the decision-making weaknesses of the legislature from a variety of perspectives. A leading student of development policy in Malaysia has said: "Through centralized party control and strict party discipline, reinforced by respect and deference for authority, Parliament has been weak and manipulated by the senior political leadership" (Esman, 1972:64). Another scholar has offered this description of the situation in 1969: "Legislators have played less of a role in actual decisions and have considerably less influence than the bureaucracy on the development plans and projects in their own areas. The Parliament has, however, legitimized decisions made elsewhere in the system and served as a formal reminder of the multiracial character of the government" (Grossholtz, 1970:108). Regardless of their assessments of the sources of the weakness, or of their perceptions of alternative roles for the legislature, previous observers would lead us to expect little parliamentary involvement in explicit policy decisions.

A review of the fall 1974 budget meeting of the Dewan Rakyat largely confirms these impressions, though space permits only brief references.[9, 10] Both the National Front and opposition MPs complained vigorously about deficiences in development administration in their constituencies. In the last two days of the meeting, a few government bills were debated and passed without change by party-line votes. The lengthiest debate—and the only spirited one— occurred on a bill that increased allowances for MPs. Following Malaysian practice (a departure from the British system), no bill was subjected to scrutiny in select committees.

That Parliament is not centrally involved in the decision-making phase of policy making is further confirmed by the perceptions of our respondents. When asked to describe the job of being a legislator by identifying "the most important things you do here," only one legislator responded that "law making or exercising the power of legislation" constituted an important part of his job. Seven responses were classifiable as referring to "policy making, participation in key governmental decisions, or setting the national priorities." In all, some 78 important activities associated with their job were identified by our sample; only about 10 percent were related to the collective responsibilities of law making and policy decisions.

A more specific behavioral indicator of the importance of various components of the legislator's role is the amount of time actually devoted to specific activities. Table 11.1 displays the pattern of responses for our sample of legislators when asked to rank a number of activities according to the amount of the legislator's time they occupy. The first activity listed, "debating and amending bills," represents the core of the collective decision-making activities of the legislature; the remaining items represent activities which may engage the time of individual legislators but which are peripheral to legislative decision making. The first column indicates the percentage of respondents classifying a particular activity as most demanding of their time, the second column indicates the distribution of activities ranked second, and the third column presents third-ranked items. The final column indicates the proportion of first, second, and third choices accounted for by each activity. What stands out is the extreme lack of attention to debating and amending bills. In every column this item is reported to consume far less of a legislator's time than any other activity.

Of course, time demands on a legislator may not reflect what he perceives as most important to his role. The actual time allocated to a task reflects a multitude of expectations and responsibilities which constrain an MP and may prevent him from spending time according to his own preferences (see Table 11.2). However, Malaysian legislators not only spend relatively little time debating and amending bills, they are predominantly content with the allocation of their time in that area. Over 60 percent of the legislators indicated that they would *like* to spend about the same amount of time on this collective activity. Thus, there is no evidence that Malaysian legislators are anxious to take a greater part in legislative rule making.

The acceptance of a minimal role in basic policy decisions is accompanied by the perception that the important decisions are not made on the parliamentary floor, nor even in legislative committees, but in the cabinet or government. When asked where the most important decisions or actions were taken on some ninety problems identified by sample members as most important during the budget meeting of the Dewan Rakyat, 86.3 percent of the responses placed these actions in the cabinet or government. By contrast, only 7.5

TABLE 11.1

**RANKINGS OF ACTIVITIES ACCORDING TO THE AMOUNT OF THE LEGISLATOR'S TIME THEY REQUIRE**

| | Percentage of legislators ranking the activity | | | |
|---|---|---|---|---|
| Activity | First (N=48) | Second (N=47) | Third (N=47) | First three combined (N=142) |
| Debating and amending bills | 6.3% | 2.1% | 6.4% | 4.9% |
| Explaining government policy to voters | 25.0 | 23.4 | 12.8 | 20.4 |
| Expressing the view of my district on policies | 4.2 | 27.7 | 19.1 | 16.9 |
| Insuring a fair amount of government resources for my district | 14.6 | 17.0 | 29.8 | 20.4 |
| Interceding with civil servants on behalf of constituents | 20.8 | 19.1 | 17.0 | 19.0 |
| Resolving local conflicts | 29.2 | 10.6 | 14.9 | 18.3 |

percent of the important actions were reported to have occurred on the floor.

In summary, whether considering legislators' activities, actual or preferred allocations of time, or the locus of policy-making power, the members of the Dewan Rakyat do not perceive a major contribution to collective decision making. Nevertheless, Parliament's lack of vigorous involvement in policy decisions as a collective body might be interpreted as a sign of consensus among its members. Though the MPs see economic development as a crucial problem, it is conceivable that they agree on development policies. This question deserves brief exploration.

The preceding section began with a discussion of the importance of economic questions in Malaysian public policy, with particular reference to the relation between growth and distribution. We can agree with Uphoff and Ilchman (1972:77–78) that

> . . . production and distribution are separable only analytically and even then often inappropriately. Any serious consideration of productivity has to take into account the varying productivity of different distributions of what is produced and the fact that different modes of production lead to differing distributions. Production and distribution are aspects of a single process, each affecting the other.

**TABLE 11.2**

**MALAYSIAN LEGISLATORS' OPINIONS ABOUT WHETHER THEY SHOULD SPEND MORE OR LESS TIME ON SPECIFIED ACTIVITIES**

| Activity | (N) | Percent of MPs desiring | | |
|---|---|---|---|---|
| | | Less Time | Same | More Time |
| Debating and amending bills | (46) | 8.7% | 60.9% | 30.4% |
| Explaining government policy to the voters | (47) | 4.3 | 48.9 | 46.8 |
| Expressing my district's views on policies | (46) | 6.5 | 39.1 | 54.3 |
| Insuring a fair amount of government resources for my district | (47) | — | 36.1 | 63.9 |
| Interceding with civil servants on behalf of constituents | (47) | 17.0 | 34.0 | 48.9 |
| Resolving local conflicts | (46) | 30.4 | 28.3 | 41.3 |

Nevertheless, choices must be made, and the balance of production and distribution constitutes a critical area of decision making in Malaysian economic policy.

Malaysian MPs display a diversity of opinion with respect to this fundamental policy choice. The MPs were almost equally split between approving and disapproving of the primacy of growth in government policies. The intricate interplay of political cleavages and economic policy, suggested in the beginning of this section, is also confirmed in these responses. Distribution policies are of particular importance to Malays.[11] Our data reveal that the policy preferences of Malay representatives and MPs from the other ethnic communities contrast sharply; nearly 70 percent of the Malay representatives feel that the government should *not* emphasize economic growth before economic equality while only one third of the MPs from non-Malay districts voice this opinion.[12] There is no consensus on strategies of economic development in the Malaysian legislature, and differences on preferred policy appear to be related at least partly to Malaysia's underlying political cleavages.[13]

In the implementation phase of legislative policy making as described in Mezey's model, legislators either oversee administrative action or explain policies to constituents in order to mobilize support for and compliance with the policies. So described, virtually no involvement with implementation is found in the collective activities of the Dewan Rakyat. Legislative committees, which are often influential in the supervision of federal agencies in the United States and have a more limited role in Great Britain, are of little consequence in Malaysia. The Public Accounts Committee might be relevant to an oversight function, but its review of administrative financial records lags three or four years behind (as an inspection of the reports reveals), and it is chaired by a government supporter rather than a member of the opposition, as in the parliamentary systems of Great Britain and Canada.

Thus, an examination of the collective role of the Dewan Rakyat in economic policy making confirms the observations offered by other students in legislatures in developing settings. The MPs consistently minimize the importance of the major decision-making role conventionally assigned to legislative bodies. Even when the search for meaningful involvement is carried to the pre- and postdecision phases there is virtually no evidence of formal legislative involvement. The fruitlessness of our search, however, may still reflect our preconceptions about where we should look. We have been looking for evidence of the impact of the Dewan Rakyat as a legislative *body*, a concept which inevitably emphasizes the process of deliberation among Parliament's members and seeks to analyze its activities primarily as a collective product. Representatives in the United States Congress, for instance, have long acted individually as advocates for their constituents before the administrative branch. Our analysis to this point, then, should not lead us to conclude that the Dewan Rakyat has no impact on economic policy. The elimination of collective policy making as a major preoccupation of the Malaysian MP leaves unanswered the further question—do the individual activities of members of the Dewan Rakyat have an effect on economic policy?

4. *When the individual activities of the Malaysian MPs are framed by an expanded conception of policy making, the MPs' involvement in policy making, particularly through linkage activities, is indicated.*

Recent research on legislatures in developing nations indicates that individual legislators perform a number of important functions for the government and polity. It has been argued persuasively that, with respect to many particularized local political demands, "the burden of response has fallen to the individual legislator" (Mezey, 1972:698). Our treatment of these activities is restricted to those which stand in a particularly important relationship to policy making.

The individual legislators may act as a major political influence in the local community. The legislator who stands for election and is frequently well known to the local constituency is an important representative of public authority. For a plurality (29.2 percent) of the MPs interviewed in this study, efforts at resolving local conflicts represent the single greatest expenditure of their time (Table 11.1). However, involvement in local disputes holds a relatively low position in the preferences of the legislators. Almost one third of our respondents (30.4 percent) expressed their dissatisfaction with this activity by indicating that they would prefer to devote *less* time to it (Table 11.2).

Barkan (1975:22) characterizes the involvement of MPs in the resolution of local conflict as a "nonlinkage activity" in contrast to a collection of individual legislative activities that serve to link a central government and the periphery. Increasingly, it has been observed that the legislator may become an important point of communication between local constituents and the national government in polities which lack the extensive nongovernmental linkages found in developed democracies. Malaysia, of course, lacks such organized linkages and Malaysian MPs do engage in a number of activities which serve to link local constituents and government. There are, however, some differences in the allocation of time between specific linkage activities.

Inevitably, problems occur in development administration and MPs are available to intercede. Possibly because of its impact on only a limited number of constituents, this linkage activity is not as popular as others with MPs.[14] The legislators in our sample also act as a communications channel from the government to constituents, 25 percent reporting that "explaining government to voters" places the greatest demands on their time (Table 11.1).

Two other activities are distinguished by the fact that a majority of our respondents would like to spend more time on them than they now do (Table 11.2). MPs are particularly anxious to devote greater efforts to "entrepreneurial" activities—securing central government resources for their districts. Barkan (1975) and Hopkins (1975b) have noted a similar emphasis among East African MPs and ascribe it to the importance attached to this service by the constituents themselves. Delivering resources is an important criterion for judging an MP's success. A majority of the MPs would also like to "express the view" of their districts more actively, even though it currently consumes less of their time than other linkage activities.

In sum, an analysis of reported time allocation indicates that Malaysian MPs spend most of their time, and would prefer spending even more time, in individual activities which serve to link center and periphery. Linkage activities are of particular interest not only because of their prevalence in the behavior of Malaysian MPs but also because of their potential contribution to policy making. Voicing local demands and advancing the interests of constituents may help shape government policy in the formulation stage or modify its implementation, even though the formal involvement of the MP in actual policy decisions is minimal.

In order to assess more specifically the relation of legislators to economic policy making in Malaysia, it is necessary to examine their activities with respect to particular issues. In the interviews, information was gathered on legislative involvement in two government initiatives in economic policy that occurred during the fall 1974 meeting. (The eleven deputy ministers and parliamentary secretaries in the sample were not asked about these matters because it was presumed that their access to program information would be significantly greater than for rank-and-file MPs, and that their subsequent actions would be affected by their ministerial positions.) The programs chosen provide contrast in the economic problem addressed, and in the manner in which they were introduced. The first—a "new approach" in government policy on housing—received mention in the King's Address (Throne Speech) at the opening of Parliament. This program was intended to apply primarily to urban economic development. The second program, referred to as the Green Book, was designed to stimulate a massive effort to improve agricultural productivity in the rural areas. The Green Book was announced by Prime Minister Tun Abdul Razak in his keynote address opening a special assembly of the United Malay National Organization on December 6, 1974 (*New Straits Times*, Dec. 7, 1974). Though neither of these programs required formal legislation to be enacted, their importance in Parliament is evidenced by the mention they received as "major problems" considered in the fall 1974 meeting.

The announcement of a new housing policy in the Throne Speech touched on an issue which was of deep concern to many members of Parliament, and, in effect, recognized the inability of the housing program to keep abreast of requirements.[15] During the fall meeting, both leaders and rank-and-file members spoke out on the housing plight. Deputy Prime Minister Datuk Hussein Onn (who became prime minister in January 1976 upon the death of Razak) characterized the housing situation in Johore as "very serious" and as requiring increased federal and state action (*New Straits Times*, Nov. 25, 1974). Speaking before the Parliament, a National Front MP compared the allocation of $35 million for housing under the Ministry of New Villages with a drop of water in the ocean, considering the 400 new villages in West Malaysia (*New Straits Times*, Nov. 21, 1974).

Housing was clearly a prominent concern for the MPs in our sample. Some 41 percent of the 39 nonministerial respondents recalled speaking on the urgency of providing public housing in the debates on the Throne Speech and/or the budget. Approximately half (49 percent) of the nonministerial MPs had received complaints on housing from their constituents prior to the king's announcement. As a further indicator of how seriously these comments were regarded, eighteen of the nineteen MPs receiving complaints reported taking further action—primarily communicating them to district officers, higher officials, or Parliament.

The prevalence of legislators' complaints does not tell us whether the government was responding to their demands in its "new approach" or taking an initiative based on other motivations. Our interviews do, however, indicate that many Malaysian MPs feel that their requests for action are influential with the government. In response to questions concerning the floor debates on the Throne Speech and the Budget, about three-fourths of our respondents indicated that they had recommended or requested action(s) by the government.[16] Of those making recommendations, over half (57 percent) felt that the government had taken some action on their requests. Nearly as many (50 percent) felt that the government's action was, to some extent, prompted by what they had said.

Though the government may have been responding to the public demands of individual legislators in its "new approach" to housing, there is clear evidence that Parliament as a body played no significant role in the formation of policy. Though there were complaints, there was certainly no parliamentary discussion of a planned change in housing policy. Only seven MPs (about 18 percent of the nonministerial members) reported any knowledge of the new policy before it was announced by the king. The Dewan Rakyat had not been consulted in the formulation of policy changes.

Once the policy had been announced by the government, nonministerial MPs saw their role from a variety of perspectives.[17] Many members perceived a role in furthering the implementation of the "new approach." As stated by one respondent, he felt obligated to insure that the policy is "not just paper" and is "translated into action."

When presented with a number of possible responsibilities in the implementation of the policy, many MPs agreed that activities involving communication between government and constituents were part of their rule as members of Parliament. Over one-third (35.9 percent) of the nonministerial members felt that making "recommendations to the government" was one responsibility to the "new approach." Just under one-quarter (23.1 percent) agreed that "explain[ing] the policy to the people" or "report[ing] the people's reactions to the government" were important aspects of their role in implementation. A smaller number indicated a responsibility to "make recommendations to [my] party" (17.9 percent) or to "report the people's reactions to [my] party" (15.4 percent). Thus, MPs saw a variety of linkage activities as important to their role in the implementation of the housing policy.

The lack of legislative involvement in the formulation of the Green Book is more evident than for housing policy. Only six MPs reported any advance knowledge of the policy, two of them being briefed by the prime minister prior to the speech. Fully 38 percent of the non-ministerial members of the Dewan Rakyat heard of the policy for the first time through the mass media (newspapers, radio, and television).

Rural food production was not a matter of vocal concern to as many individual legislators as was housing; only six MPs reported having made recommendations on the topic before the prime minister made his speech. Still, the Green Book addressed matters of great concern. As noted above, Malay students had protested against alleged starvation among rural residents; it was undoubtedly more than coincidence that, in the same speech in which the Green Book was announced, the prime minister excoriated the students for these demonstrations. The issue was particularly sensitive because of its salience for the rural Malay majority which provides the political base for the government.

In announcing the Green Book, the prime minister expressed the hope of bringing two million idle acres into cultivation (*New Straits Times*, Dec. 21, 1974). Given the clamor for opening up more land—voiced by legislators at various times during the fall session—this aspect of the plan may have been overmphasized by the public and contributed to expectations which could not be fulfilled. Some months after the Green Book was launched, Prime Minister Razak warned that the people should not misunderstand it and rush to apply for new land rather than working existing idle land or land around their homes (*New Straits Times*, Apr. 8, 1975).

Twenty-five MPs (out of thirty-nine nonministerial MPs in the sample) reported that the Green Book had been applied in their districts. Despite their lack of involvement prior to the announcement, the MPs from those districts in which the plan was applied were very actively involved in its implementation. Following the announcement, 92 percent spent time explaining the plan in their district, 80 percent were spoken to about the plan by people in their district, and 68 percent acted on suggestions or complaints by passing them on to government officials. Again, MPs contributed to the linking of central government to the periphery by explaining policy to their constituents, listening to their reactions and complaints, and communicating them to officials.

The foregoing analysis of the involvement of individual legislators in economic policies attests to the appropriateness and utility of Mezey's dissection of the policy process. In our examples, active involvement occurred either prior to the policy announcement (i.e., in the formulation stage) or after the fact (in the implementation stage). The concentration of MP activities did vary somewhat between the two policies. A substantial number of MPs heard complaints about housing difficulties in their districts and communicated them to the central government, where policy changes ensued. As to the Green Book, there was little legislative involvement prior to the policy announcement, but, in those districts where the plan was applied, MPs were almost unanimously involved in its implementation. Thus, the Malaysian MP does orient his individual activities to either the formulation or implementation stages of policy making or to both. By calling public attention to problems festering within his constituency or by keeping an eye on the implementation of a policy, the MP provides a link between the government and the governed. Identifying the conditions contributing to different patterns of linkage activity, and assessing the impact of these activities on policy decisions are challenging questions for further research on the roles of legislatures in developing countries.

## CONCLUSION

This paper has focused on the Malaysian Parliament's role in economic policy making. Such a study, it was assumed, should go beyond the making of laws in order to explore the full range of possible connections of MPs with economic policy making. Hence, a three-stage model of policy making was employed to examine both collective and individual legislative activities. In glimpsing the Dewan Rakyat at work, principal reliance was placed on the results from an interview schedule dealing with about one-third of the body.

Our analysis of the collective activities of the Dewan Rakyat in the three stages of economic policy making showed a limited involvement. Though economic policy making was seen as important by the legislators, their involvement in its formulation appears to be inconsequential. In the decision-making phase, they have the responsibility of passing statutes, but this occasion is not employed in a manner to make power accrue to the Parliament. The MPs' own perceptions of their place in decision making confirm this judgment. Evidence was found that a consensus on economic policy making among legislators does not explain their peripheral role. As to the third, or implementation phase of decision making, the conclusion was similar. Though MPs use scheduled debate and question times to bring complaints about economic problems, there appears to be no machinery for a systematic and timely examination of such problems.

By contrast, the MPs themselves perceived their individual activities as the principal avenue for contributing to economic policy making. Recent reports on other developing countries' legislators were confirmed by our data. Broadly speaking, Malaysian MPs consider it their responsibility to represent the voters and the special interest groups in their constituencies, to educate their constituents about the development programs, to listen attentively to complaints, to attend meetings in their constituencies at which suggestions and complaints can be processed, and to communicate back to the center those matters that resist settlement at local levels.

Focusing on the MPs' perceptions of economic policy making, we asked them about their actions in relation to two specific programs. They obviously had had no role in formulating the programs, one of which was even announced in a party forum rather than the legislature. Though the legislators had no policy-making responsibilities for either program, they had voiced constituency complaints about problems addressed in the housing program, and made major efforts to follow through with their constituents once the programs had been announced. This was particularly noticeable in the case of the Malay MPs and the Green Book, a program that emphasized the strong connection between economics and ethnicity.[18]

Other recent studies of developing countries appear to relate to our findings. David Morell (chapter 13, this volume) found that legislative influence over Thailand's economic decisions during 1969–71 varied in three process areas: planning (almost no role); policy formulation (considerable influence in some policy areas); and program implementation (great influence). Legislators influenced the location of development projects in their constituencies by working closely with administrative officials in the field or, in the case of some MPs, by means of membership on the Budget Scrutiny Committee. In analyzing the legislatures of Kenya and Tanzania, Raymond Hopkins (chapter 6, this volume) found that activities in the legislature (committees, speeches, voting) had less influence upon development policies than activities outside of it (broker, entrepreneur, member of local government units). An activity which had the high influence on development ascribed to the chief executive and bureaucracy in Kenya was that of serving as broker between the government and the citizenry, and this is accomplished in a variety of ways. Joel Barkan (chapter 10, this volume) has maintained that in the dual economies of East Africa, legislators are superior to bureaucrats and party workers in promoting rural development. In Kenya, by mobilizing the resources of his community for small to medium size self-help projects and extracting financial support from the center, legislators can develop an elaborate network of patron-client relationships because of the absence of central party control. Both Hopkins (chapter 6) and Barkan (chapter 10) emphasize the importance which the Kenyan MPs must attach to being active in the constituency to play the roles described above. Even for Tanzania, which has a less open political system and firm one-party control, MPs can press for government assistance for their constituencies directly with ministries and have some voice in allocating development funds disbursed by the central government.

Turning once more to Malaysia, it is relevant to note that beginning with the 1974 election, government leaders made greater efforts than previously to transform the National Front MPs into linkage activists. The prime minister has publicly exhorted them to work in their constituencies, their increased allowances were justified on the basis of the cost of doing such work, and their positions as ex-officio members of field committees dealing with development problems was strongly emphasized.[19] Enforcement of these norms is said to be backed up with signed resignations in the hands of the leadership for use if necessary. As compared with an earlier period, local party wheelhorses are increasingly being replaced.

Linkage activities often have a general political motivation, i.e., the central government's anxiety about maintaining good relations with the periphery. Yet, the connection with policy making should not be overlooked. Trimming policy to meet the objections of those on whom it operates is one of the best ways for the government to maintain these good relations. (They are particularly difficult to maintain when the presumed beneficiaries are widely scattered as in the case of rural development policies.)

As suggested above, the Malaysian government wishes to make the MP into more of a service instrument through enhancing linkage activities. Furthermore, our data suggest that these activities have an association with policy making, at least in the formulation and implementation phases. There is an implicit ultimate conflict in this approach, of course. If legislators extend their policy making influence beyond the details and publicly and noisily raise questions about basic policy, they will, from the government's standpoint, nullify their usefulness as a link to the political base. Given the strong tradition of party discipline and the relatively weak tradition of collective policy making, this is not a likely eventuality in Malaysia.

## NOTES

1. We recognize fully the frequent legislative roles in interest articulation and aggregation, representation, political socialization and education, and supervision, scrutiny, and surveillance. See LaPalombara, 1974:134–166.

2. Extensive descriptions of these and other Malaysian matters are found in Ratnam, 1965; Means, 1970; Vasil, 1971; Esman, 1972; Milne and Ratnam, 1974; and von Vorys, 1975.

3. Only Malacca and Penang in West Malaysia and the two East Malaysian states do not have such rulers.

4. See Milne, 1967, p. 128. The Dewan Negara is composed of 26 elected members, two from each state, and 32 members appointed by the king upon the prime minister's recommendation. The elected members are not chosen by the electorate but by the state legislatures and are often members of those bodies.

5. Of Malaysia's population of 10,839,025 in December 1971, 46.72 percent were Malays, 34.45 percent were Chinese, 8.92 percent were Indians and Pakistanis. The remainder (9.91 percent), categorized as "Others" in the population reports, were almost exclusively non-Malay indigenes, of whom more than 99 percent lived in Sabah and Sarawak. Only 4.20 percent of Malays, 13.10 percent of Chinese, and a negligible percentage of Indians and Pakistanis lived in Sabah and Sarawak (Malaysia, Department of Statistics, 1974:1).

6. The life of each Parliament is up to five years. Each year constitutes a "session." Parliament meets only fifty to sixty days a year. The budget "meeting" lasts a month or more, but the other meetings are of only about a week's duration. Each day the Parliament meets is called a "sitting."

7. Close contact was maintained throughout the study with the University of Iowa investigators, whose help is gratefully acknowledged.

8. In addition to one of the authors and his wife, the interviewers consisted of four faculty members at the National Institute of Public Administration. Their facility in Malay overcame such language problems as existed.

9. Thirty-eight of 50 MPs interviewed mentioned this problem in response to the following statement: "Now let me ask you more directly about the problems that the Dewan Rakyat dealt with in the November-December meeting. What would you say were the two or three most important problems that came up?"

10. Reliance was placed on the *Parliamentary Debates* and on comprehensive accounts of the daily sittings in the *New Straits Times*.

11. Esman (1972:55) has stated: "If a choice must be made, Malays to a man are more interested in reducing through institutional changes the present socioeconomic dualism, which so closely matches communal lines, than in overall economic growth, though they would like to reconcile these two desirable goals."

12. The contrast of views from Malay and non-Malay representatives yields a chi-square value of 5.97. At one degree of freedom, the between-groups difference would be statistically significant at the .01 level of probability.

13. Our interviews contain information which allows an analysis of the interplay of political parties, ethnic community, and the role of the Malaysian MP. While illuminating, this material is not central to the questions addressed here, and its inclusion is prohibited by space limitations. These data will be explored subsequently.

14. Note that apparently some of the MPs find interceding with the civil service to be an onerous task; 17 percent would prefer to spend less time on this activity. The percentage desiring to spend less time on the other linkage activities is negligible or nonexistent.

15. The Treasury's Economic Report, 1974–75 (p. 93) stated that in Kuala Lumpur "the percentage of squatter houses to the total number of living quarters in the city area is between 30 percent and 35 percent."

16. In keeping with this chapter's focus on economic development, it might be noted that two-thirds of these requests referred specifically to economic matters.

17. Several MPs denied being involved in implementation because there was no housing problem in their constituency. Another reason for lack of involvement was cited by a few opposition party members. They argued that, in fact, there was no meaningful policy and the so-called "new approach" was "all propaganda."

18. The interrelation of economic issues and ethnic community in Malaysia is salient to the specific policies examined in this paper. Complaints about housing conditions, for instance, emanated predominantly from Chinese constituencies; 75 percent of the representatives of nonministerial Chinese districts received complaints compared to fewer than one-third (30 percent) of the non-Chinese districts. The importance of the Green Book for rural Malays is also evident in the application of the policy; the plan was implemented in nearly 80 percent of the nonministerial Malay districts in the sample (11 of 14), but in barely over half (13 of 25) of the non-Malay districts. The mix of economics and ethnicity has important implications for the dyanmics of legislative politics in Malaysia, but its full explication is complex and goes beyond the purposes of this chapter. These topics must await further analyses.

19. Following the National Front's sweeping victory in the 1974 election, Prime Minister Razak announced his intention of seeing to it that MPs would truly become individuals who serve their constituents (*New Straits Times*, Oct. 21, 1974). In more specific terms, both National Front MPs and state assemblymen were told, according to a cabinet minister, that they faced ouster from their positions if they failed to serve adequately (*New Straits Times*, Sept. 18, 1974). A spokesman for the prime minister justified increased allowances for MPs mainly on the basis of the cost of looking after their constituencies (*New Straits Times*, Nov. 22, 1974). The National Front MP is an ex-officio member of a district action committee and is urged to make sure that problems and requests from constituents are made known to the committee and that government projects are carried out in his constituency. The MP is also a member of the National Front State Liaison Committee, which is headed by the chief minister of the state in which his constituency is located. Through both committees, requests gathered by the MPs are channeled to the proper authorities. According to the secretary-general of UMNO, himself an MP, involving MPs in administrative work was designed to overcome some problems that had been ignored. The people, however, having elected the MPs, held them responsible for the difficulties (interview with Senu Abdul Rahman Datuk, Kuala Lumpur, Malaysia, Apr. 24, 1975). For further background, see Ong (1976) and Puthucheary (1970:177).

*Chapter 12*

# THE ROLE OF THE NATIONAL ASSEMBLY IN KUWAIT'S ECONOMIC DEVELOPMENT: NATIONAL OIL POLICY

ABDO I. BAAKLINI

ALIA ABDUL-WAHAB

Kuwait's economic development and prosperity directly depend on its oil resources, and oil policy is undoubtedly the country's major political issue. Since the production and marketing of oil are regulated by agreements between the Kuwaiti government and a number of foreign oil companies, the revision of these agreements to attain more favorable terms became the principal preoccupation of the government when Kuwait achieved independence in 1962. For several reasons, these efforts intensified toward the end of the 1960s and in the early 1970s. This chapter will review in detail the role of the Kuwaiti National Assembly in revising these agreements and in establishing a new oil policy. Rather than deal with the role of the Assembly in terms of abstractions such as "policy initiation," "ratification," "amendment," or "legitimization," we shall review instead the actual debates and other activities which the Assembly undertook to effect a new oil policy.[1]

## THE KUWAITI NATIONAL ASSEMBLY: A BACKGROUND STATEMENT

From its inception in 1963 to its dissolution in 1976, the National Assembly was a political force in the country. A unicameral body, its fifty members were elected every four years in ten districts through universal manhood suffrage. Each district sent five members to the Assembly, each member representing fewer than ten thousand citizens. In view of the small area of Kuwait, the homogeneity of its population, and the tightly knit family structure, elections have been more of a family affair than a political campaign run by formal political parties. Each district was normally inhabited by a group of families that had close blood relationships and, therefore, tended to be represented by the leaders of the families. Thus, it was typical for each legislator to combine roles as leader of his family and his district.

The Constitution of Kuwait, itself drafted by an elected constitutional assembly in 1962, attempted to introduce responsible representative government while maintaining the traditional social structure and political institutions cherished by the Kuwaiti. The outcome was a distinctive blend of parliamentary, presidential, and constitutional monarchical forms of government. The selection of the chief executive, although still the inherited right of the House of al-Sabbah, required the approval of the Assembly. Since there are no primogeniture rules in Islamic jurisprudence, the ruler could nominate any of his brothers or sons as his successor.[2] If the Assembly rejected the nominated candidate, the Emir submitted three other names from which the Assembly chose one.

The Constitution provided for a cabinet to be selected by the ruler and headed by a prime minister, usually the crown prince. Cabinet ministers could be members of the Assembly. Since members of the Sabbah family usually shunned running for election (to keep the elections free from government pressure and to maintain their role as arbitrators), and since there was no upper house to which they could be nominated, one-third of the members of the cabinet usually belonged to the royal family.

The prime minister and the ministers assumed their responsibilities after they presented their program to the Assembly for debate and approval. Since the Assembly was composed of fifty elected members and since cabinet members appointed from outside the Assembly had the right to participate in the Assembly's general debate, including the right to vote on bills, the Constitution stipulated that the number of cabinet members could not exceed one-third of the total number of elected Assembly members. Cabinet ministers, however, were not allowed to hold membership or voting rights in the committees of the

Assembly. Furthermore, when the Assembly discussed a vote of confidence in a certain minister, the other ministers had no right to vote.

Although the Kuwaiti Constitution did not require the cabinet to receive a formal vote of confidence when appointed, it nonetheless gave the Assembly certain options tantamount to the power of voting no confidence. If the Assembly felt that it could not cooperate with the prime minister, it could, by an absolute majority vote, indicate so to the Emir. In such a case, the Emir could either ask the prime minister to resign or could dissolve the Assembly and call for a new election, though he could not dissolve the Assembly for the same reason twice. If the Emir called a new election, it had to be within two months or the dissolved Assembly could call itself into session and resume its work as if it had not been dissolved. If a new election in fact took place and the new Assembly affirmed by majority vote its intention not to cooperate with the executive, the prime minister had to submit his resignation.

Article 70 of the Constitution bestowed on the Assembly the right to approve all treaties entered into by the executive before they became effective. A treaty or an agreement became binding only after the Assembly had approved it and only after it had been promulgated by the Emir in the official gazette like any other law. All treaties involving peace, alliances, the leasing of or giving of concessions on land, properties, natural resources, or the sovereignty of the state or the public and private rights of citizens; all commercial, trade and navigational agreements with foreign powers or institutions, and any treaty or agreement involving expenditures not specifically allocated in the budget document were considered illegal unless passed as a law in the Assembly. Thus, any new oil concessions or amendments to existing concessions had to secure the approval of the Assembly before they became binding.

Laws and treaties passed by the Assembly were referred to the Emir for promulgation. The Emir was constitutionally required to promulgate regular laws within thirty days. However, if the Assembly by a simple majority decided to classify a law as urgent, the Emir was obligated to promulgate it within seven days. Laws that were neither promulgated within the legal limit nor returned to the Assembly for reconsideration became de facto laws. If the Emir decided not to promulgate a law, he could return it with the reasons for his decision to the Assembly within the legal limit, and request reconsideration. If the Assembly reaffirmed its position by a two-thirds majority, the Emir had to promulgate the law. If, on the other hand, the Assembly failed to muster the two-thirds majority, the law was shelved and could not be discussed again in that legislative session. However, if the Assembly affirmed the law by a simple majority during the following legislative session, the Emir had to promulgate it within the legal period.

Finally, for the purpose of our analysis here, we should note that the Assembly was constitutionally empowered to meet each year in October upon the request of the Emir. The legislative session was scheduled to last for a minimum of eight months. If the Emir delayed his call, the Assembly was constitutionally empowered to call itself into session. Furthermore, the Emir, or the Assembly, upon the request of the majority of its members, could call for an extraordinary session. The Constitution, however, allowed the Emir, under extraordinary circumstances, to request the Assembly to postpone its meeting for a month. Any further postponement had to receive the approval of the Assembly and could last only one month, after which the Assembly was obligated to meet.

We also should note that since there were no formal political parties between 1963 and 1976 and the Assembly sought to reach its decision by consensus, a determined minority of deputies which felt strongly on a particular issue (as was the case in the oil participation agreement debate) could wield power disproportionate to its size. The position of this minority on the issue of asserting Kuwaiti national rights on foreign oil concessions enjoyed some significant popular support and added to its importance. The absence of parties and the search for consensus had another consequence. Project laws reported by legislative committees, normally composed of from three to five legislators, were not automatically approved in the floor debate. The small size of the Assembly in Kuwait allowed for a lengthy and lively debate on all issues, including bills reported by legislative committee. The search for consensus dictated that, even when it had the votes of the majority of the Assembly members on such sensitive issues as foreign policy and oil, the government strived for a compromise solution rather than a confrontation. This explained why the Assembly, under the leadership of a vocal minority, was able to force the government to withdraw and amend the participatory oil agreement bill without a confrontation through formal voting.

## THE OIL CONCESSIONS IN KUWAIT: HISTORICAL BACKGROUND

As with other oil concessions in the region, the Kuwaiti oil agreements were worked out over a long period of time. During much of this time, the country had little control over its natural resources. In the latter part of the nineteenth century, the rising influence of Great Britain in the gulf area coincided with the continuous decline of the Ottoman Empire and the widening rift among its various national elements, including the Arab region. The growing Arab national movement hoped that Great Britain could be an ally in its struggle against the Ottomans for national independence and unity. Therefore, soon after Sheikh Mubarak al-Sabbah became the ruler of Kuwait in 1896, he made an agreement with Britain giving it exclusive economic and diplomatic privileges in Kuwait. In this agreement, he and his successors agreed never "to cede, sell, lease, mortgage, or give for occupation or for any other purpose any of his territory to the government or subjects of any power without the consent of her majesty's government" (Stocking, 1970:109).

Thus, when oil was first discovered in 1934, Kuwait was still largely tied to the authority and interests of Great Britain. On December 23, 1934, the ruler of Kuwait, Ahmad Bin Jaber, gave the Kuwait Oil Company, Ltd.[3] (jointly owned by the Anglo-Iranian Oil Company and the Gulf Oil Corporation) an exclusive concession to "explore for, produce, and market Kuwait's oil" (Stocking, 1970:108). In 1946, after twelve years of diligent exploration, the Kuwait Oil Company celebrated its first occasion to market and export oil to other countries. Eventually Kuwait became a major oil producer in the Middle East (Naufal, 1969:202).

For a long time British and American interests remained in control of the vast reserves of oil in Kuwait and other Middle East countries. They not only set the prices unilaterally, but also determined the quantity of oil that would be pumped and where it would be shipped; all this was in exchange for royalties which averaged only 21 cents a barrel (Diamond, 1974:29).

As Charles Issawi notes in "The Washington Papers: Oil, the Middle East and the World," these agreements may have been tolerable in times when "demand was slow, prices were fluctuating or dropping, prospects for discovering oil were uncertain and huge capital investments were needed" (Diamond, 1974:29). However, at the end of World War II prices rose drastically, thus lowering the value of fixed royalties (Diamond, 1974:29). As a result of these changes, the oil producing countries began to pressure the companies for a larger share, and by the early 1950s all the producing countries managed to negotiate agreements for a 50–50 division of oil revenues between an oil-producing country and an oil company. These agreements, raising payments to 70–80 cents per barrel, resulted in a tenfold increase of revenues between 1948 and 1960 for the Middle Eastern oil-producing countries (Diamond, 1974:29).

## THE EMERGENCE OF OPEC

In 1959 and 1960 the oil companies arbitrarily and unilaterally slashed posted prices, the basis of royalty and tax payments to the oil producing countries. Greatly affected by this move, Kuwait joined Iran, Iraq, Saudi Arabia, and Venezuela in forming the Organization of Petroleum Exporting Countries (OPEC). These five countries "agreed to prorate their future production based on 1960 production levels, and to pool and prorate any future increases in world market demands" (Diamond, 1974:29). By 1974, OPEC included seven other countries: Ecuador, Indonesia, Libya, Nigeria, Qatar, and the United Arab Emirates.[4] Although OPEC was unsuccessful in maintaining prices at their earlier level and in limiting oil production, it was able to prevent future cuts in posted prices.

In June 1968, OPEC held its first conference (in Vienna) and "agreed on pricing objectives, which included a minimum taxation rate of 55 percent, establishment of more uniform pricing practices, a general increase in the posted or tax reference prices in all member countries and elimination of allowances granted to oil companies" (Diamond, 1974:29). After the 1968 conference Libya took the lead in demanding higher prices from the oil companies. In 1970 the Libyan government cut production for a period of seven months, after which the oil companies agreed to raise the posted price by 30 cents a barrel (Diamond, 1974:29). Libya's successful move encouraged countries of the Arabian Gulf to take similar steps.

The Tehran agreement signed in February 1971 by Kuwait, Iran, Iraq, Abu-Dhabi, Qatar, and Saudi Arabia raised the "basic posted price of oil 35–40 cents per barrel and contained a formula for a four-step increase in posted prices through 1975" (Diamond, 1974:29). Furthermore, "the Tehran agreement hiked the countries' taxes from 50 percent to 55 percent of the net taxable income and established a system for adjusting the posted price according to the oil's gravity" (Diamond, 1974:29). In 1972 a Geneva agreement between Kuwait, Abu-Dhabi, Iran, Iraq, Qatar, Saudi Arabia, and the major oil companies adjusted prices to compensate for the dollar devaluation of December 1971 (Diamond, 1974:29).

## THE 1972 PARTICIPATORY AGREEMENT

By mid-1972 the Arab oil producing countries further accelerated their demands. Led by Saudi Arabia, Kuwait, Qatar, and Abu Dhabi, they demanded "participation," i.e., part ownership in the oil companies operating in their countries, and on December 21, 1972, they signed such agreements with their respective oil companies. This gave Kuwait, Saudi Arabia, Abu Dhabi, and Qatar an immediate 25 percent interest in company ownership with an increase of up to 51 percent by 1982. In return the Kuwaiti government agreed to compensate the companies appropriately. Since the Kuwaiti Constitution required Assembly consent and approval before any financial and economic agreement became legally binding, the participatory agreement was presented for discussion in the Assembly on January 21, 1973.

A thorough review of the Parliamentary Proceedings clearly indicates that discussions of the participatory agreement reflect legislative confrontation with the executive regarding Kuwait's oil policies. For example, several deputies made it clear that the cabinet's threat to resign if the Assembly refused to ratify the agreement would not obstruct their judgment of how it might affect Kuwait's national interest. (Kuwait National Assembly, Parliamentary Proceedings [hereafter P.P.], no. 292, Feb. 6, 1973:140). Furthermore, assemblymen emphasized that, far from being mere sounding boards for the government, they represented the public that elected them and which overwhelmingly opposed the present agreement (P.P., no. 292, Feb. 6, 1973:156). Several deputies confronted the Minister of Oil and Finance, Abdul Rahman al-Atiki, accusing him of obstructing the discussions by frequent speeches (P.P., no. 292, Feb. 6, 1973:109). They also denounced his insufficient understanding of the implications of the agreement (P.P., no. 292, p. 140) and accused him of favoring the oil companies (by which he previously had been employed) rather than the Kuwaiti nation (P.P., no. 292, p. 149).

LEGAL AND CONCEPTUAL AMBIGUITIES

One basic criticism of the agreement concerned its vagueness and complexity. In a long speech, Deputy Badir al-Ajeel took up specific articles and tried to show in detail that their abstruseness may have been intended to disguise the interests of the oil companies. According to al-Ajeel, this vagueness in the agreement meant that:

1. It represented a change over previous agreements only in spelling out certain specific and special conditions of the concessionary rights.

2. Implementation was left to the government which, in its negotiated implementation agreement with the companies, might give them the upper hand.

3. Rights to natural gas deposits, which earlier the Assembly had indicated should be developed solely by the state, would be shared with the companies.

4. The government's right to limit production levels would be restricted (P.P., no. 292, Feb. 6, 1973:124–133).

ECONOMIC DRAWBACKS OF THE AGREEMENT

The Kuwaiti deputies also questioned the agreement's far-reaching economic implications. Several assemblymen rebutted the government's argument that 25 percent participation was the most that the government could extract from the oil companies. Deputy Khalid Massoud reminded the government that the oil agreements of 1934 and 1954 were signed when Kuwait was still under the British mandate, and Iran, with its strong political and economic ties with the U.S.A., already had taken steps that would ensure complete nationalization of its oil industries by 1979. There was no justification, he concluded, for not starting participation at 51 percent (P.P., no. 292, Feb. 6, 1973:139–143, 147–151). Deputy Ahmad al-Nafisi argued that the signatures of other OPEC members on the pact did not necessarily justify Kuwait's decision to sign it. Any agreement, he asserted, must take into account Kuwait's small size and population, limited resources, and, above all, its dependency on oil as the major source of income (P.P., no. 292, p. 121).

Deputy al-Nafisi called attention to the likelihood that the agreement permitted the oil companies the opportunity to exploit the oil during its best years at very minimum prices. Though a beginning participation of 25 percent would increase only to 35 percent by 1979, by that year, according to the government's own reports, the level of oil production (at present 3 million barrels a day) would have decreased significantly (P.P., no. 292, p. 122).

Deputy Massoud indicated that the oil companies had manipulated and misused statistical information in order to disguise the eventual depletion of oil over the next ten years. Assuming his facts were correct, by 1982, when Kuwait would have attained the 51 percent ownership, the quality and quantity of oil would have declined substantially. Massoud was also concerned that the 1972 agreement would not enable the government to increase its monetary reserves, but that each year reserves could be increased two and one-half to three times what they then were if participation started with 51 percent and if, contrary to the agreement, no compensation was paid to the oil companies (P.P., no. 292, p. 144).

## THE INTERNATIONAL IMPLICATIONS

Attempting to understand the agreement within an international perspective, the deputies were convinced that, rather than reflecting the national interests of Kuwait, the agreement was tailored to fit the needs of the Western countries, and specifically the United States. Deputy al-Nafisi stated that the agreement would fulfill the goals of the United States by guaranteeing that oil would keep pumping regularly throughout ten of the following fifteen years when the U.S. would be depending heavily on Middle Eastern oil, by assuring that the price of oil would remain reasonably low; and by ensuring that Kuwait would not seize the opportunity of the present situation to control its oil production (P.P. no. 292, pp. 117–118).

## SUSPENSION OF THE 1972 AGREEMENT

The events that followed the parliamentary session of February 6, 1973, tended to bear out the deputies' arguments regarding the participatory agreement of 1972. By June 1973, four months after the February parliamentary session, the Arabs' demands accelerated rapidly. Libya nationalized the assets of the Nelson Bunker Hunt Company, a Dallas-based independent producer, and, in addition, took over 51 percent of several major oil companies (*Newsweek*, 1973:34). The deputies' expectations about the prospects of increasing prices were also realized. In June 1973, a second Geneva agreement on dollar devaluation and raising the posted price of crude oil was reached (Diamond, 1974:30). The agreement "also set a new formula under which posted prices would reflect more fully and rapidly any changes in the dollar's value" (Diamond, 1974:31). Iraq cancelled all foreign oil concessions and took over its oil resources. In March the Shah of Iran nationalized the oil industry in his country, and in May he signed a twenty-year agreement which allowed the National Iranian Oil Company to "take control of all operations and facilities of the oil companies, with the consortium to have the role of technical adviser" (Diamond, 1974:31).

The Kuwaiti Assembly's independent stand and its persistent pressures against the agreement were beginning to have an effect. By June 30, the Minister of Oil and Finance, Abdul Rahman al-Atiki, issued a declaration suspending the 1972 agreement and conceding that its terms did not serve the interests of the Kuwaiti nation adequately. In their parliamentary session of June 30, 1973, Deputy Ali Ghanem demanded that Mr. al-Atiki hand in his resignation and that a committee of young Kuwaiti experts be organized to establish guidelines for a new oil agreement (P.P., no. 311, June 30, 1973:56). Deputy al-Nafisi reminded the government that negotiations for the new agreement should be open and its proceedings available to the public (P.P., no. 311, p. 24).

### OIL IN THE ASSEMBLY'S BUDGET DEBATE

Despite suspension of the 1972 agreement, the oil issue remained paramount in parliamentary discussion of the executive budgetary proposal, among the most important issues being production, dollar devaluation, prices, and natural gas.

Regarding production, many deputies pointed out the dangers of the government's intent, as expressed in the executive budget, to increase the level of oil production (P.P., no. 311, p. 24). Many deputies argued for decreasing production because: (1) any increase in the level of production would lead to oil depletion in five years (P.P., no. 311, p. 25); (2) it would enable the government to sell a barrel of oil after three to five years at double its present price (Dr. Ahmad al-Khatib, P.P., no. 311, p. 25); and (3) the frequent dollar and sterling devaluations made keeping the oil in the wells the most beneficial policy at present. Some deputies demanded that the level of production be decreased to two million barrels per day (P.P., no. 312, July 2, 1973:54).

In reference to dollar devaluation, Deputy Ali Ghanem observed that while the last Geneva agreement had stipulated increases in the posted price to cover losses through dollar devaluation, these increases had not been entered into the revenue section, and this caused the budget to show a discrepancy of approximately 48 million dollars (P.P., no. 311, p. 49). The government was also accused of being responsible for heavy financial losses because of its laxity regarding the burning of natural gas, thereby disregarding Assembly proposals that the government exploit this resource. Thus, the government's unwise policies had resulted in a total loss of 600 million dinars: 48 million dinars from dollar devaluation, 60–70 million dinars from sterling devaluation, and 400–500 million dinars from the burning of natural gas (P.P., no. 311, pp. 54–55).

On a more positive note, deputies suggested: establishment of a separate Ministry of Oil in recognition of its importance to the national economy; establishment of colleges offering specializations in oil industry marketing, production, etc., in anticipation of the eventual nationalization of oil; creation of a comprehensive oil planning policy in order to avoid the present financial losses; synchronization of Kuwait's oil policy with the policies of other countries of the Gulf region; and exploration of the possibility of an economic union (P.P., no. 311, p. 3).

## OIL AFTER THE OCTOBER ARAB-ISRAELI WAR

The Arabs' relatively favorable military performance in the 1973 October war gave the oil question a new dimension. Conscious of their strength and of the spiraling Western demand for oil, the Arab countries formally decided to use oil as a weapon to achieve vital national objectives. At an OAPEC meeting in Kuwait on October 17, 1973, "The members agreed to cut production monthly by 5 percent over the previous month's sales until Israel had withdrawn from the Arab territories it had occupied since the 1967 war and had agreed to respect the rights of Palestinian refugees" (Diamond, 1974:31). On October 20 (one day after Nixon asked for $2.2 billion in assistance for Israel) Saudi Arabia enforced a total embargo against the U.S.A. Qatar, Kuwait, Bahrain, and Dubai followed suit on October 21. The Netherlands, Portugal, Rhodesia, and South Africa were also placed on the list. The countries most affected by this move were Japan and those of Western Europe.

The embargo proved to be effective. Despite American denunciation of it, the embargo was the driving force behind U.S. peace-keeping in the Middle East. Furthermore, countries of the Atlantic Alliance could not be stopped by Washington from bending to Arab pressure. "On November 6, representatives of the European Economic Community meeting in Brussels adopted a statement calling on Israel and Egypt to return to the October 22 cease-fire lines, end the occupation since the 1967 war, and declare that Palestinian rights have to be taken into consideration" (Diamond, 1974:33). With some progress made toward a peace settlement, the embargo against the U.S.A. was formally lifted at an OAPEC meeting in Vienna on March 18, 1974.

## THE GOVERNMENT RESCINDS THE BILL OF THE PARTICIPATORY AGREEMENT OF 1972

The Assembly's refusal to ratify the 1972 participatory agreement was based on future projections regarding oil. Assemblymen argued that increases in demand for oil would change the traditional balance of supply and demand and result in an increase in posted prices, nationalization of the oil companies, and manipulation of oil to extract political concessions. In the few months that followed, many of these projections were realized. The Assembly played a leading role in the government's decision, on November 14, 1973, to rescind the bill for the participatory agreement.

Several deputies demanded that the government issue an explanatory declaration for the rescision of the bill which previously it had defended adamantly (P.P., no. 319, Nov. 27, 1973:94). One group proposed that to present a unified bloc in the new negotiations with the oil companies, the government and the Assembly should cooperate in setting the general guidelines for an oil policy before a new agreement was signed (Ali Ghanem, P.P., no. 315, Nov. 20, 1973: 32; Yusuf al-Rifaii and Ahmad al-Nafisi, P.P., no. 319, Nov. 27, 1973: 93 and 101).

### PREPARATORY DISCUSSIONS FOR A NEW AGREEMENT

In its negotiations with the government to set the guidelines for a new oil agreement, the demands of the Assembly accelerated. The former insistence on 51 percent participation was abandoned, in favor of total nationalization of the oil companies. The proposal to keep production at 3 million barrels a day was changed to 1.5 million barrels a day. A strong and persistent request to enter the neglected fields of oil production, refining, and transportation began to be voiced.

The deputies argued that decreasing production was more urgent than it had been six months ago and production should, therefore, be maintained at the minimal level that would cover Kuwait's national developmental needs (Ali Ghanem, P.P., no. 315, Nov. 20, 1973:44–45; Salem Marzouk, p. 47; Abdul Latif al-Kazimi, p. 69; Abbas Mounawar, p. 104). Deputy Ali Ghanem calculated that as much as 1,500 million dinars could be saved even at the level of 1.5 million barrels per day.

The need to increase prices for crude oil remained a major issue. Yusuf al-Rifaii complained that comparisons with prices of other countries suggested that, by following the terms of the 1954 agreement, the government had been causing a loss estimated at $6 per barrel (P.P., no. 319, Nov. 27, 1973:90). Therefore, many deputies demanded that prices be increased to $9–10 per barrel (p. 90).

Possibly the most important appeal was the call to nationalize the two major oil companies, Gulf Oil and British Petroleum. In urging nationalization, assemblymen were well aware that several developments (e.g., the October War; the ever-increasing demand for oil; rising prices; nationalization by Libya, Iraq, and Iran) had strengthened Kuwait's bargaining position (Yusuf al-Rifaii, P.P., no. 315, Nov. 20, 1973:58; Abdul Latif al-Kazimi, p. 68; Ibrahim Khoraibat, p. 77; Ali Ghanem, p. 35; Ahmad al-Nafisi, P.P., no. 319, p. 93). Several deputies also argued in this regard that profits made by the oil companies were tantamount to support for Israel (P.P., no. 315, Nov. 20, 1973:49, 77; P.P., no. 319, Nov. 27, 1973:92).

Recognizing that nationalization would require adequate planning, Deputy Jassem Ismail accused the government of delaying the development of the proper national machinery, expertise, and cadre to administer the oil industry (P.P., no. 315, p. 72). Deputy Karim al-Hujaile asserted that the government had allowed the oil companies to favor Americans, Japanese, and Indians in employment rather than Arabs (P.P., no. 315, p. 62), and proposed establishing Kuwaiti colleges that would specialize in oil production, industry, and marketing (al-Hujaile, P.P., no. 315, p. 62).

Assembly members proposed no longer restricting the government's role to producing and selling crude oil. They began to envision enlarging activities to include petroleum refining, marketing, transportation, etc. (P.P., no. 315, pp. 70, 140; no. 319, p. 86). Abdullah al-Nibari urged the government to exploit the rising profits of petrochemical industries (P.P., no. 315, p. 42). Ahmad al-Nafisi stated that with adequate planning the possibility of exporting electricity could be realized (P.P., no. 319, p. 93).

## THE 1974 PARTICIPATORY AGREEMENT

On January 29, 1974, a new participatory agreement giving the government 60 percent ownership was signed with the British Petroleum Company and the Gulf Oil Company. On February 19, 1974, the agreement was presented to the Kuwaiti Assembly for approval. Although the agreement partially reflected their demands, some deputies still criticized it because they felt that the rights obtained were not commensurate with the new developments. Ali Ghanem, indicating that the representatives of the Kuwaiti Oil Ministry in the negotiations were foreigners, demanded that the government submit to the Assembly the names of all participants in the negotiations (P.P., no. 330D, Mar. 5, 1974:25). Other deputies requested that the government present the Assembly with any correspondence related to the agreement and the proceedings of the meetings that preceded it (P.P., no. 330D, p. 24).

Deputy Ali Ghanem asserted that participation does not merely mean increasing the government's revenues, but means joining the oil companies in managerial control of oil production, refining, transporting, and marketing (P.P., no. 330D, pp. 26–27). Taking this into consideration, some deputies asserted that several features of the agreement rendered participation meaningless despite 60 percent government ownership:

1. Article One, stating that participation should take effect on January 1, 1974, should set a beginning date one year earlier so that the oil companies could not continue to reap the profits accruing from earlier agreements (Abdul Latif al-Kazimi and Mohammad Rashid, P.P., no. 330B, Feb. 19, 1974:81).

2. Article Two, declaring that in return for participation the government should pay the companies 112 million dollars in compensation, was viewed as an indirect annulment of the rights of the Kuwaiti government to control its natural resources (P.P., no. 330D, Mar. 5, 1974:19–21).

3. Article Four, stipulating that each party to the agreement set the limits of production, was interpreted as limiting the government's prerogative to define the level of oil production unilaterally as it deems necessary (Abdul Latif al-Kazimi, P.P., no. 330B, Feb. 19,

1974:80–81). That article, in declaring that whatever remains of the share of one party's oil will be sold to the other party in accordance with commercial prices, also was seen as depriving the government of its right to sell where it wished and limiting its discretion in determining the price of crude oil (Ali Ghanem, P.P., no. 330D, p. 29; Abdul Latif al-Kazimi, P.P., no. 330B, p. 8). Finally, Deputy Ghannam Jamhour asserted that the oil companies had collaborated with the government so that, despite appearances, this agreement offered the companies more profits than the 1972 agreement (P.P., no. 330D, pp. 23, 30, 36).

4. Article Five, stipulating that the administrative committee was to be made up of two company and two Kuwaiti government representatives, meant that participation at 60 percent did not give the government a stronger say in the decision-making process (Abdullah al-Nibari, P.P., no. 330B, p. 81; Mohammad Rashid, P.P., no. 330D, p. 21).

5. Finally, Abdullah al-Nibari noted the absence of a stipulation that assured the future nationalization of the oil companies. The agreement stated only that negotiations would be resumed in 1979, when participation could be kept at 60 percent (P.P., no. 330D, p. 33).

### FROM FINANCIAL AND ECONOMIC COMMITTEE TO FURTHER DISCUSSIONS

Following established parliamentary procedures, the 1974 participatory agreement was submitted to the Assembly's Committee of Economics and Finance for review and amendment. The Assembly convened on April 13, 1974, to discuss the committee's report before its final enactment.

The committee made few changes in the new agreement. The most important was that nationalization of the oil companies should be attained by 1979. The report also recommended that negotiations between British Petroleum, Gulf Oil, and the Kuwaiti government be resumed to enact changes which would require that the language of the agreement be in Arabic and that any judicial proceedings regarding implementation be handled in the Kuwaiti court system (P.P., no. 338, Apr. 13, 1974:29–31).

Many assemblymen believed that the new agreement basically continued to restrict the government's freedom of action with its 60 percent share. Assemblymen once more expressed dissatisfaction, accusing the government of intentionally concealing the proceedings of the negotiating meetings and blaming the Finance and Economic Committee for not insisting on having them be made available (Ghannam al-Jamhour, P.P., no. 338, p. 12; Mohammad Rashid, pp. 23–24). Many again demanded the immediate resignation of the Minister of Oil and Finance, Abdul Rahman al-Atiki (P.P., no. 338, p. 13).

The discussions centered around nationalization. The Assembly was more adamant than ever that nationalization was the next logical step. Disagreements among deputies were only on the question of timing (P.P., no. 338, pp. 22–24, 37, 53). A number of deputies argued that the committee's amendment did not rectify the agreement's basic drawback, i.e., the restrictions placed on the government's rights to attain full managerial control of the oil industry. Without complete management and control of the oil industry, including processing, refining, marketing, and transporting, participation would not be a transition toward nationalization but a substitute for it (P.P., no. 338, pp. 30, 47).

Deputies also criticized the committee's acceptance of the arrangement to pay the oil companies 112 million dollars in return for the 60 percent government participation, asserting that on several bases it was unfairly arrived at and not justified (P.P., no. 338, pp. 35, 38, 39).

This review of the Kuwaiti parliamentary proceedings clearly indicates a dynamic assembly which, until it was dissolved, played a major role in setting the guidelines for the country's oil policy. The debates demonstrate that while the executive was relatively cautious and accommodating in dealing with the oil companies, the Assembly was more assertive and well aware of new national and international developments. This awareness accelerated the deputies' demands. Their claim for 51 percent participation in 1973 was replaced by a proposal in 1974 for total nationalization. Their requirement in 1973 that production be limited to three million barrels a day was reduced further in 1974 by a proposal for one and one-half million barrels per day. Their preoccupation in 1973 with the mere selling of oil was replaced in 1974 by a call for full managerial control over the Kuwait Oil Company, including refining, marketing, exporting, and processing.

In order to assess the Assembly's success in influencing Kuwait's national oil policy, the following developments should be noted:

1. The 1972 participatory agreement was rescinded approximately six months after it was reached.

2. A decision to separate the oil and finance posts was announced

on February 6, 1975. The Ministry of Finance and Oil, which Mr. al-Atiki headed for eight years, was divided into two ministries, one for finance headed by him and the other for oil headed by Abdel-Muttaleh al-Kazimi, a deputy who had served as chairman of the Assembly's finance committee (*New York Times*, Feb. 17, 1975).

3. The 1974 oil agreement was replaced on March 5, 1975, by a tentative decision to nationalize the Kuwait Oil Company (*New York Times*, Mar. 5, 1975).

4. From 2.2 million barrels a day in 1974, the level of production was decreased to one and one-half million barrels a day (*New York Times*, Mar. 6, 1975).

5. On March 5, 1975, Ali Khalifa, a prominent member of the oil ministry, announced that the government was "drafting a detailed plan for the management of Kuwait's oil and gas in accordance with the country's national aspirations" (*New York Times*, Mar. 6, 1975).

6. It was also announced that Exxon would buy 100,000 barrels per day under a three-year contract starting in July 1975. The same arrangement was given to Shell Oil Company for 400,000 barrels daily after October 1. The effect of the arrangements was to allow Kuwait greater independence in marketing.

## CONCLUSIONS

This analysis of debates of the National Assembly in Kuwait is intended to be a departure from the abstract approach that sometimes characterizes studies of legislatures in developing countries. Before this study can be concluded, however, two interrelated questions need to be considered. The first concerns the reasons for the success of the Kuwaiti legislature in asserting a position on a vital policy, and the second relates to the applicability of the findings to other legislatures in developing countries.

As to the first question, it can be contended that certain unique national background factors were helpful:

1. Kuwait, for historical reasons, did not experience the devastating effects of colonialism on its national institutions and leadership. Lacking economic incentives in the country, the colonialists left Kuwait relatively free to manage its own affairs under its own leadership and laws. Thus, the governmental institutions established after independence were not derived from foreign inheritance but were built on the stable indigenous institutions of the country. Their legitimacy was well grounded in the historical memory and tradition of the

people, and they came to reflect the real power structure in the country.

2. Through the closely knit social structure of Kuwait, the leadership remained closely involved in the life of the people. The alienated and alienating elite that developed under colonialism elsewhere failed to emerge and to hold power. Kuwait was blessed with a leadership close to and accepted by the people.

3. Again, due to colonial neglect, a strong bureaucracy—both civilian and military—failed to emerge. Thus, when independence came, the country was spared the bureaucratic struggle for power experienced by many developing countries. In other words, the socioeconomic and ideological bases for a bureaucratic class were absent in Kuwait at the time of independence. This vacuum enabled the traditional institutions and subsequently the general populace of Kuwait to play an active role in choosing the system of government that suited it.

4. The economy of abundance based on its oil resources that Kuwait has enjoyed since independence acted as a catalyst for the legislature. Compromises can be reached more easily under conditions of abundance than under conditions of scarcity. The leadership of Kuwait was able to satisfy the socioeconomic needs of the population, and, thus, to strengthen its political power and legitimacy. Thanks to the economy of abundance, the politics of turmoil were side-stepped in Kuwait.

While these circumstances may explain partially the strong stand of the legislature in the oil case, they do not provide adequate answers to a number of significant questions. Who are the members of the Kuwaiti legislature who led the campaign against the participatory agreement? Do they constitute a counterelite to the executive branch? Are they the majority in the legislature? What is the source of their information, especially with regard to highly technical economic matters? Why were they able to succeed in their campaign? What are the bases of their power and influence?

To answer these questions, extensive meetings with leading deputies who directed the campaign against the agreement, and with legislative staff members, were held during the summer of 1975 in Kuwait. The following picture emerged. Though it is difficult to assign a distinct political identity to the group of deputies that led the fight against the agreement (since organized political parties in Kuwait do not exist), it is generally known in Kuwait that most of its members share a strong pro-Arab nationalist sentiment, particularly with regard to such issues of national significance as oil policies, foreign affairs, and defense matters. In no sense, however, can the group—which usually numbers ten to fifteen—be considered a counterelite either to the executive branch or to the majority of members in the legislative branch. Political leadership and institutions in Kuwait, as we have tried to suggest, are characterized by continuity and evolutionary change rather than by discontinuities and counterpolitical cultures or leaders. The majority of these leaders are still in their upper thirties and forties. All have completed secondary education and many of them have completed an undergraduate degree at some university in the West. Some of them have completed graduate degrees. They come from prominent Kuwaiti families that are at the core of the political system and their supporters, therefore, include "traditional" as well as "modernistic" elements. Many of them had extensive experience in the bureaucracy before they were elected. Many still continue to be prominent as university professors, journalists, and/or rich independent businessmen. Since Kuwait has made it possible for all classes of the population to receive free education, and in view of their family connections, political power base, and professional and business orientation, it is hard to conceive of this group as a counterelite with a definite ideology and a different power base and appeal. Thus, while this group maintains some sort of solidarity with regard to pan-Arab issues, it is less unified with regard to local Kuwaiti matters.

There are a number of reasons for the group's success on the oil issue. Contrary to what might be concluded from the debate, both the executive and the legislature wanted to strike the best deal with the oil companies. The difference, however, was in the political means available to each and the constraints under which each institution operates. In a sense, the executive welcomed the intense opposition coming from the legislature and tried to use it as leverage in dealing with the oil companies. The debate in the Parliament and the widespread press coverage it received actually mobilized popular political support that the executive was able to capitalize on in dealing with the oil companies. Thus, rather than conceive of the Parliament as an adversary to the executive, it is more appropriate to look at its activities as having been complementary to the work of the executive in extracting additional concessions from the oil companies. Both participants in the apparent conflict stood to gain from a change in oil policy. The rhetorical question usually asked—as to whether the executive ultimately could force the legislature to acquiesce—is not only rhetorical but frequently irrelevant. In this case, had the executive wanted a showdown, most likely it would have been able to muster a majority in the Assembly to support its position. However, the executive did not want a showdown because the opposition in the Assembly gave it political muscle to deal with the oil companies.

Even if the executive had wanted to force a showdown with the legislature, the political price it would have had to pay would have been prohibitive. Any political regime associated with the protection of foreign exploitation of natural resources undoubtedly will be contributing to its own demise. A showdown, furthermore, would undermine the Kuwaiti norm of reaching sensitive decisions through consensus.

This reasoning leads to a provocative conclusion—in opposing the executive, legislatures may strengthen the executive and, more important, contribute to the survival of the political system as a whole. What appears to be a legislative-executive conflict turns out to be integrated activity in the political system.

Another reason for the success of this group of legislators with regard to the oil policy was the tremendous influence it exercised in the press of Kuwait. The Kuwaiti press has been dominated by expatriates from Arab countries and normally has taken a very nationalistic position with regard to pan-Arab issues. Oil is such an issue and, consequently, the position of this group was popular both in the Kuwaiti and the Arab press. The executive in Kuwait, as well as the majority of the members of the Assembly, could not disregard the wishes of Kuwaiti and Arab public opinion on this issue without committing political suicide. Furthermore, as we noted at the beginning of this analysis, the succession of political events in the Arab world and the position that such Arab oil-producing countries as Iraq, Libya, Algeria, and Saudi Arabia were adopting toward the oil companies exercised tremendous pressure on the Kuwaiti leadership to follow suit.

Undoubtedly, therefore, at least the outcome in this case would not be typical of all legislative-executive conflicts. When legislative-executive conflict is over priorities and scope of public policies, a legislature is likely to follow different strategies to influence executive proposals. Nonetheless, regardless of the success or failure of attempts at legislative influence, the present study provides a typical illustration of some of the ways the legislature in Kuwait interacted with the executive, even on a divisive domestic issue.

A major question remains. In the Assembly debates the members displayed a large amount of technical information and remarkable sophistication, awareness, and clarity on the issues under discussion and the various consequences of alternate courses of action. While it is understandable that a legislator was well informed about problems and issues of his constituency, particularly in a country as small as Kuwait, informed opinions are more rare on such an intricate and complex matter as oil and its political, international, and economic implications. Where did the legislators receive their information?

Before answering the question two general observations about legislatures will be noted. Some evidence suggests that legislators in developing countries reveal an entrepreneurial spirit dealing with economic development.[5] Also, as legislatures are collegial rather than hierarchical (as bureaucracies are), important issues often can come to the fore when raised by only a handful of legislators. In Kuwait, where there were no organized political parties, the leadership of the institution, elected every two years by the membership at large, was in no position to impose its agenda. Furthermore, the legislature's rules guaranteed each member the right to propose, suggest, and debate any issue he saw fit.[6] As a matter of fact, in the debate no more than five members dominated the discussions and displayed a high degree of expertise on the subject. The rest of the members, regardless of their own expertise on this particular issue, were willing to listen and to follow the lead of these experts among their colleagues.

Four sources of information were significant for the members who took the lead in the debate. One legislator had been in the Ministry of Finance and had served as a liaison between the ministry and the oil companies. He, therefore, had intimate information and knowledge of the actual operation of these companies. He is a university graduate with an emphasis in economics, and a leading journalist. In view of the importance of oil to the Kuwaiti economy, he read whatever is published in Arabic or English on this subject. He politicized the oil issue in his press reports, and as a deputy he tried to translate the technical issues into political positions and programs. Thus, prior experience and contact with the executive bureaucracy was one source of information.

Others received their information from the press and political writings in the country. For over a quarter of a century Arab writers and politically oriented intellectuals have been debating the oil question and its national, political, and economic significance. Therefore, there already was a general awareness of the importance of oil by interested politicians.

Political and cultural clubs provided a third source of information. The Arab Cultural Club, for example, included leading intellectuals in many Arab countries. It attempted to create a community of shared interests among Arab intellectuals. Frequently it sponsored symposia, lectures, and discussions on such important national issues as oil. Some of the members of the group that led the debate were associated with such clubs.

Finally, professionals at the universities and other academic institutions provided needed information and interpretations of this information. In a small country, such as Kuwait, the political and intellectual elite either overlap or are in close contact through various social groups. The Dean of the School of Economics, Commerce, and Political Science of the University of Kuwait, for example, and many of his faculty had strong personal friendships with many members of the Assembly. Quite often, either informally or by invitation, they advise on particular issues under discussion.

With regard to the applicability of the findings to other legislatures in developing countries, the Kuwaiti experience is hard to generalize outside the Gulf area and perhaps some other countries in the Arab Middle East. Nonetheless, a few methodological observations and tentative substantive hypotheses for further investigations can be advanced.

Methodologically, this chapter highlights the importance of intensive empirical studies of political institutions in developing countries as a means of arriving at an understanding of the nature of their activities. Perhaps a period of restraint is in order, during which we refrain from judgmental conclusions. Instead of posing abstract questions and offering abstract prescriptions for development, we might better ask what developing countries are doing and why. Such a shift in perspective might provide a more accurate understanding and appreciation of what development is.

One may conclude tentatively that legislatures in developing countries perform functions meaningful within the context in which they operate. In this particular study the Kuwaiti National Assembly, in its review of the oil policy that Kuwait should adopt, performed functions such as the mobilization of public opinion in favor of certain policies, communication with the public and the government regarding vital public issues, advocacy and defense of the public interest, review and oversight of government policies, and initiation of legislation. If one looks at this legislature's role in defending and safeguarding the public interest against foreign exploitation, it becomes apparent why colonial regimes were hostile toward independent-minded legislatures in their former colonies or in countries where they had substantial economic and political interests. Similarly, dictators may abolish legislatures not because they are obstacles to development nor because "the people are not yet prepared for democracy," but because legislative institutions in developing countries may take their responsibility in defending the public interest very seriously and thereby incur dictatorial wrath.

## NOTES

1. The present study started in the summer of 1974 and is based on such primary sources as parliamentary debates and the reports of committees. One of the authors also spent part of the summer attending the sessions and interviewing the leadership and members of the Assembly. We would like to express our appreciation to Dr. James J. Heaphy, the director of the Comparative Development Studies Center, State University of New York, Albany, for his encouragement and financial support for this study. Our thanks also to the then president of the Kuwaiti National Assembly, His Excellency Khalid Saleh al-Ghaneim and to Mr. Abdul Latif al Fuleij.

2. In the case of Kuwait, however, regulation of succession is governed by an elaborate law.

3. Kuwait Oil Company was later owned by British Petroleum Company and Gulf Oil Company.

4. Early in 1968 Saudi Arabia, Libya, and Kuwait formed the Organization of Arab Petroleum Exporting Countries (OAPEC). In 1974 OAPEC included Algeria, Bahrain, Egypt, Iraq, Qatar, Syria and UAE.

5. The tentative findings of a group of political scientists at the University of Iowa support this position. The data gathered from Kenya, South Korea and Turkey tend to show that legislatures play a leading entrepreneurial role in many aspects of development. In particular, see a recent paper by Kihl (1975).

6. For the organizational characteristics of the legislature and the implications of these characteristics for the operations of the legislature see Heaphey (1975).

*Chapter 13*

## THAILAND'S LEGISLATURE AND ECONOMIC DEVELOPMENT DECISIONS

DAVID MORELL

In a country ruled primarily by military officers for the past four and one-half decades, Thailand's elected National Assembly—when in existence—has evinced a surprisingly large role in and influence over decisions regarding economic development: plans, programs, projects, locations, specific budgetary allocations, and so on. This analysis of such legislative influence has focused primarily on the 1969–71 period, from election of the House of Representatives in February 1969 to its dissolution by a military coup some 33 months later.[1] Comparative information has been included on the impact of the House of Representatives elected in January 1975 and dissolved by the military coup of October 1976.

The analysis is concerned particularly with the question of how Thailand's occasional legislative component has really functioned with respect to economic development decisions, as opposed to how this process has been set forth in theory. In this regard it parallels Jain's chapter on the Lok Sabha. Although the military have remained the dominant element in the Thai political process, elected legislatures—when present—have had a major impact.

One finds in the Thai case a clear distinction between legislative influence over economic development decisions in three process areas: national development planning, formulation of economic policies, and program (or project) implementation. Elected representatives played a minimal role in economic development planning, a function under the purview of the National Economic and Social Development Board (NESDB). Greater involvement and influence were seen with respect to formulation of specific economic policies—not across the board impact, but selective control over such critical issues as the tax increase proposed by the cabinet in 1970. Finally, in the area of project implementation, the MPs evidenced a great deal of influence over such matters as project locations and budgetary allocations. Members of the government political party, in fact, were able to support with central government funds a large number of rural development projects of their own choosing. This support was accomplished both through legislative scrutiny of the executive's proposed annual development budgets, and through the MPs' own use of special provincial development funds. Some of the apparent reasons for these distinctions in levels and types of influence have been identified in the concluding section, along with analysis of the Parliament's overall role in the process of reaching decisions on development issues in Thailand.

Thai politics since the military intervention of June 24, 1932, ended centuries of rule by absolute monarchy and provide an example of political competition between strong, unified armed forces and aspiring civilian leaders in occasional representative institutions, each seeking personal and institutional access to principal sources of authority. Even when military hegemony was complete (approximately 37 of the past 45 years), pressures for some form of a constitution and legislative institution were ever-present. Constitutional forms, elections, political parties, and interventionist legislatures have emerged periodically as alternatives to total military rule, all within the rubric of monarchical political legitimacy and patron-client factional maneuvering. Similarly, during the much briefer and often turbulent periods of civilian (or shared) rule, the dominant power reality has remained the military's intentions.

Some rather unique characteristics of the Thai situation provide the basis for that nation's experience in executive-legislative relations to date, and suggest caution in drawing generalizations from the Thai model alone. Foremost are the tandem influences of the monarchy and the absence of a colonial heritage. The royalty in Thailand continues to perform vital political functions, particularly as the source of legitimacy, cohesive national identity, and politically relevant social status. The fragmentation of ethnic/political components and the quest for a modicum of legitimacy so typical of most developing polities simply are not major problems for Thailand. The continuing importance and inherent power of the monarchy in Thai politics place distinct constraints on both the military and the legislature, limiting the degree to which a military or parliamentary leader can exercise national charisma and render the armed forces liable to the palace for continuing recognition of their legitimate political role. Cessation of this royal recognition in 1973, seen as necessary to quell student dissidence and to punish military intransigence and brutality, brought down the Thanom/Praphat regime; and the return to a military/palace alliance in October 1976 allowed the armed forces to resume their leadership role.

In addition, Thailand is unusual since it escaped colonization. The typical model of a weak parliamentary and party system collapsing after independence, with the military taking over, simply does not fit this case. The military coup of 1932, rather than a thrust to independence from colonial rule, brought the country its first constitution, replacing absolute monarchy and rule by the princes with constitutional monarchy and rule by the praetorians. Ever since, Thai politics has remained elite politics, a post-1932 version of palace intrigue. Other significant characteristics of the Thai situation include a relatively high degree of ethnic homogeneity, combined with a rather well-integrated overseas Chinese minority; a continued tolerance for paternalistic authoritarianism in the political culture; and an increasing gap between urban (Bangkok) and rural polities.

## THE SETTING FOR LEGISLATIVE ACTIVITY IN 1969

In 1968 Thailand was completing a decade of absolute military rule, first under Field Marshal Sarit Thanarat and subsequently under Field Marshal Thanom Kittikachorn. These military leaders had ruled through martial law decrees, relying on the acquiesence of their nation's "bureaucratic polity" (Riggs, 1966) for continued stability and tolerance. Even during this period, however, legislative institutions were present in the form of an all-appointed Constituent Assembly created by Sarit to perform two functions: (1) passage of laws and acts proposed by the cabinet and its military leaders, thus providing a semblance of legitimacy to the regime; and (2) development and approval of a new constitution for the nation.

In the early 1960s Thailand began a conscious effort to develop its national economy. Sarit considered achievement of a developed economy an essential prerequisite to a more open political system. He established a Bureau of the Budget (BOB) and the NESDB, both within the immediate office of the prime minister. The NESDB began to carry out development planning, producing the nation's first five-year plan in 1961.[2]

On June 20, 1968, King Phumiphon promulgated Thailand's eighth constitution, an amalgam of concepts and structures borrowed from various western nations and from earlier Thai constitutions. This document established a bicameral National Assembly, composed of an elected 219-member House of Representatives and an appointed Senate of 164 members (three-fourths the size of the House). Votes of nonconfidence in the cabinet required two-thirds of a joint sitting; otherwise each house could defeat legislation approved by the other.

Of the sizeable number of political parties which emerged in 1968 to contest the February 10, 1969, national election, the following were of later importance in the House:

1. The Saha Pracha Thai (SPT) party, formed and led by Thanom and the senior members of his cabinet, and referred to as the "government political party."
2. The Democrat party, traditional (and conservative) "loyal opposition" in Thai legislatures, with its principal electoral base in Bangkok.
3. The Liberal party, a reflection of factionalism within the ranks of the ruling groups, composed of MPs elected in 1969 as independents, many of whom owed their allegiance to General Praphat Charusathien rather than to Thanom.
4. The Economist United Front, a left-wing, quasi-socialist party with its electoral base in the Northeast.

Party composition in the House changed considerably from February 1969, just after the election, to November 1971, just before the coup. At the earlier date, of the 219 members, 75 belonged in the SPT, 57 to the Democrats, and 73 were Independents. Less than three years later the first and second groups had changed to 127 and 50 respectively, the Independents had dropped to 22, and affiliation with minor parties had become slightly more substantial and widespread. Concomitant with this shift was a sharp turnaround from the boom economy of the late 1960s (Ingram, 1971) to declining growth rates and sharp losses in international reserves.

During the 1969–71 parliamentary period, as described below, elected representatives participated in various ways in the formulation of economic development policy, plans and programs. In general, these attempts by MPs to carve out for themselves and for the parliamentary institution a meaningful role in national economic policy and in rural development programming resulted in bringing elected representatives into direct conflict with the bureaucratic and military elite, whose prerogatives were increasingly threatened by legislative "interference." In November 1971 the military again resorted to armed intervention to regain total control over the political process; abolishing the legislature; abrogating the constitution; forbidding political parties, organizations and even discussions; and returning the country to governance via martial law and decree.

## LEGISLATIVE IMPACT ON ECONOMIC POLICY AND DEVELOPMENT PLANNING

The legislature had relatively little impact on the economic planning process.[3] Contacts by elected representatives with NESDB officials during 1969 and 1970 were minimal, primarily involving proposed locations for development projects rather than macroeconomic planning or economic policy issues. Officials in the development agencies, including NESDB, had become accustomed in the previous decade to implementing their plans and programs alone, without interference from elected representatives (Hatzfeldt, 1968). Three years was too short a time for this situation to change in any major way, at least at the policy level.

Most MPs were interested in projects which directly affected development of their own provinces. As one senior NESDB official said: "Very few MPs are concerned with issues of national development and national planning, or even with the nationwide expenditures of a particular agency. They always ask: 'What difference will this program make for my own province?'" In explaining their relative lack of attention to policy issues, the MPs claimed that they had little power to implement changes at the "macro" level. As a minor party leader from the Northeast stated: "The House has had very little impact on the government's macroeconomic policy. The MPs can discuss plans, especially within the framework of the budget process. We can state that our constituents want this or that, or prefer more emphasis on one approach than another. More than just talking about economic policies, however, there is little we can do."

The inexperience of most MPs in economic matters also limited their attention to economic policy issues. The businessmen, lawyers, and long-term politicians who comprised the majority of the legislature had little practice in coping with the complexities of revenue collection, balance of payments deficits, price inflation, foreign investment, or even budget allocation procedures.

Elected representatives were formally included in the approval process for the third plan (1971–76). Although they did not participate in preparing this document, upon its completion in September 1971 the plan was submitted for approval to the Joint Economic Committee, composed of 8 MPs and 7 officials from development agencies, chaired by the NESDB secretary-general. Although no significant changes in the third plan were made by this group, nor by the SPT party's economic planning group, MPs were given a formal opportunity in both of these forums to review this planning document and note their comments or reservations.

### DIVISION OF THE BUDGET BETWEEN DEFENSE AND DEVELOPMENT

One of the crucial economic policy issues in any nation is the division of the budget between rival claimants in the Ministry of Defense and the Ministry of Development.[4] This issue is particularly interesting in a country like Thailand, ruled by the military for nearly forty years and yet committed to accelerated economic development. Presence of an elected legislature brought into the open this latent conflict between the development budget and the continuing demands of the military establishment.

There was a clear difference of opinion on this issue between elected representatives and government officials. Of 51 MPs interviewed during the research on which this analysis is based, 45 commented on this question; 87 percent (39) felt that more money ought to be spent on development (especially at the village level) and less on national security. Government officials, both civilian and military, generally took the opposite position, citing communist threats to the nation, both from outside and within, as providing a clear need for greater defense expenditures.

### EXPORTS, FOREIGN TRADE AND ASSISTANCE TO SPECIFIC INDUSTRIES

On occasion, the legislators intervened in foreign economic policy issues. As an official in the Ministry of Economic Affairs noted, however: "The MPs lack knowledge in these areas; they generally defer to the government's experts." MPs were concerned with the rice trade, especially on the marketing side; a number themselves owned rice mills. The representatives reacted strongly to proposals from the cabinet for nationalization of the rice trade and elimination of existing middlemen; and they were successful in deferring action on these proposals.

Many MPs agitated for removal of the long-standing rice premium (export tax), hoping to provide greater return to the farmers and stimulate export volume.[5] The cabinet in 1971 finally acceded to pressure for elimination of the premium, coming not only from the legislature but from NESDB, the Bank of Thailand, the Board of Export Promotion, the banking community and other influential groups. The premium was finally reduced on all but the two top grades of rice, those for which demand was relatively constant and price-inelastic.

MPs during the last several months of the parliamentary era were urging the government to open trade relationships with mainland China. In the wake of announcement of the Nixon visit to Peking and China's acceptance into the United Nations, pressure began to build for Sino-Thai trade. SPT MPs were particularly aggressive in calling for trade with China. Of the 18 SPT MPs interviewed in the course of this study, 13 (72 percent) favored immediate steps to initiate such trade.

As with legislators throughout the world, Thai representatives became involved in economic issues of direct relevance to strong interest groups in their own constituencies. For example, 40 representatives from the country's eastern provinces asked the prime minister in July 1970 to approve proposed use of a $6 million supplementary fund to purchase local sugar for export.[6] These eastern provinces are the site of most of Thailand's sugar production, and the cooperation of MPs from different political parties on this issue was indicative of its importance to a broad range of their potential supporters. A similar issue arose with respect to maize exports, an increasingly important component of the Thai balance of payments in recent years.

At times, the representatives advocated government efforts to aid specific industries,[7] often those located in their home provinces. Southern MPs, for example, expressed interest in steps to help rubber planters faced with declining prices for their products.[8] An MP from

Chonburi (an eastern province which produces sugar) was quoted in *Siam Rath* on December 8, 1969, to the effect that "sugar cane planters are suffering from low prices."

## ACCELERATED ECONOMIC ASSISTANCE TO FARMERS

The principal economic themes of the elected representatives throughout the 1969–71 legislative period were that additional resources must be shifted to the village level, more aid provided to the farmers, and steps taken to reduce income disparities.[9] Because most of their constituents were rural, and because most MPs themselves came from the provinces rather than the Bangkok area, they emphasized rural attitudes and aspirations.

This perspective placed the representatives in direct conflict with the national bureaucracy, whose ethos consists of centralized administration of the nation from Bangkok. The nature and extent of aid flowing to the villages are determined in a highly paternalistic manner by officialdom; seldom are villagers' views taken into account. And when villagers' desires or aspirations are solicited, the mechanisms for including them in the decision-making process are so laborious and so dominated by officials that these demands get lost in the flow of committee decisions wending their tedious way up the bureaucratic ladder.

The representatives, in a highly imperfect manner, were beginning by 1971 to make a mark on this issue, one of the central political problems facing Thailand. The MPs were articulating rural grievances and aspirations to the central bureaucracy and, in terms of economic development, were trying to shift the government's development effort down to the people themselves, away from visibly impressive projects and construction efforts whose primary purpose is often the provision of a vehicle for kickbacks to the officials concerned. Though the MPs were not fully successful in these attempts, the very severity of official reaction suggests that they were striking at a most sensitive nerve.

Throughout the period, representatives evidenced their concern over the economic status of the rice farmer. They were particularly concerned about declining prices being received by the farmers for their paddy, and focused on excessive middleman profits as the key to the problem.[10] This activity produced little change in the content of government economic programs; despite legislative pressure, the price of paddy continued to decline during this period. Nevertheless, the administrative branch stood warned of the interest of the parliamentarians in this subject, one of obvious concern to the vast majority of the Thai population (and electorate). The MPs had taken hold of a potentially devastating political issue.

## INCREASED TAXES: A MAJOR LEGISLATIVE-EXECUTIVE CONFRONTATION

The single greatest confrontation between the elected representatives and the cabinet during the 1969–71 constitutional era took place in mid-1970, over a proposal to raise import duties and excise taxes on more than 200 commodities.[11] The cabinet, acting in secrecy, decided to use a selective tax increase to solve its twin economic problems of an international payments deficit and a domestic revenue shortage. The measure was announced by Finance Minister Serm after midnight on July 1, 1970, in the form of a Royal Decree (thus receiving the appelation "The Midnight Decree"). The constitution had provided that, in matters of national security or urgent fiscal operations, new laws (Emergency Decrees) could be announced unilaterally; they had to be approved by the legislature at its next session or, as in this case when the legislature was in session, the decree had to be submitted to the Assembly within two days of its promulgation in the Government Gazette (Sandhikshetrin, 1968:articles 146 and 147).[12]

Although Serm and Thanom justified the measure to the public, they chose an unfortunate tactic, stressing the security threat to the nation in the wake of the crisis in Cambodia and the necessity of raising additional revenue to combat the communist threat. The government's explanation of the requirements for a tax increase placed little attention on the balance of payments problem, either because the leaders felt that the people would not understand the complexities of this situation or, more probably, because the prime minister himself did not fully comprehend the issues involved. One senior official in the economic and finance field in fact placed much of the blame for the resultant controversy on the cabinet leaders themselves: "The leaders did not do their fiscal or political homework, did not consult with any of the leading MPs in advance to explain the purposes of the tax bill, and hoped that use of the nationalism issue would be sufficient to gain adherence for the measure from the Parliament and the general public." The bill included increased excise taxes on soft drinks. As an example of the techniques utilized by the government to gain support, the public was told that, in this time of crisis, they should "drink Pepsi to help the country" (*dum Pepsi chuay chat*).

Many MPs reacted negatively to the proposed tax increase, feeling that additional revenues ought to be raised by creation and enforcement of a more equitable income tax and by new taxes on land, property and inheritance. Such measures, they felt, would begin to reduce the maldistribution of income which had come to characterize Thailand in the post-Sarit period. The cabinet's tax increase, on the contrary, appeared to raise even more revenue from the "little man," at least in the cities. Many felt that it would worsen the income distribution problem. As one frank official of the Bank of Thailand stated privately, "The government was chasing the skinny cow while the fat cat went untouched." The politicized public agreed with these criticisms and was urged to action by MPs, who were vigorously supported by the press.

This episode provides the best example from the 1969–71 constitutional era of the symbiotic, mutually supportive relationship between the legislature and the press. Alone, each was weak and vulnerable to coercion and co-optation; together, they had the potential to wield sizeable political power independent of the bureaucracy. In their response to the 1970 tax increase, MPs and journalists together managed to create a political crisis. As one Community Development Department official later stated, "The 1970 tax increase episode was a demonstration of incipient Thai-style democracy at work."

There were indications in 1970 that the House of Representatives might refuse to approve the overall tax increase bill, precipitating a constitutional crisis more serious (overtly) than any of the events which immediately preceded the November 1971 army coup. For the first time since the 1969 elections, in mid-1970 there were strong rumors in Bangkok of possible dissolution of the legislature. The uproar over the tax measure in the SPT party culminated in three tumultuous party meetings, with shouting and threats on both sides. Some SPT MPs were particularly angry that they had not been consulted in advance. As one senior SPT member said angrily in an interview: "This indicated that we were not trusted by the Cabinet. . . . They treated us as if we were the opposition." Party factions began to examine their options and to weigh continuance of the parliamentary experiment against the desirability of returning to pure military rule.

By late August the cabinet had agreed to compromise in order to gain parliamentary support for the bill. In return for SPT party support of the tax bill in the House, the prime minister agreed to rescind the two largest increases, on gasoline and cement. These two tax items had been selected for special attack by the MPs because they felt an increase in their price would have a multiplier effect throughout the economy, leading to a price rise for all commodities. Also, these two commodities represented the two largest increases in terms of total revenue, thus forming a most dramatic target (a total of $20 million out of an expected total revenue increase of $75 million). Even this concession was almost not sufficient to guarantee passage of the measure, which sneaked through the House by a margin of only one vote (102–101), indicating the defection of some government party MPs to vote with the opposition.[13]

The cabinet's concession on gasoline and cement tax increases illustrated the extent of the power which the House of Representatives had begun to wield, as well as what one senior official privately termed "the weak, ineffective leadership at the top of the Thai government." In the absence of an elected House, the "Midnight Decree" would have been enforced unilaterally, with little if any visible political opposition. But in mid-1970 the MPs were able to compel significant changes in this major item of legislation. Some representatives undoubtedly were concerned about the economic effects of the tax increase, sincerely feeling that it would lead to higher prices of commodities and a burden on the consumer. They also reflected the widespread opinion among their constituents that new tax measures ought to lessen rather than widen the income distribution gap. Another sizeable group of MPs seized on this issue not because of its intrinsic economic merits but because of the opportunity it afforded them to enhance their political reputations, gain newspaper headlines and earn popular acclaim. Members of the press were eager to support the representatives in this campaign, each enhancing the power of the other.

In the short run, the MPs won this battle, one of the 1969–71 legislature's few major victories over the cabinet. But though a tactical victory, it may have been a strategic defeat. The MPs, playing politics with the nation's economic operations, further reduced the overall legitimacy of the legislative institution in the military elite's eyes. Confrontation over the tax increase measure set the stage for dissolution of the House some 16 months later. The cabinet and military leadership began, from mid-1970, to consider seriously the possibility of ending the experiment. Each further annoyance built upon the base of anger at parliamentary independence and audacity in challenging executive branch prerogatives established by the tax increase conflict.

In August 1971, the cabinet rejected a proposal from the Ministry of Finance that taxes be increased, calling it "politically unwise and untimely." The ministers, obviously concerned about legislative reaction, were reportedly of the opinion that the government should cover the budget deficit with additional loans rather than increased taxes. Revenue Department officials were instructed "to work hard to get all taxes due paid up" and to plug tax loopholes. The ministers felt that a tax increase in 1971 would damage the SPT party's chances in the general election scheduled for early 1973. As a senior party source stated, "if taxes were increased, most SPT party members would not get re-elected" (*Bangkok Post*, Aug. 30, 1971).

By mid-November 1971, however, the cabinet had decided to proceed with the tax increase measure, and was trying to push its bill through the House of Representatives in the face of strong opposition from the MPs, especially those in the government's own party. The coup on November 17, of course, ended this legislative opposition to the cabinet's fiscal, financial and monetary proposals. In December 1971, the military leadership indicated that a 50 percent increase in the gasoline tax was imminent (*The Nation*, Dec. 29, 1971).

## COOPERATION BETWEEN MPs AND DEVELOPMENT AGENCIES

As the 1969–71 period of representative government progressed, there were indications of some mutually cooperative efforts between elected representatives and development agencies. It would be quite wrong to view the process entirely as one of conflict and competition.

Community Development (CD) officials reported that many MPs were interested in the CD program, devising cooperative working relationships with CD officials in their provinces. The MPs and CD had many of the same ultimate objectives in rural areas: improvement and democratization. Though their approaches were quite different, the similarity of objectives made cooperation mutually beneficial. The CD Department in Bangkok requested its provincial officers to make a special effort to inform MPs about the CD program: projects underway, their locations, results and so on. A special CD information pamphlet was prepared and distributed to all MPs. MPs were invited to comment on projects proposed to provincial CD coordinating committees. Although in theory this invitation was to be extended to all MPs, in reality only SPT members were invited to the meetings. Other MPs, including some from outside the government political party, were invited to address village and *tambon* council meetings convened under CD auspices. At times, MPs were able to use their political organization to raise additional money to help villagers complete a particular project.

The Bangkok headquarters of the Accelerated Rural Development (ARD) program also encouraged its provincial officers to work closely with MPs. The representatives were to be invited along on inspection visits to ARD project sites and consulted on planning for future project locations because, as the chief of ARD's Public Information Division told reporters,

> the MPs' familiarity with local development needs qualified them for advisory and other work in the office of ARD. Most MPs had served as provincial assemblymen before their election to the House and are experts on the needs of their provinces. . . . In addition to advising the ARD, the representatives will serve as inspectors of road construction and other ARD projects (*Bangkok World*, Sept. 9, 1970).

It was left up to individual ARD provincial officers to decide which MPs would be invited to participate. MPs from all political parties were invited to attend meetings at ARD headquarters.

A senior ARD official estimated that over half of the 26 ARD provinces evidenced "good" or "excellent" cooperation between MPs and ARD provincial officials. He related an incident from Nakhon Phanom province in the Northeast in which ARD road construction equipment had been used in a special project initiated by an MP. In this case, ARD provided the construction equipment while the MP paid for gasoline and per diem for ARD employees.

The Ministry of National Development also made a concerted effort to open channels of communication with elected representatives. On several occasions MPs were invited to the ministry to attend briefings and to air their complaints about MOND operations. These meetings included opposition members as well as government party MPs. Some of these meetings became quite heated. For example, in August 1969 one representative questioned the minister and the director-general of the Royal Irrigation Department about delays in compensating villagers for expropriated land. Another MP at the same meeting reportedly asked "whether equipment available for reservoir and dam construction is still being used in improving the land of some high-ranking officials?" (*Daily News*, Aug. 7, 1969).[14]

As a result of this meeting, the national development minister established new guidelines for payment for expropriated land (*Siam Rath*, Aug. 13, 1969).

## MP ACTIVITY IN DEVELOPMENT PROJECT IMPLEMENTATION

Though restricted in their overall impact on national economic policy, the elected representatives were able to wield direct, tangible influence over the location of development projects in their home provinces. Priorities for water projects were shifted, roads were built to link Village X instead of Village A with the main highway, and so on; all at the insistence of individual MPs.

An independent MP from the Northeast related his role in influencing project locations to the functions of interest articulation and grievance resolution. This MP, and others, felt that their efforts should concentrate on the district office, where most project implementation decisions are made. Accordingly, they spent much of their time visiting villages in the province and then discussing their findings with the district officer and his staff. Another focus of their attention was the provincial administrative officer and the provincial council.[15]

One official of the CD Department described the activities of an SPT party representative from a central province.

> This man, also the Lord Mayor of the provincial town, ran for election as a government party candidate, promising to improve the living conditions of city dwellers. Within two weeks of his election this MP dispatched municipal workers to repair one of the main roads into the town, putting asphalt on the road to keep down the dust. He personally supervised the construction work, which was completed in only a few days. The residents of _____ were most impressed with the ability of their new representative to perform.

### CHANGES TO PROJECT LOCATIONS

Locations of many regular development projects were altered in response to MP pressure. Officials of development agencies stated in interviews that "many projects had been affected."[16] Estimates ranged from a low of 10 percent to a high of 40 to 50 percent of all project locations. Some of these changes were made during budget review hearings, others after personal contact between an MP and a government official, either in Bangkok or in the provinces.

The process of MP intervention in locational decisions may be illustrated in the water projects area. The NESDB, along with the Sanitary Engineering Division of the Ministry of Public Health, had established criteria for determining water project locations, including availability of water, population density in the area to be served, adequacy of existing community facilities, and willingness of the people to help meet project costs. Based on these criteria, locations for future water projects were listed on a priority basis. Beginning in 1969, MPs began to intervene in the process, superimposing a set of political criteria and making extensive changes in water project locations.[17] During this period, Thailand had about 5,000 water projects underway annually, ranging from hand-dug wells to large municipal water systems and major irrigation projects. NESDB officials estimated that in 1970 the locations of about one-third of all the water projects in the kingdom (or some 1,600) were altered due to recommendations, pressure or influence from the elected representatives.

An SPT MP from the North described his activities in trying to induce the government to build a small water reservoir in his province. He said that the villagers in one of his districts had been requesting the project from local officials for several years. After the election, the villagers asked their MP to join them in a new request. In response, the government finally agreed to carry out a feasibility survey. At the time this MP was interviewed (August 1971), the survey had been completed with favorable results; but construction work had not yet been started. The MP vowed that "if construction for this project is not included in the FY72 budget, I will go after the officials again."[18] In the opinion of two senior NESDB officials, the same one-third ratio applied to MP-initiated changes of locations of rural road projects.

SPT party members, especially members of the Budget Scrutiny Committee, were the most involved in attempts to alter development project locations. Many changes in the location of development projects were made during the budget hearings. MPs identified projects in their home provinces which they felt, for whatever reason, would be better implemented in a different district or village. Many such projects were shifted to the site where the MP felt some political benefit could be gained.

At times, an individual MP or group of MPs sent a letter to the prime minister or to the minister directly concerned, advocating a new project location. SPT MPs raised these issues in party meetings. In terms of their frequency, however, modifications to project priorities made during the budget review process were more significant. This is a further reason why a position on the Budget Scrutiny Committee was so desirable, providing an MP with the means to achieve greater usefulness to his constituents; and why membership changed each year to provide opportunities to SPT members. Much of the problem was caused by the inability of SPT MPs to stop boasting to their constituents that they were personally responsible for bringing a new project into the province.

In at least one instance, a representative of the government party objected to a locational change approved by the Ministry of National Development at the urging of an opposition MP. The SPT MP accused the deputy minister of national development of diverting funds from a dam project near the provincial seat to another project in an outlying district of the province. This latter project apparently had been favored by a Democrat MP who was a native of the outlying district (*Bangkok Post*, Jul. 8, 1971).

The revised FY70 budget indicated the extensive changes made by MPs to project locations, with sizeable increases in projects located in provinces represented by MPs who had a seat on the Budget Scrutiny Committee. The pork-barrel political appropriations process clearly was operating in Thailand's elected legislature, as MPs on the Budget Scrutiny Committee reduced some appropriations in order to increase others in their own constituencies (the overall budget total remained constant).

With a few notable exceptions, press reaction to the legislature's role in altering locations of development projects was consistently negative, paralleling the reactions of military leaders and the political elite in general. Newspaper editorials capsulized the elitist view of development in Thailand. "Experts" and "technicians" must be accorded autonomy from "politicians" who, although elected to represent the people, "lack specialized knowledge." The experts ought to decide on project locations without "interference" from the representatives, whose purpose is seen as solely symbolic, "representing" the people—without any power to affect their welfare or modify the activities of their government and its officials.

Many officials and the political elite in general took the stance that legislative politics are dirty, unfair, "political." No notice is taken of the politics of the bureaucratic allocation process (Samudavanija, 1971a), the inequities in a development strategy determined solely by self-appointed leaders, their own "special partiality" to certain interest groups, or the degree to which personal interests of bureaucratic officials determine project locations. All these problems, endemic in Thai development to date, are shoved under the table in these attacks on "the legislative role."

When everything else has been studied, considered, and discussed, the analyst of Thai political development cannot avoid returning to these attitudes of the elite to explain episodes of military intervention, bureaucratic corruption, and legislative nonviability in Thailand over the past 45 years.

## LARGE VS. SMALL INFRASTRUCTURE PROJECTS

One of the most significant elements of the MPs' project implementation strategy was their attack on large infrastructure projects, which have been the focus of Thailand's national development effort (Ingram, 1971; Hatzfeldt, 1968). The MPs talked constantly about small dams, little irrigation canals, and feeder roads, and were beginning to redirect the emphasis toward smaller construction efforts. They perceived this type of development project as having greater benefit to their constituents, Thailand's rural citizenry. One government party MP, for example, was quoted as stating that government should "stop concentrating on the beauty of official buildings rather than their usefulness to the people" (*Chao Thai*, Jan. 15, 1970). As a Democrat MP from the Northeast stated, "We trimmed the budgets of big projects and shifted the funds to smaller ones."

When infrastructure projects were to be implemented in their own provinces, of course, even the most outspoken "pro-farmer" MPs were prone to support these construction efforts. But most of the time, elected representatives were pushing the government to shift its development emphasis down to the villages and their residents.

In retrospect, the time available was far too short to change the project decision-making system, and powerful groups and individuals had a vested interest in continuing large projects. A Democrat MP from the South noted that the Irrigation Department continued to operate much as before, "continuing to let contracts for massive facilities as in the past. . . . The MPs could talk and raise questions, but they could not really control government project implementation." In the end, perhaps the legislators' major achievement was to further annoy the bureaucratic elite.

UTILIZATION OF PROVINCIAL DEVELOPMENT FUNDS BY SPT MPs

One unique feature of the 1969–71 legislative experiment in Thailand was the provision of special funds to members of the government's SPT party for their use in implementing development projects in their own constituencies: a legalized party pork barrel. These funds were to become the single most controversial component of the entire process of executive-legislative interaction, and by November 1971 "excessive MP demands" had become totally unacceptable to the nation's military leaders. The funds were available only to MPs from the government party; no opposition members had access to such government largess. In fact, the development funds were a principal mechanism by which the SPT party grew from 75 to 127 parliamentary members.

Starting the FY70, each MP in the government party was allotted $15,000 for use in carrying out development projects of his own choosing in his home province. Special provisions for members of the Budget Scrutiny Committee, however, soon became apparent. These representatives, as an added incentive to pass the FY70 budget, began to receive $50,000 each. Therefore, when the budget came up for review on the floor of the House, other SPT MPs objected to this inequity within their party; over 100 SPT MPs demanded—and received—the full $50,000.

For a while, government party leaders tried to deny the existence of these special allowances for SPT MPs. As time passed, however, the party's leaders became more open about their development funds effort. In August 1970, "high party sources" were quoted as stating that these funds

> were *political in objective*, while they also made possible the construction of certain roads, bridges, wells or other utilities for the benefit of an SPT member's constituents. *This is the party system in operation.* . . . Any representative who desires the same privilege for his constituents should *consider joining the SPT (Bangkok Post*, Aug. 9, 1970; emphasis added).

*Objectives of the Development Funds Effort.* This pork-barrel approach to political and economic development was designed to encourage recalcitrant party members to support the government's budget requests and other legislation, and to increase the size of the SPT party's representation in the House. As a *Bangkok World* reporter noted:

The government has reportedly notified SPT members of the National
Assembly that, if they permit the [budget] committee to cut the budget
heavily, they will not get the money needed for their 'development programs' (*Bangkok World*, Sept. 12, 1970).

The funds gave MPs a tangible device to prove to villagers, unaccustomed to legislative representation after a decade without it, that
their MP was a man worthy of attention. SPT members were not
permitted to criticize the government openly. The development funds
represented a device to increase their competitive advantage over
their Democrat, Economist United Front, Democratic Front or other
opponents in the next electoral contest. The funds were also useful in
expanding local political organization in the districts, *tambons*, and
villages.

The process did induce expansion of SPT parliamentary membership. For example, one MP elected as a Democrat from the Northeast
province of Roi Et explained openly that he had switched to the SPT
party in order to obtain access to $50,000 for local development
projects. He said he planned to use these funds mostly for "road,
bridge, and culvert construction in remote areas" (*Bangkok World*,
Jul. 4, 1970). Predictably, the opposition cried foul.

*Techniques of SPT Project Implementation.* Due to political sensitivity, an SPT MP using his special funds to implement a development
project had to follow an intricate process. His allowance was provided not in the form of cash but as a "line of credit" at the provincial
level, against which the MP could draw for project implementation.
One of the MP's local supporters might recommend that an improvement project be carried out in a particular village or *tambon*, as a
means of enhancing the representative's image in that area. This
supporter, or the MP himself, might further propose that contractor X
from the provincial town be given the contract. In theory, the MP was

required to hold close consultations with the Governor, District officials
and local leaders in his constituency, to ensure the greatest benefit to the
inhabitants. [Furthermore], the recommended projects [will be]
scrutinized by the National Economic Development Board to certify their
feasibility and usefulness (*Bangkok Post*, Aug. 9, 1970).

In practice, however, such coordination and control were seldom
enforced. The MP would request a specific project directly from the
governor's office (actually from an official of the Provincial Administrative Organization—PAO). As long as the project fell within the

MP's annual appropriation, the proposal was not scrutinized nor was competitive bidding requested. The PAO signed a contract with contractor X, who proceeded with the work. This leniency made it quite easy for an MP who so desired to sponsor "padded" projects, with formal costs in excess of actual operations. The contractor might be a brother-in-law or a political supporter, or might simply agree to kick back some of the proceeds to the MP. These projects were later subject to the same postaudit investigations as are other government construction efforts;[19] the difference was in the absence of preaudit scrutiny.

SPT party officials recognized the dangers of corruption inherent in this process. In late 1970, for example, an "SPT source" was quoted as saying that senior SPT leaders were concerned about possible misuse of the development funds. Until they dissolved the legislature and reinstated martial law, however, SPT party leaders took no concerted measures to control misuse of these funds. They were either unable or unwilling to use this unique party device effectively, maximizing the gains from these funds in economic and political development while minimizing the losses from MP corruption. Yet, as shown in Table 12.1 on page 354, the MPs were dealing on a modest scale as compared with the vast resources available for use, both above-board and under-the-table, by ministers, generals, and bureaucrats.

Some SPT development projects involved plans already scheduled by the development agencies, with MPs taking credit for accelerating project implementation; others, however, reflected the ideas of the villagers or local political supporters of a particular MP. Some projects were suggested by a governor or district officer, who used the MPs' access to special resources as a means to accelerate implementation of a particular effort not included in the regular budget. Other projects were inserted by the MPs directly from Bangkok, in conversations with a director-general or a minister. Most projects started in Bangkok were carried out under DOLA auspices, since the bulk of MP funds were hidden in the large DOLA appropriation. Temple repairs were a popular way to use the funds, and the only one which differed in type from development projects normally undertaken by government agencies. Money for temple repairs was buried in the regular appropriation of the Department of Religious Affairs, Ministry of Education, whose representative in the province had authority to finance the project.

No data are available on the exact division between types of projects. The most popular projects, in order, were identified in interviews as: (1) roads, (2) temples, (3) wells, (4) dams, and (5) schools. One senior NESDB official stated that a large proportion of the funds were used to purchase construction equipment, the machinery being presented to the PAO in a ceremony designed to gain publicity for the MP.[20] Agricultural implements, such as tractors, were purchased by MPs for use by farmers' associations. As for geographic dispersion, in 1971 only six of the country's 71 provinces had no SPT representation: two in the Northeast, three in the South, and Bangkok. Two other Northeast provinces each had five SPT representatives, thus receiving $250,000 worth of special development assistance.

Within a province, interview data indicate that the MPs, perhaps reflecting traditional Thai conservatism, chose a defensive rather than an aggressive strategy. They concentrated on implementing projects in areas of strong support in the 1969 election, paying back an implicit (and at times explicit) promise to "do something for the people who supported me." Projects in these areas helped enhance an existing local political organization which had proved its ability to deliver votes in the last election, something quite new for rural Thailand. Local supporters suggested development projects as a way of increasing the reputation of the MP (and their own role) in the area. Few SPT MPs took advantage of these funds to open up new areas where

TABLE 12.1

**BUDGET APPROPRIATIONS FOR DEVELOPMENT AGENCIES, DEFENSE, AND ESTIMATED COST OF SPT PARTY DEVELOPMENT FUNDS (IN MILLIONS OF US DOLLARS)**

|                                          | FY70  | FY71  | FY72   |
|------------------------------------------|-------|-------|--------|
| Accelerated Rural Development (ARD)       | 14.3  | 14.0  | 16.4   |
| Community Development (CD)                | 4.8   | 5.3   | 5.3    |
| Department of Local Administration (DOLA) | 159.9 | 187.0 | 189.3  |
| Ministry of Defense (MOD)                | 232.3 | 253.4 | 263.4  |
| SPT Party Development Funds              | 1.1[a] | 5.0[b] | 12.5[c] |

One U.S. dollar equals 20 Thai baht.
a. Assuming 75 MPs, at 300,000 baht per man.
b. Assuming 100 MPs, at 1,000,000 baht per man.
c. Assuming 125 MPs, at 2,000,000 baht per man (the FY72 program was never implemented).
Sources: Royal Thai Government, *Budget Act*: FY 1970, FY 1971, and FY 1972.

they did not receive strong support in 1969. They preferred to "build on strength" for the 1973 contest, rather than trying to expand their base of support into other districts, *tambons*, and villages. The validity of this strategy, which characterizes all 18 SPT MPs interviewed, would have been tested had the 1973 election been held.

*Impact of the SPT Development Funds Effort.* For the rural citizenry, creation of these special funds meant an increase in the total amount of small-scale development projects being carried out in their villages. Most provincial development funds were used for minor construction and repair projects: an improved road from a village to the main highway; a new well in the village; repairs to the schoolhouse; construction of a new village meeting hall; repairs to the village temple.

Attempts to obtain data on the exact uses of these funds, even in an anonymous sample province, proved futile, primarily reflecting government sensitivity over the charge that national revenues were being employed for partisan political gain. Nevertheless, based on interviews with MPs and officials it is possible to conclude that projects paid for by these funds represented a net addition to total village project implementation, not a diversion of appropriations from the Community Development Department, the Department of Local Administration or the Accelerated Rural Development program, the three regular efforts which carry out most village projects. Table 12.1 lists appropriations for these departments in FY70–72, in comparison with the estimated cost of SPT development project funds (in fact, there is surely some double counting, for the development funds were buried in other appropriations, especially DOLA). The Ministry of Defense budget also is shown, for comparative purposes.

It appears the projects funded by SPT MPs were either a net addition to the efforts of these government departments (perhaps at the expense of large infrastructure projects), or a reshuffling of priorities for approved projects by these agencies. Many projects originally had been requested through CD channels or included in ARD provincial development plans; MP intervention accelerated their implementation.

Even if they did not represent a diversion of resources, many political and economic observers questioned the efficacy of these projects. Critics argued that the benefit/cost ratio was very low, and that too much money was being spent on each project, wasting scarce government resources. One analyst, a Chulalongkorn University professor of political science, worried that economic development might be hampered by "this attention to minuscule projects: a few tiles for the roof of a temple; 1,000 baht to build a wooden bridge across a canal. Spending money on projects of this kind dissipates it too widely to really assist the nation's economic development." He felt that it would be preferable to add these funds into the operations of regular, planned rural development efforts.

Many observers, including some in the military elite, felt that the process led to increased corruption and was out of keeping with the correct role of legislators. It was urged that MPs urge provincial officials to consider various development projects carefully and assist them in determining project priorities. There were also worries about the duplication of legislative and executive functions. The former should tell the officials what the people want, the latter should actually implement the project. Many in the elite believed sincerely that legislators should spend their time and energy controlling the administrative branch, not implementing projects of their own. They claimed that use of provincial development funds by government party MPs destroys unity and cohesion within the legislature and the country at large and comes close to producing two categories of MPs,[21] those with access to budget resources and those without.

For the cabinet and the military leadership, the provincial funds issue by 1971 had become an intolerable annoyance. Party members were demanding that their allowances be doubled to $100,000 per MP, to improve their election prospects (a total of some $12.5 million). The Budget Scrutiny Committee set aside $14 million for this purpose. Some MPs, apparently as many as 28, threatened to vote with the opposition against the FY72 budget bill unless their doubling request was met. The MPs contended that the FY72 budget was the last complete one before the next national election, scheduled for February 1973, and that they needed the extra assets to enhance their preelection image. The ministry had $14 million transferred to the military's budget for "urgent national security expenditures." SPT leaders were quoted in the *Bangkok World* on November 16, 1961 (the day before the coup) as

> accusing the complaining MPs . . . of trying to create trouble in the party. This has caused great anxiety to the government, a reliable SPT source said, because there is fear that these dissenters might vote against the budget bill in its second or third readings. The source admitted that the trouble stemmed from the fact that the military has taken the 280 million baht set aside for electioneering.

The final resolution of this dilemma, a competition between rural-based demands by elected representatives and "security requirements" as perceived by the military elite, culminated the next day in dissolution of the legislature, party, and constitution.[22]

### THE 1975 LEGISLATURE AND ECONOMIC DEVELOPMENT DECISIONS

In October 1973, the lingering animosity toward the military leaders who had carried out the November 1971 coup and ruled in a repressive style thereafter exploded in a cataclysm of violence (Race, 1974). Student-led demonstrations, initially seeking only a new constitution, mushroomed into violence in the streets and ended only with the king's personal intervention to dispatch into exile the three most prominent military leaders: Field Marshals Thanom and Praphat and Thanom's son (Praphat's son-in-law), Colonel Narong. A civilian prime minister, closely associated with the king, was appointed; he presided over the familiar process of drafting a new constitution and convening elections for a new National Assembly.

Forty-two political parties formally entered 2,193 candidates in the election for the new 269-member House of Representatives, held on January 26, 1975. The election proceeded with relatively little difficulty, but voter turnout was low even by comparison with previous Thai elections. No party (or likely multiparty coalition) gained a majority position (135) in the new House. Twenty-two parties had at least one representative elected, with nine having double-digit representation (ranging from Democrat party, 72; Social Justice party, 45; Thai Nation party, 28, to six others between 19 and 10). Only 69 of the House members elected (26 percent) had previously served in Parliament; all 200 others were newcomers.

These results led to a series of negotiations among party leaders in the days following the election. Finally, on February 13, former prime minister and long-time Democrat party leader M.R. Seni Pramoj was formally selected by the House as prime minister and asked to form a cabinet. His coalition included MPs from the Democrat, Social Agrarian, Social Action, New Force, United Socialist Front, and three minor parties. Seni's cabinet was announced on February 26; then on March 6 the House in the required confidence vote overthrew the new government, 152–111.

After the collapse of Seni's coalition, three major parties on the right (Social Justice, Thai Nation and Social Nationalist), plus the

Social Action party (SAP) and 10 minor parties, supported Seni's brother M.R. Kukrit Pramoj as head of a new coalition government. Kukrit, leader of SAP, is a respected and influential author, publisher, newspaper columnist, and advisor to the king. He has been frankly supportive in the past of the military's "men of action," and disdainful of civilian politics and politicians. In 1946, he founded the country's first political party, but he never actively reentered politics until 1974 when he founded SAP. He was president of the indirectly elected National Assembly which served as the nation's legislature during 1974.

Kukrit presented his government's policies to the House on March 19, in a spectacular one-man show. In contrast to his brother, who had allowed each minister to respond to questions in his own policy area, Kukrit dominated the floor during the entire 12-hour debate. Several aspects of his economic policies are worthy of special attention. They were not only unexpected and overwhelming in scope, but also serve to illustrate the vital latent influence which representative political institutions can wield over the economic policies or decisions of a regime dependent on a parliament for its tenure in office.

The Kukrit government proposed establishment of a national minimum wage of $50 per month for each employed individual at least 20 years of age. (Thailand's per capita annual income is only barely above $100). Two potentially contradictory targets were established: achievement of full employment within five years, along with total eradication of inflation. Perhaps of greatest immediate significance, the government proposed to assist the rural sector by allocating a special fund of $125 million for development projects in the country's 5,000 *tambons* (subdistricts); this is ten times the size of the SPT party's development funds program proposed but not implemented in 1971. Project development grants of $25,000 were to be made available to each *tambon*, to be spent as the *tambon* council—a quasi-elected body—saw fit. This is infinitely more money than these rural leaders have ever before been allocated by the central government for project initiation.[23] Urban residents, however, were not neglected in the Kukrit government's largess. The new government promised to build 20,000 units of public housing a year for low-income workers; and those earning less than $50 per month were to be provided with free bus transportation.

Although many representatives from opposition parties castigated Kukrit's economic policies as unrealistic, inflationary or utopian (*Sri*

*Araya*), they certainly did achieve a broad political appeal. After the lengthy debate had wound to a conclusion, the government won its vote of confidence by a margin of 16 votes, 140–124. There seems no question but that the demands of coalition politics in a 22-party House of Representatives, along with Kukrit's own shrewd political skills, induced him to adopt such an innovative set of economic policies.

Torn by political conflict, this attempt at representative government was ended by a brutal military coup on October 6, 1976. One of the new government's first acts was to end the *tambon* development funds program.

## CONCLUSIONS: IMPACT OF AN ELECTED LEGISLATURE ON ECONOMIC DEVELOPMENT

Whenever present in the political structure, Thailand's legislators have intervened forcefully in the on-going operations of the country's development agencies, representing the interests of their rural constituents. In the 1969–71 period, they concentrated on two aspects of the economic development process. On the "macro" side, they reacted negatively to the cabinet's proposal to increase import duties and excise taxes as a principal measure to improve Thailand's balance of payments situation. In a stormy series of meetings which came close to compelling the military leaders to halt the constitutional experiment in 1970 rather than 1971, the House forced the cabinet to rescind the two largest tax increases. The amended tax increase bill then passed by only a one-vote margin.

The MPs were even more deeply involved, however, in issues of project implementation, especially in altering the locations of development projects. Their primary intent was to demonstrate tangibly to their constituents that elected representatives indeed were capable of providing useful assistance to villagers. The SPT party in 1970 initiated its controversial program of providing money from the national budget for party representatives to implement development projects of their own choosing. The underlying objectives behind this concept were to improve the capabilities and strength of the government's political party while expanding rural infrastructure.

Representatives attacked the efficiency of large infrastructure projects favored in the first and second plans, demanding more attention to small projects, village-level irrigation canals, and feeder roads, efforts which they claimed would be of greater benefit to the people. In 1971, just prior to the military coup, the MPs were urging greater expenditures on smaller projects while the cabinet was claiming the need for additional "urgent national security expenditures."

Unfortunately, there is no simple answer to the fundamental question of whether the representatives' activities helped or hindered their nation's economic progress. This would require not only measurement of technically complex macroeconomic parameters but agreement on certain definitional imperatives as well. And this brings one immediately to the contradictory perceptions of different groups, their placement of priorities on alternative goals and actions.

In the eyes of bureaucrats and military men, the MPs' interventions reduced the effectiveness of development planning and implementation and caused rates of economic progress to decline. The representatives certainly used their access to development project decisions to enhance their own political power; some surely enhanced their personal fortunes as well. At the same time, however, many MPs were convinced that they were providing important assistance to villagers: countering tax increases they considered to be unfair; agitating for increased attention to smaller projects rather than massive infrastructure; altering the locations of development projects; and even (for SPT members) implementing development projects on their own initiative.

These different perceptions lie at the heart of identifying the direction of the elected legislature's overall impact on Thailand's development. If development in the Thai context is to be stimulated best by the "trickle-down" process typified by private capital foreign investment models, then the presence of an elected legislature in Bangkok from early 1969 to late 1971 (and again in 1975–76) hindered GNP growth rates. On the other hand, if one accepts a politicized model of development emphasizing growth in the rural sector along with some expansion on the industrial/urban front—typified perhaps by China's experience since 1949—then the legislators were indeed levering the system in a "positive direction."

Three parallel dichotomies identify the MPs' role and impact on economic development:

Elite — Mass
Urban — Rural
Large Projects — Small Projects

In each paired case, the development bureaucracy and its military allies since the inception of economic planning in Thailand have stood clearly for the former value, while the legislature has come down rather strongly in support of the latter.

The most controversial aspect of MP involvement in the development process was the SPT party's use of provincial development funds, and the later focus under the elected Kukrit government on the *tambon* development funds effort. Since this money came from regular government revenues, many observers felt it should be used for the welfare of the citizenry as a whole, not restricted to use by government party MPs alone (1970–71), or allocated by members of *tambon* councils (1975–76). Others, however, view decentralization of government decisions and political party development, and especially expansion of the capabilities of a government party, as crucial to achieving a successful transition from military rule, finally institutionalizing representative, civilian government.

Thailand, to date, has been characterized by an overabundance of weak, parliamentary-based political parties. What has been most lacking is a mass-based party which would emphasize political education and mobilization of the rural electorate into political activity (Wilson, 1962). Few parliamentary parties have been interested in establishing extraparliamentary mechanisms. As a result of this characteristic of party development, political activities have remained the affair of bureaucratic officials and elected representatives, with the people remaining little more than an "audience for the political theater." Those originally disinterested in politics, remain disinterested (Thongthammachat, 1971). If Thai provincial development funds were indeed useful in expanding SPT party capabilities and producing greater party strength ("institutionalization"), they may have been a useful addition to the political process. Tangible projects, rather than vague concepts of "controlling the government by interpellation and legislation," so difficult to explain to a Thai villager unaccustomed to the democratic process, were important to the MPs in creating an identity in the eyes of their constituents as men of continuing importance and utility.

The representatives focused on administrative power rather than on policy alternatives. For a new institution, with severely constrained power of its own, perhaps this may have been the legislature's only real option. The MPs had little experience in economic matters and had no staff aides to perform research for them. More important, in a "bureaucratic polity" control over the government's administrative tasks would seem to provide the only short-term route to political power. The representatives were not content to simply legislate, interpellate, and make speeches on overall policy issues. In their attempt to institutionalize an electoral/legislative system and create for it a meaningful political role, their only alternative was to intervene directly, seeking administrative power. For a legislature to become a powerful extrabureaucratic institution in a developing country, rather than just an impotent tool of the military/bureaucratic elite, intervention in administration of development projects may be essential.

However, this MP intervention constituted a major challenge to executive branch prerogatives, even though the total amount of money involved in the SPT development funds effort was relatively small when compared with the CD program, ARD, or the Ministry of Defense budget. The gains in improved capabilities of political institutions such as the House of Representatives and the government political party, as well as the impact in providing villagers with useful development projects, may have been worth this level of expenditure. But the challenge to executive branch domination of the political system—both from the SPT effort and from other MP-induced changes to development project locations—eventually proved too severe. The final result perhaps indicates that the MPs really were having success in forging "utility function links" with their rural constituents, a rare event for a district officer or other functionary of the central bureaucracy. The terms of trade in executive-legislative competition may in 1971 have appeared so unpromising to the elite that they felt forced to preempt further accrual of MP power, rather than risk the results of the election scheduled for February 1973.

The internal organization of the legislature, its committee structure and mode of operations, also suggest a model of ad hoc intervention against targets of opportunity in the economic development sphere. Most of the influence which elected representatives had over development project decisions was wielded by members of the Budget Scrutiny Committee, not by the MPs assigned to the House Standing Committee on Economic Affairs, which met only 21 times in 33 months (Samudavanija, 1971a:18). Membership on the Budget Scrutiny Committee changed in each of the three years, reflecting intense competition for seats on this influential unit; there was no apparent demand for seats on the Economic Affairs Committee, even the chairman of which had no particular influence over economic decisions.

On balance, in terms of the overall Thai political process, the MPs' application of political criteria to issues of national *economic* policy, and to implementation of development projects, while it lasted, was probably a useful contribution to Thai *political* development. This dichotomy would seem to lie behind the others suggested above, and thus ranks as a principal latent function of the Thai legislature. The fiscal costs of introducing these rural inputs into the decision-making process, superimposing new political criteria over traditional administrative/bureaucratic ones, do not seem to have been overly large. After a gap of eleven years without elected representatives, and given the low levels of political consciousness of most rural Thais, defects in the process may have been a small price to pay for expansion of the credibility and capability of representative political institutions. It might have been preferable for local development funds to have been made available to all MPs, from whatever political party, and listed openly in the budget, not hidden away like a secret and probably corrupt expense. Such improvements were made in the later *tambon* development funds effort. The legislative branch might also have established an information/operations room, where the locations of ongoing and planned development projects could be viewed in overall perspective; and a reference service might have been established to provide legislators with reliable information on economic policy issues.

Whatever the outcome for political development, it was an historic move to permit nonofficials to introduce the interests of villagers (and of electoral politicians) into decision making on budgetary allocations and development project implementation. Unfortunately, such MP intervention so alienated the military elite and its bureaucratic allies that, though helpful to the villagers and to institutionalization of the government political party, in 1971 the price of this annoyance proved severe indeed.

## NOTES

1. Much of this material is drawn from the larger study by the author of Thai executive-legislative relations and civil-military interaction during this period; see Morell (1974).

2. A report by a World Bank study team in the late 1950s laid the basis for establishment of the NESDB and initiation of an economic planning mission; see International Bank for Reconstruction and Development (1959).

3. The role of the NESDB in economic planning and policy formulation is described in Hatzfeldt (1968); Ungphakorn (1975); Muscat (1966); and Silcock (1966:258–288).

4. The most comprehensive analysis of Thai budgetary procedures, and their political implications, is found in Samudavanija (1971b); also see Ingram (1971:175–202).

5. For a detailed examination of the rice premium, including a broader perspective on government rice policies in general, see Siamwalla (1975) (a more detailed version of this article appears in Ungphakorn, 1975). Additional information on this topic appears in Ingram (1971:36–97) and Silcock (1966:206–257).

6. Data on sugar prices and government subsidies are presented in Akrasanee (1975:41–45).

7. For an analysis of import substitution policies in Thailand and their economic impact, see Akrasanee (1977); Ingram (1971:112–148); and Silcock (1966:128–150).

8. Data on rubber prices and government subsidies are presented in Akrasanee (1975:45–46).

9. The most extensive analysis of income distribution patterns in Thailand is Meesuk (1976).

10. The perception of excessive profits being achieved by middlemen in the rice trade is seen in Ingram (1971); and Silcock (1967). A contrasting view which refutes the traditional conception of middlemen obtaining excessive profits in buying rice is expressed in Siamwalla (1976).

11. The economic impact of import tariffs in Thailand is studied in Suwankiri (1975). Thailand's overall tax structure and taxation policies are examined in Krongkaew (1975); also see Silcock (1966:151–189); and Rozenthal (1970).

12. Article 147 of the 1968 Thai Constitution stated: "If, during a session, there arises a necessity to enact a law dealing with taxes, duties or currency, which, in the interest of the state requires an urgent and confidential deliberation, the King may issue an Emergency Decree which shall provisionally have the force of an Act."

13. There could not have been many abstentions, for the total vote was 203 MPs out of a House of 219 total members (93 percent). This was the highest percentage of MPs voting on any major issue in the 1,009 days of the legislature's existence, indicating the strong feelings generated by the tax increase controversy. Compare this turnout, for example, with the vote on another issue, the power of criminal investigation, where the House split 84–82 (76 percent of the House).

14. See "The Man in the Street" Column, *Siam Rath*, Apr. 11, 1969, for a negative view of these MP-MOND sessions.

15. A number of MPs were simultaneously members of elected provincial councils, enhancing their access to its decisions.

16. A review of obstacles to project planning in an earlier period is provided in Buranasiri and Unakul (1965).

17. Political considerations, however, were not completely absent in original determinations of water project locations; but these decisions involved bureaucratic politics, not electoral/legislative politics. The balance of project expenditures between provinces was determined politically by the Ministry of Interior in Bangkok. Governors and district officers then had a great deal of flexibility in applying NESDB criteria in their areas. Many locations were chosen because the officials had a particularly close relationship with a *kamman* or *phuyaiban*, or because a local headman agreed to pay a certain fee to obtain the project for his community. This act enhanced the headman's political status in the village while providing additional revenue to the governor or district officer involved.

18. A detailed example of the elected representatives' activities in initiating changes to project locations is given in Morell (1972).

19. These postaudits notoriously have been inadequate in Thailand. Auditors examine only the papers formally submitted for the project. Whatever figures may be included in these papers are accepted as long as they are internally consistent and in accord with the total project appropriation, no matter what their discrepancy from reality. No spot checks are made to observe the quality of construction in the project or to verify the actual costs of materials.

20. This official questioned the capability of the PAOs to maintain and operate the equipment, since "over half of their existing equipment already is deadlined due to poor maintenance practices, lack of spare parts and lack of money to buy spares." Much of this PAO equipment had been provided to Thailand by the USAID program. The NESDB official questioned the efficacy

of providing even more equipment to the PAOs via the MPs, foreign aid, or whatever, since they could not adequately maintain what they already had.

21. The 1932 Constitution provided for a unicameral legislature with two categories of MPs, elected and appointed. This pattern was followed in later constitutions. In 1968, it was modified to include two houses, an elected House of Representatives and an appointed Senate.

22. In 1969, exactly 25 months before the coup, one Democrat MP, in fact, had predicted such an outcome if the government party proceeded with its "improper" development funds scheme. "Whenever there is a coup, the MPs are blamed for causing chaos and asking for money. In the past, it has been the government's own MPs who caused chaos. *The primary cause of past coups was not bad MPs, but distribution of money by the government to its MPs*" (*Siam Rath*, Oct. 17, 1969; emphasis added). A similar prediction was made in February 1970 by an independent MP, who told the press that "he disagreed with the government's distribution of money to its MP members because it will . . . lead to the MPs asking for construction contracts in the provinces. . . . *Such a practice will eventually lead to a coup*" (*Thai Rath*, Feb. 5, 1970; emphasis added).

23. The impact of this program was analysed in Chinachit (1975); also see Morell (1976:170).

# CONCLUSION

# Chapter 14

## CONCLUSION: RETROSPECT AND PROSPECT

LLOYD D. MUSOLF
JOEL SMITH

The function of this brief concluding discussion is to relate our initial ideas, as expressed in the Introduction, to the materials on legislatures and development reported in the rest of this volume. Our introductory chapter suggested that the relationship between legislatures and development, especially in the Third World, is highly malleable and that many of its aspects would tend to diverge from stereotypes of Western polities. These conventional notions have produced a one-dimensional view of legislatures only slightly caricatured as, "if they aren't the central policy-making organ, they're not worthy of attention." Such a viewpoint, we argued, pays too little attention to the subtleties of what legislatures are, how they may operate in other social systems, and the development process. Certainly the preceding chapters have illustrated (1) the enormous range of possible roles of legislatures in development, when both are viewed broadly, and (2) the need to look elsewhere than formal policy making—without slighting its importance. The intricacy of each situation permits no more than the briefest of references to the individual chapters here, but these should give a general picture of the analyses. These observations also reflect the tenor of the discussion at the four-day conference at which each chapter was discussed.

From the discussions among the participants at the conference, it appeared that some, at least, have no intellectual quarrel with the purely functional view that a legislature need not be called that to be one in effect. To be sure, the annual party convention in a one-party state without a "people's assembly" might be accepted as a structural equivalent to a legislature more easily than would a military junta in a no-party, no-legislature state. Nevertheless, if the proponents of these different views accept as a criterion for identifying a legislature that it has the potential to formulate and implement policy, there can be no sharp distinction between these two examples. When legislatures are discussed in a volume such as this, and particularly when institutions explicitly called legislatures are being related to a process (development), a nominalistic view is more manageable than a purely functional one. Of course, functionalism is hardly rejected by saying that a legislature is what a country formally designates as such. The question of what functions a recognized legislature actually performs may still be raised. A nominalistic approach does facilitate asking: (1) What is in practice ascribed to a body designated as a legislature? and (2) How do its structural features appear to relate to its ability to perform in various designated and undesignated roles and to survive? It also permits an observer to concentrate upon the appearance, disappearance, and reappearance of those legislatures that are designated as such.

Certainly the chapters confirm popular impressions that legislatures in developing countries ordinarily are not the chief movers and shakers in the political process. It is the rare legislature that lends real substance to such direct activities as prohibiting or requiring actions and appropriating or withholding funds. What is less apparent is that this does not mean that a given legislature is necessarily inconsequential. Legislatures—or, more frequently, certain of their members—enter into such indirect but critical activities as bargaining in plural societies, linkage arrangements in multiparty systems, or personal representation of citizens to administrators in virtually any type of political system. Also apparent from the chapters is the instability of developing countries' political systems. In effect, this means that no political institution can be written off, for all are caught up in the political maelstrom. Indeed, the proposition that the dilemmas of new developing states are such as to call for the coming into being of legislature-like bodies appears in one form or another in several chapters. Some attribute the frequent renascence of overthrown legislatures to these dilemmas.

The instability of the political order is more nearly the result of the grim fight for national survival than it is the product of newness and a lack of tradition, a fact that requires us to take a broad view of development. Our contributors concur that the development goals of hard-pressed nations include: (a) achieving sufficient productive capacity to increase national wealth; and (b) developing a pattern and process of distribution of the gross national product that avoids gross disparities or, more significantly, creates a strong sense of common purpose to ameliorate internal threats to national security and survival and to facilitate mobilization against external threats. Certainly the difficulties in achieving any one of these development aims is great. The effort to achieve both social redistribution and economic expansion has been more than most developing nations can tolerate without a seismic shock to their political institutions. Both of these ambitious aims, however, are generally pursued—in an age of nation states—in the context of system maintenance and national survival. Yet, the precise content given this third aim will vary in terms of the concatenation of events and the grouping of political instruments that attempt to deal with it.

What all this suggests is that the grim context in which development occurs (or at least is pursued) places a premium upon the adaptability of political institutions. It suggests, further, that legislatures have at least a potential advantage over other institutions in achieving adaptability. Adaptability implies an openness to receive informational inputs as well as to act upon them. Given the frequent lack of a sense of national identity among the populace, center-periphery disparities in economic development, and formidable communication problems, the informational outreach of any political institution may be its most crucial attribute. Whether or not it is at the center of political power, a legislature has the potential to meet these requirements. It also has a better basis than most institutions to *claim* that its participation is representative and its actions socially legitimate. It is at least conceivable that the frequent reappearance of legislatures in developing countries is based on more than the motivation to add a political institution giving the government international respectability and the trappings of legitimacy. Or, if their usefulness as the eyes and ears of the regime is not granted, it must still be acknowledged that potentially they possess this and other capacities. Because they can proceed as if they may act by choosing among a variety of alternatives, and as if nothing is finally settled before their action, they have a basis for presenting themselves as needing information, wanting to explain positions, having to bargain, and engaging in various linkage activities.

In relating these observations to the preceding chapters, it is pertinent to observe that they treat legislatures from several perspectives, which helps account for the various legislature-development relationships they reveal. In some instances, legislatures are considered as institutional, collective organizations of positions with certain pre-specified and explicit tasks. At the institutional level, all legislatures do their own housekeeping (i.e., provide internal organization and operating procedures), which is central to their capacity to conduct the routine business that permits them to serve legitimating symbolic functions. As assemblages of authoritative actors, however, they may pass bills, appropriate funds, and the like. Such externally oriented activities count a great deal, and how they are organized for substantive action and relate to other political institutions is crucial, but whatever the importance of such externally oriented activities there is evidence to suggest that some fields are less susceptible to legislative influence than others. The place of most legislatures of developing countries in fertility control, for example, has been minor. The explanation rests partly upon the absence or weakness of legislatures, partly upon the fact that the major impetus for fertility control has come from foreign rather than domestic sources (McCoy, chapter 9). The advent of national planning also has tended to aggrandize the role of the executive. The rise of a national planning, antipolitics ideology in Chile's executive branch apparently contributed significantly to the erosion of the congressional arena as the key compromise center on economic policies (Valenzuela and Wilde, chapter 7). The Indian and Thai legislatures have operated only at the fringes of planning in those countries (Jain, chapter 8; Morell, chapter 13). By contrast, the Thai legislature has had considerable influence over certain economic policies and great influence over the implementation of development projects.

In contrast to discussions that focus on these internally and externally oriented activities of legislatures, there are others that focus on the individual legislator. Many of the functions that can be attributed to the legislatures of developing countries follow from these activities. Legislative contributions to rural development in Africa are almost entirely a function of individual legislator's attempts to establish linkages between their constituencies and government agencies, that is, between the periphery and the center (Barkan, chapter 10). Important variables which affect this process are the availability and extent of resources at the center for distribution to the periphery, the nature and goals of the governing party, bureaucracy-legislature relations, and the nature of the electoral process. The differences between the legislatures of Kenya and Tanzania are explained partly by differences in the informal and indirect functions of the individual legislators of the two countries (Hopkins, chapter 6). Furthermore, of the development outcomes that can be attributed directly to the legislature in these African nations, most appear to be by-products of the activities of individual legislators pursuing essentially non-lawmaking tasks (compare the case made in the Malaysian context [Musolf and Springer, chapter 11] for subsuming such activities under a policy-making framework).

Nevertheless, it scarcely can be maintained that every legislature contributes to development, no matter how broadly the legislature-development syndrome is viewed. The Jordanian legislature has been little more than a sounding board, and a very muted one at that (Jaber, 1975). In Francophone Africa, many legislatures that had promising beginnings as training grounds for native elites were dismantled or emasculated by these same elites once they gained power and moved from the assemblies (Le Vine, chapter 5). There and elsewhere, authoritarian regimes have tended to keep legislatures on a short tether. They may be mere appendages of a ruling party. Where such a party is only one of many components of a conservative regime which feels a need to give representation to the diverse forces associated with it, variations of corporativism may be employed. In Spain this has meant the use of the legislature for intricate functional representation (Linz, chapter 4). Though such legislatures thus have some limited representational functions, it is obvious that authoritarian regimes will use every means to rig them both to be compliant instruments and to depoliticize the populace. Authoritarian Latin-American regimes find legislatures useful in (a) serving as part of a broad organizational framework through which ideological messages, symbolic rewards, and interpretations of specific events are conveyed to the society, and (b) stimulating and conveying information from below so as to provide political elites with a sense of the popular mood and the degree to which it can be structured organizationally (Portes, 1977).

Undoubtedly these twin roles are pictured as satisfactory and acceptable by many a ruling elite. Yet, the execution is often far from perfect. For many ruling groups there may be tension between their belief that they know best how to govern and their sense of a need to keep in touch with the grassroots. The importance of the latter is enhanced through unexpected and disturbing events. Under such conditions, or as a precautionary measure, an authoritarian regime may permit or even welcome the strengthening of the constituent relations role of legislators. Small development projects may even be placed under the control of legislators. Thus, in Kenya, legislators initiate community development projects and then obtain a variety of matching grants from the government to sustain them (Barkan, chapter 10). In the somewhat looser but authoritarian Thai regime of 1969–71, legislators exercised influence over budgetary allocations and development project locations (Morell, chapter 13). In Kuwait, a handful of legislators apparently were able to exercise a decisive role in important oil policy decisions because of their expertise and contacts (Baaklini and Abdul-Wahab, chapter 12). It can be argued that the collegial nature of a legislature permits views of its members to surface more easily than those of functionaries in a hierarchical administrative structure (Baaklini and Abdul-Wahab, chapter 12).

The issue of legislatures and development is marked by ferment. Clearly there are disagreements at various levels among our contributors—from specific judgments about the roles of specific legislatures and/or about the developmental meaning of specific activities, to general judgments about the nature, importance, and direction of legislative roles. Disagreement, however, has a positive function, the identification of high priority needs—in this case a careful review and synthesis of the extant literature; perhaps the creation of running, cumulative bibliographies. Illustrative of the concrete issues on which there is disagreement is the question of whether legislative blocking of executive action usually impedes development, or whether in the uncertain circumstances of evolving developing states, it makes a more positive contribution to development in the long run. Rather than try to review every possible disagreement, we shall reexamine briefly the issues implied that seem to us to be particularly seminal in their implications—which are, metaphorically speaking, the wine of the ferment.

1. The literature needs to be reviewed as just indicated, not only because it is already scattered and critical pieces for an argument may be overlooked, but also because the definition of "relevant literature" is changing. If, as we have argued, all change may need to be considered because often only time will tell whether a policy or program is developmental and what, if any, the legislative role therein may have been, it follows that some literature on change that would have been ignored because it did not deal explicitly with "legislatures" and "development" may turn out to be pertinent.

2. Value questions need to be separated from empirical questions. We can only study what happens or does not happen and try to reconstruct the process analytically. Whether programs or decisions are developmental involves a double value judgment, what we consider development and how we judge the facts of the case by our own criterion.

3. We need to be more systematic about the distinction between what is necessary and what is sufficient for development, or, to use our own designation, for an effort at managing change. Our contributors have shown that legislatures may be involved in both. To varying degrees the authors suggest that in some cases, even if legislatures do nothing directly about change, they do help keep nations going and, thereby, provide other agencies the opportunity to attempt change. The issue, though, is not whether one is more or less important. Rather, it is what do legislatures have to do with each.

4. Development goals, and, hence, development efforts are changing. Cambodia develops by emptying cities whereas Canada develops by building them. Not only are there differences in approach represented by liberal, Marxist, and corporative-statist thinking, but, perhaps more important, there is an alternative image of national condition implied in the rapidly emerging set of concepts that scholars, Latin Americanists in particular, are designating as dependency theory.

5. The tempo of change (as well as its direction and implications) remains largely ignored. Basically, most scholars take for granted how long a period needs to be considered before judging the developmental outcome of change—and study of the literature would show that their decisions on an appropriate time frame diverge. The tempo of change, in addition, is linked to whether changes become firmly established. Some of our participants suggest that periods of slowdown facilitate adjustment and deter reaction to important programs of change. Whether any of this speculation about time frames is valid is inseparable from the need to be aware of the impact of the time span selected for study on judgments as to the direction and magnitude of change.

This list could go on extensively if not endlessly. However, involved in all these and any other issues and any strategy for dealing with them is that they do not call for simple, absolute right or wrong judgments. Rather, the questions themselves involve variable and conditional dimensions (e.g., in this period of time . . . , from what I have read . . . , if development is defined in this fashion . . .). Accordingly, questions as to the roles of legislatures in development can only be answered with conditional formulations, i.e., under these 'X' conditions legislatures are more likely to play these 'Y' roles with respect to these 'Z' outcomes. As the formulations of the proposition change, one indeed is likely to perceive sharp contrast and contradictions in the roles of legislatures in development.

In closing it is important to emphasize how misleading it would be to focus on legislatures alone even if they are the occasion for this volume. It is helpful, for example, to regard both military intervention and the establishment and reestablishment of legislatures as integral parts of the process of political development (Kornberg and Pittman, chapter 3). To understand legislatures and development ultimately requires understanding change and the forces and constraints that shape its thrust. It is unfortunate that this may mean scholarship will be at the case level and that there will be few general propositions for a long period.

In bringing together these discussions and keynoting them, we dare to hope that henceforth the relation between legislatures and development will be viewed broadly. Governmental structure, party system, problem-solving methods, and, in a larger sense, the shape of the economy and the society, all these and more inevitably affect the relationship. Whatever the state of a developing nation's legislature, its situation is obviously at least as responsive to contextual reality as to anything in the essence of the institution. Whatever potentialities (or limits) legislatures may have must encounter the realities faced by the new states. Few attain the level of political development that would enable the authors of one of the papers in this volume to call these legislatures "viable" (Sisson and Snowiss, chapter 2). Nor can we quarrel with the view that legislatures usually are not prime movers in socioeconomic development. Important as these judgments are, they take second place, we think, to the following: the relation between legislatures and development can best be viewed in dialectical terms and both the challenge of development and the contributions which legislatures potentially can make justify attention to the relationship.

# REFERENCES

ADELMAN, I., and C.T. MORRIS (1973) Economic Growth and Social Equity. Stanford, Calif.: Stanford University Press.

Africa Research Bulletin. Political, Social and Cultural Series (1964–1975) Exeter and London: African Research Ltd.

AGOR, W. H. (1971a) The Chilean Senate. Austin, Texas: University of Texas Press.

——— (1971b) "Senate: integrative role in Chile's political development," pp. 245–260 in H. H. Hirsch and M. D. Hancock (eds.) Comparative Legislative Systems. New York: Free Press.

——— (1970) "The decisional role of the Senate in the Chilean political system," pp. 228–272 in A. Kornberg and L. D. Musolf (eds.) Legislatures in Developmental Perspective. Durham, N.C.: Duke University Press.

AGUILAR, M. (forthcoming) Las ultimos Cortes del franquismo. n.p.

———, and C. MARTÍNEZ (1975) "Durante el año del aperturismo: 239 procuradores mudos." Posible 12 (April 3–9): 6–9.

AKRASANEE, N. (1977) "Industrialization and trade policies and employment effects in Thailand," in N. Akrasanee, S. Naya, and V. Vichitvadakarn (eds.) Proceedings of the Eighth Pacific Trade and Development Conference, Pattaya, Thailand, July 1976: UN Asian Development Institute.

——— et al. (1975) The Structure of Differential Incentives and Effects on Industrialization and Employment: A Case Study of Thailand. Report of the Council for Asian Manpower Studies, Project No. 74–5–02. Bangkok: Faculty of Economics, Thammasat University (December).

ALBA, C. (1975) A Spanish Strategic Elite: The Directores Generales (1938–1974). New Haven, Conn.: Yale University, Department of Political Science research paper.

ALCANDE, S. (1957) La République Autonome du Togo: de la fiction à la réalité. Paris: Maspero.

ALMOND, G. (1969) "Political development: analytical and normative perspectives." Comparative Political Studies 1 (January): 447–470.

————, and J. S. COLEMAN (eds.) (1960) The Politics of Developing Areas. Princeton, N.J.: Princeton University Press.

AMELLER, M. (1966) Parliaments: A Comparative Study on the Structure and Functioning of Representative Institutions in Fifty-five Countries. London: Cassell for the Inter-Parliamentary Union.

American Universities Field Staff (1972–74) Population Perspective, 1971, 1972, 1973. San Francisco: Freeman, Cooper.

AMUNÁTEGUI SOLAR, D. (1946) La democracia en Chile: teatro político 1810–1910. Santiago: Universidad de Chile.

ANSPRENGER, F. (1961) Politik im Schwarzen Afrika. Cologne and Opladen: Westdeutscher Verlag.

APTER, D. (1973) "The premise of parliamentary planning." Government and Opposition 8 (Winter): 3–23.

———— (1972) Ghana in Transition. Princeton, N.J.: Princeton University Press.

———— (1971) Choice and the Politics of Allocation: A Developmental Theory. New Haven, Conn.: Yale University Press.

———— (1965) The Politics of Modernization. Chicago: University of Chicago Press.

AQUARONE, A. (1965) L'Organizzazione dello' Stato Totalitario. Torino: Einaudi.

ARENDT, H. (1968) The Origins of Totalitarianism. New York: Harcourt, Brace, and World.

ASHFORD, D. (1967) National Development and Local Reform: Political Participation, Morocco, Tunisia, and Pakistan. Princeton, N.J.: Princeton University Press.

Asian Recorder (1955–1975). New Delhi, India: Recorder Press.

Associated Press (April 14, 1975).

ASTIZ, C. A. (1973) "The decay of Latin American legislatures," pp. 114–126 in A. Kornberg (ed.) Legislatures in Comparative Perspective. New York: David McKay.

AUSTIN, D. (1967) "Opposition in Ghana 1947–67." Government and Opposition 2 (July): 539–555.

BADGLEY, J. (1971) Asian Development: Problems and Prognosis. New York: Free Press.

BANADOS ESPINOSA, J. (1894) Balmaceda, su gobierno y la revolución de 1891. 2 vols. Paris: n.p.

BANFIELD, E. (1958) The Moral Basis of a Backward Society. New York: Free Press.

Bangkok Post (1970) August 9.

———— (1971) July 8; August 30; October 26.

Bangkok World (1970) June 23; July 2; July 4; July 26; August 14; September 9; September 12.

———— (1971) January 3; July 16; November 15; November 16; December 3.

BAÑÓN MARTÍNEZ, R. B. (1974) "El Proyecto de léy de incompatibilidades de los procuradores in Cortes: un comentario sobre la presencia en la Cámara de la burocracia española." Revista Española de la Opinión Pública 38 (October-December): 77–91.

BARKAN, J. D. (1976) "Political knowledge and voting behavior in rural Kenya." American Political Science Review 70 (June): 452–455.

———— (1975) An African Dilemma. New York and Nairobi: Oxford University Press.

————, and J. J. OKUMU (1974) "Political linkage in Kenya: citizens, local elites and legislators." Paper presented at the American Political Science Association meetings, Chicago.

BAYLY, C. A. (1971) "Local control in Indian towns: the case of Allahabad, 1880–1920." Modern Asian Studies 5 (October): 289–311.

BEER, S. H. (1966) "The British legislature and the problem of mobilizing consent," pp. 30–48 in E. Frank (ed.) Lawmakers in a Changing World. Englewood Cliffs, N.J.: Prentice-Hall.

—— (1965) British Politics in the Collectivist Age. New York: Knopf.

BEINEN, H. (1968) The Military Intervenes: Case Studies in Political Development. New York: Russell Sage Foundation.

BENDIX, R. (1969) Nation-Building and Citizenship. New York: Doubleday Anchor.

BENNINGTON, H. (1968) "Partnership and dissidence in the nineteenth-century House of Commons." Parliamentary Affairs 2 (Autumn): 338–374.

BERELSON, B. (1970) "The present state of family planning programs." Studies in Family Planning 1 (September): 1–11.

BERG, E. (1971) "Structural transformation versus gradualism: recent economic development in Ghana and the Ivory Coast," pp. 187–230 in P. Foster and A. Zolberg (eds.) Ghana and the Ivory Coast. Chicago: University of Chicago Press.

BERGER, R. (1974) Executive Privilege: A Constitutional Myth. Cambridge, Mass.: Harvard University Press.

BETTS, R. (1961) Assimilation and Association in French Colonial Theory, 1890–1914. New York: Columbia University Press.

Bhartiya Jana Sangh (1962) Bhartiya Jana Sangh Election Manifesto. Bombay Central Office: Bhartiya Jana Sangh.

BICHENO, H. E. (1972) "Anti-parliamentary themes in Chilean history: 1920–70." Government and Opposition 7 (Summer): 351–388.

BIENEN, H. (1974) Kenya: The Politics of Participation and Control. Princeton, N.J.: Princeton University Press.

—— (1967) Tanzania: Party Transformation and Economic Development. Princeton, N.J.: Princeton University Press.

BILL, J. A. (1971) "The politics of legislative monarchy: the Iranian Majlis," pp. 360–369 in H. Hirsch and M. D. Hancock (eds.) Comparative Legislative Systems. New York: Free Press.

BINDER, L. (ed.) (1971) Crises and Sequences in Political Development. Princeton, N.J.: Princeton University Press.

BLACK, C. E. (1966) The Dynamics of Modernization: A Study in Comparative History. New York: Harper and Row.

BLAKEMORE, H. (1964) "The Chilean revolution of 1891 and its historiography." Hispanic American Historical Review 45 (August): 393–421.

BLONDEL, J. (1973) Comparative Legislatures. Englewood Cliffs, N.J.: Prentice-Hall.

BOEKE, J. H. (1953) Economics and Economic Policy of Dual Societies as Exemplified by Indonesia. New York: International Secretariat, Institute of Pacific Relations.

BOENINGER, E., and O. SUNKEL (1972) "Structural changes, development strategies and the planning experience in Chile, 1938–69," in M. Faber and D. Seers (eds.) The Crisis in Planning, Vol. 2. Sussex, England: Sussex University Press.

BONJEAN, C., and M. GRIMES (1970) "Bureaucracy and alienation: a dimensional approach." Social Forces 48 (March): 365–373.

BOYNTON, G. R., and G. LOEWENBERG (1973) "The development of public support for parliament in Germany, 1951–59." British Journal of Political Science 3 (April): 169–189.

BRACHER, K. D. (1964) "Problems of parliamentary democracy in Europe." Daedalus 93 (Winter): 179–198.

BRETTON, H. (1973) Power and Politics in Africa. Chicago: Aldine.

BROOMFIELD, J. H. (1968) Elite Conflict in a Plural Society: Twentieth Century Bengal. Berkeley and Los Angeles: University of California Press.

BRUNSCHWIG, H. (1966) French Colonialism 1871–1914. London: Pall Mall.

BRUNTON, D., and D. PENNINGTON (1954) Members of the Long Parliament. London: George Allen and Unwin.

BUDGE, I. (1970) Agreement and the Stability of Democracy. Chicago: Markham.

BURANASIRI, P., and S. UNAKUL (1965) "Obstacles to effective planning encountered in the Thai planning experience." The Philippine Economic Journal 4: 327–340.

BUTT, R. (1967) The Power of Parliament. London: Constable.

CALLARD, K. (1957) Pakistan: A Political Study. London: Allen and Unwin.

CATROUX, G. (1953) "The French union." International Conciliation No. 495 (November).

Centro de Investigaciones Sociológicas (1977) La reforma política la ideologia política de los españoles. Madrid: CIS.

Chao Thai (1970) January 15.

CHARLES, B. (1972) La République de Guinee. Paris: Berger-Levrault.

CHAUDHURY, G. W. (1965) The Last Days of United Pakistan. Bloomington, Ind.: Indiana University Press.

CHINACHIT, S. (1975) The Tambon Project Funds. Bangkok: Bank of Thailand, Special Report (in Thai).

CHINWEIZU (1975) The West and the Rest of Us. New York: Random House-Vintage.

CHOPRA, P. (1974) "The Malaysian miracle—and dilemma." The World Today 30 (May): 199–205.

CHRISTOPH, J. (1965) "Consensus and cleavage in British political ideology." American Political Science Review 59 (September): 629–642.

CLIFFE, L. (ed.) (1967) One Party Democracy: The 1965 Tanzanian General Elections. Nairobi: East Africa Publishing House.

COHEN, A. (1959) British Policy in Changing Africa. London: Routledge and Kegan Paul.

COHEN, M. A. (1974) Urban Policy and Political Conflict in Africa. Chicago: University of Chicago Press.

COLEMAN, J. S. (1970)"Political Money." American Political Science Review 64 (December): 1074–1087.

——— (1956) Togoland. New York: Carnegie Endowment for International Peace.

———, and C. ROSBERG (1964) Political Parties and National Integration in Tropical Africa. Berkeley: University of California Press.

CONTRERAS STRAUCH, O. (1971) Antecedents y perspectivas de la planificación en Chile. Santiago: Editorial Jurídica.

CORREA BRAVO, A. (1914) Comentario y concordancia de la ley de organización y atribuciones de las municipalidades. [3rd ed.] Santiago: Librería Tornero.

CORTES, L., and J. FUENTES (1967) Diccionario político de Chile. Santiago: Editorial Orbe.

CRANE, R. I. (1964) "The transfer of western education to India," pp. 108–138 in W. B. Hamilton (ed.) The Transfer of Institutions. Durham, N.C.: Duke University Press.

CRICK, B. (1970) "Parliament in the British political system," pp. 33–54 in A. Kornberg and L. D. Musolf (eds.) Legislatures in Developmental Perspective. Durham, N.C.: Duke University Press.

——— (1968) The Reform of Parliament. London: Cox and Wyman.

CROPSEY, J. (1963) "The right of foreign aid," pp. 109–130 in R. A. Goodwin (ed.)

Why Foreign Aid? Chicago: Rand McNally.
CROWDER, M. (1965) "Independence as a goal in French West Africa politics: 1944–1960," pp. 15–44 in W. H. Lewis (ed.) French-Speaking Africa; The Search for Identity. New York: Walker.
Cuadernos para el Diálogo (1967) "Representación familiar: análysis juridíco de las normas electorales." 47–48 (August-September): 12–14.
CUTRIGHT, P. (1965) "Political structure, economic development, and national social security programs." American Journal of Sociology 70 (March): 537–550.
——— (1963) "National political development: measurement and analysis." American Sociological Review 28 (April): 253–264.
DAALDER, H. (1974) "The consociational democracy theme." World Politics 26 (July): 604–621.
——— (1966) "Parties, elites and political developments in western Europe," pp. 43–77 in J. LaPalombara and M. Weiner (eds.) Political Parties and Political Development. Princeton, N.J.: Princeton University Press.
DAHL, R. (1971) Polyarchy. New Haven, Conn.: Yale University Press.
——— (1961) Who Governs? New Haven, Conn.: Yale University Press.
——— (1956) A Preface to Democratic Theory. Chicago: University of Chicago Press.
Daily News (Bangkok) (1969) August 7.
DALY, H. E. (1970) "The population question in northeast Brazil: its economic and ideological dimensions." Economic Development and Cultural Change 18 (July): 536–574.
DAVIDSON, R. (1969) The Role of the Congressman. New York: Pegasus.
DAVIS, K. (1967) "Population policy: will current programs succeed?" Science 158 (November): 730–739.
——— (1949) Human Society. New York: Macmillan.
Deadline Data in World Affairs. (n.d.) Greenwich, Conn.: McGraw-Hill.
DE ESTEBAN, J., S. VARELA, F. J. GARCÍA FERNÁNDEZ, L. L. GUERRA, and J. L. G. RUIZ (1973) Desarrollo político y constitución española. Esplugues de Llobregat, Barcelona: Ariel.
DE GRAZIA, A. (1962) Political Organization. New York: Free Press.
——— (1951) Public and Republic: Political Representation in America. New York: Knopf.
DE JOUVENAL, B. (1957) Sovereignty. Chicago: University of Chicago Press.
——— (1949) Power: The Natural History of Its Growth. New York: Viking Press.
DELAVIGNETTE, R. (1962) L'Afrique noire française et son destin. Paris: Gallimard.
DE MIGUEL, J. M., and J. J. LINZ (1975a) "Las Cortes españolas 1943–1970: un análisis de cohortes. I las cohortes." Sistema 8 (January): 85–110.
——— (1975b) "Las Cortes españolas 1943–1970: un análisis de cohortes. II las elites." Sistema 9 (April): 103–123.
DEUTSCH, K. W. (1961) "Social mobilization and political development." American Political Science Review 55 (September): 493–514.
——— (1953) Nationalism and Social Communication. Cambridge, Mass.: Massachusetts Institute of Technology Press.
DIAMOND, R. A. (ed.) (1974) The Middle East: U.S. Policy, Israel, Oil, and the Arabs. Washington, D.C.: Congressional Quarterly.
DIAMONT, A. (1960) Austrian Catholics and the First Republic: Democracy, Capitalism and Social Order, 1918–1934. Princeton: Princeton University Press.
DIAZ-NOSTY, B. (1972) Las Cortes de Franco. 30 años orgánicos. Barcelona: DOPESA.
DIX, R. (1973) "Latin America: oppositions and development," pp. 261–303 in

R. Dahl (ed.) Regimes and Opposition. New Haven, Conn.: Yale University Press.

DUBEY, S. N. (1975) "Environment, technology and decision-making in Panchayati Raj institutions." Economic and Political Weekly (Bombay) 10 (January): 75–84.

DUMONT, R. (1969) False Start in Africa. New York: Praeger.

DURKHEIM, E. (1947) The Division of Labor in Society. New York: Free Press.

DUVERGER, M. (1961) Political Parties. London and New York: Methuen and Wiley.

EBANKS, G. E., P. M. GEORGE, and C. E. NOBLE (1975) "Emigration and fertility decline: the case of Barbados." Demography 12 (August): 431–445.

ECHEVERRIA, A., and L. FREI (eds.) (1974) 1970–73: La lucha por la juricidad en Chile, Vol. 3. Santiago: Editorial del Pacífico.

ECKSTEIN, H. (1973) "Authority patterns: a structural basis for political inquiry." American Political Science Review 67 (December): 1142–1161.

EDELMAN, M. (1964) The Symbolic Uses of Politics. Urbana, Ill.: University of Illinois Press.

EDWARDS, A. (1917) "Nuestro régimen tributario en los últimos 40 años." Revista Chilena 1 (April): 337–356.

EIDELBERG, P. (1968) The Philosophy of the American Constitution. New York: Free Press.

EISENSTADT, S. N. (1966) Modernization: Protest and Change. Englewood Cliffs, N.J.: Prentice-Hall.

ELDRIDGE, H. T. (1968) "Population policies," pp. 381–388 in D. Sills (ed.) International Encyclopedia of the Social Sciences, Vol. 12. New York: Macmillan.

ELYAS, O. (1974) "Policy analysis and development in Malaysia." Paper prepared for a colloquium on policy analysis and development sponsored by the Asian Centre for Development Administration, Kuala Lumpur, Malaysia (November 25–28).

ENCINA, F. (1942) Historia de Chile. Santiago: Editorial Nacimiento.

Equipo Data (1969) Quién es quién en las Cortes. Madrid: Edicusa.

ESMAN, M.J. (1972) Administration and Development in Malaysia: Institution Building and Reform in a Plural Society. Ithaca, N.Y.: Cornell University Press.

ESTRENA CUESTA, R. E. (1974) "La jefatura del estado," pp. 975–1026 in M. Fraga Iribarne (ed.) La España de los años 70. Madrid: Moneda y Crédito.

Europa Yearbook (1975) London: Europa Publications.

EVANS DE LA CUADRA, E. (1973) Chile, hacia una constitución contemporánea. Santiago: Editorial Jurídica.

FABER, M., and D. SEERS (eds.) (1972) The Crisis in Planning. 2 vols. Sussex, England: Sussex University Press.

FEITH, H. (1962) The Decline of Constitutional Government in Indonesia. Ithaca, N.Y.: Cornell University Press.

FELDMAN, D. (1969) "The economics of ideology: some problems of achieving rural socialism in Tanzania," pp. 85–111 in C. Leys (ed.) Politics and Change in Developing Countries. Cambridge, England: Cambridge University Press.

FELICE, R. de (1974) Mussolini il duce. Gli anni del consenso 1929–1936. Torino: Einaudi.

——— (1968) Mussolini il facista. L'organizzazione dello Stato fascista 1925–1929. Torino: Einaudi.

FERNÁNDEZ-CARVAJAL, R. (1969) La Constitución española. Madrid: Editora Nacional.

FINER, S. M. (1962) The Man on Horseback: The Role of the Military in Politics. New York: Praeger.

FLERON, F. (ed.) (1969) Communist Studies and the Social Sciences: Essays on Methodology and Empirical Theory. Chicago: Rand McNally.

FOLTZ, W. (1973) "Political opposition," pp. 143–170 in R. Dahl (ed.) Regimes and Opposition. New Haven, Conn.: Yale University Press.

FRAGA IRIBARNE, M. (1959) El reglamento de las Cortes españolas. Madrid: Servicio de Información y Publicaciones de la Organización Sindical.

FRAILE CLIVILLÉS, M. M. (1974) La Comisión Permanente de las Cortes. Madrid: Editoria Nacional.

FRANCO BAHAMONDE, F. (1943) Palabras del Caudillo, 19 April 1937–7 December 1942, Tercera Edición. Madrid: Editora Nacional.

FREI, E. (1970) "La reforma constitucional en su contexto histórico político," pp. 19–51 in E. Frei et al. (eds.) Reforma Constitucional 1970. Santiago: Editorial Jurídica.

FREY, F. (1965) The Turkish Political Elite. Cambridge, Mass.: Massachusetts Institute of Technology Press.

FRIEDRICH, C. J. (1940) "Public policy and the nature of administrative responsibility," pp. 3–24 in C. J. Friedrich and E. S. Mason (eds.) Public Policy. Cambridge, Mass.: Harvard University Press.

FURNIVALL, J. S. (1948) Colonial Policy and Practice: A Comparative Study of Burma and Netherlands India. Cambridge, England: Cambridge University Press.

GARCÍA CANALES, M. (1977) La teoría de la representación en la España del siglo XX (De la crisis de la Restauración a 1936). Murcia: Universidad de Murcia, Publicaciones del Departamento de Derecho Político.

GARRORENA MORALES, A. (1977) Autoritarismo y control parlamentario en las Cortes de Franco. Murcia: Departamento de Derecho Político, Universidad de Murcia.

GASCÓN HERNÁNDEZ, J. (1945) "Caracteres y funciones de la presidencia de las Cortes españolas." Revista de Estudios Políticos 10 (January-April): 141–147.

GEERTZ, C. (1963) "The integrative revolution," pp. 105–157 in C. Geertz (ed.) Old Societies and New States. New York: Free Press.

GELLAR, S. (1973) "State-building and nation-building in West Africa," pp. 403–409 in S. N. Eisenstadt and S. Rokkan (eds.) Building States and Nations, Vol. 2. Beverly Hills, Calif.: Sage.

GERMANI, G., and K. SILVERT (1961) "Politics, social structures and military intervention in Latin America." Archives Européennes de Sociologie 2 (Spring): 62–81.

GHAI, Y. P., and N. P. W. B. McAUSLEN (1970) Public Law and Political Change in Kenya. Nairobi: Oxford University Press.

Ghana Today (1961) Supplement. (July 19): 3.

GIL, F. (1966) The Political System of Chile. Boston: Houghton Mifflin.

GODFREY, E. M., and G. C. M. MUTISO (1974) "The political economy of self-help; Kenya's 'Harambee' institutes of technology." Canadian Journal of African Studies 8: 109–133.

GOGUEL, F. (1971) "Parliament under the fifth republic: difficulties in adapting to a new role," pp. 84–96 in G. Loewenberg (ed.) Modern Parliaments: Change or Decline? Chicago: Aldine-Atherton.

GOMEZ-RIENO, M., F. ANDRES ORIZO, and D. VILA (1976) "Sociología politica," pp. 1145–1319 in Fomento de Estudios Sociales y de Sociología Aplicada (FOESSA), Estudios sociológicos sobre la situación social de España, 1975. Madrid: Euramérica.

GONIDEC, P. F. (1971) La République du Tchad. Paris: Berger-Levrault.

——— (1968) La République du Senegal. Paris: Berger-Levrault.

GONZÁLEZ CERRUTTI, R., and S. B. KAR (1975) "Venezuela." Country Profiles (June), A Publication of the Population Council.

GOODY, J. (1968) "Consensus and dissent in Ghana." Political Science Quarterly 83

(September): 337–351.

GOULD, H. (1973) "Local government roots of contemporary Indian politics." Economic and Political Weekly 6 (February): 457–464.

Government and Opposition (1967) 2: 491–619.

Great Britain. Indian Statutory Commission (1930) Report of the Indian Statutory Commission. London: H. M. Stationery Office.

Great Britain. Secretary of State for India (1918) Report on Indian Constitutional Reforms. Calcutta: Superintendent of Government Printing.

GREEN, R. H. (1972) "The parastatal corporation as an element in the quest for national development: Tanzania, 1967–1972." Paper presented at UN African Institute (IDEP/ET/CS/2365–26).

——— (1971) "Reflections on economic strategy, structure, implementation, and necessity: Ghana and the Ivory Coast," pp. 231–264 in P. Foster and A. Zolberg (eds.) Ghana and the Ivory Coast: Perspectives on Modernization. Chicago: University of Chicago Press.

GROSSHOLTZ, J. (1970) "Integrative factors in the Malaysian and Philippine legislatures." Comparative Politics 3 (October): 93–113.

GROTH, A. J., R. J. LIEBER, and N. I. LIEBER (1976) Contemporary Politics: Europe. Cambridge, Mass.: Winthrop.

GRUMM, J. (1973) A Paradigm for the Comparative Analysis of Legislative Systems. Sage Research Papers in the Social Sciences. Beverly Hills, Calif.: Sage.

GUTTSMAN, W. L. (1963) The British Political Elite. London: MacGibbon and Kee.

HAKES, J. E. (1968) "Recruitment of ministers from the Kenyan Parliament," unpublished manuscript. Durham, N.C.: Duke University.

———, and J. HELGERSON (1973) "Bargaining and parliamentary behavior in Africa: a comparative study of Zambia and Kenya," pp. 335–362 in A. Kornberg (ed.) Legislatures in Comparative Perspective. New York: David McKay.

HAMPTON, W. (1970–71) "Democratic planning." Parliamentary Affairs 24 (Autumn): 338–346.

HANSON, A. H. (1966) The Process of Planning. London: Oxford University Press.

HARBESON, J. W. (1971) "Land reforms and politics in Kenya, 1954–1970." Journal of Modern African Studies 9 (August): 231–251.

HART, H. (1971) "Parliament and nation-building: England and India," pp. 111–140 in G. Loewenberg (ed.) Modern Parliaments: Change or Decline? Chicago: Atherton.

HATZFELDT, H. (1968) "Economic development planning in Thailand." Bangkok: The Ford Foundation, mimeo.

HAUG, M. (1967) "Social and cultural pluralism as a concept in social systems analysis." American Journal of Sociology 73 (November): 294–304.

HAUSER, P. M. (1971) "World Population: Retrospect and Prospect," pp. 103–122 in National Academy of Sciences, Washington, D.C., Rapid Population Growth: Consequences and Policy Implications. Baltimore: Johns Hopkins University Press.

HAWLEY, A. (1950) Human Ecology: A Theory of Community Structure. New York: Ronald Press.

HEAPHEY, J. J. (1975) "Legislative staffing: organizational and philosophical considerations," pp. 1–22 in J. J. Heaphey and A. P. Balutis (eds.) Legislative Staffing: A Comparative Perspective. Beverly Hills, Calif.: Sage.

HECHT, L. (n.d.) The Cortes Españolas. New Haven, Conn.: Yale University honors paper.

HELLEINER, G. K. (1972) "Socialism and economic development in Tanzania." Journal of Development Studies 8 (January): 183–204.

HERMAN, V., and F. MENDEL (1976) Parliaments of the World. Berlin: De Gruyter.

HERMET, G. (1974) "Electoral trends in Spain: an appraisal of the polls conducted under the Franco regime." Iberian Studies 3: 55–59.

HOCKIN, T. A. (1971–72) "The roles of the loyal opposition in Britain's House of Commons: three historical paradigms." Parliamentary Affairs 25 (Winter): 50–68.

HODGKIN, T. (1961) "A note on the language of African nationalism," pp. 22–40 in K. Kirkwood (ed.) St. Anthony's Papers, Number 10: African Affairs, Number 1. Carbondale, Ill.: Southern Illinois University Press.

HOPKINS, R. F. (1975a) "The Kenyan legislature: political functions and citizen perceptions," pp. 207–231 in G. R. Boynton and C. L. Kim (eds.) Legislative Systems in Developing Countries. Durham, N.C.: Duke University Press.

——— (1975b) Kenyan Politics: Citizen Expectation and Regime Support. Unpublished manuscript.

——— (1975c) "Political roles: micro analysis and macro process," pp. 244–267 in G. D. Brewer and R. D. Brunner (eds.), Political Development and Change: A Policy Approach. New York: Free Press.

——— (1972) "Equality, structure and legitimation: alternative development paths in Kenya and Tanzania." Paper presented at the American Political Science Association meetings, Washington, D.C.

——— (1970) "The role of the M.P. in Tanzania." American Political Science Review 64 (September): 754–771.

HUGHES, S. W. (1971) Governmental Decision Making in Chile: The Relative Decisional Positions of the Executive Legislature. Unpublished Ph.D. dissertation, University of North Carolina, Chapel Hill.

HUNTINGTON, S. P. (1968) Political Order in Changing Societies. New Haven, Conn.: Yale University Press.

——— (1966) "Congressional responses to the twentieth century," pp. 30–48 in D. B. Truman (ed.) The Congress in America's Future. Englewood Cliffs, N.J.: Prentice-Hall.

———, and C. MOORE (eds.) (1970) Authoritarian Politics in Modern Society. New York: Basic Books.

HYDEN, G., and C. LEYS (1972) "Elections and politics in single-party systems: the case of Kenya and Tanzania." British Journal of Political Science 2 (October): 389–420.

IBRD. See International Bank for Reconstruction and Development.

IGLESIAS SELGAS, C. (1968) La vía española a la democracia. Madrid: Editora Nacional.

INGRAM, J. C. (1971) Economic Change in Thailand, 1850–1970. Stanford, Calif.: Stanford University Press.

Instituto Administracion [INSORA] (1969) Unpublished study, University of Chile.

International Bank for Reconstruction and Development [IBRD] (1974) Tanzania: Agricultural and Rural Development Sector Study, 3 Vols. Washington, D.C.: IBRD.

——— (1959) A Public Development Program for Thailand. Baltimore: Johns Hopkins University Press.

International Planned Parenthood Federation [IPPF] (1974) Family Planning in Five Continents. London: IPPF.

The International Yearbook and Statesman's Who's Who (1974) London: Mercury House Reference Books.

IRSCHICK, E. F. (1969) Politics and Social Change in South India: The Non-Brahman Movement and Tamil Separatism, 1916–1929. Berkeley and Los Angeles: University of California Press.

ISMAEL, T. Y. (1970) Government and Politics of the Contemporary Middle East. Homewood, Ill.: Dorsey Press.

JABER, K. S. A. (1975) The parliament of the Hashemite kingdom of Jordan: its role in social and economic development. Unpublished paper, University of Jordan, Amman, Jordan.

JACKSON, D. (1971) "Economic development and income distribution in Eastern Africa." Journal of Modern African Studies 9 (December): 531–542.

JAHAN, R. (1973) Pakistan: The Failure of National Integration. New York: Columbia University Press.

JAIN, R. B. (1975) "Innovations and reforms in the Indian parliament." Paper presented at the Second International Conference on Legislative Development. Albany, N.Y. (January 20–24).

JAMES, J. (1972) "Legislatorial decision-making role perceptions in Kenya." Paper presented at the annual meeting of the African Studies Association. Philadelphia (November ).

JANOS, A. C. (1970) "The one-party state and social mobilization: East Europe between the wars," pp. 204–238 in S. P. Huntington and C. H. Moore (eds.) Authoritarian Politics in Modern Society: The Dynamics of Established One-Party Systems. New York: Basic Books.

JANOWITZ, M. (1964) The Military in the Political Development of New Nations: An Essay in Comparative Analysis. Chicago: University of Chicago Press.

JEWELL, M. E. (1977) "Legislative representation and national integration," pp. 13–53 in A. Eldridge (ed.) Legislatures in Plural Societies. Durham, N.C.: Duke University Press.

——— (1973) "Linkages between legislative parties and external parties," pp. 203–234 in A. Kornberg (ed.) Legislatures in Comparative Perspective. New York: David McKay.

JHANGIANI, M. A. (1969) Jana Sangha and Swatantra: A Profile of the Rightist Parties in India. Bombay: Manaktalas.

JOHNSON, G. (1971) "Notes on wages, employment and income distribution in Kenya." Nairobi: University of Nairobi.

JOHNSON, S. (1970) Life Without Birth. Boston: Little, Brown.

JOXE, A. (1970) Las fuerzas armadas en el sistema político Chileno. Santiago: Editorial Universitaria.

JUDD, G. P. (1955) Members of Parliament, 1734–1832. New Haven, Conn.: Yale University Press.

KABWEGYERE, T. B. (1974) The Politics of State Formation: The Nature and Effects of Colonialism in Uganda. Nairobi: East African Literature Bureau.

KAHANE, R. (1973) The Problems of Political Legitimacy in an Antagonistic Society: The Indonesian Case. Beverly Hills, Calif.: Sage.

KASFIR, N. (1974) "Departicipation and political development in Black African politics." Studies in Comparative International Development 9 (Fall): 3–25.

KEARNEY, R. H. (1967) Communalism and Language in the Politics of Ceylon. Durham, N.C.: Duke University Press.

KENDALL, W. (1960) "The two majorities." Midwest Journal of Political Science 4 (November): 317–345.

KENT, R. (1962) From Madagascar to the Malagasy Republic. New York: Praeger.

KEY, V. O., Jr. (1964) Public Opinion and American Democracy. New York: Knopf.

KIHL, Y. W. (1975) "Local elites, power structures and the legislative process in Korea." Comparative Legislative Research Center Occasional Paper #8. Iowa City, Iowa: University of Iowa, mimeo.

KILSON, M. (1966) Political Change in a West African State: A Study of the Modernization Process. Cambridge, Mass.: Harvard University Press.

Kingdom of Thailand (1970–72) Royal Thai Government Budget Act: Fiscal Years 1970, 1971, 1972.

KJECKSHUS, H. (1974) Parliament in a one-party state—the Bunge of Tanzania. Journal of Modern African Studies (March):19–43.

KOCHANEK, S. A. (1968a) The Congress Party of India; the Dynamics of One-party Democracy. Princeton, N.J.: Princeton University Press.

——— (1968b) "The relations between social background and attitudes of Indian legislators." Journal of Commonwealth Political Studies 6 (March): 34–53.

KOHN, M. (1971) "Bureaucratic man: a portrait and an interpretation." American Sociological Review 36 (June): 461–474.

KOFF, D., and G. VON DER MUHLL (1971) "Political socialization in Kenya and Tanzania," in K. Prewitt (ed.) Education and Political Values. Nairobi: East African Publishing House.

KOLATA, G. (1974) !Kung hunter-gatherers: feminism, diet, and birth control." Science 185 (September): 932–934.

KORNBERG, A., and S. M. HINES (1977) "Parliament's role in the integration-modernization of Canadian society, 1865–1876," pp. 201–232 in A. F. Eldridge (ed.) Legislatures in Plural Societies. Durham, N.C.: Duke University Press.

———, S. M. HINES, and J. SMITH (1973) "Legislatures and the modernization of societies." Comparative Political Studies 5 (January): 471–491.

———, and L. D. MUSOLF (1970) Legislatures in Developmental Perspective. Durham, N.C.: Duke University Press.

KORNHAUSER, W. (1959) The Politics of Mass Society. New York: Free Press.

KRAUS, J. (1971) "Political change, conflict, and development in Ghana," pp. 33–72 in P. Foster and A. Zolberg (eds.) Ghana and the Ivory Coast: Perspectives on Modernization. Chicago: University of Chicago Press.

KRONGKAEW, M. (1975) The Incidence of Taxes in Thailand. Unpublished Ph.D. dissertation, Michigan State University.

KUPER, L., and M. G. SMITH (1971) Pluralism in Africa. Berkeley: University of California Press.

Kuwait National Assembly (1973–1974) Parliamentary Proceedings. Nos. 292, 311, 312, 315, 319, 330B, 330D, 338.

KUZNETS, S. (1959) Six Lectures on Economic Growth. Glencoe, Ill.: Free Press.

LAMPUE, P. (1961) "Les Constitutions des états Africains d'expression française." Revue juridique et politique d'outre-mer 15 (October–December): 513–556.

LaPALOMBARA, J. (ed.) (1974) Politics Within Nations. Englewood Cliffs, N.J.: Prentice-Hall.

——— (1971) "Penetration," pp. 205–232 in L. Binder et al. (eds.) Crises and Sequences of Political Development. Princeton, N.J.: Princeton University Press.

——— (1965) Bureaucracy and Political Development. Princeton, N.J.: Princeton University Press.

LASKI, H. J. (1928a) "The British cabinet: a study of its personnel, 1801–1924." Fabian Society Tract 233. London: The Fabian Society.

——— (1928b) "The personnel of the English cabinet, 1801–1924." American Political Science Review 22 (February): 12–31.

LASSWELL, H. D., and R. SERENO (1966) "The Fascists: the changing Italian elite," pp. 178–193 in H. Lasswell and D. Lerner (eds.) World Revolutionary Elites. Cambridge, Mass.: M.I.T. Press.

LASSWELL, H. D., and A. KAPLAN (eds.) (1950) Power and Society. New Haven and London: Yale University Press.

Latin America (1967–1975). London: Latin America Newsletters.

LAVROFF, D. G., and G. PEISER (1961) Les constitutions africaines. Paris: A. Pedone.

LEE, J. M. (1963) "Parliament in republican Ghana." Parliamentary Affairs 16 (Autumn): 376–395.

LEE, R. (1972) "Population growth and the beginnings of sedentary life among the !Kung bushmen," pp. 329–342 in B. Spooner (ed.) Population Growth: Anthropological Implications. Cambridge, Mass.: Massachusetts Institute of Technology Press.

LEFEVER, E. W. (1970) Spear and Sceptre: Army, Policy, and Politics in Tropical Africa. Washington, D.C.: The Brookings Institution.

LEITES, N. (1959) On the Game of Politics in France. Stanford, Calif.: Stanford University Press.

LERNER, D. (1958) The Passing of Traditional Society. New York: Free Press.

——, and R. D. ROBINSON (1960) "Swords and ploughshares: the Turkish army as a modernizing force." World Politics 12 (October): 19–44.

LE VINE, V. T. (1975) "Leadership transition in Black Africa: elite generations and political succession." Munger Africana Library Notes No. 30 (May).

—— (1971) "The political cultures of French-speaking Africa." Ghana Social Science Journal 1 (November): 1–17.

—— (1968) "Political elite recruitment and political structure in French-speaking Africa." Cahiers d'études Africaines 31; 8: 369–389.

—— (1964) The Cameroons from Mandate to Independence. Berkeley: University of California Press.

LEYS, C. (1975) The Underdevelopment of Kenya. Berkeley: University of California Press.

—— (1970) "Politics in Kenya: the development of peasant society." Nairobi: Institute of Development Studies, Discussion paper no. 102.

LIJPHART, A. (1969) "Consociational democracy: types of western democratic systems." World Politics 21 (January): 207–225.

—— (1968) The Politics of Accommodation: Pluralism and Democracy in the Netherlands. Berkeley: University of California Press.

Link (1975) 25th Anniversary Issue. New Delhi (January 26).

LINTON, R. (1947) "The change from dry to wet rice cultivation in Tanala-Betsileo," pp. 45–51 in T. M. Newcomb and E. L. Hartley (eds.) Readings in Social Psychology. New York: Henry Holt.

LINZ, J. (1978) The Breakdown of Democratic Regimes: Crisis Breakdown and Reequilibration. Baltimore: Johns Hopkins University Press.

—— (1976) The Breakdown of Competitive Democratic Regimes. New Haven, Conn.: Yale University Press.

—— (1975a) "La caduta dei regimi democratici." Revista Italiana De Scienze Politica 1 (April): 7–44.

—— (1975b) "Totalitarian and authoritarian regimes," pp. 175–411 in F. I. Greenstein and N. W. Polsby (eds.) The Handbook of Political Science, Vol. III. Reading, Mass.: Addison-Wesley.

—— (1973) "Opposition in and under an Authoritarian Regime: The Case of Spain," pp. 171–259 in R. Dahl (ed.) Regimes and Oppositions. New Haven, Conn.: Yale University Press.

—— (1972) "Continuidad y discontinuidad en la élite política española. De la Restauración al Régimen actual," in Libro-Homenaje al Prof. Carlos Ollero. Madrid: Graficas Carlavilla.

—— (1970a) "An authoritarian regime: the case of Spain," pp. 251–283, 374–381 in E. Allardt and S. Rokkan (eds.) Mass Politics: Studies in Political Sociology. New York: Free Press.

—— (1970b) "From Falange to Movimiento-Organización: the Spanish single party and the Franco regime, 1936–1968," pp. 128–201 in S. P. Huntington and C. H. Moore (eds.) Authoritarian Politics in Modern Society: The Dynamics of Established One-Party Systems. New York: Basic Books.

———— (1967) "The party system of Spain: past and future," pp. 197–282 in S. M. Lipset and S. Rokkan (eds.) Party Systems and Voter Alignments. New York: Free Press.

———— (1966) "Michels e il suo contributo alla sociologia politica," Introduction to R. Michels, La sociologia del partito politico nelle democrazia moderna. Bologna: Il Mulino.

LIPSET, S. M. (1962) "Introduction," to R. Michels, Political Parties: A Sociological Study of Oligarchic Tendencies of Modern Democracy. New York: Collier.

———— (1960) Political Man; The Social Bases of Politics. Garden City, N.Y.: Doubleday.

———— (1959) "Some social requisites of democracy: economic development and political legitimacy." American Political Science Review 53 (March): 69–105.

————, and S. ROKKAN (1967) "Cleavage structures, party systems, and voter alignments: an introduction," pp. 26–29 in S. M. Lipset and S. Rokkan (eds.) Party Systems and Voter Alignments. New York: Free Press.

LOEWENBERG, G. (1973) The institutionalization of parliament and public orientations to the political system," pp. 142–156 in A. Kornberg (ed.) Legislatures in Comparative Perspective. New York: David McKay.

———— (1971a) "The influence of parliamentary behavior on regime stability: some conceptual clarifications." Comparative Politics 3 (January): 177–200.

———— (ed.) (1971b) Modern Parliaments: Change or Decline? Chicago: Aldine-Atherton.

———— (1971c) "The role of parliaments in modern political systems," pp. 1–20 in G. Loewenberg (ed.) Modern Parliaments: Change or Decline? Chicago: Aldine-Atherton.

———— (1967) Parliament in the German Political System. Ithaca, N.Y.: Cornell University Press.

LOFCHIE, M. (1967) "Representative government, bureaucracy, and political development: the African case." Journal of Developing Areas 2 (October): 37–56.

LOPEZ PINA, A., and LOPEZ ARANGUREN, E. (1976) La cultura polítíca de la España de Franco. Madrid: Taurus.

LUCAS VERDÚ, P. (1976) La Octava Ley Fundamental: Crítica juridico-politica de la reforma Suárez. Madrid: Tecnos.

LUCHAIRE, F. (1958) Les institutions politiques et administratives des territoires d'outre-mer après la loi-cadre. Paris: Librairie générale de droit de jurisprudence.

LUTTWAK, E. (1968) Coup d'Etat: A Practical Handbook. London: Allen Lane.

MABILEAU, A. (1967) "Les états d'Afrique noire du succession française," pp. 13–35 in A. Mabileau and J. Meyriat (eds.) Decolonisation et régimes politiques en Afrique noire. Paris: Armand Colin.

MACRIDIS, R., and B. BROWN (1960) The DeGaulle Republic: A Quest for Unity. Homewood, Ill.: Dorsey Press.

MAHESHWARI, S. R. (1972) Government Through Consultation: Advisory Committees in Indian Government. New Delhi: Indian Institute of Public Administration.

MAHIOU, A. (1969) L'avènement du parti unique en Afrique noire. Paris: Librairie générale de droit et de jurisprudence.

MAINE, H. (1931) Ancient Law. London: Oxford University Press.

MAJUMDAR, B. B. (1965) Indian Political Association and Reform of Legislatures, 1818–1917. Calcutta: Firma K. L. Mukhapadhyay.

Malaysia (1971) Second Malaysia Plan. Kuala Lumpur: Government Printer.

Malaysia. Department of Statistics (1974) Annual Statistical Bulletin, Malaysia, 1973. Kuala Lumpur: Government Printer.

Malaysia. Parliament (1975) Parliamentary Debates, Dewan Rakyat, Fourth Parliament, First Session.

Malaysia. Treasury (1974) Economic Report, 1974–75. Kuala Lumpur: Government Printer.

MANSFIELD, H. J., Jr. (1968a) "Impartial representation," pp. 91–114 in R. A. Goldwin (ed.) Representation and Misrepresentation. Chicago: Rand McNally.

——— (1968b) "Modern and medieval representation," pp. 55–82 in J. R. Pennock and W. Chapman (eds.) Representation. New York: Atherton.

——— (1965) Statesmanship and Party Government. Chicago: University of Chicago Press.

MARSHALL, D. B. (1973) The French Colonial Myth and Constitution-Making in the Fourth Republic. New Haven, Conn.: Yale University Press.

MARTIN, B., Jr. (1961) New India, 1885: British Official Policy and the Emergence of the Indian National Congress. Berkeley and Los Angeles: University of California Press.

MARTÍNEZ CUADRADO, M. (1974) "Representación. Elecciones. Referéndum," pp. 1371–1439 in M. Fraga Iribarne (ed.) La España de los años 70, Vol. III. Madrid: Moneda y Crédito.

——— (1970) "Cambio social y modernización política," pp. 331–362 in M. Martínez Cuadrado (ed.) Anuario político español 1969. Madrid: Edicusa.

MARTÍNEZ SOSPEDRA, M. M. (1974) "El consejo del Reino," pp. 1241–1290 in M. Fraga Iribarne (ed.) La España de los años 70, Vol. III. Madrid: Moneda y Crédito.

MARTÍNEZ VAL, J. M. 1975) ¿Por qué no fue posible la Falange? Barcelona: DOPESA.

MARX, K. (1955) The Eighteenth Brumaire of Louis Bonaparte. Pp. 243–344 in K. Marx and F. Engels, Selected Works, Vol. I. Moscow: Foreign Languages Publishing House.

MAUDLIN, P., N. CHOUCRI, F. W. NOTESTEIN, and M. TEITELBAUM (1974) "A report on Bucharest." Studies in Family Planning 5 (December): 357–395.

MAZRUI, A. A. (1976) "Soldiers as traditionalizers: military rule and the re-Africanization of Africa." World Politics 28 (January): 246–272.

McCOY, T. L. (1975) "A framework for comparing national fertility policies," pp. 47–74 in R. K. Godwin (ed.) Comparative Policy Analysis: The Study of Population Policy Determinants in Developing Countries. Lexington, Mass.: Lexington Books.

——— (1974) "Linkage politics and Latin American population policies," pp. 59–94 in T. L. McCoy (ed.) The Dynamics of Population Policy in Latin America. Cambridge, Mass.: Ballinger.

McCULLY, B. (1940) English Education and the Origins of Indian Nationalism. New York: Columbia University Press.

MEADOWS, D., D. MEADOWS, J. RANDERS, and W. BEHRENS (1972) The Limits to Growth: A Report for the Club of Rome's Project on the Predicament of Mankind. New York: Universe Books.

MEANS, G. (1970) Malaysian Politics. London: University of London Press.

MEESUK, O. (1976) Income Distribution in Thailand. Bangkok: Faculty of Economics, Thammasat University, Discussion Paper No. 50 (January).

MERTON, R. (1957) Social Theory and Social Structure (Revised ed.). Glencoe, Ill.: Free Press.

Metra-Seis (1975a) "Los Españoles, ante las asociaciones." Informaciones (January 20).
—— (1975b) "Según una en cuesta de opinión: Los españoles, a favor de la democracia." Informaciones (May 31).
MEZEY, M. L. (1974) "The policy-making role of legislatures in developing political systems." Unpublished paper.
—— (1972) "The functions of a minimal legislature: role perceptions of Thai legislators." Western Political Quarterly 25 (December): 686–701.
MICKS, U. (1961) Development from Below. New York: Oxford University Press.
MILL, J. S. (1958) Representative Government. New York: Liberal Arts Press.
MILLER, N. (ed.) (1969) Research in Rural Africa. East Lansing, Mich.: Michigan State University Press.
MILNE, R. (1967) Government and Politics in Malaysia. Boston: Houghton Mifflin.
——, and K. J. RATNAM (1974) Malaysia—New States in a New Nation: Political Development of Sarawak and Sabah in Malaysia. London: Frank Cass.
MINOQUE, M., and J. MALLOY (eds.) (1974) African Aims and Attitudes. London: Cambridge University Press.
MISRA, B. B. (1961) The Indian Middle Classes: Their Growth in Modern Times. London: Oxford University Press.
MOE, R. C., and R. TEEL (1971) "Congress as policy maker: a necessary reappraisal," pp. 32–52 in R. C. Moe and R. Teel (eds.) Congress and the President. Pacific Palisades, Calif.: Goodyear.
MORELL, D. (1976) "Political conflict in Thailand." Asian Affairs 3 (January-February): 151–184.
—— (1974) Power and Parliament in Thailand: The Futile Challenge, 1968–1971. Unpublished Ph.D. dissertation, Princeton University.
—— (1972) "Legislative intervention in Thailand's development process: a case study." Asian Survey 12 (August): 627–646.
MORGENTHAU, R. S. (1964) Political Parties in French-Speaking West Africa. Oxford: The Clarendon Press.
MORIS, J. R. (1974) "The voters' view of the elections," pp. 349–350 in The Election Study Committee (eds.) Socialism and Participation: Tanzania's 1970 National Elections. Dar-es-Salaam: Tanzanian Publishing House.
MORRIS-JONES, W. H. (1971) The Government and Politics of India. London: Hutchinson University Library.
—— (1957) Parliament in India. London: Longmans Green.
MORTIMER, E. (1969) France and the Africans 1944–1960: A Political History. London: Faber and Faber.
MOYA FIGUEROA, L. (1901) Estudio comparativo de la ley de municipalidades de 22 Diciembre de 1891. Santiago: Editorial Universiteria.
MUSCAT, R. J. (1966) Development Strategy in Thailand. New York: Praeger.
NAMIER, L. B. (1957) The Structure of Politics at the Accession of George III. New York: St. Martin's Press.
The Nation (Bangkok) (1971) December 12.
NAUFAL, S. (1969) Al Khlij al-Arabi (The Persian Gulf) Beirut: Dar al-Talia.
NDEGWA, D. N. (1971) Report of the Commission of Inquiry. Nairobi: Government Printer.
NEALE, J. E. (1963) The Elizabethan House of Commons. Hammondsworth, England: Penguin Books.
NEEDLER, M. C. (ed.) (1970) Political Systems of Latin America. (2nd ed.) New York: Van Nostrand Reinhold.
NESS, G. (1967) Bureaucracy and Rural Development in Malaysia. Berkeley: Uni-

versity of California Press.

NEUBERGER, B. (1974) "Has the single-party state failed in Africa?" African Studies Review 17 (April): 173–178.

NEUMANN, F. (1944) Behemoth: The Structure and Practice of National Socialism, 1933–1944. New York: Oxford University Press.

New Straits Times (Malaysia) (1974) April 8, September 18, October 21, November 21, November 22, November 25, December 7, December 12, December 21.

New York Times (1975) February 17, March 5, March 6, May 2, June 12, October 17.

Newsweek (1973) July 23.

NICHOLSON, N. (1972) "Factionalism and the Indian council of ministers." Journal of Commonwealth Political Studies 10 (November): 179–197.

NOHLEN, D. (1969) "Spanien," pp. 1229–1284 in A. Sternberger and B. Vogel (eds.) Die Wahl der Parlamente und Anderer Staatsorgane: Ein Handbuch. (Bd. 1. Europa. H.B. 2). Berlin: De Gruyter.

―――― (1966) Monarchischer Parlamentarismus und parlamentarische Regierung im Spanien des 19. Jahrhunderts. Ph.D. dissertation: Universität von Heidelberg.

NORDLINGER, E. A. (1972) Conflict Resolution in Divided Societies. Cambridge, Mass.: Harvard University, Center for International Affairs.

―――― (1970) "Soldiers in mufti: the impact of military rule upon economic and social change in the non-western states." American Political Science Review 64 (December): 1131–1148.

NORTMAN, D. (1974) "Population and family planning programs: a factbook." Reports on Population/Family Planning, No. 2 (6th ed.) (December).

NYERERE, J. K. (1968a) Freedom and Socialism. Dar-es-Salaam: Oxford University Press.

―――― (1968b) Ujamaa: Essays on Socialism. Dar-es-Salaam: Oxford University Press.

―――― (1965) "Address at the opening of the National Assembly." Dar-es-Salaam: Ministry of Tourism and Information.

―――― (1963) "Democracy and the party system." Dar-es-Salaam: Standard Press.

OAKESHOTT, M. (1961) "The masses in representative democracy," pp. 151–170 in A. Hunold (ed.) Freedom and Serfdom. Dordrecht, The Netherlands: Reidel.

O'CONNELL, J. (1971) "Authority and community in Nigeria," pp. 514–527 in R. Melson and H. Wolpe (eds.) Nigeria: Modernization and the Politics of Communalism. East Lansing, Mich.: Michigan State University Press.

OLLERO, C. (1974) "Desarrollo político y constitución española," pp. 1441–1466 in M. Fraga Iribarne (ed.) La españa de los años 70, Vol. III. Madrid: Moneda y Crédito.

ONG, M. H. C. (1976) "The member of parliament and his constituency: the Malaysian case." Legislative Studies Quarterly 1 (August): 405–422.

ORTÍ BORDÁS, J. M. O. (1974) "El movimiento y su consejo nacional," pp. 1165–1234 in M. Fraga Iribarne (ed.) La España de los años 70, Vol. III. Madrid: Moneda y Crédito.

PACKENHAM, R. A. (1974) "How legislatures do and do not help development: an approach and some hypotheses." Unpublished paper presented at a seminar on legislative development in Rio de Janeiro, August 12–14, 1974.

―――― (1970) "Legislatures and political development," pp. 521–582 in A. Kornberg and L. D. Musolf (eds.) Legislatures in Developmental Perspective. Durham, N.C.: Duke University Press.

PARSONS, T. (1971) The System of Modern Societies. Englewood Cliffs, N.J.: Prentice-Hall.

―――― , and E. SHILS (eds.) (1962) Toward a General Theory of Action. New York: Harper and Row.

PASCAL, R. (1965) La République Malagache. Paris: Berger-Levrault.

PATTERSON, M. L. (1954) "Caste and political leadership in Maharashtra." Economic Weekly 6 (September): 1066–1067.

PATTERSON, S. C. (1970) "Congressional committee professional staffing: capabilities and constraints," pp. 391–428 in A. Kornberg and L. D. Musolf (eds.) Legislatures in Developmental Perspective. Durham, N.C.: Duke University Press.

——, and G. R. BOYNTON (1969) "Legislative recruitment in a civic culture." Social Science Quarterly 50 (September): 243–263.

——, J. WAHLKE, and G. R. BOYNTON (1973) "Dimensions of support in legislative systems," pp. 282–313 in A. Kornberg (ed.) Legislatures in Comparative Perspective. New York: David McKay.

PAYNE, J. (1968) Patterns of Conflict in Colombia. New Haven, Conn.: Yale University Press.

PERERA, V. (1975) "Law and order in Chile." New York Times Magazine (April 13): 15 and 24–27.

PHILIPPI, J. (1916) "La nueva ley de contribuciones." Revista de Gobierno Local 1 (June): 9–10.

PIEDRABUENA RICHARDS, G. (1970) La reforma constitucional. Santiago: Ediciones Encina.

PIKE, F. (1974) "The new corporatism in Franco's Spain and some Latin American perspectives," pp. 171–210 in F. B. Pike and T. Stritch (eds.) The New Corporatism: Social-Political Structures in the Iberian World. Notre Dame, Ind.: University of Notre Dame Press.

—— (1967) Chile and the United States 1880–1962. South Bend, Ind.: University of Notre Dame Press.

PIPER, D., and T. COLE (eds.) (1964) Post-Primary Education and Political and Economic Development. Durham, N.C.: Duke University Press.

PITKIN, H. F. (1969) "The concept of representation," pp. 1–23 in H. F. Pitkin (ed.) Representation. New York: Atherton.

PLUMB, J. H. (1967) The Origins of Political Stability in England, 1675–1725. Boston: Houghton Mifflin.

POLSBY, N. W. (1975) "Legislatures," pp. 257–319 in F. I. Greenstein and N. W. Polsby (eds.) The Handbook of Political Science, Vol. V. Reading, Mass.: Addison-Wesley.

—— (1971) "Strengthening congress in national policy making," pp. 3–13 in N. W. Polsby (ed.) Congressional Behavior. New York: Random House.

—— (1968) "The institutionalization of the U. S. House of Representatives." American Political Science Review 62 (March): 144–168.

Population Council, New York (1969–1) Country Profiles.

PORTES, A. (1977) Legislatures under authoritarian regimes: the case of Mexico. Journal of Political and Military Sociology 5 (Fall):185–201.

POTHOLM, C. (1970) Four African Political Systems. Englewood Cliffs, N.J.: Prentice-Hall.

Prachathipati (1970) November 12.

PREWITT, K. (1971) "Schooling, stratification and equality: notes for research." Unpublished paper, Nairobi: Institute of Development Studies.

PROCTOR, J. H. (1973) "The national members of the Tanzanian parliament: a study of legislative behavior." African Review 3 (March): 1–19.

PROTHRO, J. W., and C. M. GRIGG (1960) "Fundamental principles of democracy: bases of agreement and disagreement." Journal of Politics 22 (May): 276–294.

PUTHUCHEARY, M. (1970) "The operations room in Malaysia as a technique in administrative reform," in H.-B. Lee and A. G. Samonte (eds.) Administrative

Reforms in Asia. Manila: Eastern Regional Organization for Public Administration.

PUTNAM, R. (1973) The Beliefs of Politicians: Ideology, Conflict and Democracy in Britain and Italy. New Haven, Conn.: Yale University Press.

PYE, L. (1966) Aspects of Political Development. Boston: Little Brown.

——— (1962) "The sovereignty of politics in impeding developments," pp. 80–96 in his Politics, Personality, and Nation Building: Burma's Search for Identity. New Haven, Conn.: Yale University Press.

RACE, J. (1974) "Thailand 1973: 'We certainly have been ravaged by something. . . .'" Asian Survey 14 (February): 192–203.

RAE, D. (1967) The Political Consequences of Electoral Laws. New Haven, Conn.: Yale University Press.

———, and M. TAYLOR (1970) The Analysis of Political Cleavages. New Haven, Conn.: Yale University Press.

RAMIREZ NECOCHEA, H. (1951) La Guerra Civil de 1891: Antecedentes Economicos. Santiago: n.p.

RAPOPORT, D. C. (1968) "The political dimensions of military usurpation." Political Science Quarterly 83 (December): 551–572.

RATNAM, K. J. (1965) Communalism and the Political Process in Malaya. Kuala Lumpur: University of Malaya Press.

REISSMAN, L. (1949) "A study of role conceptions in bureaucracy." Social Forces 27 (March): 305–310.

Republic of Chile. Congreso (1965) Diario de Sesiones (December 27).

——— (1959) Diario de Sesiones (January 28).

Republic of Chile. Junta de Gobierno (1973a) Declaración de principios de Chile. Santiago: Editorial Lord Cochrane S.A.

——— (1973b) 100 primeros decretos leyes dictados por la Junta de Gobierno de la República de Chile. Santiago: Editorial Jurídica.

Republic of Chile. ODEPLAN (1971) Plan de la economia nacional: antecedentes sobre el desarrollo chileno 1960–1970. Santiago: ODEPLAN.

Republic of Chile. Ministerio de Hacienda (1973) Balance consolidado del sector público de Chile. Santiago: Ministerio de Hacienda.

——— (1968) Ley de presupuesto del ministerio de obras públicas y transportes: Año 1969. Santiago: Talleres Gráficos La Nación.

Republic of Chile. Parlamento (1952–1973) Boletines de Sesiones.

Republic of France. Ministry of Overseas France (1953) "La situation économique et sociale de Madagascar." Notes et Études Documentaries 1 (November): 799.

Republic of India. Administrative Reforms Commission (1968) Report on Machinery and Planning. Delhi: Manager of Publications.

——— (1967) Interim Report of the Study Team on the Machinery of Planning. Delhi: Manager of Publications.

Republic of India. Department of Parliamentary Affairs (1958–1959) Report. Delhi: Manager of Publications.

Republic of India. Lok Sabha (1969) Debates. May 8: cols. 202–207. Delhi: Manager of Publications.

——— (1961) Debates. August 23: cols. 4296–4316. Delhi: Manager of Publications.

——— (1960) Debates. August 22: cols. 4069–4082. Delhi: Manager of Publications.

——— (1958) Debates. Delhi: Manager of Publications.

——— (1956) Debates. May 11: cols. 7986–7993. Delhi: Manager of Publications.

——— Business Advisory Committee (1956) 35th Report Presented to the House. May 9. Delhi: Manager of Publications.

——— Committee "A" on Draft Fifth Five Year Plan (1974a) Synopsis of Proceedings. Delhi: Manager of Publications.

—— Committee "E" on Draft Fifth Five Year Plan (1974b) Synopsis of Proceedings. Delhi: Manager of Publications.

—— Estimates Committee (1958) Twenty-First Report on Planning Commission. Delhi: Manager of Publications.

Republic of Kenya (1974) Development Plan 1974–78. Nairobi: Government Printer.

—— (1969) Development Plan 1970–74. Nairobi: Government Printer.

RESNICK, I. (1968) Tanzania: Revolution by Education. Arusha: Longmans of Tanzania.

RICH, W. (1973) Smaller Families Through Social and Economic Progress. Washington, D.C.: Overseas Development Council.

RIELES, H. (1974) "La legitimidad de la Junta de Gobierno," pp. 112–130 in Republic of Chile, Junta de Gobierno, Algunos Fundamentos de la Intervención Militar en Chile. (2nd ed.) Santiago: Editora Nacional Gabriela Mistral.

RIGGS, F. W. (1974) "Legislative origins: a contextual approach." Mimeo.

—— (1973) "Legislative structures: some thoughts on elected national assemblies," pp. 36–93 in A. Kornberg (ed.) Legislatures in Comparative Perspective. New York: David McKay.

—— (1969) "Bureaucratic politics in comparative perspective." Journal of Comparative Administration 1 (May): 5–38.

—— (1966) Thailand: The Modernization of a Bureaucratic Polity. Honolulu: East-West Center Press.

RIVAS VICUÑA, M. (1964) Historia política y parlamentaria de Chile. 3 vols. Santiago: Editorial Nascimiento.

ROBINSON, F. (1973) "Municipal government and Muslim separatism in the United Provinces, 1883–1916," pp. 69–122 in J. Gallagher, G. Johnson, and A. Seah (eds.) Locality, Province and Nation: Essays on Indian Politics, 1870–1940. London: Cambridge University Press.

ROBINSON, J. (1970) "Staffing the legislature," pp. 366–390 in A. Kornberg and L. Musolf (eds.) Legislatures in Developmental Perspective. Durham, N.C.: Duke University Press.

ROBINSON, K. E. (1965) The Dilemmas of Trusteeship: Aspects of British Colonial Policy Between the Wars. London: Oxford University Press.

—— (1960) "Senegal: the elections to the territorial assembly, March 1957," pp. 281–390 in W. J. M. MacKenzie and K. E. Robinson (eds.) Five Elections in Africa. London: Oxford University Press.

—— (1958) "Constitutional reform in French tropical Africa." Political Studies 6 (February): 45–69.

—— (1956) "Local government reform in French tropical Africa." Journal of African Administration 8 (October): 179–185.

—— (1955) "Political development in French West Africa," pp. 157–168 in C. W. Stillman (ed.) Africa in the Modern World. Chicago: University of Chicago Press.

RODRIGUEZ BRAVO, J. (1921 and 1926) Balmaceda y el conflicto entre el congreso y el ejecutivo. 2 vols. Santiago: n.p.

RODWIN, L. (1970) Nations and Cities: A Comparison of Strategies of Urban Growth. Boston: Houghton Mifflin.

ROKKAN, S. (1968) "The structure of mass politics in the smaller European democracies: a developmental typology." Comparative Studies in Society and History 10 (January): 173–210.

ROSBERG, C. B., Jr. (1964) "Democracy and the new African states," pp. 23–53 in K. Kirkwood (ed.) St. Antony's Papers, No. 15: African Affairs, No. 2. Carbondale, Ill.: Southern Illinois University Press.

ROSE, R. (1969) "Dynamic tendencies in the authority of regimes." World Politics 21 (July): 602–608.

ROSELLO GARCÍA, J. L. R. (ed.) (1962) DICODI: directorio de consejeros y directores, 1961–1962. Madrid: DICODI.

ROSSITER, C. (ed.) (1961) The Federalist Papers. New York: New American Library.

ROTHCHILD, D. (1969) "Ethnic inequalities in Kenya." Journal of Modern African Studies 7 (December): 689–711.

ROZENTHAL, A. A. (1970) Finance and Development in Thailand. New York: Praeger.

RUBIN, L., and B. WEINSTEIN (1974) Introduction to African Politics: A Continental Approach. New York: Praeger.

RUBIO, F., and M. ARAGON (1977) "La legalización del P.C.E. y Suincidencia en el estatuto juridico de los partidos politicos en España," pp. 219–237 in P. de Vega (ed.) Teoria y practica de los partido politicos. Madrid: Edicusa.

RUDOLPH, L., and S. RUDOLPH (1967) The Modernity of Tradition. Chicago: University of Chicago Press.

RUSTOW, D. (1970) "Transitions to democracy: toward a dynamic model." Comparative Politics 2 (April): 337–363.

SABINE, G. H. (1952) "The two democratic traditions." Philosophical Review 61 (October): 451–474.

SAINZ DE VARANDA, R., et al. (1957) Colección de leyes Fundamentales. Zaragoza: Acribia.

SAMUDAVANIJA, C. (1971a) Development of the Legislative Institution (Kan Pattana Onkorn Nithibanyat). Bangkok: National Institute of Development Administration (in Thai).

——— (1971b) The Politics and Administration of Thailand's Budget Process. Unpublished Ph.D. dissertation, University of Wisconsin.

SANCHEZ AGESTA, L. (1964) Historia del constitucionalismo español. Madrid: Instituto de Estudios Políticos.

SANDHIKSHETRIN, K. (Tr.) (1968) Constitution of the Kingdom of Thailand. Bangkok: Thammasat University Press (in Thai and English).

SARTORI, G. (1965) Democratic Theory. New York: Praeger.

——— (1960) "European political parties: the case of polarized pluralism," pp. 137–176 in J. LaPalombara and M. Weiner (eds.) Political Parties and Political Development. Princeton, N.J.: Princeton University Press.

SCHMITTER, P. (1975a) Corporatism and Public Policy in Authoritarian Portugal. Beverly Hills: Sage Contemporary Political Sociology Series, Vol. I, pp. 85–131.

——— (1975b) "Liberation by Golpe: retrospective thoughts on the demise of authoritarian rule in Portugal." Armed Forces and Society 2(1):2–33.

——— (1974) "Still the century of corporatism?" in F. B. Pike and T. Stritch (eds.) The New Corporatism: Social-Political Structures in the Iberian World. Notre Dame, Ind.: University of Notre Dame Press.

SCHNEIDER, H. (1968) "Das Ermächtigungsgesetz vom 24 Marz 1933," pp. 405–442 in J. Gotthard (ed.) Von Weimar zu Hitler 1930–1933. Cologne: Keipenheuer und Witsch.

SCOTT, J. C. (1972) "Patron-client politics and political change in Southeast Asia." American Political Science Review 66 (March): 91–113.

SCHWARZ, M. (1965) Mitglied des Reichstages: Biographisches Handbuch der Reichstage. Hannover: Verlag für Literatur und Zeitgeschehen.

SEAL, A. (1968) The Emergence of Indian Nationalism: Competition and Collaboration in the Later Nineteenth Century. London: Oxford University Press.

Sécretariat général du gouvernement (1963) "Les constitutions des républiques Africaines et Malagache d'expression française." La documentation française: notes et études documentaries. Nos. 2994 and 2995.

SEGAL, A. (1967) "The politics of land in East Africa." Africa Report 12 (April): 46–50.

SEN, S. R. (1974) "Formulation of the national plan—the basic process and the machinery," pp. 53–58 in V. A. Pai Panandiker (ed.) Development Administration in India. Delhi: Macmillan.

SHAKDHER, S. L. (1974) "The parliament and the plan." Journal of Parliamentary Information 20 (July-September): 515.

SHILS, E. (1962) "The military in the political development of the new states," pp. 7–67 in J. Johnson (ed.) The Role of the Military in Underdeveloped Countries. Princeton, N.J.: Princeton University Press.

––––– (1961) "Centre and periphery," pp. 117–130 in The Logic of Knowledge: Essays Presented to Michael Polanyi. New York: Free Press.

––––– (1960) Political Development in the New States. The Hague: Mouton.

Siam Rath (1969) April 11, June 16, August 13, October 17, December 8.

SIAMWALLA, A. (1976) "Agricultural commodities in farmers and middle men," pp. 1–34 in N. Akrasanee and R. Thanapornpun (eds.) Essays in Honor of Puey Ungphakorn (Rak Muang Thai), Bangkok: Thai Wattana Panich (March) (in Thai).

––––– (1975) "A history of rice policies in Thailand." Food Research Institute Studies 14:233–249.

SILCOCK, T. H. (ed.) (1966) Thailand: Social and Economic Studies in Development. Canberra: Australian National University Press.

SILVA CIMMA, E. (1968) Derecho administrativo Chileno y comparado, (3rd ed.) Vol. 1. Santiago: Editorial Jurídica.

SILVA, L. (1974) Allende: El fin de una aventura. Santiago: Edicones Patria Nueva.

SIMMEL, G. (1964) Conflict and the Web of Group Affiliations (K. H. Wolff and R. Bendix eds.). New York: Free Press.

––––– (1950) The Sociology of Georg Simmel (K. H. Wolff ed.). New York: Free Press.

––––– (1908) Sociologie. Leipzig: Duncker und Humblot.

––––– (1900) Philosophie des Geldes. Leipzig: Duncker und Humblot.

SINGHVI, L. M. (1976) "Parliament in the Indian political system," pp. 179–227 in A. Kornberg and L. D. Musolf (eds.) Legislatures in Developmental Perspective. Durham, N.C.: Duke University Press.

SISSON, R. (1973) "Comparative legislative institutionalization: a theoretical exploration," pp. 17–38 in A. Kornberg (ed.) Legislatures in Comparative Perspective. New York: David McKay.

––––– (1972) The Congress Party of Rajasthan. Berkeley and Los Angeles: University of California Press.

––––– (1969) "Peasant movements and political mobility: the Jats of Rajasthan." Asian Survey 9 (December): 946–963.

SMELSER, N. J. (1962) Theory of Collective Behavior. New York: Free Press.

SMEND, R. (1955) "Massstäbe des Parliamentarischen Wahlrechts in der deutschen Staatstheorie des 19. Jahrhunderts," pp. 19–39 in R. Smend, Staatsrechtliche Abhandlungen und Andere Aufsätze. (Originally published 1912). Berlin: Duncker und Humblot.

SMITH, A. K. (1969) "Socio-economic development and political democracy: a causal analysis." Midwest Journal of Political Science 13 (February): 95–125.

SMITH, D. E. (1963) India as a Secular State. Princeton, N.J.: Princeton University Press.

The Statesman's Yearbook, 1975–1976 (1975) New York: St. Martin's Press.

––––– 1974–1975 (1974) New York: St. Martin's Press.

STAUFFER, R. (1970) "Congress in the Philippine political system," pp. 334–365 in A. Kornberg and L. D. Musolf (eds.) Legislatures in Developmental Perspective.

Durham, N.C.: Duke University Press.

STEBBINS. R. D., and A. AMOIA (eds.) (1973) The World This Year, 1973. New York: Council on Foreign Relations.

STEINER, H., and D. TRUBECK (1971) "Brazil—all power to the generals." Foreign Affairs 49 (April): 464–479.

STEPAN, A. (1978) The State and Society: Peru in Comparative Perspective. Princeton: Princeton University Press.

—— (1971) The Military in Politics: Changing Patterns in Brazil. Princeton, N.J.: Princeton University Press.

STEWART, J. D. (1958) British Pressure Groups: Their Role in Relation to the House of Commons. Oxford: Clarendon Press.

STULTZ, N. M. (1970) "The National Assembly in the politics of Kenya," pp. 303–333 in A. Kornberg and L. D. Musolf (eds.) Legislatures in Developmental Perspective. Durham, N.C.: Duke University Press.

—— (1969) "Parliament in a tutelary democracy: a recent case in Kenya." Journal of Politics 31 (February); 95–118.

—— (1968) "Parliaments in former British Black Africa." Journal of the Developing Areas 2 (July): 479–494.

STOCKING, G. (1970) Middle East Oil. Nashville, Tenn.: Vanderbilt University Press.

STOCKTON, R. (1971) "Aspects of Nyeri leadership." Nairobi: Institute of Development Studies, Staff Paper No. 107.

STYCOS, J. M. (1974) "Politics and population control in Latin America," pp. 3–35 in T. L. McCoy (ed.) The Dynamics of Population Policy in Latin America. Cambridge, Mass.: Ballinger.

STYSKAL, R. A. (1969) "Philippine legislators' reception of individuals and interest groups in the legislative process." Comparative Politics 1 (April): 405–422.

SUWANKIRI, T. (1975) The Cost of Protection. Unpublished Ph.D. dissertation, University of Hawaii.

Swatantra Party (1962) The Election Manifesto. Bombay: Central Office.

TACHAU, F., and M.-J. D. GOOD (1973) "The anatomy of political and social change: Turkish parties, parliaments, and elections." Comparative Politics 5 (July): 551–573.

TAPIA VALDÉS, J. (1966) La tecnica legislativa. Santiago: Editorial Jurídica.

TEITELBAUM, M. S. (1974) "Population and development: is a consensus possible?" Foreign Affairs 52 (July): 742–760.

Thai Rath (1970) February 5, February 7.

—— (1969) June 12.

THOMAS, D. B. (1974) "Political development theory and Africa: toward a conceptual clarification and comparative analysis." Journal of Developing Areas 8 (April): 375–394.

THOMAS, J. A. (1939) The House of Commons, 1852–1901: A Study of Its Economic and Functional Character. Cardiff: University of Wales Press.

THOMPSON, V. (1973) "Supplement," pp. 172–231 in R. Galize (ed.) The Politics of Congo-Brazzaville. Stanford, Calif.: Hoover Institution Press.

——, and R. ADLOFF (1958) French West Africa. London: Allen and Unwin.

THONGTHAMMACHAT, K. (1971) The Legislature in the Governing System of Thailand. (Rathasapha Nai Rabop Kan Muang Khong Thai) Bangkok: Faculty of Political Science, Chulalongkorn University (in Thai).

TOMÁS VILLARROYA, J. (1974) "El gobierno," pp. 1027–1082 in M. Fraga Iribarne (ed.) La España de los años 70, Vol. III. Madrid: Moneda y Crédito.

TORDOFF, W. (1965) "Parliament in Tanzania." Journal of Commonwealth Political Studies 3 (July): 85–103.

TURNER, F. C. (1974) Responsible Parenthood: The Politics of Mexico's New

Population Policies. Washington, D.C.: American Enterprise Institute for Public Policy Research.

UNGPHAKORN, P., et al. (eds.) (1975) Finance, Trade and Economic Development in Thailand. Bangkok: Sompong Press.

UNICA (1976) "Population policies and programs in the Caribbean: committee report of workshop proceedings held April 9–10, 1976, Santo Domingo, Dominican Republic." Santo Domingo, Dominican Republic: Association of Caribbean Universities and Research Institutes [UNICA].

United Nations (1975) Yearbook of National Account Statistics, 1974, Vol. III. Department of Economic and Social Affairs. New York: United Nations Publishing Service.

——— (1974) UN Statistical Yearbook. New York: United Nations Publishing Service.

United Republic of Tanzania (1970) Economic Survey and Annual Plan 1970–71. Dar-es-Salaam: Government Printer.

——— (1969) Second Five Year Plan for Economic and Social Development, July 1969–June 1974. Vols. I and II. Dar-es-Salaam: Government Printer.

——— (1965) Report of the Presidential Commission on the Establishment of a Democratic One Party State. Dar-es-Salaam: Government Printer.

United States. Agency for International Development. Office of Population (1969–1973) Population Program Assistance. Washington, D.C.: United States Government Printing Office.

United States. Domestic Council Committee on Illegal Aliens (1976) Preliminary Report. Washington, D.C.; United States Domestic Council Committee on Illegal Aliens.

UPADHYAHA, D. D. (1958) The Two Plans: Promises, Performance, Prospects. Lucknow: Rashtradharma Prakashan.

UPHOFF, N. I., and W. F. ILCHMAN (eds.) (1972) The Political Economy of Development. Berkeley: University of California Press.

URZÚA VALENZUELA, G., and A. GARCIA BARZELATTO (1971) Diagnóstico de la burocracia Chilena (1818–1969). Santiago: Editorial Jurídica.

VALDERRAMA, A. (1915) Album político. Santiago: n.p.

VALENCIA AVARÍA, L. (ed.) (1951) Anales de la república, Vol. II. Santiago: Imprenta Universitaria.

VALENZUELA, A. (1978) The Breakdown of Democratic Regimes: Chile. Baltimore: Johns Hopkins University Press.

——— (1977) Political Brokers in Chile: Local Government in a Centralized Society. Durham, N.C.: Duke University Press.

——— (1975) "Il crollo di la democrazia in Cile." Revista Italiana di Scienza Política 5 (April): 83–129.

———, and J. S. VALENZUELA (1975) "Visions of Chile." Latin American Research Review 10 (Fall): 155–175.

VALENZUELA, S. (1972) "Determinants of suffrage expansion in Chile: the 1874 electoral law." Unpublished manuscript, Columbia University.

VASIL, R. K. (1971) Politics in a Plural Society: A Study of Non-Communal Political Parties in West Malaysia. London: Oxford University Press.

VERNER, J. G. (1977) "Legislative perspectives on population growth and development: the case of El Salvador," pp. 82–95 in S. W. Schmidt and H. H. Schmidt (eds.) Latin America: Rural Life and Agrarian Problems. Ames, Iowa: Iowa State University Research Foundation.

——— (1975) "Legislative attitudes toward overpopulation: the case of El Salvador." Journal of Developing Areas 10 (October): 61–76.

VICKERS, M. (1970) "Competition and control in modern Nigeria: origins of the war with Biafra." International Journal 25 (Summer): 603–633.

VLARD, R. (1963) La fin de l'empire colonial français. Paris: G. P. Maisonneuve et Larose.

VOEGLIN, E. (1936) Der Autoritäre Staat: Ein Besuch über das österreichische Staats-problem. Vienna: Springer.

VON DER MEHDEN, F. D. (1969) Politics of the Developing Nations. Englewood Cliffs, N.J.: Prentice-Hall.

VON VORYS, K. (1975) Democracy Without Consensus. Princeton. N.J.: Princeton University Press.

––––– (1959) "The legislator in underdeveloped countries." Prod 3 (November): 23–26.

WADE, N. (1974) "Green revolution (I): a just technology, often unjust in use." Science 187 (December): 1093–1096.

WAHLKE, J. C. (1971) "Policy demands and system support: the role of the represented." British Journal of Political Science 1 (July): 271–290.

WANG, G. (ed.) (1964) Malaysia: A Survey. New York: Praeger.

WASHBROOK, D. A. (1973) "The influence of government institutions on provincial politics and leadership in Madras C. 1880–1925." Paper presented to seminar on Leadership in South Asia, Centre of South Asian Studies, School of Oriental and African Studies, University of London. (January).

WATSON, W. B., and R. J. LAPHAM (eds.) (1975) "Family planning programs: world review, 1974." Studies in Family Planning 6 (August): 206–322.

WEBER, M. (1968) Economy and Society (G. Roth and C. Wittich eds.). New York: Bedminster.

––––– (1967) On Law in Economy and Society. M. Reinstein (ed.). New York: Simon and Schuster.

––––– (1947) The Theory of Social and Economic Organization. Glencoe, Ill.: Free Press.

WEINBAUM, M. (1972) "Afghanistan: nonparty parliamentary democracy." Journal of the Developing Areas 7 (October): 57–74.

WHEARE, J. (1950) The Nigerian Legislative Council. London: Faber and Faber.

WHITAKER, C. S. (1970) The Politics of Tradition, Continuity and Change in Northern Nigeria: 1946–1960. Princeton, N.J.: Princeton University Press.

WIARDA, H. J. (1974) "Corporatism and development in the Iberic-Latin world: persistent strains and new variations," pp. 3–33 in F. B. Pike and T. Stritch (eds.) The New Corporatism: Social-Political Structures in the Iberian World. Notre Dame, Ind.: Notre Dame University Press.

WIARDA, I. S. (1974) "Approaches and strategies of population policy-making in a democratic context: the case of Venezuela," pp. 323–352 in T. L. McCoy (ed.) The Dynamics of Population Policy in Latin America. Cambridge, Mass.: Ballinger.

WIGHT, M. (1947) The Gold Coast Legislative Council. London: Faber and Faber.

––––– (1946) Development of the Legislative Council, 1606–1945. London: Faber and Faber.

WILLIAMS, P. (1964) Crisis and Compromise. Hamden, Conn.: Archon Books.

WILSON, D. (1962) Politics in Thailand. Ithaca, N.Y.: Cornell University Press.

WRIGGINS, W. (1960) Ceylon: Dilemmas of a New Nation. Princeton. N.J.: Princeton University Press.

YOUNG, J. (1966) The Washington Community 1800–1828. New York: Columbia University Press.

ZOLBERG, A. (1971) "Political development in the Ivory Coast since independence," pp. 9–32 in P. Foster and A. Zolberg (eds.) Ghana and the Ivory Coast: Perspectives on Modernization. Chicago: University of Chicago Press.

––––– (1966) Creating Political Order; the Party States of West Africa. Chicago: Rand McNally.

––––– (1964) One-Party Government in the Ivory Coast. Princeton, N.J.: Princeton University Press.

# INDEX